Oxon, 1961

The World's Classics

303
LIVES
BY
IZAAK WALTON

Oxford University Press, Amen House, London E.C.4

GLASGOW NEW YORK TORONTO MELBOURNE WELLINGTON
BOMBAY CALCUTTA MADRAS KARACHI CAPE TOWN IBADAN

Geoffrey Cumberlege, Publisher to the University

THE LIVES OF

JOHN DONNE
SIR HENRY WOTTON
RICHARD HOOKER
GEORGE HERBERT &
ROBERT SANDERSON

BY IZAAK WALTON
WITH AN INTRODUCTION
BY GEORGE SAINTSBURY

The World's Classics

Geoffrey Cumberlege
OXFORD UNIVERSITY PRESS
London New York Toronto

IZAAK WALTON

Born, Stafford   9 August 1593
Died, Winchester   15 December 1683

*The first four of these Lives were first published in
1640, 1651, 1655, and 1670 respectively, and were
first published together in one volume in 1670. The
life of Dr. Robert Sanderson was first published in 1678.
In The World's Classics they were first published in
1927 and reprinted in 1936, 1940, 1947, 1950,
and 1956.*

INTRODUCTION

IN a fairly extensive range of knowledge of books and authors I cannot find any of the latter who can match Izaak Walton in having obtained and retained fame by a pair of books so different in character and treatment of subject as *The Compleat Angler* and the collection of short biographies which we here present once more for public delectation. That there is the same *spirit* in both is of course true, but that is another matter : and it would be a rather positive critic who should declare that the merits of the one book prepared him for those of the other before he read it.

The charms of the *Angler* are indeed various in themselves, and of various appeal to different classes of readers. But to some of us it presents itself, first of all, and perhaps most constantly, as a wonderful and delightful panorama in letters, requiring no "illustrations" because it is all, or almost all, illustration itself. You *see* the road and the travellers, the river and the meadows, the gear to catch the fish, and the fish the gear catches, Maudlin and mine hostess. As the verses are set to the prose, so is the prose itself set as letterpress to a picture, the lines and colours of which, invisible to the senses of the body, are vividly present to those of the mind.

The appeal of the *Lives* is quite different. There are vivid pictures in them : but it is perhaps not idle to point out that the most vivid are chiefly to be found in the one case in which Walton had no direct knowledge of his man. The vision of good Bishop Jewel supplying the boy undergraduate Hooker with the wooden horse in the shape of a stick, and the ten-silver-groat equipage to it, is pleasing; and the still more famous but tragicomic ones—of the author of not the least great book of English prose and Christian argument literally keeping sheep because Mrs Hooker wanted the shepherd, and when relieved of that duty, being promptly set to rock the cradle—are all clear enough to the mind's eye; as also is the wholly tragic and rather ghostly one of Donne rehearsing his enshroudment. One might almost say that there is a touch of Walton's pictorial magic, as well as of his peculiar suppressed humour, in the single line where he tells us how that robustious person Andrew Melville (or as he calls him Melvin) "remained, *very angry*, for three years" in the Tower. It must be a sadly weak imagination which cannot fill in the two words "very angry" with a string of various exhibitions of the three-years-long anger.

But these are the merest accidents—not in the least the substance—of the book. Whether Walton deliberately chose his subjects so as to form a group, one does not know: and it is hardly likely. But it is observable that he takes some trouble to explain *why* he undertook the various pieces: a proceeding which, when followed in more modern times, once drew down the wrath of a martinet reviewer. And there is no doubt about the strange flood of light which the book pours on the more contemplative side of English life in the seventeenth century. Not the contemplative only: for Donne was, in a restless and defeated manner, a man of action for a long time; it is pretty evident, though Walton disguises the fact a little, that Herbert would have liked to be one; and Wotton diversified his famous occupation of "*lying* abroad for the good of his country" with other activities of the most business-like sorts. But none of them was, in that century of perpetual warfare, a regular soldier; all of them (for Wotton took deacon's Orders after he went to Eton) were clerics; and practically all of them (though Wotton the least) displayed that singular union of spiritual and less spiritual thought for which the century is distinguished among all centuries with us. Three were poets: from Donne, the "best poet in the world for some things" (including some that Ben hardly knew), through Herbert's graceful divinity, to the few but charming verses that give Wotton a safe seat in the skirts of Parnassus. Hooker and Donne rank—the one continuously, the other in higher and lower strains by turns—among the greatest prose-writers of that our greatest prose time. And Walton's own prose, though there have been some perhaps unnecessary squabbles as to the proportions of art and nature in it, proves itself as effectual for delineation of character as it is, in the other book, for rendering of the outside of persons and places and things.

Perhaps the most successful of the five pieces in this principal respect is what must have been the most difficult—the first. That it is neither the most accurate nor the most complete in detail further researches, culminating in those of Sir Edmund Gosse for the life and those of Professor Grierson for the work, have shown; on the work indeed Walton gives us very little; and next to nothing, even on the Sermons to which his composition was prefixed, of a really critical kind. Indeed English criticism was only being born and passing through its adolescence during his time. It happens that the present writer, familiar with the *Compleat Angler* from his childhood, had paid hardly any attention to the *Lives* till after he had come under the spell of Donne's poems: yet he found the impression, which these poems had produced, confirmed in the most singular way by Walton's presentation of the poet. There is a curious kind of *awe* in this presentation: which, in the wrong hands, might have slipped into mere inadequacy, into positive silliness, or into pretentious rhetoric. Walton's art or nature keeps it free of all these, and diffuses it as a sort of atmosphere throughout or all over the portrait. As this portrait is, at the same time, the most intimate of the whole set, it is not difficult to understand that it could hardly have been hit off at one draft: and accordingly we find some notable insertions in its later editions bringing out the "strange kind of irresistible art" which pervaded Donne's expressions of himself in life and literature.

Some of these insertions belong to a class which possesses more than the individual interest of its members: that is to say the letters here and there given in whole or part. Thanks to a bit of good nature of Boswell's, the credit of utilising letters in biography is generally given to Mason in respect of his Life of Gray. But Walton, a full hundred years earlier, had anticipated "Skroddles" in using correspondence, though the small scale of his *Lives* precluded voluminous employment of it. He has laid Donne under contribution in this way more than once, and to great effect: particularly in the group of letters to Lady Magdalen Herbert cited in the Life of her son George. But in Donne's own Life he has not neglected the device; the most admirable specimen being the extract (p. 36) beginning "For we hardly discover." The earlier part of this can scarcely be surpassed even in the Sermons, as an example of that long-drawn, echoing, melancholy music which so often lends an almost uncanny charm to its author's prose : and which contrasts, whether designedly or not, with the harmonious but not in the least mysterious simplicity of Walton's.

But whether this contrast was designed or not, there can hardly have been a total absence of design in the direct transition from Donne to Wotton. That the knight-Provost had been one of the most intimate friends of the Dean, and that Walton had in a manner acted as substitute to the former in the office of biographer to the latter, may have had something to do with this, but hardly all. Wotton was a good man and a pious man ; you could not easily be good without being pious in the seventeenth century, whatever may have been or be the case in others. But he was eminently a man of the world : and there was nothing, even in the very pretty little bits of poetry already mentioned, in the least mysterious about him. On the other hand his biographer had plenty of interesting stuff to hand : and it could only have been his own fault if he did not make good use of it. No such fault can be laid to Walton's charge.

One can see, even from Sir Henry's portrait, though it is by no means a grinning one, that he was not only a good and pious, but like Juliet's nurse's husband "a merry man" : and his biographer brought, as has been said, a good deal of suppressed humour to make concatenation with this. It has indeed seemed to some that there is something wrong about the ambassador story (*v. inf.*, p. 121). If Wotton originally wrote in Latin, not only is it no wonder that James was annoyed, but also the play certainly on the English "lie" and possibly on the technical term "lieger" (resident) applied to ministers abroad * disappears for everybody except those who can and do translate it into English. But the account of his behaviour at a certain crisis when (*v. inf.*, pp. 108-9) "so soon as the Earl [Essex] was apprehended he did very quickly and as privately glide through Kent to Dover," paid mariners liberally and got to France in sixteen hours from London——only to hear that the Earl was beheaded and their common friend, Mr Cuffe of Merton, hanged——is either the most unintelligible piece of "simplicity" or the most successful one of quiet irony that one can easily imagine. Evidently Wotton was cut out for a diplomatist: and, we may add, Walton for a biographer.

Not indeed that——as perhaps some biographers, eager to escape the common charge of idolatry, have done——he makes hits at his subject. Sir Henry could have done neither Devereux nor Cuffe the least good by staying, and was quite guiltless of any share in their treason. On the other hand the transaction (*v. inf.*, p. 125) in which, receiving a thousand pounds worth of diamonds from the Emperor, he handed them over † to a lady and his hostess, and justified the double proceeding——because he would neither insult the Emperor by refusing his gift nor profit himself by a gift from the Queen of Bohemia's enemy—— is the kind of thing that does one's heart good in these days. This is the True Romance: which never dies though it may seem sometimes to sleep, and while it sleeps men scoff at it.

There is a sentence, not the least amusing in

---

* And (wickedly) by Bishop King (or some one else) to hangmen. See *Minor Caroline Poets* (Oxford), vol. iii. p. 264.

† He was, all his life, a poor man.

Walton's work, and not the least characteristic of him, in which (*v. inf.*, p. 196) he begs of his Reader to let him digress, and then he will "presently lead" that reader "back to Mr Hooker." The fact is that this process pervades the third of the *Lives*: and if you were to cut out the digressions it would be, instead of about the longest as it is, by far the shortest of all. There never was an author who was—let us not say more dependent upon personal familiarity with the things and persons he wrote about, but—more inclined to prefer subjects with which he was familiar, than Walton. He did not and could not well know anything personally of Hooker, who died when Izaak was seven years old: though he knew Hooker's favourite pupils George Cranmer and Edwin Sandys well, and received from them the lamentable stories of the great man's domestic polity. But there could not be much else to tell of such a private life: and there was nothing public to talk about except change of benefices, and that singular spiritual duel with Travers at the Temple which communicated a profane interest to attending church twice a day during its period. Accordingly Walton gives himself frequent opportunities of "coming back to Mr Hooker" by going away from him. The very quaint beginning, "It is not to be doubted but that Richard Hooker was born at Heavitree," arouses a suspicion that the writer is not so *very* sure of himself, and would like to catch hold of things about which he is sure. So we get not merely the passages, anecdotic and epistolary, from Sandys and Cranmer; not merely an Appendix about Hooker's will and a not very thoroughgoing touch at the still, I believe, not fully settled problem of the later books of the *Polity*; not only a not quite irrelevant but certainly disproportionately long account of the rise of the Puritans; but something like a short biography of Archbishop Whitgift—Queen Elizabeth's "little black husband"—and his letters to Her Majesty, and the Hospital which he built and which some of the good people of Croydon are so anxious to pull down; and other things which either have no connexion at all, or the very slightest connection, with "Mr" Richard Hooker.

Nevertheless it is by no means the least interesting of the set. The simplicity of the learned is not merely an old joke but a present truth; I have known a person of brains, knowledge and taste far above the common who was as much surprised as pleased by being told that he could cash an American draft in England without going over to New York to do so. But still, because your landlady, quite a stranger to you, has tucked you comfortably up when you came in from a wet walk, to empower her to choose you a wife, without apparently any idea that she would, or desire that she should, choose her own daughter, seems to be going incredibly far. Yet if we may believe not merely common fame, but two known and respectable witnesses, it happened. On the other hand, for serious historical and theological students, Walton's account of Cartwright and Travers and their fellows is specially attractive. He was quite opposed to their views; he had seen and deplored the mischief which their followers did; but he is not at all savage towards them. On a pure question of argument one would not perhaps attach much importance to Walton, whatever side he took: but as an example of Charity—here as elsewhere but even more than elsewhere—he is rather precious.

It seems that he knew no more personally of Herbert than of Hooker, except that he had seen him. But they were contemporaries; and they had many and important friends in common, including both Wotton and Donne. The latter indeed is laid under contribution, in Walton's special manner, to this Life, for we get through it those most interesting letters of Donne's to George Herbert's mother, Magdalen * Newport, Herbert, and Danvers, who figures largely here. Indeed, she would seem, in some odd fashion, to have suggested the whole thing: for in his Introduction he dwells, otherwise with apparent irrelevance, on her patron or patroness Saint, with a striking touch of that pictorial faculty which has been noticed in him, in respect of *the* Magdalen both before and after her reaching a state of sanctity. The absence, however, of direct personal knowledge may perhaps account for something like a recurrence of the discursive quality of the "Hooker." One never knows exactly where *not* to have a seventeenth-century writer: and it may be that an additional suggestion occurred from the Magdalen's two lives in respect of Herbert's undoubtedly rather rapid change from a life of Court and University business to one of spiritual occupation. Izaak does not insist very much on the point of the change: but it no doubt justified in his mind the large digression on Nicholas Ferrer of Little Gidding, whose influence, partly at least, occasioned or directed it. His account of the poet-parson's courtship and marriage is odd; there is always a touch of oddity in Walton's accounts of courtships and marriages; and in particular I doubt whether he in the least understood Donne's attitude to the matter. Nor except the "very angry" noted

---

* They called her and we still sometimes as above call her *Lady* Magdalen Herbert: but it does not seem that, according to the stricter modern valuation, she had a right to this title, though she became Lady Danvers by her second marriage.

already is there anything so strongly pictorial here as
the disgust of Hooker's good clerk when, in the time
of the Puritan tyranny, the intrusive minister ordered
him at Communion time to "bring Joint stools and
cushions—*not* to kneel upon"—a most characteristic
Waltonism. But the description of "the Country
Parson's" actual ruling of his parish at Bemerton is a
classic—indeed the very *locus classicus*—of the subject.
Here as elsewhere Walton, though he may speak about
his author's books, indulges in practically nothing of
what may be called literary criticism on the subject.
Critics sometimes nowadays class Herbert with Donne
in poetry; it would have been interesting to hear
what Walton thought on that subject—a subject for
which he did care, as we know from his remarks upon,
and his preservation of, the mysterious Jo. Chalkhill.

To the average modern reader (nothing foolish or
uppish is intended in the use of this phrase) the fifth
of the *Lives* is probably the least interesting. People
used at one time to write as if Donne were chiefly worth
notice because Walton wrote about him; but we have
pretty well changed that, to do us justice. The
variety and distinction of Wotton, in his several
capacities, must always give him interest with any one
whose attention is not merely devoted to things
modern. The literary position of Hooker in English
prose must always keep him alive, whether interest in
theology wanes or waxes: and Herbert divides with
Keble the summit of popularity as regards English
sacred verse. But with Sanderson it is different. You
may indeed still find a "greatest" attached to his name
in books of reference: but it is also attached to the
noun "casuist." Now casuistry in its strict sense, and
as applied to his work, is, if not utterly dead, pretty
fast asleep in England to-day. You may still find it

in law courts and questionable forms of it in political speech : while what is called psycho-analysis might be described as a bastard Greek name for not so much psychical as physical explanations of abnormal or eccentric " cases." But *pure* casuistry—that is to say the discussion of cases of conduct, thought, or speech with reference to accepted laws of morality or religion, especially if the cases seem to be in conflict with these laws—is not now " a popular pie," as the late Shakespearian scholar Grant White once heard a little American boy describe the food put before him in an eating-house. As what we may call a grammarian of Logic, Sanderson was succeeded by Aldrich, who was succeeded by Mansel, who has been succeeded by— whom shall we say ? As a mere life, too, his had no particular interest except as an example of regular academic and ecclesiastical progress. He was not even deprived during the Rebellion, like other Royalist Churchmen, though he had to suffer a little from those intermeddlings of Cromwellian warriors which Scott has utilised so well in *Woodstock*. Walton knew him, took an interest in him, and has after his fashion made that interest contagious in a certain degree.* But almost the only *lively* passage is that which tells how Gilbert Sheldon, afterwards to be one of the most sumptuous and imperious of the Archbishops of

---

* For the perhaps not numerous but not wholly contemptible readers who like logical reasoning Sanderson has plenty of intrinsic interest. The six volumes of his *Works* (W. Jacobson, Oxford, 1854) may be alarming : but the chief of these works, the Oxford Lectures *De Obligatione Conscientiæ*, is accessible in two modern forms—the original Latin with a somewhat compressed English *Précis* and a few notes by Whewell (Cambridge, 1851), and an older English translation revised by Bishop Christopher Wordsworth (Rivingtons, 1877). The Latin is the better ; but the English is quite good.

Canterbury, passed, when he was an undergraduate, an exceedingly bad night, because Sanderson had sent to request a visit from him next morning. Now the future Bishop of Lincoln was at the time proctor : and the future Archbishop of Canterbury had " run into some irregularity, such as made him conscious he had transgressed his statutes." Walton is tantalising and does not tell us what the " irregularity " was.

> Had he played marbles on the sacred steps ?
> Had he worn garments that were not subfusc ?

as the poet asks. But in the circumstances one can imagine considerable discomfort on the undergraduate's part. As a matter of fact Sanderson had not sent as proctor and knew nothing of any crime of Sheldon's, but was kindly fulfilling a petition from the boy's father to look after him.

That Walton's faculty of anecdote in this fashion has a good deal to do with the singular readableness of his work there is no doubt. But it is questionable whether it would be anything like so effective if he could not, like Shakespeare in the famous description, though not quite in the same way, be " wholly serious " also. It is the combination—in fact the interpenetration—of the two moods and modes that constitutes his almost unique attraction. When he wrote the " Sanderson " he was midway between eighty and ninety, and perhaps the treatment, as well as the subject, is not quite up to the standard of the others. Yet, in a certain way, it completes the set and it is not easy to suggest a better substitute. Walton was no coward : during the time when he took charge of Charles the Second's " George " (the Garter jewel) after Worcester he must have been perfectly sure of being hanged or shot in case of discovery. He could never have been a Pacifist in the modern sense : but it is quite clear that Peace was his favourite Goddess, and War not a God of his at all.   With an active soldier, or even an active politician, however much he agreed with the side they took, he could never have been in full sympathy.   But with that union of learning and piety which was so distinctively characteristic of the seventeenth century, and of which Donne, Hooker, Sanderson and Herbert were such eminent examples, while Wotton was not lacking in it, Izaak was as much at home spiritually as he was socially in the Bishop's houses where he spent so much of his life.   And he has rendered it for us with that extraordinary *naturalness* which, as has been said, is probably his greatest charm and in which he has few if any equals.   If you go to him with the modern rage for accurate and abundant fact, you may be disappointed, even disgusted : hardly so if you want natural and individual treatment of fact or not-fact. There are forms of this naturalness—perhaps one should rather call them failures of it—which are puerile or forced : but Walton's is never either. There are, of course, other forms, not failures at all, as in all the greatest poets and some of the greatest prose-writers, which are not unnatural, but which transcend ordinary nature.   Walton cannot reach these. But if he never rises to the heights he never sinks to the depths, and is always restful and refreshing to read.

GEORGE SAINTSBURY

1927

CONTENTS

CONTENTS

THE
LIVES

Of
- Dr. *John Donne,*
- Sir *Henry Wotton,*
- Mr. *Richard Hooker,*
- Mr. *George Herbert.*

Written by *IZAAK WALTON.*

The Fourth Edition.

Eccles. XLIV. 7.
These were Honourable Men in their Generations.

LONDON,
Printed by *Tho. Roycroft* for *Richard Marriot.*
Sold by most Booksellers. 1675.

B

To the Right Honourable

And

Reverend Father in *GOD*,

GEORGE

Lord Bishop of *Winchester*, and *Prelate of the most noble Order of the Garter.*

My Lord,

I Did some years past, present You with a plain relation of the Life of Mr. *Richard Hooker,* that humble man, to whose memory, *Princes* and the most *learned of this Nation* have paid a reverence at the mention of his Name.—And, now, with Mr. *Hookers* I present You also, the Life of that *pattern of primitive Piety,* Mr. *George Herbert*; and, with his, the Life of Dr. *Donne,* and your friend Sir *Henry Wotton,* all reprinted.—The two first were written under your roof : for which reason, if they were worth it, you might justly challenge a Dedication : And indeed, so you might of Dr. *Donnes,* and Sir *Henry Wottons* : because, if I had been fit for this Undertaking, it would not have been by acquir'd Learning or Study ; but, by the advantage of forty years friendship, and thereby with hearing and discoursing with Your Lordship, that hath inabled me to make the Relation of

3

these Lives passable (if they prove so) in an eloquent and captious Age.

And indeed, my Lord, though, these relations be well-meant Sacrifices to the Memory of these Worthy men: yet, I have so little Confidence in my performance, that I beg pardon for superscribing your Name to them; And, desire all that know your *Lordship*, to apprehend this not as a Dedication, (at least, by which you receive any addition of Honour;) but rather, as an humble, and a more publick acknowledgment of your long continued, and, your now daily Favours to

My Lord,

Your most affectionate

and

most humble Servant

Izaak Walton.

TO THE
READER.

Though, the several Introductions to these several Lives, have partly declared the reasons how, and why I undertook them: yet, since they are come to be review'd, and augmented, and reprinted; and the four are now become one Book; I desire leave to inform you that shall become my Reader, that when I sometime look back upon my education and mean abilities, 'tis not without some little wonder at my self, that I am come to be publickly in print. And though I have in those Introductions declar'd some of the accidental reasons that occasioned me to be so: yet let me add this to what is there said: that, by my undertaking to collect some notes for Sir Henry Wottons writing the Life of Dr. Donne, and by Sir Henry's dying before he perform'd it, I became like those men that enter easily into a Law-sute, or a quarrel, and having begun, cannot make a fair retreat and be quiet, when they desire it.——— And really, after such a manner, I became ingag'd, into a necessity of writing the Life of Dr. Donne: Contrary, to my first Intentions: And that begot a like necessity of writing the Life of his and my ever-honoured friend, Sir Henry Wotton.

And, having writ these two lives; I lay quiet twenty years, without a thought of either troubling my self or others, by any new ingagement in this kind, for I thought I knew my unfitness. But, about that time, Dr. Gauden

(*then Lord Bishop of* Exeter) *publisht* the Life of Mr.
Richard Hooker, (*so he called it*) *with so many dangerous
mistakes, both of him and* his Books, *that discoursing of
them with his* Grace, Gilbert *that now is Lord Archbishop of* Canterbury ; *he, injoined me to examine some
Circumstances, and then rectifie the Bishops mistakes, by
giving the World a fuller and a truer account of* Mr.
Hooker *and his* Books, *then that Bishop had done, and,
I know I have done so.   And, let me tell the Reader, that
till* his Grace *had laid this injunction upon me, I could
not admit a thought of any fitness in me to undertake it :
but, when he had twice injoin'd me to it, I then declin'd
my own, and trusted his judgment, and submitted to his
Commands :   concluding, that if I did not, I could not
forbear accusing my self of disobedience :   And indeed of*
Ingratitude *for his many favours.*   Thus I became ingaged into the third Life.

For the Life of that great example of holiness Mr.
George Herbert, *I profess it to be so far a* Free-will-offer-
ing, *that it was writ, chiefly to please my self : but, yet,
not without some respect to posterity ; for though he was
not a man that the next age can forget ; yet, many of his
particular acts and vertues might have been neglected, or
lost, if I had not collected and presented them to the
Imitation of those that shall succeed us : for I humbly
conceive writing to be both a safer and truer preserver of
mens Vertuous actions, then tradition, especially as 'tis
manag'd in this age.   And I am also to tell the Reader,
that though this Life of* Mr. Herbert *was not by me writ
in haste, yet, I intended it a Review, before it should be
made publick : but, that was not allowed me, by reason
of my absence from* London *when 'twas printing ; so
that the Reader may find in it, some mistakes, some double
expressions, and some not very proper, and some that
might have been contracted, and, some faults that are not*

justly chargable upon me but the Printer: and yet I hope none so great, as may not by this Confession purchase pardon, from a good natur'd Reader.

And now, I wish that as that learned Jew, Josephus and others, so these men had also writ their own lives: but since 'tis not the fashion of these times, I wish their relations or friends would do it for them, before delays make it too difficult. And I desire this the more: because 'tis an honour due to the dead, *and a generous* debt due to those that shall live, and succeed us: *and, would to them prove both a content and satisfaction. For, when the next age shall* (as this do's) *admire the Learning and clear Reason which that excellent Casuist Doctor Sanderson (the late Bishop of Lincoln) hath demonstrated in his Sermons and other writings; who, if they love vertue, would not rejoice to know that this good man was as remarkable for the* meekness and innocence of his life, *as for his great and useful learning; and indeed, as remarkable for his* Fortitude, *in his long and* patient *suffering (under them, that then call'd themselves the Godly Party) for that Doctrine, which he had* preach'd and printed, *in the happy days of the Nations and the Churches peace: And, who would not be content to have the like account of* Doctor Field, *that great Schoolman, and others of noted learning? And, though I cannot hope, that my example or reason can perswade to this undertaking, yet, I please my self, that I shall conclude my Preface*, with wishing that it were so.

J. W.

To my Old, and most Worthy Friend, Mr. *IZAAK WALTON*, on his Life of Dr. *DONNE*, &c.

WHen to a Nations loss, the Vertuous dye,
  There's justly due, from every hand, and eye,
  That can, or write, or weep, an Elegy.

Which though it be the poorest, cheapest way,
The Debt we owe, great merits to defray,
Yet, it is almost all, that most men pay.

And, these are Monuments of so short date,
That, with their birth, they oft receive their fate:
Dying, with those, whom they would celebrate.

And, though to Verse, great reverence is due;
Yet, what most Poets write, proves so untrue,
It renders truth in Verse, suspected too.

Something more sacred then, and more intire,
The memories of Vertuous men require,
Then what may with their Funeral-torch expire.

This, History can give : to which alone,
The priviledge to mate oblivion
Is granted, when deny'd to brass and stone.

Wherein, my Friend, you have a hand so sure,
Your truths so candid are, your stile so pure,
That what you write, may Envies search endure.

8

Your Pen, disdaining to be brib'd or prest,
Flows without vanity, or interest:
A Vertue, with which few good Pens are blest.

How happy was my Father then! to see
Those men he lov'd, by him he lov'd, to be
Rescu'd from frailties, and mortality.

Wotton and Donne, to whom his soul was knit:
Those twins of Vertue, Eloquence, and Wit,
He saw, in Fames eternal Annals writ.

Where one, has fortunately found a place,
More faithful to him, than his * Marble was:
Which eating age, nor fire, shall e're deface.

* His Monument in St. *Pauls* Church, before the late dreadful fire, 1665.

A Monument! that, as it has, shall last
And prove a Monument to that defac't:
It self, but with the world, not to be rac'd.

And, even, in their flowry Characters,
My Fathers grave, part of your Friendship shares:
For, you have honour'd his in strewing theirs.

Thus, by an office though particular,
Vertues whole Common-weal obliged are:
For, in a vertuous act, all good men share.

And, by this act, the world is taught to know,
That, the true friendship we to merit owe,
Is not discharg'd by complement, and show.

But, yours is Friendship of so pure a kind,
From all mean ends, and interest so refin'd,
It ought to be, a pattern to mankind.

For, whereas, most mens friendships here beneath,
Do perish with their friends expiring breath,
Yours, proves a Friendship living after death.

By which, the generous Wotton, *reverend* Donne,
Soft Herbert, *and, the Churches Champion*
Hooker, *are rescued from oblivion.*

For, though they each of them, his time so spent,
As rais'd unto himself, a Monument
With which Ambition might rest well content!

Yet, their great works, though they can never dye:
And are in truth superlatively high,
Are no just scale, to take their vertues by.

Because, they show not how th' Almighties grace,
By various, and more admirable ways,
Brought them to be the Organs of his praise.

But, what their humble modesty wou'd hide,
And was by any other means deny'd,
Is by your love, and diligence supply'd.

Wotton, *a nobler soul was never bred!*
You, by your narratives most even thred,
Through all his Laborinths of Life have led.

Through his degrees of Honour, and of Arts:
Brought him, secure from Envies venom'd darts;
Which are still level'd, at the greatest parts.

Through, all th' employments of his Wit, and Spirit:
Whose great effects, these kingdoms still inherit;
The trials then, now, trophies of his merit.

Nay, through disgrace; which oft the worthiest have:
Through all state-tempests, through each wind, and wave,
And, laid him, in an honourable grave.

And, yours, and the whole Worlds beloved Donne,
When he, a long, and wild carere had run
To the Meridian of his glorious Sun:

And, being then an object of much ruth,
Led on, by vanities, error, and youth,
Was long e're he did find the way to truth;

By the same Clew, after his youthful swing,
To serve at his Gods Altar here you bring:
Where, an once-wanton-Muse, doth Anthems sing.

And, though by Gods most powerful grace alone,
His heart was setled in Religion:
Yet, 'tis by you, we know how it was done.

And know, that having crucifi'd vanities,
And fixt his hope, he clos'd up his own eyes:
And then, your Friend, a Saint and Preacher dyes.

The meek, and Learned Hooker *too, almost*
I'th Churches ruines over-whelm'd and lost,
Is, by your Pen, recover'd from his dust.

And Herbert : *he, whose education,*
Manners, and parts, by high applauses blown,
Was deeply tainted with Ambition;

And fitted for a Court, made that his aim:
At last, without regard to Birth or Name,
For a poor Country-Cure, does all disclaim.

Where, with a soul compos'd of Harmonies,
Like a sweet Swan, *he warbles, as he dies*
His makers praise, and, his own obsequies.

All this you tell us, with so good success,
That our oblig'd posterity shall profess,
T'have been your Friend, was a great happiness.

And now !
        When many worthier, would be proud
T'appear before you, if they were allow'd,
I, take up room enough to serve a croud.

Where, to commend what you have choicely writ,
Both my poor testimony, and, my wit,
Are equally invalid, and unfit:

Yet this, and much more, is most justly due:
Were what I write, as Elegant *as true,*
To the best friend, I now, or ever knew.

But, my dear friend, 'tis so, that you and I,
By a condition of mortality,
With all this great, and more proud world, must dye;

In which estate, I ask no more of Fame,
Nor, other Monument of Honour claim,
Then that, of your true Friend, *t'advance my name.*

And, if your many merits, shall have bred
An abler Pen, to write your Life when dead;
I think, an honester cannot be read.

Jan. 17. 1672.

Charles Wotton.

The Copy of a Letter writ to Mr. Izaak Walton, *by Doctor* King *Lord Bishop of* Chichester.

Honest Izaak,

THough a Familiarity of more then Forty years continuance, and the constant experience of your Love even in the worst of the late sad times, be sufficient to endear our Friendship; yet, I must confess my Affection much improved, not only by Evidences of private Respect to many that know and love you, but by your new Demonstration of a publick Spirit, testified in a diligent, true, and useful Collection of so many Material Passages as you have now afforded me in the Life of Venerable Mr. *Hooker*; of which, since desired by such a Friend as your self, I shall not deny to give the Testimony of what I know concerning him and his learned Books: but, shall first here take a fair occasion to tell you, that you have been happy in choosing to write the Lives of three such Persons, as Posterity hath just cause to honour; which they will do the more for the true Relation of them by your happy Pen; of all which I shall give you my unfeigned Censure.

I shall begin with my most dear and incomparable Friend Dr. *Donne*, late Dean of St. *Pauls* Church, who not only trusted me as his Executor, but three days before his death delivered into my hands those

excellent Sermons of his now made publick: professing before Dr. *Winniff*, Dr. *Monford*, and, I think,
your self then present at his bed side, that it was by
my restless importunity, that he had prepared them
for the Press; together with which (as his best Legacy)
he gave me all his Sermon-Notes, and his other Papers,
containing an Extract of near Fifteen hundred Authors.
How these were got out of my hands, you, who were
the Messenger for them, and how lost both to me
and your self, is not now seasonable to complain:
but, since they did miscarry, I am glad that the general
Demonstration of his Worth was so fairly preserved,
and represented to the World by your Pen in the
History of his Life; indeed so well, that beside others,
the best Critick of our later time (Mr. *John Hales* of
Eaton Colledge) affirm'd to me, *He had not seen a Life
written with more advantage to the Subject, or more
reputation to the Writer, then that of Dr.* Donnes.

After the performance of this task for Dr. *Donne*,
you undertook the like office for our Friend Sir *Henry
Wotton*: betwixt which two there was a Friendship
begun in *Oxford*, continued in their various Travels,
and more confirmed in the religious Friendship of
Age: and doubtless this excellent Person had writ the
Life of Dr. *Donne*, if Death had not prevented him;
by which means his and your Pre-collections for that
Work fell to the happy Menage of your Pen: a Work
which you would have declined, if imperious Persua-
sions had not been stronger then your modest Resolutions against it. And I am thus far glad, that the first
Life was so imposed upon you, because it gave an
unavoidable Cause of Writing the second: if not? 'tis
too probable, we had wanted both, which had been
a prejudice to all Lovers of Honour and ingenious
Learning. And let me not leave my Friend Sir *Henry*

without this Testimony added to yours; That he was a man of as Florid a Wit and as Elegant a Pen, as any former (or ours which in that kind is a most excellent) Age hath ever produced.

And now having made this voluntary Observation of our two deceased Friends, I proceed to satisfie your desire concerning what I know and believe of the ever-memorable Mr. *Hooker,* who was *Schismaticorum Malleus,* so great a Champion for the Church of *Englands* Rights against the Factious Torrent of Separatists, that then ran high against Church-Discipline: and in his unanswerable Books continues to be so against the unquiet Disciples of their Schism, which now under other Names still carry on their Design; and, who (as the proper Heirs of their Irrational Zeal) would again rake into the scarce closed Wounds of a newly bleeding State and Church.

And first, though I dare not say that I knew Mr. *Hooker;* yet, as our Ecclesiastical History reports to the honour of S. *Ignatius, that he lived in the time of St. John, and had seen him in his Childhood;* so, I also joy that in my Minority I have often seen Mr. *Hooker* with my Father, who was after Bishop of *London;* from whom, and others, at that time, I have heard most of the material passages which you relate in the History of his Life; and, from my Father received such a Character of his *Learning, Humility,* and other Virtues, that like Jewels of unvaluable price, they still cast such a lustre as Envy or the Rust of Time shall never darken.

From my Father I have also heard all the Circumstances of the Plot to defame him; and how Sir *Edwin Sandys* outwitted his Accusers, and gained their Confession; and I could give an account of each particular of that Plot, but that I judge it fitter to be forgotten, and rot in the same grave with the malicious Authors.

I may not omit to declare, that my Fathers Knowledge of Mr. *Hooker* was occasioned by the Learned Dr. *John Spencer*, who after the Death of Mr. *Hooker* was so careful to preserve his unvaluable Sixth, Seventh, and Eighth Books of *ECCLESIASTICAL POLITY*, and his other Writings, that he procured *Henry Jackson*, then of *Corpus Christi* Colledge, to transcribe for him all Mr. *Hookers* remaining written Papers; many of which were imperfect, for his Study had been rifled, or worse used, by Mr. *Chark*, and another, of Principles too like his: but these Papers were endeavoured to be compleated by his dear friend Dr. *Spencer*, who bequeathed them as a precious Legacy to my Father, after whose Death they rested in my hand, till Dr. *Abbot*, then Archbishop of *Canterbury*, commanded them out of my custody, by authorizing Dr. *John Barkeham* to require, and bring them to him to his Palace in *Lambeth*; at which time, I have heard, they were put into the Bishops Library, and that they remained there till the Martyrdom of Archbishop *Laud*; and were then by the Brethren of that Faction given with all the Library to *Hugh Peters*, as a Reward for his remarkable Service in those sad times of the Churches Confusion; and though they could hardly fall into a fouler hand; yet, there wanted not other Endeavors to corrupt and make them speak that Language for which the Faction then fought, which indeed was *To subject the Soveraign Power to the People*.

But I need not strive to vindicate Mr. *Hooker* in this particular; his known Loyalty to his Prince whilest he lived, the Sorrow expressed by King *James* at his Death, the Value our late Soveraign (of ever-blessed Memory) put upon his Works, and now, the singular Character of his Worth by you given in the passages of his Life, especially in your *Appendix* to it, do sufficiently clear him from that Imputation : and I am glad you mention how much value *Thomas Stapleton*, Pope *Clement* the VIII. and other Eminent men of the Romish Perswasion, have put upon his Books : having been told the same in my Youth by Persons of worth that have travelled *Italy*.

Lastly, I must again congratulate this Undertaking of yours, as now more proper to you then any other person, by reason of your long Knowledge and Alliance to the worthy Family of the *Cranmers* (my old Friends also) who have been men of noted Wisdom, especially Mr. *George Cranmer*, whose Prudence added to that of Sir *Edwin Sandys*, proved very useful in the Completing of Mr. *Hookers* matchless Books ; one of their Letters I herewith send you, to make use of, if you think fit. And let me say further ; you merit much from many of Mr. *Hookers* best Friends then living ; namely, from the ever renowned Archbishop *Whitgift*, of whose incomparable Worth, with the Character of the Times, you have given us a more short and significant Account then I have received from any other Pen. You have done much for the Learned Sir *Henry Savile*, his Contemporary and familiar Friend ; amongst the surviving Monuments of whose Learning (give me leave to tell you so) two are omitted ; his Edition of *Euclid*, but especially his Translation of *King James his Apologie for the Oath of Allegeance* into elegant Latine ; which flying in that dress as far as *Rome*, was by the Pope and Conclave sent to *Salamanca* unto *Franciscus Suarez* (then residing there as President of that Colledge) with a Command to answer it. And 'tis worth noting, that when he had perfected the Work, which he calls *Defensio Fidei Catholicæ*, it was transmitted to *Rome* for a view of the Inquisitors; who according to their custom blotted out what they pleased, and (as Mr. *Hooker* hath been used since his Death) added whatsoever might advance the Popes Supremacy, or carry on their own Interest: commonly coupling together *Deponere & Occidere*, the Deposing, and then Killing of Princes. Which cruel and unchristian Language Mr. *John Saltkel*, the *Amanuensis* to *Suarez*, when he wrote that answer (but since a Convert and living long in my Fathers house) often professed, the good Old man (whose Piety and Charity Mr. *Saltkel* magnified much) not only disavowed, but detested. Not to trouble you further; your Reader (if according to your desire, my Approbation of your Work carries any weight) will here find many just Reasons to thank you for it; and possibly for this Circumstance here mentioned (not known to many) may happily apprehend one to thank him, who heartily wishes your happiness, and is unfainedly,

Chichester,
Novem. 17.
1664.

Sir,

Your ever-faithful and

affectionate old Friend,

Henry Chichester.

THE
LIFE
OF
Dr. *JOHN DONNE*,
Late Dean of St. *Paul's* Church,
LONDON.

The Introduction.

*I*F *that great Master of Language and Art, Sir* Henry
Wotton, *the late Provost of* Eaton Colledge, *had
liv'd to see the Publication of these Sermons, he had
presented the World with the* Authors Life *exactly
written ; And, 'twas pity he did not ; for it was a work
worthy his undertaking, and he fit to undertake it :
betwixt whom, and the Author, there was so mutual a
knowledge, and such a friendship contracted in their
Youth, as nothing but death could force a separation.
And, though their bodies were divided, their affections
were not : for that learned Knight's love followed his
Friends fame beyond death and the forgetful grave ;
which he testified by intreating me, whom he acquainted
with his design, to inquire of some particulars that concern'd it, not doubting but my knowledge of the Author,
and love to his memory, might make my diligence useful :*

I did most gladly undertake the employment, and continued it with great content 'till I had made my Collection ready to be augmented and compleated by his matchless Pen : but then, Death prevented his intentions.

When I heard that sad news, and heard also that these Sermons were to be printed, and want the Authors Life, which I thought to be very remarkable : Indignation or grief (indeed I know not which) transported me so far, that I reviewed my forsaken-Collections, and resolv'd the World should see the best plain Picture of the Authors Life that my artless Pensil, guided by the hand of truth, could present to it.

And, If I shall now be demanded as once Pompey's *poor bondman was*, " (The grateful wretch*   * Plutark. *" had been left alone on the Sea-shore, with " the forsaken dead body of his once glorious lord and " master : and, was then gathering the scatter'd pieces " of an old broken boat to make a funeral pile to burn " it (which was the custom of the Romans) who art thou that alone hast the honour to bury the body of* Pompey *the great ? so, who am I that do thus officiously set the Authors memory on fire ? I hope the question will prove to have in it, more of wonder then disdain ; But wonder indeed the Reader may, that I who profess my self artless should presume with my faint light to shew forth his Life whose very name makes it illustrious ! but be this to the disadvantage of the person represented : Certain I am, it is to the advantage of the beholder, who shall here see the Authors Picture in a natural dress, which ought to beget faith in what is spoken : for he that wants skill to deceive, may safely be trusted.*

And if the Authors glorious spirit, which now is in Heaven ; can have the leasure to look down and see me, the poorest, the meanest of all his friends, in the midst of this officious duty, confident I am, that he will not disdain this well-meant sacrifice to his memory : for, whilst his Conversation made me and many others happy below, I know his Humility and Gentleness was then eminent ; and, I have heard Divines say, those Vertues that were but sparks upon Earth, become great and glorious flames in Heaven.

Before I proceed further, I am to intreat the Reader to take notice, that when *Doctor Donn*'s Sermons were first printed, this was then my excuse for daring to write his life ; and, I dare not now appear without it.

The LIFE.

MAster *John Donne* was born in *London*, in the year 1573. of good and vertuous Parents: and, though his own Learning and other multiplyed merits may justly appear sufficient to dignifie both Himself and his Posterity: yet, the Reader may be pleased to know, that his Father was masculinely and lineally descended from a very antient Family in *Wales*, where many of his name now live, that deserve and have great reputation in that Countrey.

By his Mother he was descended of the Family of the famous and learned Sir *Thomas Moor*, sometime Lord *Chancellour* of *England*: as also, from that worthy and laborious *Judge Rastall*, who left Posterity the vast Statutes of the Law of this Nation most exactly abridged.

He had his first breeding in his Fathers house, where a private Tutor had the care of him, until the tenth year of his age; and, in his eleventh year, was sent to the University of *Oxford*; having at that time a good command both of the French and Latine Tongue. This and some other of his remarkable Abilities, made one then give this censure of him; *That this age had brought forth another* Picus Mirandula; of whom Story says, *That he was rather born, than made wise by study.*

There he remained for some years in *Hart-Hall*, having for the advancement of his studies Tutors of several Sciences to attend and instruct him, till time made him capable, and his learning expressed in publick exercises declared him worthy to receive his first degree in the Schools, which he forbore by advice from his friends, who being for their Religion of the *Romish* perswasion, were *conscionably* averse to some parts of the Oath that is alwaies tendered at those times; and not to be refused by those that expect the titulary honour of their studies.

About the fourteenth year of his age, he was transplanted from *Oxford* to *Cambridge*; where, that he might receive nourishment from both Soils, he staied till his seventeenth year; all which time he was a most laborious Student, often changing his studies, but endeavouring to take no degree, for the reasons formerly mentioned.

About the seventeenth year of his age, he was removed to *London*, and then admitted into *Lincolns-Inne*, with an intent to study the *Law*; where he gave great testimonies of his Wit, his Learning, and of his Improvement in that profession: which never served him for other use than an Ornament and Self-satisfaction.

His Father died before his admission into this Society; and being a Merchant, left him his portion in money (it was 3000 l.). His Mother and those to whose care he was committed, were watchful to improve his knowledge, and to that end appointed him Tutors both in the *Mathematicks*, and in all the other *Liberal Sciences*, to attend him. But with these Arts they were advised to instil into him particular Principles of the *Romish Church*; of which those Tutors profest (though secretly) themselves to be members.

They had almost obliged him to their faith; having for their advantage, besides many opportunities, the example of his dear and pious Parents, which was a most powerful perswasion, and did work much upon him, as he professeth in his Preface to his *Pseudo-Martyr*; a Book of which the Reader shall have some account in what follows.

He was now entered into the eighteenth year of his age; and at that time had betrothed himself to no Religion that might give him any other denomination than *a Christian*. And Reason, and Piety had both perswaded him, that there could be no such sin as *Schism*, if an adherence to some visible Church were not necessary.

About the nineteenth year of his age, he, being then unresolv'd what Religion to adhere to, and, considering how much it concern'd his soul to choose the most Orthodox, did therefore (though his youth and health, promised him a long life) to rectifie all scruples that might concern that, presently lay aside all study of the Law: and, of all other Sciences that might give him a denomination; and begun seriously to survey, and consider the Body of Divinity, as it was then controverted betwixt the *Reformed* and the *Roman Church*. And as *Gods blessed Spirit did then awaken him to the search, and in that industry did never forsake him,* (they be his own words *) *so he calls the same holy Spirit to witness this Protestation; that, in that disquisition and search, he proceeded with humility and diffidence in himself; and, by that which he took to be the safest way; namely, frequent Prayers, and an indifferent affection to both parties*; and indeed, truth had too much light about her to be hid from so sharp an Inquirer; and, he had too much ingenuity, not to acknowledge he had found her.

* In his Preface to *Pseudo-Martyr*.

Being to undertake this search, he believed the

Cardinal Bellarmine to be the best defender of the *Roman cause*, and therefore betook himself to the examination of his Reasons. The Cause was weighty: and wilful delays had been inexcusable both towards God and his own Conscience; he therefore proceeded in this search with all moderate haste, and about the twentieth year of his age, did shew the then *Dean* of *Gloucester* (whose name my memory hath now lost) all the Cardinals works marked with many weighty observations under his own hand; which works were bequeathed by him at his death as a Legacy to a most dear Friend.

About a year following he resolved to travel; and the Earl of *Essex* going first the *Cales*, and after the *Island voyages*, the first *Anno* 1596. the second 1597. he took the advantage of those opportunities, waited upon his Lordship, and was an eye-witness of those happy and unhappy employments.

But he returned not back into *England*, till he had staid some years first in *Italy*, and then in *Spain*, where he made many useful observations of those Countreys, their Laws and manner of Government, and returned perfect in their Languages.

The time that he spent in *Spain* was at his first going into *Italy* designed for travelling to the *Holy Land*, and for viewing *Jerusalem* and the Sepulchre of our Saviour. But at his being in the furthest parts of *Italy*, the disappointment of Company, or of a safe Convoy, or the uncertainty of returns of Money into those remote parts, denied him that happiness: which he did often occasionally mention with a deploration.

Not long after his return into *England*, that exemplary Pattern of Gravity and Wisdom, the Lord *Elsemore*, then Keeper of the Great Seal, and *Lord Chancellour of England*, taking notice of his Learning,

Languages, and other Abilities, and much affecting his Person and Behaviour, took him to be his chief Secretary; supposing and intending it to be an Introduction to some more weighty Employment in the State; for which, his Lordship did often protest, he thought him very fit.

Nor did his Lordship in this time of Master *Donne's* attendance upon him, account him to be so much his Servant, as to forget he was his Friend; and to testifie it, did alwayes use him with much courtesie, appointing him a place at his own Table, to which he esteemed his Company and Discourse to be a great Ornament.

He continued that employment for the space of five years, being daily useful, and not mercenary to his Friends. During which time he (I dare not say unhappily) fell into such a liking, as (with her approbation) increased into a love with a young Gentlewoman that lived in that Family, who was Niece to the Lady *Elsemore*, and Daughter to Sir *George Moor*, then Chancellor of the Garter and Lieutenant of the Tower.

Sir *George* had some intimation of it, and knowing prevention to be a great part of wisdom, did therefore remove her with much haste from that to his own house at *Lothesley*, in the County of *Surry*; but too late, by reason of some faithful promises which were so interchangeably passed, as never to be violated by either party.

These promises were only known to themselves, and the friends of both parties used much diligence, and many arguments to kill or cool their affections to each other: but in vain; for love is a flattering mischief, that hath denied aged and wise men a foresight of those evils that too often prove to be the children of that blind father, a passion! that carries us to commit *Errors* with as much ease as whirlwinds

remove feathers, and begets in us an unwearied industry to the attainment of what we desire. And such
an Industry did, notwithstanding much watchfulness
against it, bring them secretly together (I forbear to
tell the manner how) and at last to a marriage too,
without the allowance of those friends, whose approbation always was, and ever will be necessary, to make
even a vertuous love become lawful.

And that the knowledge of their marriage might
not fall, like an unexpected tempest, on those that
were unwilling to have it so : and, that preappre-
hensions might make it the less enormous, when it was
known : it was purposely whispered into the ears of
many that it was so, yet by none that could affirm it.
But, to put a period to the jealousies of Sir *George*
(Doubt often begetting more restless thoughts then the
certain knowledge of what we fear) the news was in
favour to Mr. *Donne,* and with his allowance, made
known to Sir *George,* by his honourable friend and
neighbour *Henry* Earl of *Northumberland* : but it was
to Sir *George* so immeasurably unwelcome, and, so
transported him ; that as though his passion of anger
and inconsideration, might exceed theirs of love and
errour, he presently engaged his Sister the Lady
Elsemore, to join with him to procure her Lord to
discharge Mr. *Donne* of the place he held under his
Lordship.—This request was followed with violence ;
and though Sir *George* were remembred, that Errors
might be overpunished, and desired therefore to forbear
till second considerations might clear some scruples :
yet, he became restless until his suit was granted, and
the punishment executed. And though the *Lord
Chancellor* did not at Mr. *Donnes* dismission, give him
such a Commendation as the great Emperour *Charles*
the fifth, did of his Secretary *Eraso,* when he presented

him to his Son and Successor *Philip* the Second, saying, *That in his* Eraso, *he gave to him a greater gift then all his Estate, and all the Kingdoms which he then resigned to him*: yet the Lord *Chancellor* said, *He parted with a Friend; and such a Secretary as was fitter to serve a King then a Subject.*

Immediately after his dismission from his service, he sent a sad Letter to his Wife, to acquaint her with it: and, after the subscription of his name, writ,

John Donne, Anne Donne, Vn-done,

and God knows it proved too true.

For this bitter Physick of Mr. *Donnes* dismission was not strong enough to purge out all Sir *George's* choler; for, he was not satisfied till Mr. *Donne* and his sometime Compupil in *Cambridge* that married him; namely, *Samuel Brook* (who was after Doctor in Divinity, and Master of Trinity Colledge) and his brother Mr. *Christopher Brook*, sometime Mr. *Donnes* Chamber-fellow in *Lincolns-Inn*, who gave Mr. *Donne* his Wife, and witnessed the marriage, were all committed, to three several prisons.

Mr. *Donne* was first enlarged, who neither gave rest to his body or brain, nor to any friend in whom he might hope to have an interest, until he had procured an enlargement for his two imprisoned friends.

He was now at liberty; but his days were still cloudy: and being past these troubles, others did still multiply upon him; for his wife was (to her extream sorrow) detained from him; and though with *Jacob* he endured not an hard service for her, yet he lost a good one, and, was forced to make good his title, and to get possession of her by a long and restless suit in Law; which proved troublesome and sadly-chargeable to him, whose youth, and travel, and needless bounty, had brought his estate into a narrow compass.

It is observed, and most truly, that silence and submission are charming qualities, and work most upon passionate men ; and it proved so with Sir *George* ; for these, and a general report of Mr. *Donnes* merits, together with his winning behaviour (which when it would intice, had a strange kind of elegant irresistible art) these, and time had so dispassionated Sir *George*, that as the world had approved his Daughters choice, so he also could not but see a more then ordinary merit in his new son : and this at last melted him into so much remorse (for Love and Anger are so like Agues, as to have hot and cold fits ; and love in Parents, though it may be quenched, yet is easily rekindled, and expires not, till death denies mankind a natural heat) that he laboured his Sons restauration to his place ; using to that end, both his own and his Sisters power to her Lord ; but with no success ; for his Answer was, *That though he was unfeignedly sorry for what he had done, yet it was inconsistent with his place and credit, to discharge and readmit servants at the request of passionate petitioners.*

Sir *Georges* endeavour for Mr. *Donnes* readmission, was by all means to be kept secret (for men do more naturally reluct for errors, then submit to put on those blemishes that attend their visible acknowledgment.) But however it was not long before Sir *George* appeared to be so far reconciled, as to wish their happiness ; and not to deny them his paternal blessing, but yet, refused to contribute any means that might conduce to their livelyhood.

Mr. *Donnes* estate was the greatest part spent in many and chargeable Travels, Books and dear-bought Experience : he out of all employment that might yield a support for himself and wife, who had been curiously and plentifully educated; both their natures generous, and accustomed to confer, and not to receive Courtesies: These and other considerations, but chiefly that his wife was to bear a part in his sufferings, surrounded him with many sad thoughts, and some apparent apprehensions of want.

But his sorrows were lessened and his wants prevented by the seasonable courtesie of their noble kinsman Sir *Francis Wolly* of *Pirford* in *Surry*, who intreated them to a cohabitation with him; where they remained with much freedom to themselves, and equal content to him for some years; and, as their charge encreased (she had yearly a child) so did his love and bounty.

It hath been observed by wise and considering men, that Wealth hath seldom been the Portion, and never the Mark to discover good People; but, that Almighty God, who disposeth all things wisely, hath of his abundant goodness denied it (he only knows why) to many, whose minds he hath enriched with the greater Blessings of *Knowledge* and *Vertue*, as the fairer Testimonies of his love to Mankind; and this was the present condition of this man of so excellent Erudition and Endowments; whose necessary and daily expences were hardly reconcileable with his uncertain and narrow estate. Which I mention, for that at this time there was a most generous offer made him for the moderating of his worldly cares; the declaration of which shall be the next employment of my Pen.

God hath been so good to his Church, as to afford it in every age some such men to serve at his Altar as have been piously ambitious of doing good to mankind, a disposition that is so like to God himself, that it

owes it self only to him who takes a pleasure to behold
it in his Creatures. These times * he did
bless with many such; some of which still
live to be Patterns of Apostolical Charity, and of more
than Humane Patience. I have said this, because I
have occasion to mention one of them in my following
discourse; namely, Dr. *Morton*, the most laborious
and learned Bishop of *Durham*; one, that God hath
blessed with perfect intellectuals, and a chearful heart
at the age of 94 years (and is yet living :) one, that
in his days of plenty had so large a heart as to use his
large Revenue to the encouragement of *Learning* and
Vertue, and is now (be it spoken with sorrow) reduced
to a narrow estate, which he embraces without repining; and still shews the beauty of his mind by so
liberal a hand, as if this were an age in which *to morrow
were to care for it self.* I have taken a pleasure in
giving the Reader a short, but true character of this
good man, my friend, from whom I received this
following relation.——He sent to Mr. *Donne*, and
intreated to borrow an hour of his time for a Conference the next day. After their meeting, there was
not many minutes passed before he spake to Mr.
Donne to this purpose; ' Mr. *Donne*, The occasion of
' sending for you is to propose to you what I have
' often revolv'd in my own thought since I last saw
' you : which nevertheless, I will not declare but upon
' this condition, that you shall not return me a pre-
' sent answer, but forbear three days, and bestow
' some part of that time in Fasting and Prayer; and
' after a serious consideration of what I shall propose;
' then return to me with your answer. Deny me
' not, Mr. *Donne*; for, it is the effect of a true love,
' which I would gladly pay as a debt due for yours
' to me.

* 1548.

This request being granted, the
Doctor exprest himself thus:

'Mr. *Donne*, I know your Education and Abilities;
'I know your expectation of a State-employment;
'and I know your fitness for it; and I know too, the
'many delays and contingencies that attend Court-
'promises; and let me tell you that, my love begot by
'our long friendship, and your merits, hath prompted
'me to such an inquisition after your present temporal
'estate, as makes me no stranger to your necessities;
'which I know to be such as your generous spirit
'could not bear, if it were not supported with a pious
'Patience: you know I have formerly perswaded you
'to wave your Court-hopes, and enter into holy
'Orders; which I now again perswade you to
'embrace, with this reason added to my former re-
'quest: The King hath yesterday made me Dean of
'*Gloucester*, and I am also possessed of a Benefice,
'the profits of which are equal to those of my
'Deanry; I will think my Deanry enough for my
'maintenance (who am and resolve to dye a single
'man) and will quit my Benefice, and estate you in it,
'(which the Patron is willing I shall do) if God
'shall incline your heart to embrace this motion.
'*Remember*, Mr. *Donne*, no mans Education or
'Parts make him too good for this employment,
'*which is to be an Ambassadour for the God of glory,*
'*that God who by a vile death opened the gates of life*
'*to mankind.* Make me no present answer; but
'remember your promise, and return to me the third
'day with your Resolution.'

At the hearing of this, Mr. *Donne*'s faint breath and
perplext countenance gave a visible testimony of an
inward conflict; but he performed his promise and

303 c

departed without returning an answer till the third day, and then his answer was to this effect;

'My most worthy and most dear friend, since I
'saw you, I have been faithful to my promise, and
'have also meditated much of your great kindness,
'which hath been such as would exceed even my
'gratitude; but that it cannot do; and more I cannot
'return you; and I do that with an heart full of
'Humility and Thanks, though I may not accept of
'your offer; but, Sir, my refusal is not for that I think
'my self too good for that calling, for which Kings, if
'they think so, are not good enough: nor for that
'my Education and Learning, though not eminent,
'may not, being assisted with God's Grace and
'Humility, render me in some measure fit for it:
'but, I dare make so dear a friend as you are my
'Confessor; some irregularities of my life have been
'so visible to some men, that though I have, I thank
'God, made my peace with him by penitential resolu-
'tions against them, and by the assistance of his Grace
'banish'd them my affections; yet this, which God
'knows to be so, is not so visible to man, as to free me
'from their censures, and it may be that sacred call-
'ing from a dishonour. And besides, whereas it is
'determined by the best of *Casuists*, that *Gods Glory*
'*should be the first end, and a maintenance the second*
'*motive to embrace that calling*; and though each
'man may propose to himself both together; yet the
'first may not be put last without a violation of
'Conscience, which he that searches the heart will
'judge. And truly my present condition is such,
'that if I ask my own Conscience, whether it be
'reconcileable to that rule, it is at this time so per-
'plexed about it, that I can neither give my self nor
'you an answer. You know, Sir, who sayes, *Happy*

'*is that man whose Conscience doth not accuse him for*
'*that thing which he does.* To these I might add other
'reasons that disswade me; but I crave your favour
'that I may forbear to express them, and, thankfully
'decline your offer.

This was his present resolution; but, the heart of
man is not in his own keeping; and he was destined
to this sacred service by an higher hand; a hand so
powerful, as at last forced him to a compliance: of
which I shall give the Reader an account before I shall
give a rest to my Pen.

Mr. *Donne* and his wife continued with Sir *Francis
Wolly* till his death: a little before which time, Sir
Francis was so happy as to make a perfect reconcilia-
tion betwixt Sir *George* and his forsaken son and
daughter; Sir *George* conditioning by bond, to pay to
Mr. *Donne* 800 l. at a certain day, as a portion with
his wife, or 20 l. quarterly for their maintenance: as
the interest for it, till the said portion was paid.

Most of those years that he lived with Sir *Francis*,
he studied the *Civil* and *Canon Laws*; in which he
acquired such a perfection, as was judged to hold
proportion with many who had made that study the
employment of their whole life.

Sir *Francis* being dead, and that happy family dissolved, Mr. *Donne* took for himself a house in *Micham*
(near to *Croydon* in *Surrey*) a place noted for good
air, and choice company: there his wife and children
remained: and for himself he took lodgings in *London*,
near to White-Hall, whither his friends and occasions
drew him very often, and where he was as often visited
by many of the Nobility and others of this Nation, who
used him in their Counsels of greatest consideration:
and with some rewards for his better subsistence.

Nor did our own Nobility only value and favour

him, but his acquaintance and friendship was sought for by most Ambassadours of forraign Nations, and by many other strangers, whose learning or business occasioned their stay in this Nation.

He was much importuned by many friends to make his constant residence in *London*, but he still denied it, having setled his dear wife and children at *Micham*, and near some friends that were bountiful to them and him: for they, God knows, needed it: and that you may the better now judge of the then present Condition of his mind and fortune, I shall present you with an extract collected out of some few of his many Letters.

—— *And the reason why I did not send an answer to your last weeks letter, was, because it then found me under too great a sadness ; and at present 'tis thus with me : There is not one person, but my self, well of my family : I have already lost half a Child, and with that mischance of hers, my wife is fallen into such a discomposure, as would afflict her too extreamly, but that the sickness of all her other children stupifies her : of onie of which, in good faith, I have not much hope : and these meet with a fortune so ill provided for Physick, and such relief, that if God should ease us with burials, I know not how to perform even that : but I flatter my self with this hope, that I am dying too : for I cannot waste faster then by such griefs.   As for,* ——

From my hospital
at Micham,

Aug. 10.

JOHN DONNE.

Thus he did bemoan himself: And thus in other letters.

—— *For, we hardly discover a sin, when it is but an omission of some good, and no accusing act ; with this or*

*the former, I have often suspected my self to be overtaken ;
which is*, with an over earnest desire of the next life :
*and though I know it is not meerly a weariness of this,
because I had the same desire when I went with the tide,
and injoyed fairer hopes then I now do : yet, I doubt
worldly troubles have increased it : 'tis now Spring, and
all the pleasures of it displease me ; every other tree
blossoms, and I wither : I grow older and not better ;
my strength diminisheth and my load grows heavier ; and
yet, I would fain be or do something ; but, that I cannot
tell what, is no wonder in this time of my sadness ; for,
to chuse is to do ; but, to be no part of any body, is as to
be nothing ; and so I am, and shall so judge my self,
unless I could be so incorporated into a part of the world,
as by business to contribute some sustentation to the whole.
This I made account, I began early when I understood
the study of our Laws : but was diverted by leaving that
and imbracing the worst voluptuousness,* an hydroptique
immoderate desire of humane learning and languages :
*Beautiful ornaments indeed to men of great fortunes ;
but mine was grown so low as to need an occupation :
which I thought I entred well into, when I subjected my
self to such a service as I thought might exercise my poor
abilities : and there I stumbled, and fell too : and now
I am become so little, or such a nothing, that I am not a
subject good enough for one of my own letters ;—Sir, I
fear my present discontent does not proceed from a good root,
that I am so well content to be nothing, that is, dead.
But, Sir, though my fortune hath made me such, as that
I am rather a Sickness or a Disease of the world, than any
part of it, and therefore neither love it nor life ; yet I
would gladly live to become some such thing as you should
not repent loving me : Sir, your own Soul cannot be more
zealous for your good then I am, and, God, who loves that
zeal in me, will not suffer you to doubt it : you would*

pity me now, if you saw me write, for my pain hath drawn my head so much awry, and holds it so, that my eye cannot follow my pen. I therefore receive you into my Prayers with mine own weary soul, and Commend my self to yours. I doubt not but next week will bring you good news, for I have either mending or dying on my side : but If I do continue longer thus, I shall have Comfort in this, That my blessed Saviour in exercising his Justice upon my two worldly parts, my Fortune *and my* Body, *reserves all his Mercy for that which most needs it*, my Soul! *which is, I doubt, too like a Porter, that is very often near the gate, and yet goes not out. Sir, I profess to you truly, that my lothness to give over writing now, seems to my self a sign that I shall write no more—*

Your poor friend, *and*
Gods poor patient

JOHN DONNE.

Sept. 7.

By this you have seen, a part of the picture of his narrow fortune, and the perplexities of his generous mind ; and thus it continued with him for about two years ; all which time his family remained constantly at *Micham* ; and to which place he often retir'd himself, and destined some days to a constant study of some points of Controversie betwixt the *English* and *Roman Church* ; and especially those of *Supremacy* and *Allegiance* : and, to that place and such studies he could willingly have wedded himself during his life : but the earnest perswasion of friends became at last to be so powerful, as to cause the removal of himself and family to *London*, where Sir *Robert Drewry*, a Gentleman of a very noble estate, and a more liberal mind, assigned him and his wife an useful apartment in his own large house in *Drewry lane*, and not only rent-free, but was also a cherisher of his studies, and such a friend as sympathized with him and his in all their joy and sorrows.

At this time of Mr. *Donne's*, and his wives living in Sir *Roberts* house, the Lord *Hay* was by King *James* sent upon a glorious Embassie to the then *French* King *Henry* the fourth, and, Sir *Robert* put on a suddain resolution to accompany him to the *French* Court, and, to be present at his audience there. And, Sir *Robert* put on as suddain a resolution, to solicit Mr. *Donne* to be his Companion in that Journey: And this desire was suddainly made known to his wife, who was then with Child, and otherways under so dangerous a habit of body, as to her health, that she profest an unwillingness to allow him any absence from her; saying, *her divining soul boded her some ill in his absence*; and therefore, desired him not to leave her. This made Mr. *Donne* lay aside all thoughts of the Journey, and really to resolve against it. But Sir *Robert* became restless in his perswasions for it; and, Mr. *Donne* was so generous, as to think he had sold his liberty when he received so many Charitable kindnesses from him: and, told his wife so; who did therefore with an unwilling-willingness give a faint Consent to the Journey, which was proposed to be but for two months: for about that time they determin'd their return.—Within a few days after this resolve, the *Embassador*, Sir *Robert*, and Mr. *Donne* left *London*; and were the twelfth day got all safe to *Paris*.—two days after their arrival there, Mr. *Donne* was left alone, in that room in which Sir *Robert*, and he, and some other friends had din'd together. To this place Sir *Robert* return'd within half an hour; and, as he left, so he found Mr. *Donne* alone; but, in such an Extasie, and so alter'd as to his looks, as amaz'd Sir *Robert* to behold him : insomuch that he earnestly desired Mr. *Donne* to declare what had befaln him in the short time of his absence ? to which, Mr. *Donne* was not able to make a present answer : but, after a long and perplext pause, did at last say, *I have seen a dreadful Vision since I saw you : I have seen my dear wife pass twice by me through this room, with her hair hanging about her shoulders, and a dead child in her arms : this, I have seen since I saw you.* To which, Sir *Robert* reply'd ; *Sure Sir, you have slept since I saw you ; and, this is the result of some melancholy dream, which I desire you to forget, for you are now awake.* To which Mr. *Donnes* reply was : *I cannot be surer that I now live, then that I have not slept since I saw you : and am, as sure, that at her second appearing, she stopt, and look'd me in the face, and vanisht.*——Rest and sleep, had not alter'd Mr. *Donne*'s opinion the next day : for, he then affirm'd this Vision with a more deliberate, and, so confirm'd a confidence, that he inclin'd Sir *Robert* to a faint belief that the Vision was true.——It is truly said, *that desire, and doubt, have no rest* : and it prov'd so with Sir *Robert*, for he immediately sent a servant to *Drewry* house with a charge to hasten back, and bring him word, whether Mrs. *Donne* were alive ? and if alive, in what condition she was, as to her health ? —The twelfth day the Messenger returned with this account—That he found and left Mrs. *Donne* very sad, and sick in her bed : and, that after a long and dangerous labor she had been deliver'd of a dead child. And, upon examination, the abortion prov'd to be the same day, and about the very hour that Mr. *Donne* affirm'd he saw her pass by him in his Chamber.

This is a relation that will beget some wonder : and, it well may ; for most of our world are at present possest with an opinion that *Visions* and *Miracles* are ceas'd. And, though 'tis most certain, that two Lutes, being both strung and tun'd to an equal pitch, and then, one plaid upon, the other, that is not totcht, being laid upon a Table at a fit distance, will (like an Eccho to a trumpet) warble a faint audible harmony, in answer to the same tune: yet many will not believe there is any such thing, as a *sympathy of souls*; and I am well pleas'd, that every Reader do injoy his own opinion: but if the unbelieving will not allow the believing Reader of this story, a liberty to believe that it may be true; then, I wish him to consider, many Wise men have believed, that, the ghost of *Julius Cæsar* did appear to *Brutus*, and that both St. *Austin*, and *Monica* his mother, had Visions in order to his Conversion. And, though these and many others (too many to name) have but the authority of humane story, yet, the incredible Reader may find in the Sacred story *, that *Samuel* did appear to *Saul* even after his death (whether really or not? I undertake not to determine.) And, *Bildad* in the Book of *Job*, says these words †, *A spirit passed before my face, the hair of my head stood up, fear and trembling came upon me; and made all my bones to shake.* Upon which words I will make no Comment, but, leave them to be considered by the incredulous Reader; to whom, I will also commend this following consideration: That there be many pious and learned men, that believe our merciful God hath assign'd to every man a particular *guardian Angel*, to be his constant monitor; and, to attend him in all his dangers, both of body and soul. And the opinion that every man hath his particular *Angel*, may gain some authority, by the relation of St. *Peters* miraculous deliverance out of prison ‡, not by many, *but by one Angel*. And

* 1 Sam. 28.

† Job 4.

‡ Acts 12.

this belief may yet gain more credit, by the readers considering that when *Peter* after his inlargement knockt at the door of *Mary* the mother of *John*; and *Rode* the maid servant being surpriz'd with joy that *Peter* was there, did not let him in, but ran in haste and told the Disciples (who were then, and there met together) that *Peter* was at the door: and, they not believing it, *said she was mad*: yet, when she again affirm'd it, though they then believed it not: yet, they concluded, and said: *It is his Angel.*

More observations of this nature, and inferences from them, might be made to gain the relation a firmer belief: but I forbear, lest I that intended to be but a Relator, may be thought to be an ingag'd person for the proving what was related to me; and yet, I think my self bound to declare, that though it was not told me by Mr. *Donne* himself; it was told me (*now long since*) by a Person of Honour, and of such intimacy with him, that he knew more of the secrets of his soul, then any person then living: and I think they told me the truth; for, it was told with such circumstances, and such asseveration, that (to say nothing of my own thoughts) I verily believe he that told it me, did himself believe it to be true.

I forbear the Readers farther trouble, as to the relation, and what concerns it; and will conclude mine, with commending to his view a Copy of Verses given by Mr. *Donne* to his wife at the time that he then parted from her. And I beg leave to tell, that I have heard some Criticks, learned, both in Languages and Poetry, say, that none of the Greek or Latine Poets did ever equal them.

A Valediction, forbidding to Mourn.

As vertuous men pass mildly away,
And whisper to their Souls to go,
Whilst, some of their sad Friends do say,
The breath goes now, and some say no :

So, let us melt, and make no noise ;
No wind-sighs, or tear-flouds us move,
'Twere profanation of our joys,
To tell the Laity our love.

Movings of th' earth, cause harms, and fears ;
Men reckon what they did or meant,
But trepidation of the Sphears,
Though greater far, is innocent.

Dull sublunary lovers love,
(Whose soul is sense) cannot admit
Absence : because, that doth remove
Those things that Elemented it.

But we, by a Soul so much refin'd,
That our souls know not what it is,
Inter-assured of the mind,
Care not, hands, eyes, or lips to miss.

Our two souls therefore, which are one,
Though I must go, indure not yet
A breach, but an expansion,
Like gold, to aiery thinness beat.

If we be two ? we are two so
As stiff twin-compasses are two :
Thy soul, the fixt foot, makes no show
To move, but does, if th' other do.

And, though thine in the Center sit,
Yet, when my other far does rome,
Thine leans, and hearkens after it,
And grows erect as mine comes home.

Such thou must be to me, who must
Like th'other foot, obliquely run :
Thy firmness makes my circle just,
And me to end, where I begun.

I return from my account of the *Vision*, to tell the
Reader, that both before Mr. *Donne*'s going into
France, at his being there, and after his return many
of the Nobility, and others that were powerful at
Court, were watchful and solicitous to the *King* for
some Secular imployment for him.   The *King* had
formerly both known and put a value upon his Company : and had also given him some hopes of a State-
imployment ; being always much pleas'd when Mr.
Donne attended him, especially at his meals, where
there were usually many deep discourses of general
Learning : and very often friendly disputes or debates
of Religion betwixt his Majesty and those Divines,
whose places required their attendance on him at
those times : particularly the Dean of the Chappel ;
who then was Bishop *Montague* (the publisher of
the learned and eloquent Works of his Majesty) and
the most reverend Doctor *Andrews*, the late learned
Bishop of *Winchester*, who then was the Kings
Almoner.

About this time, there grew many disputes that
concerned the *Oath of Supremacy* and *Allegiance*, in
which the King had appeared, and engaged himself
by his publick writings now extant : and, his Majesty
discoursing with Mr. *Donne*, concerning many of the

reasons which are usually urged against the taking of those Oaths; apprehended, such a validity and clearness in his stating the Questions, and his Answers to them, that his Majesty commanded him to bestow some time in drawing the Arguments into a method, and then to write his Answers to them: and, having done that, not to send, but be his own messenger and bring them to him. To this he presently and diligently applied himself, and, within six weeks brought them to him under his own handwriting, as they be now printed; the Book bearing the name of *Pseudo-martyr*, printed *anno* 1610.

When the King had read and considered that Book, he perswaded Mr. *Donne* to enter into the Ministery; to which at that time he was, and appeared very unwilling, apprehending it (such was his mistaking modesty) to be too weighty for his Abilities; and though his Majesty had promised him a favour, and many persons of worth mediated with his Majesty for some secular employment for him (to which his Education had apted him) and particularly the Earl of *Somerset*, when in his greatest height of favour; who being then at *Theobalds* with the King, where one of the Clerks of the Council died that night, the Earl posted a messenger for Mr. *Donne* to come to him immediately, and at Mr. *Donne*'s coming, said, Mr. *Donne*, *To testifie the reality of my Affection, and my purpose to prefer you, Stay in this Garden till I go up to the King, and bring you word that you are Clark of the Council: doubt not my doing this, for I know the King loves you, and know the King will not deny me.* But the King gave a positive denial to all requests, and having a discerning spirit, replied, *I know Mr.* Donne *is a learned man, has the abilities of a learned Divine; and will prove a powerful Preacher, and my* *desire is to prefer him that way, and in that way, I will deny you nothing for him.* After that time, as he professeth,* *The King descended to a perswasion, almost to a solicitation of him to enter into sacred Orders:* which though he then denied not, yet he deferred it for almost three years. All which time he applied himself to an incessant study of Textual Divinity, and to the attainment of a greater perfection in the learned Languages, *Greek* and *Hebrew*.

> * In his Book of Devotions.

In the first and most blessed times of Christianity, when the Clergy were look'd upon with reverence, and deserved it, when they overcame their opposers by high examples of Vertue, by a blessed Patience and long Suffering: those only were then judged worthy the Ministry, whose quiet and meek spirits did make them look upon that sacred calling with an humble adoration and fear to undertake it; which indeed requires such great degrees of *humility*, and *labour*, and *care*, that none but such were then thought worthy of that celestial dignity. And such only were then sought out, and solicited to undertake it. This I have mentioned because forwardness and inconsideration, could not in Mr. *Donne*, as in many others, be an argument of insufficiency or unfitness; for he had considered long, and had many strifes within himself concerning the strictness of life and competency of learning required in such as enter into sacred Orders; and doubtless, considering his own demerits, did humbly ask God with St. *Paul, Lord, who is sufficient for these things?* and, with meek *Moses, Lord, who am I?* And sure, if he had consulted with flesh and blood, he had not for these reasons put his hand to that holy plough. But God who is able to prevail, wrestled with him, as the *Angel* did with *Jacob, and marked him*; mark'd him for his own; mark'd him with a blessing; a blessing of obedience to the motions of his blessed Spirit. And then, as he had formerly asked God with *Moses, Who am I ?* So now being inspired with an apprehension of Gods particular mercy to him, in the Kings and other solicitations of him, he came to ask *King Davids* thankful question, *Lord, who am I, that thou art so mindful of me ?* So mindful of me, as to lead me for more then forty years through this wilderness of the many temptations, and various turnings of a dangerous life : so merciful to me, as to move the learned'st of Kings, to descend to move me to serve at the Altar ! so merciful to me, as at last, to move my heart to imbrace this holy motion : thy motions I will and do imbrace : And, I now say with the blessed Virgin, *Be it with thy servant as seemeth best in thy sight* : and so, *blessed Jesus*, I do take the cup of Salvation, and will call upon thy Name, and will preach thy Gospel.

Such strifes as these St. *Austine* had, when St. *Ambrose* indeavoured his conversion to Christianity; with which he confesseth, he acquainted his friend *Alipius.* Our learned Author (a man fit to write after no mean Copy) did the like. And declaring his intentions to his dear friend Dr. *King* then *Bishop* of *London,* a man famous in his generation, and no stranger to Mr. *Donne*'s abilities, (for he had been Chaplain to the Lord Chancellor, at the time of Mr. *Donne*'s being his Lordships Secretary) That Reverend man did receive the news with much gladness; and, after some expressions of joy, and a perswasion to be constant in his pious purpose, he proceeded with all convenient speed to ordain him first *Deacon,* and then *Priest* not long after.

Now the *English Church* had gain'd a second St.

Austine, for, I think, none was so like him before his Conversion : none so like St. *Ambrose* after it : and if his youth had the infirmities of the one, his age had the excellencies of the other ; the learning and holiness of both.

And now all his studies which had been occasionally diffused, were all concentred in Divinity. Now he had a new calling, new thoughts, and a new imployment for his wit and eloquence : Now all his earthly affections were changed into divine love ; and all the faculties of his own soul, were ingaged in the Conversion of others : In preaching the glad tidings of Remission to repenting Sinners, and peace to each troubled soul. To these he applied himself with all care and diligence : and now, such a change was wrought in him, that he could say with *David*, *Oh how amiable are thy Tabernacles, O Lord God of Hosts!* Now he declared openly, *that when he required a temporal, God gave him a spiritual blessing.* And that, *he was now gladder to be a door-keeper in the house of God, then he could be to injoy the noblest of all temporal imployments.*

Presently after he entred into his holy profession, the King sent for him, and made him his Chaplain in Ordinary ; and promised to take a particular care for his preferment.

And though his long familiarity with Scholars, and persons of greatest quality, was such as might have given some men boldness enough to have preached to any eminent Auditory ; yet his modesty in this imployment was such, that he could not be perswaded to it, but went usually accompanied with some one friend, to preach privately in some village, not far from *London* : his first Sermon being preached at *Paddington*. This he did, till His Majesty sent and appointed him a day to preach to him at *White-hall*, and, though much were expected from him, both by His Majesty and others, yet he was so happy (which few are) as to satisfie and exceed their expectations : preaching the Word so, as shewed his own heart was possest with those very thoughts and joys that he laboured to distill into others : A Preacher in earnest ; weeping sometimes for his Auditory, sometimes with them : always preaching to himself, like an Angel from a cloud, but in none ; carrying some, as St. *Paul* was, to Heaven in holy raptures, and inticing others by a sacred Art and Courtship to amend their lives ; here picturing a vice so as to make it ugly to those that practised it ; and a vertue so, as to make it be beloved even by those that lov'd it not ; and all this with a most particular grace and an unexpressible addition of comeliness.

There may be some that may incline to think (such indeed as have not heard him) that my affection to my Friend, hath transported me to an immoderate Commendation of his Preaching. If this meets with any such, Let me intreat, though I will omit many, yet that they will receive a double witness for what I say ; it being attested by a Gentleman of worth (Mr. *Chidley*, a frequent hearer of his Sermons) in part of a funeral Elogie writ by him on Dr. *Donne* ; and is a known truth, though it be in Verse.

———— *Each Altar had his fire*————
He kept his love, but not his object : wit,
He did not banish, but transplanted it ;
Taught it both time and place, and brought it home
To Piety, which it doth best become.
For say, had ever pleasure such a dress ?
Have you seen crimes so shap't, or loveliness
Such as his lips did clothe Religion in ?

Had not reproof a beauty, passing sin?
Corrupted nature sorrowed that she stood
So near the danger of becoming good.
And, when he preach't she wish't her ears exempt
From Piety, *that had such pow'r to tempt.*
How did his sacred flattery beguile
Men to amend?————

More of this, and more witnesses might be brought, but I forbear and return.

That Summer, in the very same month in which he entred into sacred Orders, and was made the *Kings Chaplain*, His Majesty then going his Progress, was intreated to receive an entertainment in the University of *Cambridge*. And Mr. *Donne* attending his Majesty at that time, his Majesty was pleased to recommend him to the University, to be made *Doctor* in *Divinity; Doctor Harsnet* (after Archbishop of *York*) was then *Vice-Chancellor*, who knowing him to be the Author of that learned Book the *Pseudo-Martyr*, required no other proof of his Abilities, but proposed it to the *University*, who presently assented, and exprest a gladness, that they had such an occasion to intitle him to be theirs.

His Abilities and Industry in his Profession were so eminent, and he so known, and so beloved by Persons of Quality, that within the first year of his entring into sacred Orders, he had fourteen Advowsons of several Benefices presented to him : But they were in the Countrey, and he could not leave his beloved *London,* to which place he had a natural inclination, having received both his Birth and Education in it, and there contracted a friendship with many, whose conversation multiplied the joys of his life : But, an imployment that might affix him to that place would be welcome ; for he needed it.

Immediately after his return from *Cambridge*, his wife died; leaving him a man of a narrow unsetled estate, and (having buried five) the careful father of seven children then living, to whom he gave a voluntary assurance, never to bring them under the subjection of a step-mother; which promise he kept most faithfully, burying with his tears, all his earthly joys in his most dear and deserving wives grave; and betook himself to a most retired and solitary life.

In this retiredness, which was often from the sight of his dearest friends, he became *crucified to the world*, and all those vanities, those imaginary pleasures that are daily acted on that restless stage; and they were as perfectly crucified to him. Nor is it hard to think (being passions may be both changed, and heightned by accidents) but that that abundant affection which once was betwixt him and her, who had long been the delight of his eyes, and the Companion of his youth; her, with whom he had divided so many pleasant sorrows, and contented fears, as Common-people are not capable of; not hard to think but that she, being now removed by death, a commeasurable grief took as full a possession of him as joy had done; and so indeed it did: for now his very soul was elemented of nothing but sadness; now, grief took so full a possession of his heart, as to leave no place for joy: If it did? It was a joy to be alone, where like a *Pelican in the wilderness*, he might bemoan himself without witness or restraint, and pour forth his passions like *Job* in the days of his affliction, *Oh that I might have the desire of my heart! Oh that God would grant the thing that I long for!* For then, *as the grave is become her house*, so I would hasten to make it mine also; *that we two might there make our beds together in the dark.* Thus as the *Israelites* sate mourning by the rivers of *Babylon*,

when they remembered *Sion*; so he gave some ease
to his oppressed heart by thus venting his sorrows:
Thus he began the day, and ended the night; ended
the restless night and began the weary day in *Lamentations*. And, thus he continued till a consideration of
his new ingagements to God, and St. *Pauls Wo is me,
if I preach not the Gospel*: disper'st those sad clouds
that had then benighted his hopes, and now forc'd him
to behold the light.

His first motion from his house was to preach, where
his beloved wife lay buried (in St. *Clements* Church,
near Temple-Bar *London*) and his Text was a part of
the Prophet *Jeremy*'s Lamentation: *Lo, I am the man
that have seen affliction.*

And indeed, his very words and looks testified him
to be truly such a man; and they, with the addition
of his sighs and tears, exprest in his Sermon, did so work
upon the affections of his hearers, as melted and
moulded them into a companionable sadness; and so
they left the Congregation; but then their houses
presented them with objects of diversion: and his,
presented him with nothing but fresh objects of sorrow,
in beholding many helpless children, a narrow fortune,
and a consideration of the many cares and casualties
that attend their education.

In this time of sadness he was importuned by the
grave Benchers of *Lincolns Inne*, who were once the
Companions and Friends of his youth, to accept of
their Lecture, which by reason of Dr. *Gatakers*
removal from thence was then void: of which he
accepted; being most glad to renew his intermitted
friendship with those whom he so much loved;
and where he had been a *Saul*, though not to persecute Christianity, or to deride it, yet in his irregular
youth to neglect the visible practice of it: there to

become a *Paul*, and preach salvation to his beloved brethren.

And now his life was as a *Shining light* among his old friends : now he gave an ocular testimony of the strictness and regularity of it ; now he might say as St. *Paul* adviseth his *Corinthians*, *Be ye followers of me, as I follow Christ, and walk as ye have me for an example* ; not the example of a busie-body ; but of a contemplative, a harmless, an humble and an holy life and conversation.

The love of that noble society was expressed to him many ways : for besides fair lodgings that were set apart and newly furnished for him, with all necessaries, other courtesies were also daily added ; indeed, so many, and so freely, as if they meant their gratitude should exceed his merits ; and in this love-strife of desert and liberality, they continued for the space of two years, he preaching faithfully and constantly to them, and they liberally requiting him. About which time the Emperour of *Germany* died, and the Palsgrave, who had lately married the Lady *Elizabeth* the Kings only daughter, was elected and crowned King of *Bohemia*, the unhappy beginning of many miseries in that Nation.

King *James*, whose Motto (*Beati pacifici*) did truly speak the very thoughts of his heart, endeavoured first to prevent, and after to compose the discords of that discomposed State ; and amongst other his endeavours did then send the Lord *Hay* Earl of *Doncaster* his Ambassadour to those unsetled Princes ; and by a special command from his Majesty Dr. *Donne* was appointed to assist and attend that employment to the Princes of the Union : for which the Earl was most glad, who had always put a great value on him, and taken a great pleasure in his conversation and discourse: and his friends of *Lincolns Inne* were as glad; for they feared that his immoderate study, and sadness for his wives death, would, as *Jacob* said, *make his days few*, and respecting his bodily health, *evil* too: and of this there were many visible signs.

At his going, he left his friends of *Lincolns Inne*, and they him with many reluctations: for though he could not say as S. *Paul* to his *Ephesians*, *Behold you to whom I have preached the Kingdom of God, shall from henceforth see my face no more*; yet he believing himself to be in a Consumption, questioned, and they feared it: all concluding that his troubled mind, with the help of his unintermitted studies, hastened the decays of his weak body: But God who is the God of all wisdom and goodness, turn'd it to the best; for this employment (to say nothing of the event of it) did not only divert him from those too serious studies, and sad thoughts; but seemed to give him a new life by a true occasion of joy, to be an eye-witness of the health of his most dear and most honoured Mistress the Queen of *Bohemia*, in a forraign Nation; and to be a witness of that gladness which she expressed to see him: Who, having formerly known him a Courtier, was much joyed to see him in a Canonical habit, and more glad to be an ear-witness of his excellent and powerful Preaching.

About fourteen months after his departure out of *England*, he returned to his friends of *Lincolns-Inne* with his sorrows moderated, and his health improved; and there betook himself to his constant course of Preaching.

About a year after his return out of *Germany*, Dr. *Cary* was made Bishop of *Exeter*, and by his removal the Deanry of St. *Pauls* being vacant, the King sent to Dr. *Donne*, and appointed him to attend him at Dinner the next day. When his Majesty was sate down, before he had eat any meat, he said after his pleasant manner, Dr. *Donne, I have invited you to Dinner; and, though you sit not down with me, yet I will carve to you of a dish that I know you love well; for knowing you love* London, *I do therefore make you Dean of* Pauls; *and when I have dined, then do you take your beloved dish home to your study; say grace there to your self, and much good may it do you.*

Immediately after he came to his Deanry, he employed work-men to repair and beautifie the Chapel; suffering, as holy *David* once vowed, *his eyes and temples to take no rest, till he had first beautified the house of God.*

The next quarter following, when his Father-in-law Sir *George Moor* (whom Time had made a lover and admirer of him) came to pay to him the conditioned sum of twenty pounds; he refused to receive it, and said (as good *Jacob* did, when he heard his beloved son *Joseph* was alive, *It is enough*) You have been kind to me and mine: I know your present condition is such as not to abound: and I hope mine is or will be such as not to need it: I will therefore receive no more from you upon that contract; and in testimony of it freely gave him up his bond.

Immediately after his admission into his Deanry, the Vicarage of St. *Dunstan* in the West, *London,* fell to him by the death of Dr. *White,* the Advowson of it having been given to him long before by his honourable friend, *Richard* Earl of *Dorset,* then the Patron, and confirmed by his brother the late deceased *Edward,* both of them men of much honour.

By these and another Ecclesiastical endowment which fell to him about the same time, given to him formerly by the Earl of *Kent,* he was enabled to become charitable to the poor, and kind to his friends, and to make such provision for his children, that they were not left scandalous, as relating to their or his Profession and Quality.

The next *Parliament*, which was within that present year, he was chosen *Prolocutor* to the *Convocation*; and about that time was appointed by his Majesty, his most gracious Master, to preach very many occasional Sermons, as at St. *Paul's* Cross, and other places. All which employments he performed to the admiration of the Representative Body of the whole Clergy of this Nation.

He was once, and but once, clouded with the Kings displeasure; and it was about this time; which was occasioned by some malicious whisperer, who had told his Majesty that Dr. *Donne* had put on the general humor of the Pulpits, and was become busie in insinuating a fear of the Kings inclining to *Popery*, and a dislike of his Government: and particularly, for the Kings then turning the Evening Lectures into *Catechising*, and expounding the *Prayer* of our *Lord*, and of the *Belief*, and *Commandments*. His Majesty was the more inclineable to believe this, for that a Person of Nobility and great note, betwixt whom and Dr. *Donne*, there had been a great friendship, was at this very time discarded the Court (I shall forbear his name, unless I had a fairer occasion) and justly committed to prison; which begot many rumors in the common people, who in this Nation think they are not wise, unless they be busie about what they understand not: and especially about Religion.

The King received this news with so much discontent and restlesness, that he would not suffer the Sun to set and leave him under this doubt; but sent for Dr. *Donne*, and required his answer to the Accusation; which was so clear and satisfactory, that the King said *he was right glad he rested no longer under the suspicion.* When the King had said this, Doctor *Donne* kneeled down and thanked his Majesty, and protested his answer was faithful and free from all collusion, and therefore *desired that he might not rise, till, as in like cases he always had from God, so he might have from his Majesty, some assurance that he stood clear and fair in his opinion.* At which the King raised him from his knees with his own *hands,* and *protested he believ'd him: and that he knew he was an honest man, and doubted not but that he loved him truly.* And, having thus dismissed him, he called some Lords of his Council into his Chamber, and said with much earnestness, *My Doctor is an honest man: and my Lords, I was never better satisfied with an answer then he hath now made me: and I always rejoice when I think that by my means he became a Divine.*

He was made Dean the fiftieth year of his age; and in his fifty fourth year, a dangerous sickness seized him, which inclined him to a Consumption. But God, as *Job* thankfully acknowledged, *preserved his spirit,* and kept his intellectuals as clear and perfect, as when that sickness first seized his body: but it continued long and threatned him with death; which he dreaded not.

In this distemper of body, his dear friend Doctor *Henry King* (then chief Residenciary of that Church, and late Bishop of *Chichester*) a man generally known by the Clergy of this Nation, and as generally noted for his obliging nature, visited him daily; and observing that his sickness rendred his recovery doubtful, he chose a seasonable time to speak to him, to this purpose.

'Mr. *Dean,* I am by your favour no stranger to your

'temporal estate, and you are no stranger to the Offer
'lately made us, for the renewing a Lease of the best
'Prebends Corps belonging to our Church, and you
'know, 'twas denied, for that our Tenant being
'very rich, offered to fine at so low a rate as held not
'proportion with his advantages: but I will either
'raise him to an higher sum, or procure that the other
'Residenciaries shall join to accept of what was offered:
'one of these I can and will by your favour do without
'delay, and without any trouble either to your body or
'mind; I beseech you to accept of my offer, for I know
'it will be a considerable addition to your present
'estate, which I know needs it.'

To this, after a short pause, and raising himself
upon his bed, he made this reply.

'My most dear friend, I most humbly thank you
'for your many favours, and this in particular: But,
'in my present condition, I shall not accept of your
'proposal; for doubtless there is such a Sin as *Sacri-
'ledge*; if there were not, it could not have a name
'in Scripture: And the Primitive Clergy were
'watchful against all appearances of that evil; and
'indeed then all Christians lookt upon it with horror
'and detestation: Judging it to be even an *open defiance
*of the Power and Providence of Almighty God, and a
'sad presage of a declining Religion.* But in stead of
'such Christians, who had selected times set apart to
'fast and pray to God, for a pious Clergy which they
'then did obey; Our times abound with men that
'are busie and litigious about trifles and Church-Cere-
'monies; and yet so far from scrupling *Sacriledge,*
'that they make not so much as a *quære* what it is:
'But I thank God I have; and dare not now upon
'my sick-bed, when Almighty God hath made me
'useless to the service of the Church, make any

' advantages out of it. But if he shall again restore
' me to such a degree of health, as again to serve at
' his *Altar*; I shall then gladly take the reward which
' the bountiful Benefactors of this Church have designed
' me; for God knows my Children and Relations will
' need it. In which number my Mother (whose
' Credulity and Charity has contracted a very plentiful,
' to a very narrow estate) must not be forgotten : But
' Doctor *King*, if I recover not, that little worldly
' estate that I shall leave behind me (that very little,
' when divided into eight parts) must, if you deny me
' not so Charitable a favour, fall into your hands as
' my most *faithful friend* and Executor; of whose
' Care and Justice, I make no more doubt then of
' Gods blessing on that which I have conscientiously
' collected for them; but it shall not be augmented
' on my sick-bed; and this I declare to be my unalter-
' able resolution.'

The reply to this was only a promise to observe his
request.

Within a few days his distempers abated; and as
his strength increased, so did his thankfulness to
Almighty God, testified in his most excellent Book of
Devotions, which he published at his Recovery. In
which the Reader may see, the most secret thoughts
that then possest his Soul, Paraphrased and made
publick : a book, that may not unfitly be called a
Sacred picture of Spiritual Extasies, occasioned and
appliable to the emergencies of that sickness; which
book, being a composition of *Meditations, Disquisitions* and *Prayers*, he writ on his sick-bed; herein
imitating the Holy Patriarchs, who were wont to build
their Altars in that place, where they had received
their blessings.

This sickness brought him so near to the gates of

death, and he saw the grave so ready to devour him, that he would often say, his recovery was supernatural: But that God that then restored his health continued it to him, till the fifty-ninth year of his life. And then in *August* 1630. being with his eldest Daughter Mrs. *Harvy* at Abury hatch in *Essex*, he there fell into a Fever, which with the help of his constant infirmity (vapours from the spleen) hastened him into so visible a Consumption, that his beholders might say, as St. *Paul* of himself, *He dyes daily*; and he might say with *Job*, *My welfare passeth away as a cloud, the days of my affliction have taken hold of me, and weary nights are appointed for me.*

Reader, This sickness continued long, not only weakning but wearying him so much, that my desire is, he may now take some rest: and that before I speak of his death, thou wilt not think it an impertinent digression to look back with me, upon some observations of his life, which, whilst a gentle slumber gives rest to his spirits, may, I hope, not unfitly exercise thy consideration.

His marriage was the remarkable error of his life; an error which though he had a wit able and very apt to maintain Paradoxes, yet he was very far from justifying it: and though his wives Competent years, and other reasons might be justly urged to moderate severe Censures; yet he would occasionally condemn himself for it: and doubtless it had been attended with an heavy Repentance, if God had not blest them with so mutual and cordial affections, as in the midst of their sufferings made their bread of sorrow taste more pleasantly then the banquets of dull and low-spirited people.

The Recreations of his youth were *Poetry*, in which he was so happy, as if nature and all her varieties had been made only to exercise his sharp wit, and high fancy; and in those pieces which were facetiously Composed and carelesly scattered (most of them being written before the twentieth year of his age) it may appear by his choice Metaphors, that both *Nature* and all the *Arts* joyned to assist him with their utmost skill.

It is a truth, that in his penitential years, viewing some of those pieces that had been loosely (God knows too loosely) scattered in his youth, he wish't they had been abortive, or so short liv'd that his own eyes had witnessed their funerals: But though he was no friend to them, he was not so fallen out with heavenly Poetry as to forsake that: no not in his declining age; witnessed then by many Divine Sonnets, and other high, holy, and harmonious Composures. Yea, even on his former sick-bed he wrote this heavenly *Hymn*, expressing the great joy that then possest his soul in the Assurance of Gods favour to him when he Composed it.

An Hymn to God the Father.

Wilt thou forgive that sin where I begun,
    Which was my sin, though it were done before;
Wilt thou forgive that sin through which I run,
    And do run still though still I do deplore?
        When thou hast done, thou hast not done,
            For I have more.

Wilt thou forgive that sin, which I have won
    Others to sin, and made my sin their door?
Wilt thou forgive that sin which I did shun
    A year or two, but wallowed in a score?
        When thou hast done, thou hast not done,
            For I have more.

I have a sin of fear, that when I've spun
    My last thread, I shall perish on the shore :
But swear by thy self, that at my death thy Son
    Shall shine as he shines now, and heretofore ;
    And having done that, thou hast done,
                        I fear no more.

I have the rather mentioned this *Hymn,* for that he caus'd it to be set to a most grave and solemn Tune, and to be often sung to the *Organ* by the *Choristers* of St. *Pauls* Church, in his own hearing ; especially at the Evening Service, and at his return from his Customary Devotions in that place, did occasionally say to a friend, *The words of this* Hymn *have restored to me the same thoughts of joy that possest my Soul in my sickness when I composed it. And, O the power of Churchmusick! that Harmony added to this Hymn has raised the Affections of my heart, and quickned my graces of zeal and gratitude ;* and I observe, *that I always return from paying this publick duty of* Prayer *and* Praise *to God, with an unexpressible tranquillity of mind,* and a willingness *to leave the world.*

After this manner did the Disciples of our Saviour, and the best of Christians in those Ages of the Church nearest to his time, offer their praises to Almighty God. And the reader of St. *Augustines* life may there find, that towards his dissolution he wept abundantly, that the enemies of Christianity had broke in upon them, and prophaned and ruined their *Sanctuaries* ; and because their *Publick Hymns* and Lauds were lost out of their Churches. And after this manner have many devout Souls lifted up their hands and offered acceptable Sacrifices unto Almighty God where Dr. *Donne* offered his, and now lyes buried.

But now, oh Lord, how is that place } 1656.
    become desolate.

Before I proceed further, I think fit to inform the Reader, that not long before his death he caused to be drawn a figure of the Body of Christ extended upon an Anchor, like those which Painters draw when they would present us with the picture of Christ crucified on the Cross : his varying no otherwise then to affix him not to a Cross but to an Anchor (the Emblem of hope) this he caused to be drawn in little, and then many of those figures thus drawn to be ingraven very small in *Helitropian* Stones, and set in gold, and of these he sent to many of his dearest friends to be used as *Seals*, or *Rings*, and kept as memorials of him, and of his affection to them.

His dear friends and benefactors, Sir *Henry Goodier*, and Sir *Robert Drewry*, could not be of that number ; Nor could the Lady *Magdalen Herbert*, the mother of *George Herbert*, for they had put off mortality, and taken possession of the grave before him : But Sir *Henry Wotton*, and Dr. *Hall* the then late deceased Bishop of *Norwich* were ; and so were Dr. *Duppa*, Bishop of *Salisbury*, and Dr. *Henry King* Bishop of *Chichester* (lately deceased) men, in whom there was such a Commixture of general *Learning*, of natural *Eloquence*, and Christian *Humility*, that they deserve a Commemoration by a pen equal to their own, which none have exceeded.

And in this enumeration of his friends, though many must be omitted, yet that man of primitive piety, Mr. *George Herbert* may not ; I mean that *George Herbert*, who was the Author of the *Temple*, or *Sacred Poems and Ejaculations*. A Book, in which by declaring his own spiritual Conflicts, he hath Comforted and raised many a dejected and discomposed Soul, and charmed them into sweet and quiet thoughts : A Book, by the frequent reading whereof, and the assistance of that Spirit that seemed to inspire the Author, the Reader may attain habits of *Peace* and *Piety*, and all the gifts of the *Holy Ghost* and *Heaven* : and may by still reading, still keep those sacred fires burning upon the Altar of so pure a heart, as shall free it from the anxieties of this world, and keep it fixt upon things that are above ;) betwixt this *George Herbert* and Dr. *Donne* there was a long and dear friendship, made up by such a Sympathy of inclinations, that they coveted and joyed to be in each others Company ; and this happy friendship, was still maintained by many sacred indearments ; of which, that which followeth may be some Testimony.

To Mr. *George Herbert* ; sent him with one of my Seals of the *Anchor* and *Christ*. (A sheaf of Snakes used heretofore to be my Seal, which is the Crest of our poor Family.)

Qui prius assuetus serpentum falce tabellas
    Signare, hæc nostræ Symbola parva domus
Adscitus domui domini.——

Adopted in Gods family, and so
    My old Coat lost into new Arms I go.
The Cross *my seal in Baptism spread below,*
    Does by that form into an Anchor grow.
Crosses grow Anchors, bear as thou should'st do
    Thy Cross, and that Cross grows an Anchor too.
But he that makes our Crosses Anchors thus,
    Is Christ ; *who there is crucified for us.*
Yet with this I may my first Serpents hold :
    (God gives new blessings, and yet leaves the old)
The Serpent may as wise my pattern be ;
    My poison, as he feeds on dust, that's me.

And, as he rounds the earth to murder, sure
  He is my death; but on the Cross my cure.
Crucifie nature then; and then implore
  All grace from him, crucify'd there before.
When all is Cross, and that Cross Anchor grown,
  This seals a Catechism, not a seal alone.
Vnder that little seal great gifts I send,
  Both works and prayers, pawns & fruits of a friend;
Oh may that Saint that rides on our great Seal,
  To you that bear his name large bounty deal.

John Donne.

In Sacram Anchoram Piscatoris
GEORGE HERBERT.

Quod Crux nequibat fixa clavique additi,
Tenere Christum scilicet ne ascenderet
Tuive Christum————

Although the Cross could not Christ here detain,
When nail'd unto't, but he ascends again:
Nor yet thy eloquence here keep him still,
But only whilst thou speak'st; this Anchor will:
Nor canst thou be content, unless thou to
This certain Anchor add a seal, and so
The water and the earth, both unto thee
Do owe the Symbole of their certainty.
Let the world reel, we and all ours stand sure,
This Holy Cable's from all storms secure.

George Herbert.

I return to tell the Reader, that besides these verses
to his dear Mr. *Herbert,* and that *Hymn* that I men-

tioned to be sung in the *Quire* of St. *Pauls Church*; he did also shorten and beguile many sad hours by composing other sacred Ditties ; and he writ an Hymn on his death-bed, which bears this title.

An Hymn to God, my God, in my sickness, *March* 23. 1630.

Since I am coming to that holy room,
Where, with thy Quire of Saints for evermore
I shall be made thy musique, as I come
I tune my Instrument here at the dore,
And what I must do then, think here before.

Since my Physitians by their loves are grown
Cosmographers ! and I their map, who lye
Flat on this bed————

————————————————

So, in his purple wrapt receive me, Lord !
By these, his thorns, give me his other Crown :
And, as to other souls I preach'd thy Word,
Be this my Text : my Sermon to mine own.
That, he may raise ; therefore, the Lord throws down.

If these fall under the censure of a soul, whose too much mixture with earth makes it unfit to judge of these high raptures and illuminations ; let him know that many holy and devout men have thought the Soul of *Prudentius* to be most refined, when not many days before his death *he charged it to present his God each morning and evening with a new and spiritual song*; justified, by the example of King *David* and the good King *Hezekias*, who upon the renovation of his years paid his thankful vows to Almighty God in a *royal Hymn*, which he concludes in these words, *The Lord was ready to save, therefore I will sing my songs to the stringed instruments all the days of my life in the temple of my God.*

The latter part of his life may be said to be a continued study ; for as he usually preached once a week, if not oftner, so after his Sermon he never gave his eyes rest, till he had chosen out a new Text, and that night cast his Sermon into a form, and his Text into divisions ; and the next day betook himself to consult the Fathers, and so commit his meditations to his memory, which was excellent.   But upon Saturday he usually gave himself and his mind a rest from the weary burthen of his weeks meditations, and usually spent that day in visitation of friends, or some other diversions of his thoughts ; and would say, that *he gave both his body and mind that refreshment, that he might be enabled to do the work of the day following, not faintly, but with courage and chearfulness.*

Nor was his age only so industrious, but in the most unsetled days of his youth, his bed was not able to detain him beyond the hour of four in a morning : and it was no common business that drew him out of his chamber till past ten.   All which time was employed in study ; though he took great liberty after it ; and if this seem strange, it may gain a belief by the visible fruits of his labours : some of which remain as testimonies of what is here written : for he left the resultance of 1400. Authors, most of them abridged and analysed with his own hand ; he left also sixscore of his Sermons, all written with his own hand ; also an exact and laborious Treatise concerning *Self-murther*, called *Biathanatos* ; wherein all the Laws violated by that Act are diligently surveyed and judiciously censured : a Treatise written in his younger days, which alone might declare him then not only perfect in the *Civil* and *Canon Law*, but in many other such studies and arguments, as enter not into the consideration of many that labour to be thought great Clerks, and pretend to know all things.

Nor were these only found in his study, but all businesses that past of any publick consequence, either in this, or any of our neighbour-nations, he abbreviated either in Latine, or in the Language of that Nation, and kept them by him for useful memorials. So he did the Copies of divers Letters and cases of Conscience that had concerned his friends, with his observations and solutions of them ; and divers other businesses of importance ; all particularly and methodically digested by himself.

He did prepare to leave the world before life left him ; making his Will when no faculty of his soul was damp'd or made defective by pain or sickness, or he surprized by a sudden apprehension of death : but it was made with mature deliberation, expressing himself an impartial father by making his childrens portions equal ; and a lover of his friends, whom he remembred with Legacies fitly and discreetly chosen and bequeathed. I cannot forbear a nomination of some of them ; for methinks they be persons that seem to challenge a recordation in this place ; as namely, to his Brother-in-law Sir *Thomas Grimes*, he gave that striking Clock which he had long worn in his pocket—— to his dear friend and Executor Dr. *King* (late Bishop of *Chichester*) that model of gold of the Synod of *Dort*, with which the States presented him at his last being at the *Hague*—— and the two Pictures of *Padre Paulo* and *Fulgentio*, men of his acquaintance when he travelled *Italy*, and of great

note in that Nation for their remarkable learning.——
To his antient friend Dr. *Brook* (that married him)
Master of *Trinity Colledge* in *Cambridge*, he gave the
Picture of the blessed Virgin and *Joseph*.—— To Dr.
Winniff (who succeeded him in the Deanry) he gave
a Picture called the *Sceleton*.—— To the succeeding
Dean, who was not then known, he gave many necessaries
of worth, and useful for his house; and also several
Pictures and Ornaments for the Chappel, with a desire
that they might be registred, and remain as a Legacy
to his Successors.—— To the Earls of *Dorset* and
Carlile, he gave several Pictures; and so he did to
many other friends; Legacies, given rather to express
his affection, than to make any addition to their Estates:
but unto the Poor he was full of Charity, and unto
many others, who by his constant and long continued
bounty might intitle themselves to be his Alms-people;
for all these he made provision; and so largely, as
having then six children living, might to some appear
more than proportionable to his Estate. I forbear
to mention any more, lest the Reader may think I tres-
pass upon his patience: but I will beg his favour to
present him with the beginning and end of his Will.

In the Name of the blessed and glorious Trinity, Amen.
I John Donne, *by the mercy of* Christ Jesus, *and by
the calling of the Church of* England Priest, *being at
this time in good health and perfect understanding
(praised be God therefore) do hereby make my last Will
and Testament in manner and form following:*
*First, I give my gracious God an intire sacrifice of
body and soul, with my most humble thanks for that
assurance which his blessed Spirit imprints in me now
of the salvation of the one, and the Resurrection of the
other; and for that constant and chearful resolution*

which the same Spirit hath establisht in me to live and dye in the Religion now professed in the Church of England. *In expectation of that Resurrection, I desire my body may be buried (in the most private manner that may be) in that place of St.* Pauls *Church* London, *that the now Residentiaries have at my request designed for that purpose, &c.——— And this my last Will and Testament, made in the fear of God (whose mercy I humbly beg, and constantly rely upon in Jesus Christ) and in perfect love and charity with all the world (whose pardon I ask, from the lowest of my servants, to the highest of my Superiors) written all with my own hand, and my name subscribed to every page, of which there are five in number.*

Sealed *Decemb.* 13. 1630.

Nor was this blessed sacrifice of Charity expressed only at his death, but in his life also, by a chearful and frequent visitation of any friend whose mind was dejected, or his fortune necessitous ; he was inquisitive after the wants of Prisoners, and redeemed many from thence that lay for their Fees or small Debts ; he was a continual Giver to poor Scholars, both of this and forraign Nations. Besides what he gave with his own hand, he usually sent a Servant, or a discreet and trusty Friend, to distribute his Charity to all the Prisons in *London* at all the Festival times of the year, especially at the *Birth* and *Resurrection* of our Saviour. He gave an hundred pounds at one time to an old Friend, whom he had known live plentifully, and by a too liberal heart and carelessness, become decayed in his Estate : and, when the receiving of it was denied, by the Gentlemans saying, *He wanted not* ; for the Reader may note, that as there be some spirits so generous as to labour to conceal, and endure a sad poverty, rather than expose themselves to those blushes that attend the confession of it; so there be others to whom Nature and Grace have afforded such sweet and compassionate souls, as to pity and prevent the Distresses of Mankind; which I have mentioned because of Dr. *Donne's* Reply, whose Answer was, *I know you want not what will sustain nature, for a little will do that; but my desire is, that you who in the days of your plenty have cheared and raised the hearts of so many of your dejected friends, would now receive this from me, and use it as a cordial for the chearing of your own:* and upon these terms it was received. He was an happy reconciler of many differences in the Families of his Friends, and Kindred, (which he never undertook faintly; for such undertakings have usually faint effects) and they had such a faith in his judgment and impartiality, that he never advised them to any thing in vain. He was even to her death a most dutiful Son to his Mother, careful to provide for her supportation, of which she had been destitute, but that God raised him up to prevent her necessities; who having sucked in the Religion of the *Roman Church* with her Mothers Milk, spent her Estate in forraign Countreys, to enjoy a liberty in it, and died in his house but three Moneths before him.

And to the end it may appear how just a Steward he was of his Lord and Masters Revenue, I have thought fit to let the Reader know, that after his entrance into his Deanery, as he numbered his years, he (at the foot of a private account to which God and his Angels were only witnesses with him) computed first his Revenue, then what was given to the Poor, and other Pious Uses: and lastly, what rested for him and his; and, having done that, he then blest each years poor remainder with a thankful Prayer; which, for that they discover a more than common Devotion, the Reader shall partake some of them in his own words:

So all is that remains⎫
this year   ⎭

Deo Opt. Max. benigno
Largitori, à me, & ab iis
Quibus hæc à me reservantur,
Gloria & gratia in æternum.
              Amen.

So, that this year, God hath ⎫
blessed me and mine with⎭

Multiplicatæ sunt super
Nos misericordiæ tuæ
Domine.————————

Da Domine, ut quæ ex immensa
Bonitate tuâ nobis elargiri
Dignatus sis, in quorumcunque
Manus devenerint, in tuam
Semper cedant gloriam.
              Amen.

In fine horum sex Annorum manet————

Quid habeo quod non accepi à Domino?
Largitur etiam ut quæ largitus est
Sua iterum fiant, bono eorum usu; ut
Quemadmodum nec officiis hujus mundi,
Nec loci in quo me posuit; dignitati, nec

Servis, nec egenis, in toto hujus anni
Curriculo mihi conscius sum me defuisse ;
Ita & liberi, quibus quæ supersunt,
Supersunt, grato animo ea accipiant,
Et beneficum authorem recognoscant.
                                    Amen.

But I return from my long Digression.

We left the Author sick in *Essex,* where he was
forced to spend much of that Winter, by reason of
his disability to remove from that place : And having
never for almost twenty years omitted his personal
attendance on His Majesty in that month in which
he was to attend and preach to him ; nor having ever
been left out of the Roll and number of Lent-Preachers,
and there being then (in *January* 1630.) a report
brought to *London,* or raised there, that Dr. *Donne* was
dead : That report gave him occasion to write this
following Letter to a dear friend.

Sir,

‘ This advantage you and my other friends have by
‘ my frequent Fevers, that I am so much the oftner
‘ at the gates of Heaven ; and this advantage by the
‘ solitude and close imprisonment that they reduce me
‘ to after, that I am so much the oftner at my prayers,
‘ in which I shall never leave out your happiness ; and
‘ I doubt not among his other blessings, God will add
‘ some one to you for my prayers. A man would
‘ almost be content to dye (if there were no other
‘ benefit in death) to hear of so much sorrow, and so
‘ much good testimony from good men as I (God be
‘ blessed for it) did upon the report of my death ; yet
‘ I perceive it went not through all ; for one writ to
‘ me that some (and he said of my friends) conceived

' I was not so ill as I pretended, but withdrew my self
' to live at ease, discharged of preaching.   It is an un-
' friendly, and God knows an ill-grounded interpreta-
' tion ; for I have always been sorrier when I could
' not preach, than any could be they could not hear
' me.   It hath been my desire, and God may be
' pleased to grant it, that I might dye in the Pulpit ;
' if not that, yet that I might take my death in the
' Pulpit, that is, dye the sooner by occasion of those
' labours.   Sir, I hope to see you presently after
' *Candlemas*, about which time will fall my *Lent-*
' *Sermon at Court*, except my *Lord Chamberlain* believe
' me to be dead, and so leave me out of the Roll ;
' but as long as I live, and am not speechless, I would
' not willingly decline that service.   I have better
' leisure to write, than you to read ; yet I would not
' willingly oppress you with too much Letter.   God
' so bless you and your Son as I wish, to
                    Your poor friend and servant
                        in Christ Jesus,
                            J. Donne.

   Before that month ended, he was appointed to preach
upon his old constant day, the first *Friday* in *Lent* ; he
had notice of it, and had in his sickness so prepared
for that imployment, that as he had long thirsted for
it : so he resolved his weakness should not hinder his
journey ; he came therefore to *London*, some few days
before his appointed day of preaching.   At his coming
thither, many of his friends (who with sorrow saw his
sickness had left him but so much flesh as did only
cover his bones) doubted his strength to perform that
task ; and did therefore disswade him from undertaking it, assuring him however, it was like to shorten his
life ; but he passionately denied their requests ; saying,

he would not doubt that that God who in so many weaknesses had assisted him with an unexpected strength, would now withdraw it in his last employment; professing an holy ambition to perform that sacred work.   And, when to the amazement of some beholders he appeared in the Pulpit, many of them thought he presented himself not to preach mortification by a living voice: but, mortality by a decayed body and a dying face.   And doubtless, many did secretly ask that question in *Ezekiel*; *Do these bones live?* Ezek. 37. 3. *or, can that soul organize that tongue, to speak so long time as the sand in that glass will move towards its centre, and measure out an hour of this dying mans unspent life?*   Doubtless it cannot; and yet, after some faint pauses in his zealous prayer, his strong desires enabled his weak body to discharge his memory of his preconceived meditations, which were of dying: the Text being, *To God the Lord belong the issues from death.*   Many that then saw his tears, and heard his faint and hollow voice, professing they thought the Text prophetically chosen, and that Dr. Donne *had preach't his own Funeral Sermon.*

Being full of joy that God had enabled him to perform this desired duty, he hastened to his house; out of which he never moved, till like St. *Stephen, he was carried by devout men to his Grave.*

The next day after his Sermon, his strength being much wasted, and his spirits so spent, as indisposed him to business, or to talk: A friend that had often been a witness of his free and facetious discourse, asked him, *Why are you sad?*   To whom he replied with a countenance so full of chearful gravity, as gave testimony of an inward tranquillity of mind, and of a soul willing to take a farewell of this world; And said,

' I am not sad, but most of the night past I have

' entertained my self with many thoughts of several
' friends that have left me here, *and are gone to that*
' *place from which they shall not return;* And, that
' within a few days *I also shall go hence, and be no*
' *more seen.* And my preparation for this change is
' become my nightly meditation upon my bed, which
' my infirmities have now made restless to me.   But,
' at this present time, I was in a serious contempla-
' tion of the providence and goodness of God to
' me : to me *who am less than the least of his mercies;*
' and looking back upon my life past, I now plainly
' see it was his hand that prevented me from all tem-
' poral employment;   and that it was his Will I
' should never settle nor thrive till I entred into the
' Ministry;   in which, I have now liv'd almost twenty
' years (I hope to his glory) and by which I most
' humbly thank him, I have been enabled to requite
' most of those friends which shewed me kindness
' when my fortune was very low, as God knows it
' was : and (as it hath occasioned the expression of
' my gratitude) I thank God most of them have stood
' in need of my requital.   I have liv'd to be useful
' and comfortable to my good Father-in-law Sir
' *George Moore,* whose patience God hath been pleased
' to exercise with many temporal Crosses;   I have
' maintained my own Mother, whom it hath pleased
' God after a plentiful fortune in her younger days,
' to bring to a great decay in her very old age.   I
' have quieted the Consciences of many that have
' groaned under the burthen of a wounded spirit,
' whose prayers I hope are available for me : I cannot
' plead innocency of life, especially of my youth :
' But I am to be judged by a merciful God, *who is*
' *not willing to see what I have done amiss.* And,
' though of my self I have nothing to present to him

'but sins and misery; yet, I know he looks not upon
'me now as I am of my self, but as I am in my Saviour,
'and hath given me even at this present time some
'testimonies by his Holy Spirit, that I am of the
'number of his Elect: *I am therefore full of unex-*
'*pressible joy, and shall dye in peace.*

I must here look so far back, as to tell the Reader,
that at his first return out of *Essex* to preach his last
Sermon, his old Friend and Physitian, Dr. *Fox*, a
man of great worth, came to him to consult his health;
and that after a sight of him, and some queries concerning his distempers, he told him, *That by Cordials,*
and drinking milk twenty days together, there was a
probability of his restauration to health; but he
passionately denied to drink it. Nevertheless, Dr.
Fox, who loved him most intirely, wearied him with
sollicitations, till he yielded to take it for ten days;
at the end of which time, he told Dr. *Fox, he had drunk*
it more to satisfie him, than to recover his health; and,
that he would not drink it ten days longer upon the best
moral assurance of having twenty years added to his life:
for he loved it not; and was so far from fearing death,
which to others is the King of terrors: that he long'd
for the day of his dissolution.

It is observed, that a desire of glory or commendation is rooted in the very nature of man; and that
those of the severest and most mortified lives, though
they may become so humble as to banish self-flattery,
and such weeds as naturally grow there: yet they
have not been able to kill this desire of glory, but that,
like our radical heat, it will both live and dye with
us; and many think it should do so; and we want
not sacred examples to justifie the desire of having our
memory to out-live our lives: which I mention,
because Dr. *Donne*, by the perswasion of Dr. *Fox*,

easily yielded at this very time to have a Monument made for him; but Dr. *Fox* undertook not to perswade him how, or what Monument it should be; that was left to Dr. *Donne* himself.

A Monument being resolved upon, Dr. *Donne* sent for a Carver to make for him in wood the figure of an *Vrn*, giving him directions for the compass and height of it; and to bring with it a board of the just height of his body. 'These being got: then 'without delay a choice Painter was got to be in a 'readiness to draw his Picture, which was taken as 'followeth.—— Several Charcole-fires being first made 'in his large Study, he brought with him into that 'place his winding-sheet in his hand, and, having 'put off all his cloaths, had this sheet put on him, 'and so tyed with knots at his head and feet, and his 'hands so placed, as dead bodies are usually fitted to 'be shrowded and put into their Coffin, or grave. 'Upon this *Vrn* he thus stood with his eyes shut, and 'with so much of the sheet turned aside as might 'shew his lean, pale, and death-like face, which was 'purposely turned toward the East, from whence he 'expected the second coming of his and our Saviour 'Jesus.' In this posture he was drawn at his just height; and when the Picture was fully finished, he caused it to be set by his bed-side, where it continued, and became his hourly object till his death: and, was then given to his dearest friend and Executor Doctor *Henry King*, then chief Residentiary of St. *Pauls*, who caused him to be thus carved in one entire piece of white Marble, as it now stands in that Church; and by Doctor *Donne*'s own appointment, these words were to be affixed to it as his Epitaph:

JOHANNES DONNE
Sac. Theol. Profess.

Post varia Studia quibus ab annis tenerrimis fi-
deliter, nec infeliciter incubuit;
Instinctu & impulsu Sp. Sancti, Monitu
& Hortatu

REGIS JACOBI, Ordines Sacros am-
plexus Anno sui Jesu, 1614. & suæ ætatis 42.
Decanatu hujus Ecclesiæ indutus 27. Novem-
bris 1621.

Exutus morte ultimo Die Martii 1631.
Hic licet in Occiduo Cinere Aspicit Eum
Cujus nomen est Oriens.

And now, having brought him through the many labyrinths and perplexities of a various life: even to the gates of death and the grave; my desire is, he may rest till I have told my Reader, that I have seen many Pictures of him, in several habits, and at several ages, and in several postures: And I now mention this, because I have seen one Picture of him, drawn by a curious hand at his age of eighteen; with his sword and what other adornments might then suit with the present fashions of youth, and the giddy gayeties of that age: and his Motto then was,

> *How much shall I be chang'd,*
> *Before I am chang'd.*

And if that young, and his now dying Picture, were at this time set together, every beholder might say, *Lord! How much is Dr.* Donne *already chang'd, before he is chang'd?* And the view of them might give my Reader occasion, to ask himself with some amazement, *Lord! How much may I also, that am now in health be chang'd, before I am chang'd? before this vile, this changeable body shall put off mortality?* and therefore to prepare for it.—— But this is not writ so much for my Readers *Memento*, as to tell him, that Dr. *Donne* would often in his private discourses, and often publickly in his Sermons, mention the many changes both of his body and mind: especially of his mind from a vertiginous giddiness; and would as often say, *His great and most blessed change was from a temporal, to a spiritual imployment*: in which he was so happy, that he accounted the former part of his life to be lost. And, the beginning of it to be, from his first entring into *sacred Orders*; and serving his most merciful God at his Altar.

Upon *Monday* after the drawing this Picture, he took his last leave of his beloved Study; and, being sensible of his hourly decay, retired himself to his bed-chamber: and that week sent at several times for many of his most considerable friends, with whom he took a solemn and deliberate farewell; commending to their considerations some sentences useful for the regulation of their lives, and then dismist them, as good *Jacob* did his sons, with a spiritual benediction. The *Sunday* following he appointed his servants, that if there were any business yet undone that concerned him or themselves, it should be prepared against *Saturday* next; for after that day he would not mix his thoughts with any thing that concerned this world; nor ever did : But, as *Job*, so he *waited for the appointed day of his dissolution.*

And now he was so happy as to have nothing to do but to dye ; to do which, he stood in need of no longer time, for he had studied it long ; and to so happy a perfection, that in a former sickness he called God to witness * *he was that minute ready to deliver his soul into his hands, if that minute God would determine his dissolution.* In that sickness he beg'd of God the constancy to be preserved in that estate for ever ; and his patient expectation to have his immortal soul disrob'd from her garment of mortality, makes me confident he now had a modest assurance that his Prayers were then heard, and his Petition granted. He lay fifteen days earnestly expecting his hourly change ; and, in the last hour of his last day, as his body melted away and vapoured into spirit, his soul having, I verily believe, some Revelation of the Beatifical Vision, he said, *I were miserable if I might not dye* ; and after those words, closed many periods of his faint breath, by saying often, *Thy Kingdom come, Thy Will be done.* His speech, which had long been his ready and faithful servant, left him not till the last minute of his life, and then forsook him not to serve another Master (for who speaks like him) but dyed before him, for that it was then become useless to him that now conversed with God on earth, as Angels are said to do in heaven, *only by thoughts and looks.* Being speechless, and seeing heaven by that illumination by which he saw it ; he did, as St. *Stephen, look stedfastly into it, till he saw the Son of man, standing at the right hand of God his Father* ; and being satisfied with this blessed sight, as his soul ascended, and his last breath departed from him, he closed his

* In his Book of Devotions written then.

own eyes; and then disposed his hands and body into such a posture as required not the least alteration by those that came to shroud him.

Thus *variable*, thus *vertuous* was the Life; thus *excellent*, thus *exemplary* was the Death of this memorable man.

He was buried in that place of St. *Pauls* Church which he had appointed for that use some years before his death; and by which he passed daily to pay his publick devotions to Almighty God (who was then served twice a day by a publick form of Prayer and Praises in that place) but he was not buried privately, though he desired it; for, beside an unnumbred number of others, many persons of Nobility, and of eminency for Learning, who did love and honour him in his life, did shew it at his death, by a voluntary and sad attendance of his body to the grave, where nothing was so remarkable as a publick sorrow.

To which place of his Burial some mournful Friend repaired, and as *Alexander the Great* did to the grave of the famous *Achilles*, so they strewed his with an abundance of curious and costly Flowers, which course they (who were never yet known) continued morning and evening for many days; not ceasing, till the stones that were taken up in that Church to give his body admission into the cold earth (now his bed of rest) were again by the Masons art so levelled and firm'd, as they had been formerly; and his place of Burial undistinguishable to common view.

The next day after his Burial, some unknown friend, some one, of the many lovers and admirers of his vertue and learning; writ this *Epitaph* with a cole on the wall, over his grave.

> *Reader!   I am to let thee know,*
> *Donne's Body only, lyes below:*

For, could the grave his Soul comprize,
Earth would be richer then the skies.

Nor was this all the Honor done to his reverend Ashes; for as there be some persons that will not receive a reward for that for which God accounts himself a Debtor: persons, that dare trust God with their Charity, and without a witness; so there was by some grateful unknown Friend, that thought Dr. *Donne*'s memory ought to be perpetuated, an hundred Marks sent to his two faithful Friends * and Executors, towards the making of his Monument.   It was not *Dr. King and Dr. Monfort.* for many years known by whom; but, after the death of Dr. *Fox*, it was known that 'twas he that sent it; and he lived to see as lively a representation of his dead Friend, as Marble can express; a Statue indeed so like Dr. *Donne*, that (as his Friend Sir *Henry Wotton* hath expressed himself) *it seems to breath faintly; and, Posterity shall look upon it as a kind of artificial Miracle.*

He was of Stature moderately tall, of a strait and equally-proportioned body, to which all his words and actions gave an unexpressible addition of Comeliness.

The melancholy and pleasant humor, were in him so contempered, that each gave advantage to the other, and made his Company one of the delights of Mankind.

His fancy was unimitably high, equalled only by his great wit; both being made useful by a commanding judgment.

His aspect was chearful, and such, as gave a silent testimony of a clear knowing soul, and of a Conscience at peace with it self.

His melting eye, shewed that he had a soft heart, full of noble compassion; of too brave a soul to offer injuries, and too much a Christian not to pardon them in others.

He did much contemplate (especially after he entred into his Sacred Calling) the mercies *of Almighty* God, *the* immortality *of the* Soul, *and the* joyes *of* Heaven ; *and would often say, in a kind of sacred extasie——*Blessed be God that he is God only, and divinely like himself.

He was by nature highly passionate, but more apt to reluct at the excesses of it. A great lover of the offices of humanity, and of so merciful a spirit, that he never beheld the miseries of Mankind without pity and relief.

He was earnest and unwearied in the search of knowledge ; with which, his vigorous soul is now satisfied, and employed in a continual praise of that God that first breathed it into his active body ; that body, which once was a Temple of the Holy Ghost, *and is now become a small quantity of* Christian dust :

But I shall see it reanimated.

J. W.

Feb. 15. 1639.

An EPITAPH written by Dr. *Corbet*, late Bishop of *Oxford*, on his Friend Dr. *Donne*.

H*E that wou'd write an Epitaph for thee,*
   And write it well, must first begin to be
   Such as thou wert ; for none can truly know
Thy life and worth, but he that hath liv'd so.
He must have wit to spare, and to hurl down,
Enough to keep the Gallants of the Town.
He must have Learning plenty, both the Laws,
Civil and Common, to judge any Cause.
Divinity great store above the rest,

Not of the last Edition, but the best.
He must have language, travel, all the Arts,
Judgment to use, or else he wants thy parts.
He must have friends the highest, able to do,
Such as Mecænas, *and* Augustus *too.*
He must have such a sickness, such a death,
Or else his vain descriptions come beneath.
   He that would write an Epitaph *for thee,*
   Should first be dead ; let it alone for me.

To the Memory of my ever desired Dr.
   Donne. An *Elegy* by *H. King,* late
   Bishop of *Chichester.*

TO *have liv'd eminent in a degree*
      Beyond our loftiest thoughts, that is like thee ;
      Or t' have had too much merit, is not safe,
For such excesses find no Epitaph.
   At common graves we have poetick eyes,
Can melt themselves in easie Elegies ;
Each quill can drop his tributary verse,
And pin it like the hatchments to the herse :
But at thine, Poem or Inscription
(Rich soul of wit and language) we have none.
Indeed a silence does that Tomb befit,
Where is no Herauld left to blazon it.
Widow'd invention justly doth forbear
To come abroad, knowing thou art not there :
Late her great Patron, whose prerogative
Maintain'd and cloath'd her so, as none alive
Must now presume to keep her at thy rate,
Though he the Indies *for her dower estate.*
Or else that awful fire which once did burn

In thy clear brain, now fallen into thy Vrn,
Lives there to fright rude Empericks from thence,
Which might profane thee by their Ignorance.
Whoever writes of thee, and in a stile
Vnworthy such a theme, does but revile
Thy precious dust, and wakes a learned spirit,
Which may revenge his rapes upon thy merit :
For all a low-pitch't fancy can devise,
Will prove at best but hallowed injuries.

Thou like the dying Swan *didst lately sing*
Thy mournful dirge in audience of the King ;
When pale looks and faint accents of thy breath
Presented so to life that piece of death,
That it was fear'd and prophesi'd by all
Thou thither cam'st to preach thy Funerall.
Oh hadst thou in an Elegiack knell
Rung out unto the World thine own farewell,
And in thy high victorious numbers beat
The solemn measures of thy griev'd retreat,
Thou might'st the Poets service now have mist,
As well as then thou didst prevent the Priest :
And never to the World beholden be,
So much as for an Epitaph *for thee.*

I do not like the office ; nor is't fit
Thou who didst lend our age such sums of wit,
Should'st now re-borrow from her bankrupt Mine
That oar to bury thee which first was thine :
Rather still leave us in thy debt, and know,
Exalted Soul, more glory 'tis to owe
Thy memory what we can never pay,
Than with embased Coyn those Rites defray.

Commit we then thee to thy self, nor blame
Our drooping loves that thus to thine own fame
Leave thee Executor, since but thine own
No pen could do thee Justice, nor bayes Crown

Thy vast deserts ; save that, we nothing can
Depute to be thy ashes guardian :
  So, Jewellers no Art or Metal trust
To form the Diamond, but the Diamonds dust.
                                        H. K.

An *ELEGY* on Dr. *DONNE.*

Ovr Donne *is dead ! and, we may sighing say,*
  We had that man where Language chose to stay
  And shew her utmost power.   I wou'd not praise
That, and his great Wit, which in our vain days
Make others proud ; but, as these serv'd to unlock
That Cabinet his mind, where such a stock
Of knowledge was repos'd, that I lament
Our just and general cause of discontent.

  And, I rejoyce I am not so severe,
But as I write a Line, to weep a tear
For his decease : such sad Extremities
Can make such men as I write Elegies.

  And wonder not ; for, when so great a loss
Falls on a Nation, and they slight the Cross,
God hath rais'd Prophets to awaken them
From their dull Lethargy : witness my Pen,
Not us'd to upbraid the World, though now it must
Freely, and boldly, for, the Cause is just.

  Dull age ! oh, I wou'd spare thee, but thou'rt worse :
Thou art not only dull, but, hast a Curse
Of black Ingratitude : if not, Couldst thou
Part with this matchless man, and make no vow
For thee and thine successively to pay,
Some sad remembrance to his dying day ?

Did his Youth scatter Poetry, wherein
Lay Loves Philosophy ?   Was every sin
Pictur'd in his sharp Satyrs, made so foul
That some have fear'd sins shapes, and kept their soul
Safer by reading Verse ?   Did he give days,
Past marble Monuments to those whose praise
He wou'd perpetuate ?   Did he (I fear
Envy will doubt) these at his twentieth year ?

    But more matur'd : did his rich soul conceive,
And, in harmonious holy numbers weave

• La Co-   *A* Crown *of* Sacred * Sonnets, *fit t'adorn*
rona.   *A dying Martyrs brow : or, to be worn*
      On that blest head of Mary Magdalen,
After she wip'd Christs *feet ; but not, till then.*
Did he (fit for such Penitents as she
And he to use) leave us a Letanie,
Which all devout men love : and, doubtless shall
As times grow better, grow more Classicall.
Did he write Hymns, *for Piety and Wit,*
Equal to those great grave Prudentius *writ ?*
Spake he all Languages ?   Knew he all Laws ?
The grounds and use of Physick : but, because
'Twas mercenary, wav'd it : went to see
That happy place of Christs Nativity.
Did he return and preach him ? preach him so
As since St. Paul *none ever did ! they know :*
Those happy souls that hear'd him know this truth.
Did he confirm thy ag'd ? convert thy youth ?
Did he these wonders ! and, is his dear loss
Mourn'd by so few ? few for so great a Cross.

    But sure, the silent are ambitious all
To be close Mourners at his Funerall.
If not, in common pity, they forbear

By Repetitions to renew our care:
Or knowing grief conceiv'd, and hid, consumes
Mans life insensibly (as poison fumes
Corrupt the brain) take silence for the way
T'inlarge the soul from these walls, mud, and clay,
Materials of this body: to remain
With him in heaven, where no promiscuous pain
Lessens those joyes we have: for, with him all
Are satisfied, with joyes essentiall.

*   Dwell on these joyes my thoughts: oh, do not call*
Grief back, by thinking on his Funerall!
Forget he lov'd me: waste not my swift years
Which haste to Davids seventy, fill'd with fears
And sorrows for his death: Forget his parts,
They find a living grave in good mens hearts.
And, for my first is daily paid for sin:
Forget to pay my second sigh for him.
Forget his powerful preaching: and, forget
I am his Convert.   Oh my frailty! let
My flesh be no more heard: it will obtrude
This Lethargy: so shou'd my gratitude,
My vows of gratitude shou'd so be broke;
Which, can no more be, than his vertues spoke
By any but himself: for which cause, I
Write no Incomiums, but this Elegy.
Which, as a Free-will offering, I here give
Fame and the World: and, parting with it, grieve,
I want abilities, fit to set forth,
A Monument, as matchless as his worth.

April 7. 1631.   Iz. Wa.

                FINIS.

THE
LIFE

O F

Sir *HENRY WOTTON,*

L A T E

PROVOST

O F

EATON COLLEGE.

Eccles. 44.
These were Honourable Men in their Generation.

LONDON,
Printed in the Year 1675.

THE

LIFE

OF

Sir *HENRY WOTTON.*

SIR *Henry Wotton* (whose Life I now intend to write) was born in the Year of our Redemption 1568. in *Bocton-Hall* (commonly called *Bocton,* or *Bougton*-place, or Palace) in the Parish of *Bocton Malherb,* in the fruitful Country of *Kent : Bocton-hall* being an *ancient* and *goodly Structure,* beautifying, and being beautified by the Parish Church of *Bocton Malherb* adjoyning unto it ; and both seated within a fair Park of the *Wottons,* on the Brow of such a *Hill,* as gives the advantage of a large Prospect, and of equal *pleasure* to all Beholders.

But this House and Church are not remarkable for any thing so much, as for that the memorable Family of the *Wottons* have so long inhabited the one, and now lye buried in the other, as appears by their many *Monuments* in that Church : the *Wottons* being a Family that hath brought forth divers Persons eminent for Wisdom and Valour ; whose Heroick Acts, and Noble Employments, both in *England* and in Foreign parts, have adorned themselves and this Nation; which they have served abroad faithfully, in the discharge of their great trust, and prudently in their Negotiations with several Princes; and also served at home with much Honour and Justice, in their wise managing a great part of the Publick Affairs thereof, in the various times both of War and Peace.

But lest I should be thought by any that may incline either to deny or doubt this Truth, not to have observed *moderation* in the commendation of this Family: and also, for that I believe the *merits* and *memory* of such Persons ought to be thankfully recorded, I shall offer to the consideration of every Reader, out of the testimony of their *Pedegree*, and our *Chronicles*, a part (and but a part) of that just Commendation which might be from thence enlarged, and shall then leave the indifferent Reader to judge whether my error be an *excess* or *defect* of Commendations.

Sir *Robert Wotton* of *Bocton Malherb* Kt. was born about the Year of Christ 1460: he living in the Reign of King *Edward* the Fourth, was by him trusted to be Lieutenant of *Guisnes*, to be Knight Porter, and Comptroler of *Callais*, where he died, and lies honourably buried.

Sir *Edward Wotton* of *Bocton Malherb* Knight (Son and Heir of the said Sir *Robert*) was born in the Year of Christ 1489, in the Reign of King *Henry* the Seventh: he was made Treasurer of *Callais*, and of the Privy Councel to King *Henry* the Eighth, who offered him to be Lord Chancellor of *England*; but (saith * *Hollinshed*) out of a virtuous modesty he refused it.

* *In his Chronicle.*

Thomas Wotton of *Bocton Malherb* Esquire, Son and Heir of the said Sir *Edward* (and the Father of our Sir *Henry*, that occasions this Relation), was born in the Year of Christ 1521 : he was a Gentleman excellently educated, and studious in all the *Liberal Arts*, in the knowledge whereof he attained unto a great perfection; who, though he had (besides those abilities, a very Noble and plentiful Estate, and the ancient Interest of his *Predecessors*) many invitations from Queen *Elizabeth* to change his Country Recreations and Retirement for a Court, offering him a Knight-hood (she was then with him at his *Bocton-hall*) and that to be but as an earnest of some more honourable and more profitable employment under Her; yet he humbly refused both, being *a man of great modesty*, of a most *plain and single heart*, of *an ancient freedom, and integrity of mind*. A commendation which Sir *Henry Wotton* took occasion often to remember with great gladness, and thankfully to boast himself the Son of such a Father : From whom indeed he derived that noble ingenuity that was alwayes practiced by himself, and which he ever both commended and cherished in others. This *Thomas* was also remarkable for Hospitality, a great Lover, and much beloved of his Country; to which may justly be added, that he was a Cherisher of *Learning*, as appears by that excellent Antiquary Mr. *William Lambert*, in his Perambulation of *Kent*.

This *Thomas* had four Sons, Sir *Edward*, Sir *James*, Sir *John*, and Sir *Henry*.

Sir *Edward* was Knighted by Queen *Elizabeth*, and made Comptroller of Her Majesties Houshold. He was (saith *Cambden*) a man remarkable for many and great Employments in the State, during Her Reign, and sent several times *Ambassador* into Foreign Nations. After Her death, he was by King *James* made Comptroller of his Houshold, and called to be of His Privy Council, and by him advanced to be *Lord Wotton*, *Baron* of *Merley* in *Kent*, and made Lord Lieutenant of that County.

Sir *James* (the second Son) may be numbered among the Martial Men of his Age, who was in the 38 of Queen *Elizabeths* Reign (with *Robert Earl* of *Sussex*, *Count Lodowick* of *Nassaw*, *Don Christophoro*, Son of *Antonio* King of *Portugal*, and divers other Gentlemen of Nobleness and Valour) Knighted in the Field near *Cadiz* in *Spain*, after they had gotten great Honor and Riches, besides a notable retaliation of Injuries by taking that Town.

Sir *John*, being a Gentleman excellently accomplished, both by Learning and Travel, was Knighted by Queen *Elizabeth*, and by Her look'd upon with more than ordinary favour, and with intentions of preferment; but Death in his younger years put a period to his growing hopes.

Of Sir *Henry*, my following discourse shall give an account.

The descent of these fore-named *Wottons* were all in a direct Line; and most of them and their actions, in the memory of those with whom we have conversed: But if I had looked so far back as to Sir *Nicholas Wotton* (who lived in the Reign of King *Richard* the Second) or before him, upon divers others of great note in their several Ages, I might by some be thought tedious; and yet others may more justly think me negligent, if I omit to mention *Nicholas Wotton*, the fourth Son of Sir *Robert*, whom I first named.

This *Nicholas Wotton* was *Doctor of Law*, and sometime *Dean* both of *York* and *Canterbury*: a man whom God did not only bless with a long life, but with great abilities of mind, and an inclination to imploy them in the service of his Countrey, as is testified by his several Imployments; * having been sent nine times *Ambassador* unto Forraign Princes; and by his being a Privy-*Councellor* to King *Henry* the eighth, to *Edward* the sixth, to Queen *Mary* and Queen *Elizabeth*; who also, after he had been during the Wars between *England*, *Scotland* and *France*, three several times (and not unsuccessfully) imployed in Committies for setling of peace betwixt this and those Kingdoms, died (saith learned *Cambden*) *full of Commendations for Wisdom and Piety*——He was also by the Will of King *Henry* the eighth, made one of his Executors, and chief *Secretary* of State to his Son, that pious Prince *Edward* the sixth.——Concerning which *Nicholas Wotton*, I shall say but this little more; That he refused (being offered it by Qu. *Elizabeth*) to be † *Archbishop* of *Canterbury*, and that he died not rich, though he lived in that time of the dissolution of *Abbeys*.

* *Cambden in his Britannia.*

† *Hollinshead.*

More might be added: but by this it may appear, that Sir *Henry Wotton* was a Branch of such a kindred as left a Stock of Reputation to their Posterity; such Reputation, as might kindle a generous emulation in Strangers, and preserve a noble ambition in those of his Name and Family, to perform Actions worthy of their Ancestors.

And that Sir Henry Wotton did so, might appear more perfectly then my Pen can express it, if of his many surviving friends, some one of higher parts and imployment, had been pleas'd to have commended his to Posterity; But since some years are now past, and they have all (I know not why) forborn to do it; my gratitude to the memory of my dead friend, and the renewed request of some * *that still live solicitous to see this duty performed; these have had a power to perswade me to undertake it; which, truly, I have not done, but with some distrust of mine own Abilities, and yet so far from despair, that I am modestly confident my humble language shall be*

* *Sir Edward Bish Clarentieux King of Arms, M. Charls Cotton, and, Mr. Nick Oudert sometime Sir Hen. Wotton's Servant.*

accepted, because I shall present all Readers with a Commixture of truth, and Sir Henry Wotton's merits.

This being premised, I proceed to tell the Reader, that the Father of Sir *Henry Wotton* was twice married, first to *Elizabeth*, the Daughter of Sir *John Rudstone* Knight; after whose death, though his inclination was averse to all Contentions; yet necessitated he was to several Suits in Law: in the prosecution whereof (which took up much of his time, and were the occasion of many Discontents) he was by divers of his friends earnestly perswaded to a *re-marriage*; to whom he as often answered, That if ever he did put on a resolution to marry, *he was seriously resolved to avoid three sorts of persons:*

namely, those { that had *Children*
that had *Law-suits*
that were of his *Kindred*.

And yet, following his own Law-suits, he met in *Westminster-hall* with Mrs. *Elionora Morton*, Widow to *Robert Morton* of *Kent* Esquire; who was also engaged in several Suits in Law: and, he observing her Comportment at the time of hearing one of her Causes before the Judges, could not but at the same time both compassionate her Condition, and affect her Person (for, *the tears of Lovers*, or *Beauty drest in sadness*, are observ'd to have in them a Charming Eloquence; and to become very often too strong to be resisted) which I mention, because it prov'd so with this *Thomas Wotton*, for although there were in her a concurrence of all those accidents, against which he had so seriously resolved, yet his affection to her grew then so strong, that he resolved to solicite her for a Wife; and did, and obtained her.

By her (who was the Daughter of Sir *William Finch* of *Eastwell* in *Kent*) he had only *Henry* his youngest Son.——His Mother undertook to be Tutoress unto him during much of his Childhood; for whose care and pains, he paid her each day with such visible signs of future perfection in Learning, as turned her imployment into a pleasing-trouble: which she was content to continue, till his Father took him into his own particular care, and disposed of him to a Tutor in his own House at *Bocton*.

And, when time and diligent instruction had made him fit for a removal to an higher Form, (which was very early) he was sent to *Winchester-School*: a place of strict Discipline and Order: that so, he might in his youth be moulded into a Method of living by Rule; which his wise Father knew to be the most necessary way, to make the future part of his life, both happy to himself, and useful for the discharge of all business, whether publick or private.

And that he might be confirmed in this *regularity*, he was at a fit age removed from that *School*, to be a Commoner of *New-Colledge* in *Oxford*; both being founded by *William Wickham* Bishop of *Winchester*.

There he continued, till about the eighteenth year of his Age: and was then transplanted into *Queens-Colledge*; where within that year he was by the chief

of that Colledge, perswasively injoyned to write a
Play for their private use (it was the Tragedy of
Tancredo) which was so interwoven with Sentences,
and for the Method and exact personating those
humours, passions, and dispositions, which he proposed to represent, so performed, that the gravest of
that society declared, he had in a sleight imployment,
given an early and a solid testimony of his future
abilities.   And though there may be some sowr dispositions, which may think this not worth a *memorial*;
yet that wise Knight *Baptista Guarini* (whom learned
Italy accounts one of her ornaments) thought it neither
an uncomely, nor an unprofitable imployment for his
Age.

But I pass to what will be thought more serious.

About the twentieth year of his Age, he proceeded
Master of *Arts* ; and at that time read in Latine three
Lectures *de Oculo* : wherein, he having described the
Form, the *Motion*, the curious *composure* of the *Eye* :
and demonstrated, how of those very many, every
humour and *nerve* performs its distinct Office, so as
the God of Order hath appointed, without mixture
or confusion ; and all this, to the advantage of man,
to whom the *Eye* is given, not only as the Bodies guide,
but, whereas all other of his senses require time to
inform the Soul, this in an instant apprehends and
warns him of *danger* : teaching him in the very *eyes*
of others, to discover *wit, folly, love*, and *hatred* :
After he had made these Observations, he fell to dispute this Optique Question, *Whether we see by the
Emission of the Beams from within, or Reception of
the Species from without ?* and after that, and many
other like learned disquisitions, he in the Conclusion
of his *Lectures,* took a fair occasion to beautifie his
Discourse with a Commendation of the blessing and

benefit of *Seeing*: *By which, we do not only discover* Natures Secrets: *but with a continued content (for the eye is never weary of seeing) behold the great* Light *of the* World, *and by it, discover the Fabrick of the* Heavens, *and both the Order and Motion of the* Celestial Orbs; *nay, that if the eye look but downward, it may rejoice to behold the bosome of the* Earth, *our common Mother,* embroidered *and* adorned *with numberless and various* Flowers, *which man sees daily grow up to perfection, and then silently moralize his own condition, who in a short time (like those very* Flowers*) decayes, withers, and quickly returns again to that* Earth, *from which both had their first being.*

These were so exactly debated, and so Rhetorically heightned, as, among other admirers, caused that learned *Italian, Albericus Gentilis* (then Professor of the *Civil Law* in *Oxford*) to call him *Henrice mi ocelle*; which dear expression of his, was also used by divers of Sir *Henry*'s dearest Friends, and by many other persons of Note, during his stay in the University.

But his stay there was not long; at least, not so long as his Friends once intended: for the year after Sir *Henry* proceeded Master of Arts, his Father (whom Sir *Henry* did never mention without this, or some like reverential expression; as, *That good man my Father*; or, *My Father the best of men*:) about that time, this good man changed this for a better life; leaving to Sir *Henry*, as to his other younger Sons, a Rent-charge of an hundred Mark a year, to be paid for ever, out of some one of his Mannors of a much greater value.

And here, though this good man be dead, yet I wish a Circumstance or two that concern him, may not be buried without a Relation; which I shall undertake to do, for that I suppose, they may so much concern the Reader to know, that I may promise my self a pardon for a short digression.

IN the year of our Redemption, 1553. *Nicholas Wotton* Dean of *Canterbury* (whom I formerly mentioned) being then Ambassador in *France*, dream'd, that his Nephew, this *Thomas Wotton*, was inclined to be a party in such a project, as, if he were not suddenly prevented, would turn both to the loss of his life, and ruine of his *Family*.

Doubtless, the good Dean did well know, that common Dreams are but a senseless paraphrase on our waking thoughts; or, of the business of the day past; or, are the result of our over-engaged affections, when we betake our selves to rest; and knew that the observation of them, may turn to silly Superstitions; as they too often do: But, though he might know all this, and might also believe that Prophesies are ceased; yet, doubtless he could not but consider, that all Dreams are not to be neglected or cast away without all consideration: and did therefore rather lay this Dream aside, then intend totally to lose it; and dreaming the same again the Night following, when it became a double Dream, like that of *Pharaoh* (of which double dreams, the learned have made many observations) and considering that it had no dependance on his waking thoughts, much less on the desires of his heart, then he did more seriously consider it;

St. Austin's Confession. and remembred that Almighty God was pleased in a Dream to reveal and to assure * *Monica* the Mother of St. *Austin, that he, her Son for whom she wept so bitterly, and prayed so much, should at last become a Christian*: This I believe, the good Dean considered; and considering also that Almighty God (though the causes of Dreams be often unknown) hath even in these latter times also, by a certain *illumination* of the Soul in sleep, discovered many things that humane wisdom could not foresee: Upon these considerations, he resolved to use so prudent a remedy by way of prevention, as might introduce no great inconvenience either to himself or to his Nephew. And to that end, he wrote to the *Queen* ('twas *Queen Mary*) and besought her, *That she would cause his Nephew* Thomas Wotton, *to be sent for out of* Kent: *and that the Lords of her Council might interrogate him in some such feigned Questions, as might give a colour for his Commitment into a favourable* Prison; *declaring, that he would acquaint her Majesty with the true reason of his request, when he should next become so happy as to see, and speak to her Majesty.*

'Twas done as the *Dean* desired: and in Prison I must leave Mr. *Wotton*, till I have told the Reader what followed.

At this time a Marriage was concluded betwixt our *Queen Mary*, and *Philip King* of *Spain*: And though this was concluded with the advice, if not by the perswasion of her Privy Council, as having many probabilities of advantage to this Nation: yet divers persons of a contrary perswasion, did not only declare against it, but also raised Forces to oppose it; believing (as they said) it would be a means to bring *England* to be under a subjection to *Spain*, and make those of this Nation slaves to *Strangers*.

And of this number Sir *Thomas Wyat* of *Boxley-Abbey* in *Kent* (betwixt whose Family, and the Family of the *Wottons*, there had been an ancient and entire friendship) was the principal Actor; who having perswaded many of the Nobility and Gentry (especially of *Kent*) to side with him, and he being defeated, and taken Prisoner, was legally arraigned and condemned, and lost his life: So did the Duke of *Suffolk*, and divers others, especially many of the Gentry of *Kent*, who were there in several places executed as *Wyat*'s assistants.

And of this number, in all probability, had Mr. *Wotton* been if he had not been confin'd: for, though he could not be ignorant that *another mans Treason makes it mine by concealing it*; yet he durst confess to his Uncle, when he returned into *England*, and then came to visit him in Prison, *that he had more then an intimation of* Wyat's *intentions*; and thought he had not continued actually *innocent*, if his Uncle had not so happily dream'd him into a *Prison*; out of which place, when he was delivered by the same hand that caused his Commitment, they both considered the Dream more seriously; and then, both joined in praising God for it; *That God, who tyes himself to no Rules, either in preventing of evil, or in shewing of mercy to those, whom of good pleasure he hath chosen to love*.

And this Dream was the more considerable, because that God who in the days of old did use to speak to his people in Visions, did seem to speak to many of this Family in dreams: of which I will also give the Reader one short particular of this *Thomas Wotton*, whose dreams did usually prove true, both in fore-telling things to come, and discovering things past: And the particular is this; This *Thomas*, a little before his death, dream'd that the *University Treasury* was robbed by *Townsmen*, and poor *Scholars*; and, that the number was five: And being that day to write to his Son *Henry* at *Oxford*, he thought it worth so much pains, as by a Postscript in his Letter, to make a slight enquiry of it; the Letter (which was writ out of *Kent*, and dated three days before) came to his Sons hands the very morning after the night in which the Robbery was committed; and when the City and University were both in a perplext Enquest of the Thieves, then did Sir *Henry Wotton* shew his Fathers Letter, and by it such *light* was given of this work of *darkness*, that the five guilty persons were presently discovered, and apprehended, without putting the *University* to so much trouble, as the casting of a *Figure*.

And it may yet be more considerable, that this *Nicholas* and *Thomas Wotton* should both (being men of holy lives, of even tempers, and much given to fasting and prayer) foresee and foretell the very days of their own death: *Nicholas* did so, being then Seventy years of age, and in perfect health. *Thomas* did the like in the sixty fifth year of his age; who being then in *London* (where he dyed) and foreseeing his death there, gave direction in what manner his Body should be carried to *Bocton*; and, though he thought his Uncle *Nicholas* worthy of that noble Monument which he built for him in the *Cathedral Church* of *Canterbury*; yet this humble man gave direction concerning himself, to be buried privately, and especially without any pomp at his Funeral. This is some account of this Family, which seemed to be beloved of God.

BUt it may now seem more then time that I return to Sir *Henry Wotton* at *Oxford*; where, after his optick Lecture, he was taken into such a bosom friendship with the Learned *Albericus Gentilis* (whom I formerly named) that if it had been possible, *Gentilis* would have breathed all his excellent knowledge, both of the *Mathematicks* and *Law*, into the breast of his dear *Harry* (for so *Gentilis* used to call him) and though he was not able to do that, yet there was in Sir *Henry* such a propensity and connaturalness to the *Italian* Language, and those Studies whereof *Gentilis* was a great Master, that his friendship between them did daily increase, and proved daily advantagious to Sir *Henry*, for the improvement of him in several Sciences, during his stay in the University.

From which place, before I shall invite the Reader to follow him into a Foreign Nation, though I must omit to mention divers Persons that were then in *Oxford*, of memorable note for Learning, and Friends to Sir *Henry Wotton*; yet I must not omit the mention of a love that was there begun betwixt him and Dr. *Donne* (sometimes Dean of St. *Pauls*) a man of whose abilities I shall forbear to say any thing, because he who is of this *Nation*, and pretends to Learning or Ingenuity, and is ignorant of Dr. *Donne*, deserves not to know him. The friendship of these two I must not omit to mention, being such a friendship as was generously elemented : And as it was begun in their Youth, and in an University, and there maintained by correspondent Inclinations and Studies, so it lasted till Age and Death forced a Separation.

In *Oxford* he stayed till about two years after his Fathers death ; at which time, he was about the two and twentieth year of his Age : and having to his great Wit added the ballast of Learning, and knowledge of the Arts, he then laid aside his Books, and betook himself to the useful Library of Travel, and a more general Conversation with Mankind ; employing the remaining part of his Youth, his industry and fortune, to adorn his mind, and to purchase the rich Treasure of Foreign knowledge ; of which, both for the secrets of Nature, the dispositions of many

Nations, their several Laws and Languages, he was the Possessor in a very large measure; as I shall faithfully make to appear, before I take my Pen from the following Narration of his Life.

In his Travels, which was almost nine years before his return into *England*, he stayed but one year in *France*, and most of that in *Geneva*; where he became acquainted with *Theodor Beza* (then very aged) and with *Isaac Causabon*, in whose house (if I be rightly informed) Sir *Henry Wotton* was lodged, and there contracted a most worthy friendship with that man of rare Learning and Ingenuity.

Three of the remaining eight years were spent in *Germany*, the other five in *Italy* (the Stage on which God appointed he should act a great part of his life) where both in *Rome*, *Venice*, and *Florence*, he became acquainted with the most eminent men for Learning, and all manner of Arts; as *Picture*, *Sculpture*, *Chymistry*, *Architecture*, and other manual Arts, even Arts of Inferiour nature; of all which, he was a most dear Lover, and a most excellent Judge.

He returned out of *Italy* into *England* about the thirtieth year of his Age, being then noted by many, both for his Person and Comportment; for indeed he was of a choice shape, tall of stature, and of a most perswasive behaviour; which was so mixed with sweet Discourse, and Civilities, as gained him much love from all Persons with whom he entred into an acquaintance.

And whereas he was noted in his Youth to have a sharp Wit, and apt to jest; that, by Time, Travel, and Conversation, was so polish'd, and made so useful, that his company seemed to be one of the delights of mankind; insomuch as *Robert* Earl of *Essex* (then one of the Darlings of Fortune, and in greatest favour with Queen *Elizabeth*) invited him first into a friend-ship, and after a knowledge of his great abilities, to be one of his Secretaries; the other being Mr. *Henry Cuffe*, sometimes of *Merton* Colledge in *Oxford* (and there also the acquaintance of Sir *Henry Wotton* in his Youth) Mr. *Cuffe* being then a man of no common note in the University for his Learning; nor after his removal from that place, for the great abilities of his mind; nor indeed, for the *fatalness* of his end.

Sir *Henry Wotton* being now taken into a service-able friendship with the Earl of *Essex*, did personally attend his Counsels and Employments in two Voyages at Sea against the *Spaniard*, and also in that (which was the Earls last) into *Ireland*; that Voyage where-in he then did so much provoke the Queen to anger, and worse at his return into *England*; upon whose immoveable favour the Earl had built such sandy hopes, as incouraged him to those undertakings, which with the help of a contrary Faction suddenly caused his Commitment to the Tower.

Sir *Henry Wotton* observing this, though he was not of that Faction (for the *Earls* followers were also divided into their several interests) which in-couraged the *Earl* to those undertakings which proved so fatal to him, and divers of his Confederation: yet, knowing *Treason* to be so comprehensive, as to take in even Circumstances, and out of them to make such positive Conclusions as subtle States-men shall pro-ject, either for their revenge or safety; considering this, he thought prevention by absence out of *England*, a better security then to stay in it, and there plead his innocency in a *Prison*. Therefore did he, so soon as the Earl was apprehended, very quickly, and as privately glide through *Kent* to *Dover*, without so much as looking toward his native and beloved

Bocton; and was by the help of favourable winds and liberal payment of the Mariners, within sixteen hours after his departure from *London*, set upon the *French* shore; where he heard shortly after, that the *Earl* was Arraign'd, Condemned, and Beheaded; and that his Friend Mr. *Cuffe* was hang'd, and divers other Persons of Eminent Quality executed.

The Times did not look so favourably upon Sir *Henry Wotton*, as to invite his return into *England*; having therefore procured of Sir *Edward Wotton*, his elder Brother, an assurance that his Annuity should be paid him in *Italy*, thither he went, happily renewing his intermitted friendship and interest, and indeed, his great content in a new conversation with his old Acquaintance in that Nation; and more particularly in *Florence* (which City is not more eminent for the Great Dukes Court, then for the great recourse of men of choicest note for Learning and Arts,) in which number he there met with his old Friend Signior *Vietta*, a Gentleman of *Venice*, and then taken to be *Secretary* to the Great Duke of *Tuscany*.

After some stay in *Florence*, he went the fourth time to visit *Rome*, where in the *English Colledge* he had very many Friends (their humanity made them really so, though they knew him to be a dissenter from many of their Principles of Religion,) and having enjoyed their company, and satisfied himself concerning some Curiosities that did partly occasion his Journey thither, he returned back to *Florence*, where a most notable accident befell him; an accident that did not only find new employment for his choice Abilities, but introduce him a knowledge and an interest with our King *James*, then King of *Scotland*; which I shall proceed to relate.

But first, I am to tell the Reader, That though

Queen *Elizabeth* (or she and her Council) were never willing to declare her *Successor*; yet *James* then King of the *Scots*, was confidently believed by most to be the man upon whom the sweet trouble of Kingly Government would be imposed; and the *Queen* declining very fast, both by age and visible infirmities, those that were of the *Romish* perswasion in point of Religion (even *Rome* it self, and those of this Nation) knowing that the death of the *Queen*, and the establishing of her *Successor*, were taken to be *critical* days for destroying or establishing the *Protestant* Religion in this Nation, did therefore improve all opportunities for preventing a Protestant Prince to succeed Her. And as the *Pope*'s Excommunication of *Queen Elizabeth*, had both by the judgment and practice of the Jesuited Papist, exposed her to be warrantably destroyed; so (if we may believe an angry Adversary, a * secular Priest against a *Jesuit*) you may believe, that about that time there were many indeavours, first to excommunicate, and then to shorten the life of King *James*.

* Watson
in his
Quodlibets.

Immediately after Sir *Henry Wotton*'s return from *Rome* to *Florence* (which was about a year before the death of Queen *Elizabeth*) *Ferdinand* the Great Duke of *Florence* had intercepted certain Letters that discovered a design to take away the life of *James* the then King of *Scots*. The Duke abhorring the Fact, and resolving to indeavor a prevention of it, advised with his Secretary *Vietta*, by what means a caution might be best given to that King; and after consideration, it was resolved to be done by Sir *Henry Wotton*, whom *Vietta* first commended to the *Duke*; and the *Duke* had noted and approved of above all the *English* that frequented his Court.

Sir *Henry* was gladly called by his Friend *Vietta* to the *Duke*, who after much profession of trust and friendship, acquainted him with the secret; and being well instructed, dispatched him into *Scotland* with Letters to the King, and with those Letters, such *Italian* Antidotes against poison, as the *Scots* till then had been strangers to.

Having parted from the *Duke*, he took up the Name and Language of an *Italian*; and thinking it best to avoid the line of *English* intelligence and danger, he posted into *Norway*, and through that Country towards *Scotland*, where he found the King at *Sterling*; being there, he used means by *Bernard Lindsey*, one of the Kings Bed-Chamber, to procure him a speedy and private conference with his Majesty, assuring him, *That the business which he was to negotiate, was of such consequence, as had caused the Great Duke of* Tuscany *to enjoin him suddenly to leave his Native Country of* Italy, *to impart it to his King.*

This being by *Bernard Lindsey* made known to the King, the King after a little wonder (mixt with jealousie) to hear of an *Italian* Ambassador, or Messenger, required his Name (which was said to be *Octavio Baldi*) and appointed him to be heard privately at a fixed hour that Evening.

When *Octavio Baldi* came to the Presence-Chamber-door, he was requested to lay aside his long *Rapier* (which *Italian*-like he then wore) and being entred the Chamber, he found there with the King three or four *Scotch* Lords standing distant in several corners of the Chamber: at the sight of whom he made a stand; which the King observing, *bade him be bold, and deliver his Message; for he would undertake for the secresie of all that were present.* Then did *Octavio Baldi* deliver his Letters and his Message to the King in *Italian*; which, when the King had graciously received, after a little pause, *Octavio Baldi* steps to the Table, and whispers to the King in his own Language, that he was an *English* man, beseeching Him for a more private conference with His Majesty, and that he might be concealed during his stay in that Nation; which was promised, and really performed by the King during all his abode there (which was about three Months) all which time was spent with much pleasantness to the King, and with as much to *Octavio Baldi* himself, as that Countrey could afford; from which he departed as true an *Italian* as he came thither.

To the *Duke* at *Florence* he return'd with a fair and grateful account of his imployment, and within some few Months after his return, there came certain News to *Florence*, that Queen *Elizabeth* was dead; and *James* King of the *Scots* proclaimed King of *England*. The Duke knowing travel and business to be the best Schools of wisdom, and that Sir *Henry Wotton* had been tutor'd in both, advis'd him to return presently to *England*, and there joy the King with his new and better Title, and wait there upon Fortune for a better imployment.

When King *James* came into *England*, he found, amongst other of the late Queens Officers, Sir *Edward*, who was after Lord *Wotton*, Comptroller of the House, of whom he demanded, *If he knew one* Henry Wotton, *that had spent much time in Foreign Travel?* The Lord replied, he knew him well, and that he was his Brother; then the *King* asking where he then was, was answered, at *Venice*, or *Florence*; but by late Letters from thence, he understood, he would suddenly be at *Paris*. *Send for him*, said the King, *and when he shall come into* England, *bid him repair privately to me.* The Lord *Wotton* after a little wonder, asked the King, *If he knew him?* to which the King answered, *You must rest unsatisfied of that, till you bring the Gentleman to me.*

Not many Moneths after this Discourse, the Lord *Wotton* brought his Brother to attend the King, who took him in His Arms, *and bade him welcome by the Name of* Octavio Baldi, *saying, he was the most honest, and therefore the best Dissembler that ever he met with*: And said, *Seeing I know you neither want Learning, Travel, nor Experience, and that I have had so real a Testimony of your faithfulness and abilities to manage an Ambassage, I have sent for you to declare my purpose; which is, to make use of you in that kind hereafter*: And indeed the King did so most of those two and twenty years of his Raign; but before he dismist *Octavio Baldi* from his present attendance upon him, he restored him to his old Name of *Henry Wotton*, by which he then Knighted him.

Not long after this, the King having resolved, according to his Motto (*Beati pacifici*), to have a friendship with his Neighbour-Kingdoms of *France* and *Spain*, and also for divers weighty reasons, to enter into an Alliance with the State of *Venice*, and to that end to send Ambassadors to those several places, did propose the choice of these Imployments to Sir *Henry Wotton*; who considering the smallness of his own Estate (which he never took care to augment) and knowing the Courts of great Princes to be sumptuous, and necessarily expensive, inclined most to that of *Venice*, as being a place of more retirement, and best suiting with his *Genius*, who did ever love to join with Business, Study, and a tryal of natural Experiments; for both which fruitful *Italy, that Darling of Nature, and Cherisher of all Arts, is so justly fam'd in all parts of the Christian World.*

Sir *Henry* having after some short time and consideration, resolved upon *Venice*, and a large allowance
being appointed by the *King* for his Voyage thither,
and a settled maintenance during his stay there, he left
England, nobly accompanied through *France* to *Venice*,
by Gentlemen of the best Families and breeding that
this Nation afforded ; they were too many to name,
but these two, for following reasons, may not be
omitted ; Sir *Albertus Morton* his Nephew, who went
his Secretary ; and *William Bedel*, a man of choice
Learning, and sanctified Wisdom, who went his Chaplain. And though his dear friend Dr. *Donne* (then
a private Gentleman) was not one of that number that
did personally accompany him in this Voyage, yet the
reading of this following Letter sent by him to Sir
Henry Wotton, the morning before he left *England*,
may testifie he wanted not his friends best wishes to
attend him.

S I R ,

AFter those reverend Papers, *whose soul is (name :*
    Our good, and great Kings lov'd hand, and fear'd
    By which to you he derives much of his,
    And, how he may, makes you almost the same ;

A Taper *of his* Torch : *a Copy writ*
    From his Original, and a fair Beam
Of the same warm and dazling Sun, *though it*
    Must in another Sphear his vertue stream ;

After those Learned Papers *which your hand*
    Hath stor'd with notes of use and pleasure too :
From which rich treasury you may command
    Fit matter whether you will write or do :

After those loving Papers *which Friends send*
   With glad grief to your Sea-ward-steps farewell,
And thicken on you now as prayers *ascend*
   To Heaven on *troops at a good mans* passing-Bell *.*

Admit this honest Paper *; and allow*
   It such an audience as your self would ask ;
What you would say at Venice, *this says now,*
   And has for nature *what you have for* task.

To swear much love ; nor to be chang'd before
   Honour alone will to your fortune fit ;
Nor shall I then honour your fortune *more,*
   Then I have done your honour-wanting-wit.

But 'tis an easier load (though both oppress)
   To want, then govern greatness *; for we are*
In that, our own, and only business ;
   In this, we must for others vices care.

'Tis therefore well, your spirits now are plac'd
   In their last furnace, in activity ;   *(ore-past*
Which fits them: Schools, *and* Courts, *and* Wars
   To touch and taste in any best degree.

For me ! (if there be such a thing as I)
   Fortune (if there be such a thing as she)
Finds that I bear so well her tyranny,
   That she thinks nothing else so fit for me.

But, though she part us, to hear my oft prayers
   For your encrease, *God is as near me here :*
And, to send you what I shall beg, his stairs
   In length, and ease, are alike every where.

                                     J. Donne.

SIR *Henry Wotton* was received by the State of *Venice*, with much honour and gladness, both for that he delivered his Ambassage most elegantly in the *Italian* Language, and came also in such a Juncture of time, as his Masters friendship seem'd useful for that Republick: the time of his coming thither was about the year 1604. *Leonardo Donato* being then Duke; a wise and resolv'd man, and to all purposes such (Sir *Henry Wotton* would often say it) as the State of *Venice* could not then have wanted; there having been formerly in the time of *Pope Clement* the eighth, some contests about the priviledges of Church-men, and the power of the Civil Magistrate; of which, for the information of common Readers, I shall say a little, because it may give light to some passages that follow.

About the year 1603. the Republick of *Venice* made several Injunctions against Lay-persons giving Lands or Goods to the Church, without Licence from the Civil Magistrate; and in that inhibition, they exprest their reasons to be, *For that when any Goods or Land once came into the hands of the Ecclesiasticks, it was not subject to alienation; by reason whereof (the Lay-people being at their death charitable even to excess) the Clergy grew every day more numerous, and pretended an exemption from all* publick service, and Taxes, and from all secular Judgment: *so that the burden grew thereby too heavy to be born by the Laity.*

Another occasion of difference was, That about this time complaints were justly made by the *Venetians* against two Clergy-men, the *Abbot of Nervesa*, and a *Canon of Vicenza*, for committing such sins, as I think not fit to name; nor are these mentioned with an intent to fix a Scandal upon any

Calling; (for holiness is not tyed to Ecclesiastical Orders, and *Italy* is observed to breed the most vertuous, and most vicious men of any Nation) these two having been long complained of at *Rome* in the Name of the State of *Venice*, and no satisfaction being given to the *Venetians*, they seized the persons of this *Abbot* and *Canon*, and committed them to prison.

The justice, or injustice of such or the like power, then used by the *Venetians*, had formerly had some calm debates betwixt the former Pope *Clement* the Eighth, and that *Republick*: I say, calm, for he did not Excommunicate them; considering (as I conceive) that in the late *Council of Trent* it was at last (after many Politique disturbances, and delayes, and endeavours to preserve the Popes present power) in order to a general reformation of those many Errors, which were in time crept into the Church, declar'd by that Counsel, *That though* Discipline, *and especial* Excommunication *be one of the chief sinews of Church-Government, and intended to keep men in obedience to it: for which end, it was declar'd to be very profitable; yet, it was also declar'd, and advised to be used with great sobriety and care: because experience had informed them, that when it was pronounced unadvisedly, or rashly, it became more contemn'd then fear'd.* And, though this was the advice of that Council at the Conclusion of it, which was not many years before this quarrel with the *Venetians*: yet this prudent, patient Pope *Clement* dying, *Pope Paul* the fifth, who succeeded him (though not immediately, yet in the same year) being a man of a much hotter temper, brought this difference with the *Venetians* to a much higher Contention: objecting those late acts of that State, to be a diminution of his just power, and limited a time of twenty four dayes for their revocation;

threatning, if he were not obeyed, to proceed to Excommunication of the *Republick,* who still offered to shew both reason and ancient custom to warrant their Actions. But this *Pope,* contrary to his Predecessors moderation, required absolute obedience without disputes.

Thus it continued for about a year; the Pope still threatning Excommunication, and the *Venetians* still answering him with fair speeches, and no compliance, till at last, the Popes zeal to the *Apostolick See* did make him to excommunicate the *Duke,* the whole *Senate,* and all their Dominions; and that done to shut up all their *Churches*; charging the whole Clergy to forbear all sacred Offices to the *Venetians,* till their Obedience should render them capable of *Absolution.*

But this act of the Popes did but the more confirm the *Venetians* in their resolution not to obey him; *And to that end, upon the hearing of the Popes Interdict, they presently* published by sound *of Trumpet, a Proclamation to this effect:*

That whosoever hath received from Rome *any Copy of a Papal Interdict, publish'd there, as well against the Law of God, as against the Honour of this Nation, shall presently render it to the Councel of* Ten, *upon pain of Death. And made it loss of Estate and Nobility, but to speak in the behalf of the* Jesuits.

Then was *Duado* their Ambassador call'd home from *Rome,* and the *Inquisition* presently suspended by Order of the State; and the Flood-gates being thus set open, any man that had a pleasant or scoffing wit might safely vent it against the *Pope,* either by free speaking, or by Libels in Print; and both became very pleasant to the people.

Matters thus heightned, the State advised with Father *Paul*, a Holy and Learned Frier (the Author of the *History of the Council of Trent*), whose advice was, *Neither to provoke the Pope, nor lose their own Right*: he declaring publickly in Print in the name of the State, *That the Pope was trusted to keep two Keys; one of Prudence, and the other of Power: And that if they were not both used together*, Power *alone is not effectual in an Excommunication.*

And thus these discontents and oppositions continued, till a report was blown abroad, that the *Venetians* were all turned *Protestants*: which was believed by many, for that it was observ'd, the *English* Ambassadour was so often in conference with the *Senate*, and his Chaplain Mr. *Bedel* more often with Father *Paul*, whom the People did not take to be his Friend: And also, for that the *Republick* of *Venice* was known to give Commission to *Gregory Justiniano*, then their Ambassador in *England*, to make all these Proceedings known to the King of *England*, and to crave a Promise of his assistance, if need should require: and in the mean time they required the King's advice and judgment; which was the same that he gave to *Pope Clement*, at his first coming to the Crown of *England*; (that Pope then moving him to an Union with the *Roman Church*) namely, *To endeavour the calling of a free Council, for the settlement of Peace in Christendom: and that he doubted not, but that the French King, and divers other Princes would join to assist in so good a work; and in the mean time, the sin of this Breach, both with His, and the* Venetians *Dominions, must of necessity lye at the* Pope's *door.*

In this contention (which lasted almost two years) the *Pope* grew still higher, and the *Venetians* more and more resolv'd and careless: still acquainting King

James with their proceedings, which was done by the help of Sir *Henry Wotton*, Mr. *Bedel*, and *Padre Paulo*, whom the *Venetians* did then call to be one of their Consulters of State, and with his Pen to defend their just Cause: which was by him so performed, that the *Pope* saw plainly, he had weakned his Power by exceeding it, and offered the *Venetians* Absolution upon very easie terms; which the *Venetians* still slighting, did at last obtain, by that which was scarce so much as a shew of acknowledging it: For they made an order, that in that day in which they were Absolv'd, there should be no Publick Rejoycing, nor any *Bonfires* that night, lest the Common People might judge, that they desired an Absolution, or were Absolved for committing a Fault.

These Contests were the occasion of *Padre Paulo's* knowledge and interest with King *James*, for whose sake principally *Padre Paulo* compiled that eminent History of the remarkable Council of *Trent*; which History was, as fast as it was written, sent in several sheets in Letters by Sir *Henry Wotton*, Mr. *Bedel*, *and* others, unto King *James*, and the then Bishop of *Canterbury*, into *England*, and there first made publick, both in *English* and in the universal Language.

For eight years after Sir *Henry Wotton's* going into *Italy*, he stood fair and highly valued in the Kings opinion, but at last became much clouded by an accident, which I shall proceed to relate.

At his first going Ambassadour into *Italy*, as he passed through *Germany*, he stayed some days at *Augusta*; where having been in his former Travels well known by many of the best note for Learning and Ingeniousness (those that are esteemed the *Virtuosi* of that Nation) with whom he passing an evening in merriments, was requested by *Christopher Flecamore* to write some Sentence in his *Albo*; (a Book of white Paper, which for that purpose many of the *German* Gentry usually carry about them) and Sir *Henry Wotton* consenting to the motion, took an occasion from some accidental discourse of the present Company, to write a pleasant definition of an Ambassadour, in these very words:

Legatus est vir bonus peregrè missus ad mentiendum Reipublicæ causâ.

Which Sir *Henry Wotton* could have been content should have been thus Englished:

An Embassadour is an honest man, sent to lie *abroad for the good of his Country.*

But the word for *lye* (being the hinge upon which the Conceit was to turn) was not so exprest in *Latine*, as would admit (in the hands of an Enemy especially) so fair a construction as Sir *Henry* thought in *English*. Yet as it was, it slept quietly among other Sentences in this *Albo*, almost *eight years*, till by accident it fell into the hands of *Jasper Scioppius*, a Romanist, a man of a restless spirit, and a malicious Pen: who with Books against King *James*, prints this as a Principle of that Religion professed by the King, and his Ambassador Sir *Henry Wotton*, then at *Venice*: and in *Venice* it was presently after written in several Glass-windows, and spitefully declared to be Sir *Henry Wottons*.

This coming to the knowledge of King *James*, he apprehended it to be such an oversight, such a weakness, or worse, in Sir *Henry Wotton*, as caused the King to express much wrath against him: and this caused Sir *Henry Wotton* to write two Apologies, one to *Velserus* (one of the Chiefs of *Augusta*) in the universal Language, which he caused to be Printed, and given, and scattered in the most remarkable places both in *Germany* and *Italy*, as an Antidote against the venomous Books of *Scioppius* ; and another Apology to King *James* : which were both so ingenious, so clear, and so choicely Eloquent, that his Majesty (who was a pure Judge of it) could not forbear, at the receit thereof, to declare publickly, *That Sir* Henry Wotton *had commuted sufficiently for a greater offence*.

And now, as broken bones well set become stronger, so Sir *Henry Wotton* did not only recover, but was much more confirmed in his Majesties estimation and favour then formerly he had been.

And as that Man of great Wit and useful Fancy (his Friend Dr. *Donne*) gave in a Will of his (a *Will of Conceits*) his *Reputation* to his *Friends*, and his *Industry* to his *Foes*, because from thence he received both : so those Friends, that in this time of trial laboured to excuse this facetious freedom of Sir *Henry Wottons*, were to him more dear, and by him more highly valued ; and those Acquaintance that urged this as an advantage against him, caused him by this error to grow both more wise, and (which is the best fruit error can bring forth) for the future to become more industriously watchful over his Tongue and Pen.

I have told you a part of his Employment in *Italy*, where notwithstanding the death of his Favorer, the Duke *Leonardo Donato*, who had an undissembled affection for him, and the malicious Accusation of *Scioppius* ; yet his interest (as though it had been an intail'd love) was still found to live and increase in all the succeeding Dukes, during his Employment to that State, which was almost twenty years ; all which time he studied the dispositions of those *Dukes*, and the other *Consulters* of *State* ; well knowing, that he who negotiates a continued business, and neglects the study of dispositions, usually fails in his proposed ends: But in this Sir *Henry Wotton* did not fail; for by a fine sorting of fit Presents, curious and not costly Entertainments, always sweetned by various and pleasant Discourse; with which, and his choice application of Stories, and his elegant Delivery of all these, even in their *Italian* Language, he first got, and still preserv'd such interest in the State of *Venice*, that it was observ'd (such was either his merit, or his modesty) they never denied him any request.

But all this shews but his abilities, and his fitness for that Employment: 'Twill therefore be needful to tell the Reader, what use he made of the Interest which these procured him; and that indeed was rather to oblige others then to enrich himself; he still endeavouring that the Reputation of the *English* might be maintained, both in the *German* Empire, and in *Italy*; where many Gentlemen whom Travel had invited into that Nation, received from him chearful Entertainments, advice for their behaviour, and by his interest shelter, or deliverance from those accidental storms of adversity which usually attend upon Travel.

And because these things may appear to the Reader to be but Generals, I shall acquaint him with two particular Examples; one of his Merciful Disposition, and one of the Nobleness of his Mind; which shall follow.

There had been many *English* Souldiers brought by Commanders of their own Country, to serve the *Venetians* for pay against the *Turk*: and those *English*, having by Irregularities, or Improvidence, brought themselves into several Gallies and Prisons, Sir *Henry Wotton* became a Petitioner to that State for their

Lives and Enlargement; and his Request was granted: so that those (which were many hundreds, and there made the sad Examples of Humane Misery, by hard Imprisonment, and unpitied Poverty in a strange Nation) were by his means released, relieved, and in a comfortable Condition sent to thank God and him for their Lives and Liberty in their own Country.

And this I have observed as one testimony of the compassionate Nature of him, who was (during his stay in those parts) as a City of Refuge for the Distressed of this and other Nations.

And for that which I offer as a Testimony of the Nobleness of his Mind; I shall make way to the Readers clearer understanding of it, by telling him, that beside several other Foreign Employments, Sir *Henry Wotton* was sent thrice Ambassadour to the Republick of *Venice*; and at his last going thither, he was employed Ambassadour to several of the *German* Princes, and more particularly to the Emperour *Ferdinando* the second; and that his Employment to him, and those Princes, was to incline them to equitable Conditions, for the Restauration of the Queen of *Bohemia*, and her Descendents, to their Patrimonial Inheritance of the *Palatinate*.

This was by his eight Moneths constant endeavours and attendance upon the *Emperour*, his Court and Councel, brought to a probability of a successful Conclusion without blood-shed: but there was at that time two opposite Armies in the Field; and as they were Treating, there was a Battle fought; in the managery whereof, there was so many miserable Errors on the one side, (so Sir *Henry Wotton* expresses it in a Dispatch to the King) and so advantagious Events to the Emperour, as put an end to all present Hopes of a successful Treaty: so that Sir *Henry* seeing the face of Peace altered by that Victory, prepared for a removal from that Court; and at his departure from the *Emperor*, was so bold as to remember him, *That the Events of every Battle move on the unseen Wheels of Fortune, which are this moment up, and down the next: and therefore humbly advised him to use his Victory so soberly, as still to put on thoughts of Peace.* Which Advice, though it seemed to be spoke with some Passion, (his dear Mistress the Queen of *Bohemia* being concerned in it) was yet taken in good part by the *Emperor*; who replied, *That he would consider his Advice: And though he looked on the King his Master as an Abettor of his Enemy the* Paulsgrave; *yet for Sir* Henry *himself, his behaviour had been such during the manage of the Treaty, that he took him to be a Person of much Honour and Merit, and did therefore desire him to accept of that Jewel, as a testimony of his good opinion of him*; which was a Jewel of Diamonds of more value then a Thousand Pounds.

This Jewel was received with all outward Circumstances and Terms of Honour by Sir *Henry Wotton*: but the next morning, at his departing from *Vienna*, he at his taking leave of the Countess of *Sabrina* (an *Italian* Lady, in whose House the Emperor had appointed him to be lodg'd, and honourably entertained) *he acknowledged her Merits, and besought her to accept of that Jewel, as a testimony of his gratitude for her Civilities*: presenting her with the same that was given him by the *Emperor*: which being suddenly discovered, and told to the *Emperor*, was by him taken for a high affront, and Sir *Henry Wotton* told so by a Messenger. To which he replied, *That though he received it with thankfulness, yet he found in himself an indisposition to be the better for any gift that came from an Enemy to his Royal Mistress the Queen of*

Bohemia; for so she was pleased he should always call her.

Many other of his Services to his Prince, and this Nation, might be insisted upon: as namely, his procurations of Priviledges and Courtesies with the *German* Princes, and the Republick of *Venice*, for the *English* Merchants; and what he did by direction of King *James* with the *Venetian* State, concerning the Bishop of *Spalato*'s return to the Church of *Rome*. But for the particulars of these, and many more that I meant to make known, I want a view of some Papers that might inform me, (his late Majesties *Letter Office* having now suffered a strange alienation) and indeed I want time too; for the Printers Press stays for what is written: so that I must haste to bring Sir *Henry Wotton* in an instant from *Venice* to *London*, leaving the Reader to make up what is defective in this place, by the small supplement of the Inscription under his Arms, which he left at all those Houses where he rested, or lodged, when he return'd from his last Embassie into *England*.

Henricus Wottonius *Anglo-Cantianus*, Thomæ *optimi viri filius natu minimus, à serenissimo* Jacobo I. *Mag. Britt. Rege, in equestrem titulum adscitus, ejusdemque ter ad Rempublicam* Venetam *Legatus Ordinarius, semel ad confœderatarum Provinciarum Ordines in Juliacensi negotio.   Bis ad* Carolum Emanuel, *Sabaudiæ Ducem; semel ad unitos superioris* Germaniæ *Principes in Conventu* Heilbrunensi, *postremo ad Archiducem* Leopoldum, Ducem Wittembergensem, *Civitates imperiales,* Argentinam, Vlmamque, & *ipsum* Romanorum Imperatorem *Ferdinandum secundum, Legatus Extraordinarius, tandem hoc didicit,*

Animas fieri sapientiores quiescendo.

To *London* he came the year before King *James* died; who having for the reward of his forreign service, promised him the reversion of an Office which was fit to be turned into present money, which he wanted, for a supply of his present necessities, and also granted him the reversion of the *Master of the Rolls* place, if he out-lived charitable Sir *Julius Cæsar*, who then possessed it: and then grown so old, that he was said to be kept alive beyond Natures Course, by the prayers of those many poor which he daily relieved.

But these were but in hope; and his condition required a present support: For in the beginning of these imployments he sold to his elder Brother the Lord *Wotton*, the Rent-charge left by his good Father, and (which is worse) was now at his return indebted to several persons, whom he was not able to satisfie, but by the Kings payment of his Arrears due for his forreign Imployments: He had brought into *England* many servants, of which some were *German* and *Italian* Artists; this was part of his condition, who had many times hardly sufficient to supply the occasions of the day: (For it may by no means be said of his providence, as himself said of Sir *Philip Sidney's* wit, *That it was the very measure of congruity*) He being alwayes so careless of money, as though our Saviours words, *Care not for to morrow*, were to be literally understood.

But it pleased the God of providence, that in this juncture of time, the Provostship of His Majesties Colledge of *Eaton* became void by the death of Mr. *Thomas Murray*, for which there were (as the place deserv'd) many earnest and powerful Suiters to the *King*. And Sir *Henry* who had for many years (like *Sisyphus*) rolled the restless stone of a State-imployment; knowing experimentally, that the great blessing of sweet content was not to be found in multitudes of men or business : and, that a *Colledge* was the fittest place to nourish *holy thoughts*, and to afford rest both to his body and mind, which his age (being now almost threescore years) seemed to require, did therefore use his own, and the interest of all his friends to procure that place. By which means, and quitting the King of his promised reversionary Offices, and a piece of honest policy (which I have not time to relate) he got a Grant of it from His Majesty.

And this was a fair satisfaction to his *mind* : but *money* was wanting to furnish him with those necessaries which attend removes, and a settlement in such a place ; and to procure that, he wrote to his old friend Mr. *Nicholas Pey*, for his assistance ; of which *Nicholas Pey* I shall here say a little, for the clearing of some passages that I shall mention hereafter.

He was in his youth a Clerk, or in some such way, a Servant to the Lord *Wotton*, Sir *Henry's* Brother ; and by him, when he was Comptroller of the Kings Houshold, was made a great Officer in His Majesties House. This, and other favours being conferred upon Mr. *Pey* (*in whom there was a radical honesty*) were always thankfully acknowledged by him, and his gratitude exprest by a willing and unwearied serviceableness to that Family even till his death. To him Sir *Henry Wotton* wrote, to use all his interest at Court, to procure Five hundred pounds of his Arrears (for less would not settle him in the Colledge) and the want of such a sum *wrinckled his face with care* ; ('twas his own expression) and that money being procured, he should the next day after find him in his *Colledge*, and *Invidiæ remedium* writ over his *Study*-door.

This money, being part of his Arrears, was by his own, and the help of honest *Nicholas Pey's* interest in Court, quickly procured him; and he as quickly in the *Colledge*; the place where indeed his happiness then seemed to have its beginning: the *Colledge* being to his mind, as a quiet Harbor to a Sea-faring man after a tempestuous voyage; where, by the bounty of the pious Founder, his very *Food* and *Raiment* were plentifully provided for him in kind, and more money then enough, where he was freed from all corroding cares, and seated on such a Rock, as the waves of want could not probably shake; where he might sit in a *Calm*, and looking down, behold the busie multitude turmoyl'd and tossed in a tempestuous Sea of trouble and dangers! And (as Sir *William Davenant* has happily exprest the like of another person)

> *Laugh at the graver business of the State,*
> *Which speaks men rather wise then fortunate.*

Being thus setled according to the desires of his *heart*, his first *study* was the Statutes of the *Colledge*: by which, he conceiv'd himself bound to enter into *Holy Orders*, which he did; being made *Deacon* with all convenient speed; shortly after which time, as he came in his *Surplice* from the *Church-service*, an old Friend, a person of Quality, met him so attired, and joyed him of his new habit; to whom Sir *Henry Wotton* replied, *I thank* God *and the* King, *by whose goodness I now am in this condition; a condition, which that Emperor* Charles *the Fifth seem'd to approve: who, after so many remarkable Victories, when his glory was great in the eyes of all men, freely gave up his* Crown, *and the many cares that attended it, to* Philip *his Son, making a holy retreat to a Cloysteral life, where he might by devout meditations consult with* God *(which the rich or busie men seldom do) and have leisure both to examine the errors of his life past, and prepare for that great day, wherein all flesh must make an account of their actions: And after a kind of tempestuous life, I now have the like advantage from him,* that makes the out-goings of the morning to praise him; *even from my* God, *whom I daily magnifie for this particular mercy, of an exemption from business, a quiet mind, and a liberal maintenance, even in this part of my life, when my age and* infirmities *seem to sound me a retreat from the pleasures of this world, and invite me to contemplation, in which I have ever taken the greatest felicity.*

And now to speak a little of the imployment of his *time* in the Colledge. After his customary publick Devotions, his use was to retire into his *Study,* and there to spend some hours in reading the Bible, and Authors in Divinity, closing up his meditations with private prayer; this was, for the most part, his imployment in the Forenoon: But when he was once sate to Dinner, then nothing but chearful thoughts possess'd his mind; and those still increased by constant company at his Table, of such persons as brought thither additions both of Learning and Pleasure; but some part of most days was usually spent in *Philosophical Conclusions.* Nor did he forget his innate pleasure of *Angling,* which he would usually call, *his idle time, not idly spent*; saying often, he would rather live five *May months,* then *forty Decembers.*

He was a great lover of his Neighbours, and a bountiful entertainer of them very often at his Table, where his meat was choice, and his discourse better.

He was a constant Cherisher of all those youths in that School, in whom he found either a constant diligence, or a *Genius* that prompted them to Learning; for whose encouragement, he was (beside many other things of necessity and beauty) at the charge of setting up in it two rows of *Pillars,* on which he caused to be choicely drawn, the pictures of divers of the most famous *Greek* and *Latin Historians*, *Poets*, and *Orators* ; perswading them not to neglect *Rhetorick*, because *Almighty God has left Mankind affections to be wrought upon* : And he would often say, *That none despised Eloquence, but such dull souls as were not capable of it.* He would also often make choice of some Observations out of those *Historians* and *Poets* : and would never leave the School, without dropping some choice *Greek* or *Latin Apothegm* or sentence, that might be worthy of a room in the memory of a growing Scholar.

He was pleased constantly to breed up one or more hopeful Youths, which he picked out of the *School*, and took into his own Domestick care, and to attend him at his Meals ; out of whose *Discourse* and *Behaviour*, he gathered observations for the better compleating of his intended work of *Education* : of which, by his still striving to make the whole better, he lived to leave but part to Posterity.

He was a great enemy to *wrangling Disputes* of *Religion*, concerning which, I shall say a little, both to testifie that, and to shew the readiness of his Wit.

Having at his being in *Rome* made acquaintance with a pleasant *Priest*, who invited him one Evening to hear their *Vesper Musick* at *Church*, the Priest seeing Sir *Henry* stand obscurely in a corner, sends to him by a Boy of the Quire this Question, writ in a small piece of Paper, *Where was your Religion to be found before* Luther ? To which Question Sir *Henry* presently under-writ, *My Religion was to be found* then, *where yours is not to be found* now, *in the written Word of God.*

The next Vesper, Sir *Henry* went purposely to the same Church, and sent one of the Quire-boyes with this Question, to his honest, pleasant friend, the Priest ;

Do you believe all those many thousands of poor Christians were damn'd, that were Excommunicated, because the Pope, *and the Duke of* Venice, *could not agree about their temporal power?* even those poor Christians that knew not why they quarrel'd. Speak your Conscience. To which he under-writ in *French, Monsieur, excusay moy.*

To one that asked him, *Whether a Papist may be saved?* he replied, *You may be saved without knowing that.* Look to your self.

To another, whose earnestness exceeded his knowledge, and was still railing against the *Papists*, he gave this advice, *Pray Sir forbear, till you have studied the Points better; for the wise* Italians *have this Proverb; He that understands amiss, concludes worse:* And take heed of thinking, *The farther you go from the Church of* Rome, *the nearer you are to God.*

And to another that spake indiscreet, and bitter words against *Arminius*, I heard him reply to this purpose:

In my travel towards Venice, *as I past through* Germany, *I rested almost a year at* Leyden, *where I entred into an acquaintance with* Arminius *(then the Professor of* Divinity *in that University) a man much talk'd of in this Age, which is made up of opposition and Controversie: And indeed, if I mistake not* Arminius *in his expressions (as so weak a brain as mine is may easily do) then I know I differ from him in some points; yet I profess my judgment of him to be, that he was a man of most rare Learning, and I knew him to be of a most strict life, and of a most meek spirit. And that he was so mild, appears by his Proposals to our Master* Perkins *of* Cambridge, *from whose Book*, of the Order and Causes of Salvation *(which was first writ in Latin)* Arminius *took the occasion of writing some* Queries *to him concerning the consequents of his* Doctrine; *intending them ('tis said) to come privately to Mr.* Perkins *own hands, and to receive from him, a like private and a like loving* Answer : *But Mr.* Perkins *died before those* Queries *came to him ; and 'tis thought* Arminius *meant them to dye with him ; for though he lived long after, I have heard he forbore to publish them,* (but since his death, his Sons did not.) *And 'tis pity, if God had been so pleased, that Mr.* Perkins *did not live to see, consider, and answer those proposals himself ; for he was also of a most meek* spirit, *and of great and sanctified* Learning : *And though since their deaths, many of high parts and piety have undertaken to clear the* Controversie, *yet, for the most part, they have rather satisfied themselves, then convinced the dissenting party.   And doubtless, many middle-witted men (which yet may mean well ;) many Scholars that are not in the highest Form for Learning (which yet may preach well ;) men that are but Preachers, and shall never know, till they come to Heaven, where the* Questions *stick betwixt* Arminius *and the Church of* England, *(if there be any) will yet in this world be tampering with, and thereby perplexing the* Controversie, *and do therefore justly fall under the reproof of St.* Jude, *for being* Busie-bodies, *& for medling with things they understand not.*

And here it offers it self (I think not unfitly) to tell the Reader, that a friend of Sir *Henry Wottons*, being designed for the imployment of an *Ambassador*, came to *Eaton,* and requested from him some experimental Rules for his prudent and safe carriage in his Negotiations ; to whom he smilingly gave this for an infallible *Aphorism*; *That, to be in safety himself, and serviceable to his* Country, *he should always, & upon all occasions speak the* truth (it seems a State-Paradox) *for, says* Sir Henry Wotton, *you shall never be* believed ; *and by this means, your truth will secure your self, if you shall ever be called to any account ; and 'twill also*

put your Adversaries (who will still hunt counter) to a
loss in all their disquisitions and undertakings.

Many more of this nature might be observed, but
they must be laid aside ; for I shall here make a little
stop, and invite the Reader to look back with me,
whilst according to my promise, I shall say a little of
Sir *Albertus Morton*, and Mr. *William Bedel*, whom I
formerly mentioned.

I have told you that are my Reader ; that at Sir
Henry Wotton's first going Ambassador into *Italy*, his
Cousin, Sir *Albert Morton*, went his Secretary : and am
next to tell you, that Sir *Albertus* died *Secretary of State*
to our late King ; but cannot, am not able to express
the sorrow that possest Sir *Henry Wotton* at his first
hearing the news that Sir *Albertus* was by death lost
to him and this world ; and yet, the Reader may
partly guess by these following expressions : The first
in a Letter to his *Nicholas Pey*, of which this that
followeth is a part.

——*And* my dear Nick, *When I had been here*
almost a fortnight, in the midst of my great contentment,
I received notice of Sir Albertus Morton *his departure*
out of this World, who was dearer to me, then mine own
being in it ; what a wound it is to my heart, you that
knew him, and know me, will easily believe : but our
Creators Will must be done, and unrepiningly received
by his own Creatures, who is the Lord of all Nature, and
of all Fortune, when he taketh to himself now one, and
then another, till that expected day, wherein it shall
please him to dissolve the whole, and wrap up even the
Heaven it self as a Scrole of Parchment. This is the
last Philosophy *that we must study upon Earth ; let us*
therefore that yet remain here, as our days and friends
waste, reinforce our love to each other ; which of all
vertues, both spiritual *and* moral, *hath the highest*

priviledge, *because death it self cannot end it.   And my good* Nick, *&c.*

This is a part of his sorrow thus exprest to his *Nick Pey*; the other part is in this following Elogy, of which the Reader may safely conclude, 'twas too hearty to be dissembled.

Tears wept at the Grave of Sir *Albertus Morton*, by *Henry Wotton.*

Silence in truth would speak my sorrow best,
   For deepest wounds can least their feelings tell;
   Yet let me borrow from mine own unrest,
A time to bid him whom I lov'd, farewell.

Oh, my unhappy lines! you that before
Have serv'd my youth to vent some wanton cries,
And now congeal'd with grief, can scarce implore
Strength to accent, Here my *Albertus* lies.

This is that Sable Stone, this is the Cave
And womb of Earth, that doth his Corps embrace;
While others sing his praise, let me ingrave
These bleeding numbers to adorn the place.

Here will I paint the Characters of Woe;
Here will I pay my Tribute to the Dead;
And here my faithful Tears in showres shall flow
To humanize the Flints on which I tread.

Where though I mourn my matchless loss alone,
And none between my weakness judge and me;
Yet even these pensive Walls allow my moan,
Whose doleful Ecchoes to my plaints agree.

But is he gone? and live I rhyming here,
As if some Muse *would listen to my lay?*
When all dis-tun'd sit waiting for their dear,
And bathe the Banks *where he was wont to play.*

Dwell then in endless Bliss with happy Souls,
Discharg'd from Natures *and from* Fortunes *Trust;*
Whil'st on this fluid Globe my Hour-glass rowls,
And runs the rest of my remaining dust.

                                    H. W.

This concerning his Sir *Albertus Morton.*

And for what I shall say concerning Mr. *William Bedel,* I must prepare the Reader by telling him, That when King *James* sent Sir *Henry Wotton* Ambassador to the State of *Venice,* he sent also an Ambassador to the King of *France,* and another to the King of *Spain:* with the Ambassador of *France* went *Joseph Hall* (late *Bishop* of *Norwich*) whose many and useful Works speak his great Merit: with the Ambassador of *Spain* went *Ja. Wadsworth*; and with Sir *Henry Wotton* went *William Bedel.*

These three Chaplains to these three Ambassadours, were all bred in one University, all of one *Colledge, all Benefic'd in one Diocess, and all most dear and intire Friends: But in *Spain* Mr. *Wadsworth* met with temptations, or reasons, such as were so powerful, as to perswade him (who of the three, was formerly observ'd to be the most averse to that Religion that calls it self *Catholick*) to disclaim himself a Member of the Church of *England,* and declare himself for the Church of *Rome*; discharging himself of his attendance on the Ambassador, and betaking himself to a Monasterial life; in which he lived very regularly, and so died.

* *Emanuel* Colledge *in* Cambridge.

When Dr. *Hall* (the late Bishop of *Norwich*) came into *England*, he wrote to Mr. *Wadsworth* ('tis the first Epistle in his Printed Decads) to perswade his return, or to shew the reason of his Apostasie: the Letter seemed to have in it many sweet expressions of love; and yet there was in it some expression that was so unpleasant to Mr. *Wadsworth*, that he chose rather to acquaint his old Friend Mr. *Bedel* with his motives; by which means there past betwixt Mr. *Bedel* and Mr. *Wadsworth* divers Letters, which be extant in Print, and did well deserve it; for in them there seems to be a controversie, not of Religion only, but who should answer each other with most love and meekness: which I mention the rather, because it too seldom falls out to be so in a Book-War.

There is yet a little more to be said of Mr. *Bedel*, for the greatest part of which, the Reader is referred to this following Letter of Sir *Henry Wottons*, writ to our late King *Charles* the First.

May it please Your most Gracious Majesty,

Having been informed that certain persons have, by the good wishes of the Archbishop of Armagh, *been directed hither, with a most humble Petition unto Your Majesty, that You will be pleased to make Mr.* William Bedel (*now resident upon a small Benefice in* Suffolk) *Governor of Your Colledge at* Dublin *for the good of that Society; and my self being required to render unto Your Majesty some testimony of the said* William Bedel, *who was long my Chaplain at* Venice, *in the time of my first employment there; I am bound in all Conscience & Truth (so far as Your Majesty will vouchsafe to accept my poor judgment) to affirm of him, That I think hardly a fitter man for that Charge, could have been propounded unto Your Majesty in Your whole*

Kingdom, for singular Erudition and Piety, Conformity to the Rites of the Church, and Zeal to advance the Cause of God, wherein his Travels abroad were not obscure, in the time of the Excommunication of the Venetians.

For it may please Your Majesty to know, that this is the man whom Padre Paulo *took, I may say, into his very soul, with whom he did communicate the inwardest thoughts of his heart, from whom he professed to have received more knowledge in all* Divinity, *both Scholastical and Positive, than from any that he had ever practised in his days; of which, all the passages were well known to the King Your Father, of most blessed memory. And so with Your Majesties good favour, I will end this needless Office; for the general Fame of his Learning, his Life, and Christian temper, and those Religious Labours which himself hath dedicated to Your Majesty, do better describe him then I am able.*

Your M A J E S T I E S
Most humble and faithful Servant,

H. WOTTON.

TO this Letter, I shall add this; That he was (to the great joy of Sir *Henry Wotton*) made Governor of the said Colledge; and that * after a fair discharge of his duty and trust there, he was thence removed to be *Bishop* of *Kilmore*. * In both which places, his life was so holy, as seemed to equal the primitive Christians; for as they, so he kept all the *Ember-weeks*, observed (besides his private devotions) the *Canonical* hours of Prayer very strictly,

* *August,* 1627.

* *Sept.* 3. 1629.

and so he did all the Feasts, and Fast-days of his Mother,
the Church of *England*; to which I may add, that his
Patience and Charity were both such, as shewed his
affections were set upon *things that are above*; for
indeed his whole life brought forth the *fruits of the
Spirit*; there being in him such a remarkable meekness, that as S. *Paul* advised his *Timothy* in the
Election of a *Bishop*, * *That he have a
good report of those that be without*; so   * 1 *Tim.* 3. 7.
had he; *for those that were without*, even those that
in point of Religion, were of the *Roman* perswasion
(of which there were very many in his Diocess) did
yet (such is the power of visible Piety) ever look upon
him with respect and reverence; and testified it, by
a concealing, and safe protecting him from death in
the late horrid Rebellion in *Ireland*, when the fury of
the wild *Irish* knew no distinction of persons; and
yet, there, and then, he was protected and cherished
by those of a contrary perswasion; and there and then
he died, not by violence or misusage, but by grief in
a quiet prison (1629). And with him was lost many
of his learned Writings, which were thought worthy
of preservation; and amongst the rest, was lost the
Bible, which by many years labour, and conference,
and study, he had translated into the *Irish* Tongue,
with an intent to have printed it for publick use.

More might be said of Mr. *Bedel*, who (I told the
Reader) was Sir *Henry Wottons* first Chaplain; and
much of his second Chaplain, *Isaac Bargrave*, Doctor
in *Divinity*, and the late learned and hospitable Dean
of *Canterbury*; as also of the Merit of many others,
that had the happiness to attend Sir *Henry* in his foreign
imployments: But the Reader may think that in this
digression, I have already carried him too far from
Eaton-Colledge, and therefore I shall lead him back as

gently, and as orderly as I may to that place, for a further conference concerning Sir *Henry Wotton*.

Sir *Henry Wotton* had propos'd to himself, before he entred into his Collegiate life, to write the life of *Martin Luther*; and in it, the History of the Reformation, as it was carried on in *Germany*: For the doing of which, he had many advantages by his several Embassies into those parts, and his interest in the several Princes of the Empire; by whose means he had access to the Records of all the *Hans Towns*, and the knowledge of many secret passages that fell not under common view; and in these he had made a happy progress, as was well known to his worthy friend Doctor *Duppa*, the late Reverend Bishop of *Salisbury*; but in the midst of this design, His late Majesty King *Charles* the *First*, that knew the value of Sir *Henry Wottons* Pen, did by a perswasive loving violence (to which may be added a promise of 500 *l.* a year) force him to lay *Luther* aside, and betake himself to write the History of *England*; in which he proceeded to write some short Characters of a few Kings, as a foundation upon which he meant to build; but, for the present, meant to be more large in the story of *Henry* the *sixth*, the Founder of that Colledge, in which he then enjoy'd all the worldly happiness of his present being; but Sir *Henry* dyed in the midst of this undertaking, and the footsteps of his labours are not recoverable by a more than common diligence.

This is some account both of his inclination, and the employment of his time in the Colledge, where he seemed to have his *Youth* renewed by a continual conversation with that Learned Society, and a daily recourse of other Friends of choicest breeding and parts; by which, that great blessing of a chearful heart was still maintained; he being always free, even to the last of his days, from that peevishness which usually attends Age.

And yet his mirth was sometimes damp'd by the remembrance of divers old Debts, partly contracted in his foreign Imployments, for which his just Arrears due from the *King*, would have made satisfaction; but, being still delayed with Court-promises, and finding some decays of health, he did about two years before his death, out of a Christian desire, that none should be a loser by him, make his last *Will*; concerning which, a doubt still remains, namely, whether it discovered more *holy wit*, or *conscionable policy*? But there is no doubt, but that his chief design was a *Christian* endeavour that his Debts might be satisfied.

And that it may remain as such a Testimony, and a Legacy to those that lov'd him, I shall here impart it to the Reader, as it was found writ with his own hand.

I*N the name of God Almighty and All-merciful, I Henry Wotton, Provost of his Majesties Colledge by Eaton, being mindful of mine own mortality, which the sin of our first Parents did bring upon all flesh, Do by this last Will and Testament, thus dispose of my self, and the poor things I shall leave in this World. My Soul, I bequeath to the Immortal God my Maker, Father of our Lord Jesus Christ, my blessed Redeemer, and Mediator, through his all-sole sufficient satisfaction for the sins of the whole World, and efficient for his Elect; in the number of whom, I am one by his meer grace, and thereof most unremoveably assured by his holy Spirit, the true Eternal Comforter. My body I bequeath to the Earth, if I shall end my transitory days at, or near Eaton, to be buried in the Chappel of the said Colledge, as the Fellows shall dispose thereof, with whom I have liv'd* (my God knows) *in all loving affection; or if I shall dye near* Bocton Malherb, *in the County of* Kent, *then I wish to be laid in that* Parish-Church, *as near as may be to the* Sepulchre *of my good Father, expecting a joyful Resurrection with him in the day of Christ.*

After this account of his *Faith,* and this Surrender of his *Soul* to that God that inspir'd it, and this direction for the disposal of his body, he proceeded to appoint that his *Executors* should lay over his grave a Marble stone, plain, and not costly: And considering that time moulders even Marble to dust; (for * *Monuments themselves must dye.*) Therefore did he (waving the common way) think fit rather to preserve his name (to which the Son of *Sirac* adviseth all men) by a useful *Apothegm,* then by a large enumeration of his descent or merits (of both which he might justly have boasted) but he was content to forget them, and did chuse only this prudent, pious, Sentence, to discover his Disposition, and preserve his *Memory.*

* *Juven.*

'Twas directed by him, to be thus inscribed:

Hic jacet hujus Sententiæ primus Author.

DISPUTANDI PRURITUS, EC-CLESIARUM SCABIES.

Nomen aliàs quære.

Which may be Englished thus,
Here lies the first Author of this Sentence.

THE ITCH OF DISPUTATION WILL PROVE THE SCAB OF THE CHURCH.

Inquire his name elsewhere.

And if any shall object, as I think some have, That Sir *Henry Wotton* was not the first Author of this Sentence; but, that this, or a Sentence like it, was long before his time; To him I answer, that *Solomon* says, *Nothing can be spoken, that hath not been spoken; for there is no new thing under the Sun.* But grant, that in his various reading, he had met with this, or a like Sentence; yet Reason mixt with Charity should perswade all Readers to believe, That Sir *Henry Wotton's* mind was then so fix'd on that part of the Communion of *Saints* which is above, that an holy *Lethargy* did surprize his *Memory.* For doubtless, if he had not believed himself to be the first Author of what he said, he was too prudent first to own, and then expose it to the publick view, and censure of every *Critick.* And questionless, 'twill be charity in all Readers, to think his mind was then so fix'd on Heaven, that a holy zeal did transport him: and that in this Sacred Extasie, his thoughts were then only of the Church Triumphant, (into which he daily expected his admission). And that Almighty God was then pleased to make him a *Prophet,* to tell the *Church Militant,* and particularly that part of it in this Nation where the weeds of controversie grow to be daily both more numerous, and more destructive to humble Piety: and where men have Consciences that boggle at Ceremonies, and yet scruple not to speak and act such sins as the ancient humble Christians believed to be a sin to think: and where, as our Reverend *Hooker* says, *former Simplicity, and softness of Spirit, is not now to be found, because Zeal hath drowned Charity, and Skill Meekness:* It will be good to think that these sad changes have proved this *Epitaph* to be a useful Caution unto us of this Nation; and the sad effects thereof in *Germany* have prov'd it to be a mournful *Truth.*

This by way of Observation concerning his *Epitaph*: The rest of his *Will* follows in his own words.

Further, I the said Henry Wotton, *do constitute and ordain to be joint Executors of this my last* Will *and* Testament, *my two Grand-Nephews,* Albert Morton, *second Son to Sir* Robert Morton *Knight, late deceased, and* Thomas Bargrave, *eldest son to Dr.* Bargrave, *Dean of* Canterbury, *Husband to my Right Vertuous and only Neece. And I do pray the foresaid Dr.* Bargrave, *and Mr.* Nicholas Pey, *my most faithful and chosen friends, together with Mr.* John Harrison *one of the Fellows of* Eaton Colledge, *best acquainted with my Books and Pictures, and other Vtensils, to be Supervisors of this my last* Will *and* Testament. *And I do pray the foresaid Dr.* Bargrave, *and Mr.* Nicholas Pey, *to be Solicitors for such Arrearages as shall appear due unto me from his Majesties Exchequer at the time of my death ; and to assist my fore-named Executors in some reasonable and conscientious satisfaction of my Creditors, and discharge of my Legacies now specified ; or that shall be hereafter added unto this my* Testament, *by any Codicil or Schedule, or left in the hands, or in any Memorial with the aforesaid Mr.* John Harrison. *And first, To my most dear Soveraign and Master of incomparable* Goodness (*in whose gracious opinion I have ever had some portion, as far as the interest of a plain honest man*) *I leave four Pictures at large of those Dukes of* Venice, *in whose time I was there imployed, with their Names written on the back-side, which hang in my great ordinary Dining-room, done after the Life by* Edoardo Fialetto. *Likewise a Table of the* Venetian Colledge, *where Ambassadors had their Audience, hanging over the Mantle of the Chimney in the said Room, done by the same hand, which containeth a draught*

*in little, well resembling the famous D. Leonardo
Donato, in a time which needed a wise and constant
man. It' The Picture of a Duke of Venice hanging
over against the door, done either by Titiano, or some
other principal hand long before my time. Most humbly
beseeching his Majesty that the said Pieces may remain
in some corner of any of his Houses, for a poor Memorial
of his most humble vassal.*

*It' I leave his said Majesty all the Papers and Nego-
tiations of Sir Nich. Throgmorton Knight, during his
famous imployment under Queen Elizabeth, in Scotland
and in France, which contain divers secrets of State,
that perchance his Majesty will think fit to be preserved
in his Paper-Office, after they have been perused and
sorted by Mr. Secretary Windebank, with whom I have
heretofore, as I remember, conferred about them. They
were committed to my disposal by Sir Arthur Throgmorton his Son, to whose worthy memory I cannot better
discharge my faith, then by assigning them to the highest
place of trust. It' I leave to our most Gracious and
Vertuous Queen Mary, Dioscorides, with the Plants
naturally coloured, and the Text translated by Matthiolo,
in the best Language of Tuscany, whence her said
Majesty is lineally descended, for a poor token of my
thankful devotion, for the honour she was once pleased
to do my private study with her presence. I leave to
the most hopeful Prince, the Picture of the elected and
crowned Queen of Bohemia, his Aunt, of clear and
resplendent vertues through the clouds of her Fortune.
To my Lords Grace of Canterbury now being, I leave
my Picture of Divine Love, rarely copied from one in
the Kings Galleries, of my presentation to his Majesty :
beseeching him to receive it as a pledge of my humble
reverence to his great Wisdom. And to the most worthy
L. Bishop of London, L. High Treasurer of England,*

*in true admiration of his Christian simplicity, and con-
tempt of earthly pomp, I leave a Picture of* Heraclitus
bewailing, and Democritus *laughing at the world:
Most humbly beseeching the said Lord Archbishop his
Grace, and the Lord Bishop of* London, *of both whose
favours I have tasted in my life time, to intercede with
our most gracious Soveraign after my death, in the bowels
of* Jesus Christ, *That out of compassionate memory of my
long Services (wherein I more studied the publick Honour,
then mine own Vtility) some Order may be taken out of
my Arrears due in the Exchequer, for such satisfaction
of my Creditors, as those whom I have Ordained Supervisors of this my last* Will & Testament *shall present
unto their Lordships, without their farther trouble:
Hoping likewise in his Majesties most indubitable Goodness, that he will keep me from all prejudice, which I
may otherwise suffer by any defect of formality in the
Demand of my said Arrears. To —— for a poor
addition to his Cabinet, I leave as Emblems of his
attractive Vertues, and Obliging Nobleness, my great*
Loadstone *; and a piece of* Amber *of both kinds naturally united, and only differing in degree of Concoction,
which is thought somewhat rare. Item, A piece of*
Christal Sexangular *(as they grow all) grasping divers
several things within it, which I bought among the
Rhætian Alps, in the very place where it grew : recom-
mending most humbly unto his Lordship, the reputation
of my poor Name in the point of my debts, as I have done
to the forenamed Spiritual Lords ; and am heartily
sorry, that I have no better token of my humble thankfulness to his honored Person. It' I leave to Sir* Francis
Windebank, *one of his Majesties principal Secretaries
of State (whom I found my great friend in point of
Necessity) the four Seasons of old* Bassano, *to hang near
the Eye in his Parlour (being in little form) which I*

bought at Venice, *where I first entred into his most worthy Acquaintance.*

To the abovenamed Dr. Bargrave *Dean of* Canterbury, *I leave all my* Italian *Books not disposed in this Will. I leave to him likewise my* Viol de Gamba, *which hath been twice with me in* Italy, *in which Countrey I first contracted with him an unremovable Affection. To my other Supervisor Mr.* Nicholas Pey, *I leave my Chest, or* Cabinet *of Instruments and Engines of all kinds of uses: in* the lower box whereof, are some fit to be bequeathed to none but so entire an honest man as he is. I leave him likewise forty pound for his pains in the solicitation of my Arrears, and am sorry that my ragged Estate can reach no further to one that hath taken such care for me in the same kind, during all my foreign Imployments. To the* Library *at* Eaton *Colledge I leave all my Manuscripts not before disposed, and to each of the Fellows a plain Ring of Gold, enamel'd black; all save the verge, with this Motto within,* Amor unit omnia.

* In it were Italian locks, picklocks, screws to force open doors, and many things of worth and rarity, that he had gathered in his foreign Travel.

This is my last Will *and* Testament, *save what shall be added by a Schedule thereunto annexed. Written on the first of* October, *in the present year of our Redemption* 1637. *And subscribed by my self, with the Testimony of these Witnesses.*

HENRY WOTTON.

Nich. Oudert.
Geo. Lash.

ANd now, because the mind of man is best satisfied by the knowledge of *Events*, I think fit to declare, that every one that was named in his Will, did gladly receive their Legacies; by which,

and his most just and passionate desires for the payment of his debts, they joined in assisting the Over-
seers of his Will; and by their joint endeavours to
the King (then whom none was more willing) conscionable satisfaction was given for his just debts.

The next thing wherewith I shall acquaint the
Reader, is, That he went usually once a year, if not
oftner, to the beloved *Bocton-hall*, where he would
say, *he found a cure for all cares, by the chearful company*, which he called the living furniture of that place :
and *a restoration of his strength, by the Connaturalness
of that, which he called his* genial *air*.

He yearly went also to *Oxford*.   But the Summer
before his death he changed that for a journey to
Winchester-Colledge; to which School he was first
removed from *Bocton*.   And as he returned from
Winchester, towards *Eaton*-Colledge, said to a friend,
his Companion in that Journey; *How useful was that
advice of a Holy* Monk, *who perswaded his friend* to
perform his Customary devotions in a constant place,
because in that place, we usually meet with those very
thoughts which possessed us at our last being there;
*And I find it thus far experimentally true ; that, at
my now being in that School, and seeing that very place
where I sate when I was a Boy, occasioned me to remember those very thoughts of my youth which then possessed
me ; sweet thoughts indeed, that promised my growing
years numerous pleasures, without mixtures of cares ; and
those to be enjoyed, when time (which I therefore thought
slow pac'd) had changed my youth into manhood : But
age and experience have taught me, that those were but
empty hopes : For I have always found it true, as my*
Saviour *did foretell*, Sufficient for the day is the evil
thereof.   *Nevertheless, I saw there a succession of Boys
using the same recreations, and questionless possessed*

with the same thoughts that then possessed me. Thus, one generation succeeds another, both in their lives, recreations, hopes, fears, and death.

After his return from *Winchester* to *Eaton* (which was about five Moneths before his death) he became much more retir'd, and contemplative; in which time he was often visited by Mr. *John Hales*, (learned Mr. *John Hales*) then a Fellow of that Colledge, to whom upon an occasion he spake to this purpose—— *I have in my passage to my grave met with most of those Joys of which a discoursive soul is capable : and, being entertain'd with more inferior pleasures then the sons of men are usually made partakers of : nevertheless, in this voyage I have not always floated on the calm Sea of Content ; but have oft met with cross winds and storms, and with many troubles of mind and temptations to evil. And yet, though I have been and am a man compass'd about with humane frailties, Almighty God hath by his grace prevented me from making* shipwrack *of faith and a* good Conscience *; the thought of which is now the joy of my heart, and I most humbly praise him for it ; And I humbly acknowledge that it was not my self but he that hath kept me to this great age, and let him take the glory of his great mercy.*——*And my dear Friend, I now see that I draw near my harbour of death : that harbor, that will secure me from all the future storms and waves of this restless world ; and I praise God I am willing to leave it, and expect a better ; that world, wherein dwelleth Righteousness, and I long for it.*——These, and the like expressions were then utter'd by him at the beginning of a Feavourish distemper, at which time he was also troubled with an *Asthma*, or short spitting ; but after less then twenty fits, by the help of familiar Physick and a spare Diet, this Feaver abated ; yet so, as to leave him much weaker then it

found him : and his *Asthma* seem'd also to be overcome in a good degree by his forbearing *Tobacco*,
which, as many thoughtful men do, he also had taken
somewhat immoderately.——This was his then present condition, and, thus he continued till about the
end of *October* 1639. which was about a moneth
before his death, at which time, he again fell into
a *Feaver*, which, though he seem'd to recover, yet
these still left him so weak, that they and those other
common infirmities that accompany age, and were
wont to visit him like civil friends, and after some
short time to leave him ; came now, both oftner and
with more violence, and at last took up their constant
habitation with him, still weakning his Body and
abating his chearfulness : of both which he grew more
sensible, and did the oftner retire into his Study, and
there made many Papers that had pass'd his Pen both
in the days of his youth, and in the busie part of his
life, useless, by a fire made there to that purpose.——
These and several unusual expressions to his Servants
and Friends, seem'd to foretell that the day of his
death drew near : for which, he seem'd to those many
friends that observ'd him, to be well prepar'd, & to
be both patient, and free from all fear ; as several of
his Letters writ on this his last sick-bed may testifie :
and thus he continued till about the beginning of
December following, at which time he was seiz'd more
violently with a *Quotidian Feaver*, in the tenth fit of
which Feaver, his better part, that part of Sir *Henry
Wotton* which could not dye, put off mortality with
as much content and chearfulness as humane frailty is
capable of ; being then in great tranquillity of mind,
and in perfect peace with God and man.

And thus the Circle of Sir *Henry Wotton*'s Life——
(that Circle which began at *Bocton*, and in the *Cir-*

cumference thereof, did first touch at *Winchester-School*, then at *Oxford*, and after upon so many remarkable parts and passages in *Christendom*) That *Circle* of his *Life*, was by *Death* thus closed up and compleated, in the seventy and second year of his *Age*, at *Eaton Colledge*, where, according to his Will, he now lies buried, with his Motto on a plain Grave-stone over him; dying worthy of his Name and *Family*, worthy of the love and favour of so many *Princes*, and Persons of eminent *Wisdom* and *Learning*, worthy of the trust committed unto him, for the Service of his *Prince* and *Countrey*.

And all Readers are requested to believe, that he was worthy of a more worthy Pen, to have preserved his Memory, *and commended his* Merits *to the imitation of Posterity.*

Iz. Wa.

An *ELEGY* on

Sir *HENRY WOTTON*,

WRIT

By Mr. *ABRAM COWLEY.*

WHat shall we say, since silent *now* is he,
 Who when he spoke all things would silent *be.*
 Who had so many Languages *in store,*
That only fame *shall speak of him in more:*
Whom England *now no more return'd must see:*
He's gone to Heaven, *on his* fourth Embassie.
On Earth *he travel'd often, not to say*
H'ad been abroad to pass loose time *away:*
For, in what ever Land he chanc'd to come,
He read the men *and* manners: *bringing home*
Their Wisdom, Learning, *and their* Piety,
As if he went to Conquer, *not to see.*
So well he understood the most and best
Of Tongues, *that* Babel *sent into the West:*
Spoke them so truly, that he had (you'd swear)
Not only liv'd, *but been* born, *every where.*
Justly each Nations *speech to him was known:*
Who for the World *was made, not us alone.*
Nor ought the Language *of that man be less*
Who in his brest *had all things to express:*
We say that Learning's *endless, and blame* Fate
For not allowing Life *a longer date:*
He did the utmost bounds *of* Knowledge *find;*
And found them not so large as was his mind:
But like the brave Pellean *youth did* mone:
Because that Art *had no more* Worlds *then one.*
And when he saw that he through all had past,
 He dy'd, *lest he should* Idle *grow at last.*

A. Cowley.

FINIS.

THE

LIFE

OF

Mr. *RICHARD HOOKER,*

THE

AUTHOR of those Learned Books

OF THE

𝕷𝖆𝖜𝖘 𝖔𝖋 𝕰𝖈𝖈𝖑𝖊𝖘𝖎𝖆𝖘𝖙𝖎𝖈𝖆𝖑 𝕻𝖔𝖑𝖎𝖙𝖞.

Eccles. 24. 34.
Behold! I have not labour'd for my self only:
but, for all those that seek wisdom.

Psal. 145. 4.
One Generation shall praise thy works to another.

LONDON,
Printed in the Year 1675.

THE

LIFE

OF

Mr. RICHARD HOOKER,

THE

Author of those Learned Books

OF THE

Laws of Ecclesiastical Polity.

LONDON,

Printed in the Year 1675.

To his very Worthy Friend Mr. *Izaak Walton,* upon his Writing and Publishing the L I F E of the Venerable and Judicious Mr. *Richard Hooker.*

I.

Ail, *Sacred Mother*, British Church, *all hail!*
    From whose fruitful Loins have sprung
    Of Pious Sons so great a throng,
That Heav'n t'oppose their force, of strength did fail
And let the mighty Conquerors o're Almighty arms
    prevail ;
    How art thou chang'd from what thou wert a late,
    When destitute, and quite forlorn,
(*And scarce a Child of thousands, with thee left to mourn*)
    Thy veil all rent, and all thy garments torn : (*fate ;*
With tears thou didst bewail thine own, and childrens
Too much (*alas !*) *thou didst resemble then*
Sion *thy pattern ;* Sion, *in ashes laid,*
    Despis'd, Forsaken, and betray'd :
Sion, *thou dost resemble once agen ;*
And rais'd, like her, the glory of the World art made.
    Threnes *only to thee could that time belong,*
But now, thou art the lofty Subject of my Song.

155

II.

Begin my Verse, and where the doleful Mother sate,
 (*As it in Vision was to* Esdras *shown*)
  Lamenting, with the rest, her dearest Son,
 (*Blest* Charles, *who his Forefathers has outgone,*
And to the Royal, join'd the Martyrs brighter Crown)
 Let a new City rise, with beauteous state :
And beauteous let its Temple be, and beautiful the Gate !
 Lo ! how the Sacred Fabrick up does rise !
  The Architects so skilful All,
  So grave, so humble, and so wise :
  The Axes, and the Hammers noise
Is drown'd in silence, or in numbers Musicall :
  'Tis up ; and at the Altar stand
  The Reverend Fathers, as of Old,
  With Harps, *and* Incense *in their hand :*
Nor let the pious service grow or stiff, or cold :
  Th'inferiour Priests, the while,
  To Praise continually imploy'd, or Pray,
  Need not the weary hours beguile,
 Enough's the single Duty of each day.
Thou thy self, Woodford, *on thy humbler Pipe mayst*
  And, tho' but lately entred there,   (*play ;*
 So gracious those thou honour'st all appear,
  So ready and attent to hear,
An easie part, proportion'd to thy skill, may'st bear.

III.

But where (alas!) where wilt thou fix thy choice ?
 The Subjects are so noble all,
So great their beauties, and thy art so small,
They'll judge, I fear, themselves disparag'd by thy voice:

Yet try, and since thou canst not take
A name, so despicably low,
But 'twill exceed what thou canst do,
Tho' thy whole Mite thou away at once shouldst throw,
Thy Poverty a vertue make ;
And, that thou may'st Immortal live,
(Since Immortality thou canst not give)
From one, who has enough to spare, be ambitious to re-
Of Reverend and Judicious Hooker sing ; (ceive
Hooker, does to th'Church belong,
The Church, and Hooker claim thy Song,
And inexhausted Riches to thy Verse will bring :
So far, beyond it self, will make it grow,
That life, his gift to thee, thou shalt again on him bestow.

IV.

How great, blest Soul, must needs thy Glories be,
Thy Joys how perfect, and thy Crown how fair,
Who mad'st the Church thy chiefest care ;
This Church, which owes so much to thee,
That all Her Sons are studious of thy memory.
'Twas a bold work the Captiv'd to redeem,
And not so only, but th' Oppress'd to raise,
(Our aged Mother) to that due Esteem
She had, and merited in her younger days :
When Primitive Zeal, and Piety,
Were all her Laws, and Policy,
And decent Worship kept the mean,
It's too wide stretch't Extreams between ;
The rudely scrupulous, and extravagantly vain.
This was the work of Hookers *Pen ;*
With Judgment, Candor, and such Learning writ,
Matter and words so exactly fit,

That, were it to be done agen,
Expected 'twould be, as its Answer hitherto has been

RITORNATA.

To Chelsea, Song ; there, tell Thy Masters Friend
The Church is Hookers Debtor : Hooker His ;
And strange 'twould be, if he should Glory miss,
For whom two such most powerfully contend :
*   Bid him, chear up, the Day's his own,*
*   And he shall never dye*
*   Who after Seventy's past and gone,*
*   Can all th' Assaults of Age defie :*
Is master still of so much youthful heat,
A Child, so perfect, and so sprightly to beget.

Bensted, Hants,
  Mar. 10. 16$\frac{62}{70}$.

                    Sam. Woodford.

THE
L I F E
OF
Mr. *RICHARD HOOKER.*

The Introduction.

I *Have been perswaded, by a Friend whom I rever-*
ence, and ought to obey, to write The Life of
RICHARD HOOKER, *the happy Author of*
Five (if not more) of the Eight learned Books of the
Laws of Ecclesiastical Polity. *And though I have*
undertaken it, yet it hath been with some unwillingness;
because, I foresee that it must prove to me, and especially
at this time of my Age, a work of much labour to enquire,
consider, research, and determine what is needful to be
known concerning him : For I knew him not in his Life,
and must therefore not only look back to his Death, now
64 *years past ; but almost* 50 *years beyond that, even to*
his Childhood, and Youth, and gather thence such Ob-
servations and Prognosticks, as may at least adorn, if not
prove necessary for the compleating of what I have
undertaken.

This trouble I foresee; and foresee also, that it is

impossible to escape Censures; against which, I will not hope my well-meaning and diligence can protect me, (for I consider the Age in which I live) and shall therefore but intreat of my Reader a suspension of his Censures, till I have made known unto him some Reasons, which I my self would now gladly believe do make me in some measure fit for this undertaking: and if these Reasons shall not acquit me from all Censures, they may at least abate of their severity, and this is all I can probably hope for.

My Reasons follow.

About forty years past (for I am now past the Seventy of my Age) I began a happy affinity with William Cranmer *(now with God) grand Nephew unto the great Archbishop of that name, a Family of noted prudence and resolution; with him and two of his Sisters, I had an entire and free friendship: one of them was the Wife of Dr.* Spencer, *a Bosom-friend, and sometime Com-pupil with Mr.* Hooker *in* Corpus-Christi *Colledge in* Oxford, *and after President of the same. I name them here, for that I shall have occasion to mention them in this following Discourse; as also* George Cranmer *their Brother, of whose useful abilities my Reader may have a more authentick Testimony, than my Pen can purchase for him, by that of our learned* Cambden, *and others.*

This William Cranmer, *and his two forenamed Sisters, had some affinity, and a most familiar friendship with Mr.* Hooker; *and had had some part of their Education with him in his house, when he was Parson of* Bishops-Borne *near* Canterbury, *in which City their good father then lived. They had (I say) a part of their Education with him, as my self since that time a happy Cohabitation with them; and having some years before read part of Mr.* Hookers *Works with great liking and satisfaction, my affection to them made me a diligent*

Inquisitor into many things that concerned him; as namely, of his Person, his Nature, the management of his Time, his Wife, his Family, and the Fortune of him and his. Which inquiry hath given me much advantage in the knowledge of what is now under my consideration, and intended for the satisfaction of my Reader.

I had also a friendship with the Reverend Dr. Usher, the late learned Archbishop of Armagh, and with Dr. Morton, the late learned and charitable Bishop of Durham; as also with the learned John Hales of Eaton-Colledge; and with them also (who loved the very name of Mr. Hooker) I have had many discourses concerning him: and from them, and many others that have now put off Mortality, I might have had more Informations, if I could then have admitted a thought of any fitness for what by perswasion I have now undertaken. But, though that full Harvest be irrecoverably lost, yet my Memory hath preserved some gleanings, and my Diligence made such additions to them, as I hope will prove useful to the compleating of what I intend: In the discovery of which I shall be faithful, and with this assurance put a period to my Introduction.

The *LIFE*.

IT is not to be doubted but that *Richard Hooker* was born at *Heavy-tree*, near or within the Precincts, or in the City of *Exeter*; a City which may justly boast, that it was the Birth-place of him, and Sir *Tho. Bodley*; as indeed the County may in which it stands, that it hath furnished this Nation with Bishop *Jewel*, Sir *Francis Drake*, Sir *Walter Raleigh*, and many others, memorable for their Valour and Learning. He was born about the Year of our Redemption 1553, and of Parents that were not so remarkable for their Extraction or Riches, as for their Virtue and Industry, and Gods blessing upon both; by which they were enabled to educate their Children in some degree of Learning, of which our *Richard Hooker* may appear to be one fair testimony; and that Nature is not so partial, as always to give the great blessings of Wisdom and Learning, and with them the greater blessings of Virtue and Government, to those only that are of a more high and honourable Birth.

His Complexion (if we may guess by him at the age of Forty) was Sanguine, with a mixture of Choler; and yet his Motion was slow even in his Youth, and so was his Speech, never expressing an Earnestness in either of them, but an humble Gravity suitable to the Aged. And 'tis observed (so far as Inquiry is able to look back at this distance of Time) that at his being a School-boy he was an early Questionist, quietly inquisitive *Why this was, and that was not, to be remem-*

bred? *Why this was granted, and that denied?*
This being mixt with a remarkable Modesty, and a
sweet serene quietness of Nature, and with them a
quick apprehension of many perplext parts of Learning imposed then upon him as a Scholer, made his
Master and others to believe him to have an inward
blessed Divine Light, and therefore to consider him
to a little wonder. For in that, Children were less
pregnant, less confident, and more malleable, than in
this wiser, but not better, Age.

This Meekness and conjuncture of Knowledge,
with Modesty in his Conversation, being observed by
his Schoolmaster, caused him to perswade his Parents
(who intended him for an Apprentice) to continue
him at School, till he could find out some means, by
perswading his rich Uncle, or some other charitable
person, to ease them of a part of their care and charge;
assuring them, that their son was so enriched with the
blessings of Nature and Grace, that God seemed to
single him out as a special Instrument of his Glory.
And the good man told them also, that he would
double his diligence in instructing him, and would
neither expect nor receive any other Reward, than the
content of so hopeful and happy an employment.

This was not unwelcome News, and especially to
his Mother, to whom he was a dutiful and dear
Child; and all Parties were so pleased with this
proposal, that it was resolved, so it should be. And
in the mean time, his Parents and Master laid a
foundation for his future happiness, by instilling into
his Soul *the seeds of Piety*, those conscientious principles of *loving and fearing God*; of *an early belief
that he knows the very secrets of our Souls; That he
punisheth our Vices, and rewards our Innocence; That
we should be free from hypocrisie, and appear to man*

what we are to God, because first or last the crafty man is catch't in his own snare. These seeds of Piety were so seasonably planted, and so continually watered with the daily dew of Gods blessed Spirit, that his Infant vertues grew into such holy habits, as did make him grow daily into more and more favour both with God and man; which, with the great Learning that he did after attain to, hath made *Richard Hooker* honour'd in this, and will continue him to be so to succeeding Generations.

This good Schoolmaster, whose Name I am not able to recover (and am sorry, for that I would have given him a better memorial in this humble Monument, dedicated to the memory of his Scholar), was very sollicitous with *John Hooker*, then Chamberlain of *Exeter*, and Uncle to our *Richard*, to take his Nephew into his care, and to maintain him for one Year in the University, and in the mean time to use his endeavours to procure an admission for him into some Colledge, though it were but in a mean degree; still urging and assuring him, that his Charge would not continue long, for the Lads Learning and Manners, were both so remarkable, that they must of necessity be taken notice of; and, that doubtless God would provide him some second Patron, that would free him and his Parents from their future care and charge.

These Reasons, with the affectionate Rhetorick of his good Master, and Gods blessing upon both, procured from his Uncle a faithful promise, that he would take him into his care and charge before the expiration of the Year following, which was performed by him, and with the assistance of the Learned Mr. *John Jewel*; of whom this may be noted that he left, or was about the first of Queen *Maries* Reign, expell'd out of *Corpus-Christi* Colledge in *Oxford* (of which he was a Fellow) for adhering to the Truth of those Principles of Religion, to which he had assented and given testimony in the days of her Brother and Predecessor *Edward* the Sixth ; and this *John Jewel* having within a short time after a just cause to fear a more heavy punishment than Expulsion, was forced, by forsaking this, to seek safety in another Nation ; and, with that safety, the enjoyment of that Doctrine and Worship, for which he suffer'd.

But the Cloud of that persecution and fear ending with the Life of Queen *Mary*, the Affairs of the Church and State did then look more clear and comfortable ; so that he, and with him many others of the same judgment, made a happy return into *England* about the first of Queen *Elizabeth*, in which Year this *John Jewel* was sent a Commissioner or Visitor of the Churches of the Western parts of this Kingdom, and especially of those in *Devonshire*, in which County he was born : and then and there he contracted a friendship with *John Hooker*, the Uncle of our *Richard*.

About the second or third Year of her Reign, this *John Jewel* was made Bishop of *Salisbury* ; and there being always observed in him a willingness to do good, and to oblige his Friends, and now a power added to this willingness : this *John Hooker* gave him a Visit in *Salisbury*, *and besought him for Charity's sake to look favourably upon a poor Nephew of his, whom Nature had fitted for a Scholar, but the Estate of his Parents was so narrow, that they were unable to give him the advantage of Learning ; and that the Bishop would therefore become his Patron, and prevent him from being a Tradesman ; for he was a Boy of remarkable hopes.* And though the Bishop knew, men do not usually look with an indifferent eye upon their own Children and Relations, yet he assented so far to *John*

Hooker, that he appointed the Boy and his Schoolmaster should attend him about *Easter* next following at that place: which was done accordingly; and then, after some Questions and observations of the Boys learning and gravity, and behaviour, the Bishop gave his Schoolmaster a reward, and took order for an annual Pension for the Boys Parents: promising also, to take him into his care for a future preferment, which he performed; for about the Fifteenth Year of his age, which was *Anno* 1567, he was by the Bishop appointed to remove to *Oxford*, and there to attend Dr. *Cole*, then President of *Corpus-Christi* Colledge. Which he did; and Dr. *Cole* had (according to a promise made to the Bishop) provided for him both a Tutor (which was said to be the learned Dr. *John Reynolds*) and a Clerks place in that Colledge: which place, though it were not a full maintenance, yet with the contribution of his Uncle, and the continued Pension of his Patron the good Bishop, gave him a comfortable subsistence. And in this condition he continued unto the Eighteenth Year of his age, still increasing in Learning and Prudence, and so much in Humility and Piety, that he seemed to be filled with the Holy Ghost, and even like St. *John Baptist*, to be sanctified from his Mothers womb, who did often bless the day in which she bare him.

About this time of his age he fell into a dangerous Sickness, which lasted two Months; all which time his Mother, having notice of it, did in her hourly prayers as earnestly beg his life of God, as *Monica* the Mother of St. *Augustine* did that he might become a true Christian; and their prayers were both so heard as to be granted. Which Mr. *Hooker* would often mention with much joy, *and as often pray that he might never live to occasion any sorrow to so good a Mother;* of *whom, he would often say, he loved her so dearly, that he would endeavor to be good even as much for hers, as for his own sake.*

As soon as he was perfectly recovered from this Sickness, he took a journey from *Oxford* to *Exeter*, to satisfie and see his good Mother, being accompanied with a Countreyman and Companion of his own Colledge, and both on foot; which was then either more in fashion, or want of money, or their humility made it so: But on foot they went, and took *Salisbury* in their way, purposely to see the good Bishop, who made Mr. *Hooker* and his Companion dine with him at his own Table; which Mr. *Hooker* boasted of with much joy and gratitude when he saw his Mother and Friends: And at the Bishops parting with him, the Bishop gave him good Counsel, and his Benediction, but forgot to give him money; which when the Bishop had considered, he sent a Servant in all haste to call *Richard* back to him, and at *Richards* return, the Bishop said to him, *Richard, I sent for you back to lend you a Horse, which hath carried me many a Mile, and I thank God with much ease*; and presently delivered into his hand a Walking-staff, with which he professed he had travelled through many parts of *Germany*; and he said, *Richard, I do not give, but lend you my Horse; be sure you be honest, and bring my Horse back to me at your return this way to Oxford. And I do now give you Ten Groats to bear your charges to* Exeter; *and here is Ten Groats more, which I charge you to deliver to your Mother, and tell her, I send her a Bishops Benediction with it, and beg the continuance of her prayers for me. And if you bring my Horse back to me, I will give you Ten Groats more to carry you on foot to the Colledge, and so God bless you, good* Richard.

And this, you may believe, was performed by both

Parties. But, alas! the next News that followed Mr. *Hooker* to *Oxford*, was, that his learned and charitable Patron had changed this for a *better life*. Which happy change may be believed, for that as he lived, so he dyed, in devout meditation and prayer; and in both so zealously, that it became a religious question, *Whether his last Ejaculations, or his Soul, did first enter into Heaven?*

And now Mr. *Hooker* became a man of sorrow and fear; of sorrow, for the loss of so dear and comfortable a Patron; and of fear, for his future subsistence: But Dr. *Cole* raised his spirits from this dejection, by bidding him go chearfully to his Studies, and assuring him he should neither want food nor raiment (which was the utmost of his hopes) for he would become his Patron.

And so he was for about nine months, and not longer; for about that time, this following accident did befall Mr. *Hooker*.

Edwin Sandys (sometime Bishop of *London*, and after Archbishop of *York*) had also been in the days of Queen *Mary* forced, by forsaking this, to seek safety in another Nation; where for some Years Bishop *Jewell* and he were Companions at Bed and Board in *Germany*; and, where in this their Exile they did often eat the bread of sorrow; and by that means they there began such a friendship, as lasted till the death of Bishop *Jewell*, which was in *September* 1571. A little before which time, the two Bishops meeting, *Jewell* had an occasion to begin a story of his *Richard Hooker*, and in it gave such a Character of his Learning and Manners, that though Bishop *Sandys* was educated in *Cambridge*, where he had obliged and had many Friends; yet his resolution was, that his Son *Edwin* should be sent to *Corpus-Christi* Colledge in *Oxford*,

and by all means be Pupil to Mr. *Hooker*, though his
Son *Edwin* was not much younger then Mr. *Hooker*
then was: for, the Bishop said, *I will have a Tutor
for my Son that shall teach him Learning by Instruction,
and Vertue by Example ; and my greatest care shall be
of the last ; and (God willing) this* Richard Hooker
shall be the Man into whose hands I will commit my
Edwin. And the Bishop did so about twelve months,
or not much longer, after this resolution.

And doubtless as to these two a better choice could
not be made ; for Mr. *Hooker* was now in the nineteenth year of his age, had spent five in the University,
and had by a constant unwearied diligence attained unto
a perfection in all the learned Languages ; by the help
of which, an excellent Tutor, and his unintermitted
Studies, he had made the subtilty of all the Arts easie
and familiar to him, and useful for the discovery of
such Learning as lay hid from common Searchers ;
so that by these added to his great Reason, and his
restless Industry added to both, *He did not only know
more of Causes and Effects, but what he knew, he knew
better then other men.* And with this Knowledge he
had a most blessed and clear Method of Demonstrat-
ing what he knew, to the great advantage of all his
Pupils (which in time were many) but especially to
his two first, his dear *Edwin Sandys*, and his as
dear *George Cranmer* ; of which there will be a fair
Testimony in the ensuing Relation.

This for Mr. *Hookers* Learning. And for his
Behaviour, amongst other Testimonies this still remains
of him : That in four years, he was but twice absent
from the Chappel prayers ; and that his Behaviour
there was such as shewed an awful reverence of
that God which he then worshipped and prayed to ;
giving all outward testimonies that his Affections were

set on heavenly things. This was his Behaviour towards God; and for that to Man; it is observable that he was never known to be angry, or passionate, or extream in any of his Desires; never heard to repine or dispute with Providence, but by a quiet gentle submission and resignation of his Will to the Wisdom of his Creator, bore the burthen of the day with Patience; never heard to utter an uncomly word: and by this, and a grave Behaviour, which is a Divine Charm, he begot an early Reverence unto his Person, even from those that at other times, and in other companies, took a liberty to cast off that strictness of Behaviour and Discourse that is required in a Collegiate Life. And when he took any liberty to be pleasant, his Wit was never blemisht with Scoffing, or the utterance of any Conceit that border'd upon, or might beget a thought of Looseness in his hearers. Thus mild, thus innocent and exemplary was his Behaviour in his Colledge; and, thus this good man continued till his death, still increasing in Learning, in Patience, and Piety.

In this nineteenth year of his age, he was *December* 24. 1573, admitted to be one of the twenty Scholars of the Foundation, being elected and so admitted as born in *Devon* or *Hantshire*, out of which Countries a certain number are to be elected in Vacancies by the Founders Statutes. And now, as he was much encouraged, so now he was perfectly incorporated into this beloved Colledge, which was then noted for an eminent Library, strict Students, and remarkable Scholars. And indeed it may glory, that it had Cardinal *Poole*, but more, that it had Bishop *Jewell*, Doctor *John Reynolds*, and Doctor *Thomas Jackson* of that Foundation: the first famous for his Learned Apology for the Church of *England*,

and his Defence of it against *Harding*. The Second,
for the learned and wise Menage of a publick Dispute
with *John Hart* (of the *Romish* perswasion) about the
Head and Faith of the Church, and after printed by
consent of both parties. And the Third, for his
most excellent Exposition of the Creed, and other
Treatises: All, such as have given greatest satisfaction
to men of the greatest Learning: Nor was Doctor
Jackson more Note-worthy for his Learning, than for
his strict and pious Life, testified by his abundant love
and meekness and charity to all men.

And in the year 1576. *Febr.* 23. Mr. *Hookers* Grace
was given him for *Inceptor* of Arts, Dr. *Herbert West-
phaling*, a man of note for Learning, being then Vice-
chancellor. And the Act following he was compleated
Master, which was *Anno* 1577. his Patron Doctor
Cole being Vice-chancellor that year, and his dear
friend *Henry Savill* of *Merton Colledge* being then one
of the Proctors. 'Twas that *Henry Savill*, that was
after Sir *Henry Savill*, Warden of *Merton Colledge*,
and Provost of *Eaton*: He which founded in *Oxford*
two famous Lectures, and endowed them with liberal
maintenance.

'Twas that Sir *Henry Savill*, that translated and
enlightned the History of *Cornelius Tacitus*, with a
most excellent Comment; and enriched the world
by his laborious and chargeable collecting the scattered
pieces of S. *Chrysostome*, and the publication of them
in one entire Body in Greek; in which Language he
was a most judicious Critick. 'Twas this Sir *Henry
Savill*, that had the happiness to be a Contemporary,
and familiar friend to Mr. *Hooker*; and let Posterity
know it.

And in this year of 1577. He was so happy as to
be admitted Fellow of the Colledge; happy also in

being the Contemporary and Friend of that Dr. *John Reynolds*, of whom I have lately spoken; and of Dr. *Spencer*: both which were after, and successively, made Presidents of *Corpus-Christi* Colledge; men of great Learning and Merit, and famous in their Generations.

Nor was Mr. *Hooker* more happy in his Contemporaries of his Time and Colledge, than in the Pupillage and Friendship of his *Edwin Sandys* and *George Cranmer*; of whom my Reader may note, that this *Edwin Sandys* was after Sir *Edwin Sandys*, and as famous for his *Speculum Europæ*, as his brother *George* for making Posterity beholden to his Pen by a learned Relation and Comment on his dangerous and remarkable *Travels*, and, for his harmonious Translation of the *Psalms of David*, the Book of *Job*, and other Poetical parts of Holy Writ, into most high and elegant Verse. And for *Cranmer*, his other Pupil, I shall refer my Reader to the printed Testimonies of our learned Mr. *Cambden*, of *Fines Morrison*, and others.

' This *Cranmer* (says Mr. *Cambden*, in his Annals
' of Queen *Elizabeth*) whose Christen name was
' *George*, was a Gentleman of singular hopes, the
' eldest Son of *Thomas Cranmer*, Son of *Edmund Cran-*
' *mer*, the Archbishops brother: he spent much of his
' Youth in *Corpus-Christi* Colledge in *Oxford*, where
' he continued Master of Arts for some time before he
' removed, and then betook himself to Travel, accom-
' panying that worthy Gentleman Sir *Edwin Sandys*
' into *France*, *Germany*, and *Italy*, for the space of
' three years; and after their happy return he betook
' himself to an Imployment under Secretary *Davison*
' a Privy Counsellor of note, who for an unhappy
' undertaking, became clouded and pitied, after whose
' Fall, he went in place of Secretary with Sir *Henry*

'*Killegrew* in his Embassage into *France*: and after
'his death he was sought after by the most Noble Lord
'*Mount-Joy*, with whom he went into *Ireland*, where
'he remained untill in a battel against the Rebels,
'near *Carlingford*, an unfortunate wound put an end
'both to his Life, and the great hopes that were con-
'ceived of him: he being then but in the 36 year of
'his age.

Betwixt Mr. *Hooker* and these his two Pupils, there
was a sacred Friendship; a Friendship made up of
Religious Principles, which increased daily by a
similitude of Inclinations to the same Recreations and
Studies; a Friendship elemented in Youth, and in an
University, free from self-ends, which the Friendships
of Age usually are not: and in this sweet, this blessed,
this spiritual Amity they went on for many years; and
as the Holy Prophet saith, so *they took sweet counsel
together, and walked in the House of God as Friends*.
By which means they improved this friendship to such
a degree of holy Amity as bordered upon Heaven; a
Friendship so sacred, that when it ended in this world,
it began in that next, where it shall have no end.

And though this world cannot give any degree of
Pleasure equal to such a Friendship: yet Obedience
to Parents, and a desire to know the Affairs, Manners,
Laws, and Learning of other Nations, that they might
thereby become the more serviceable unto their own:
made them put off their Gowns, and leave the Colledge
and Mr. *Hooker* to his Studies; in which he was daily
more assiduous: still enriching his quiet and capacious
Soul with the precious Learning of the Philosophers,
Casuists, and School-men; and with them, the foundation and reason of all Laws, both Sacred and Civil:
and indeed, with such other Learning as lay most
remote from the track of common Studies. And as he

was diligent in these, so he seemed restless in searching the scope and intention of Gods Spirit revealed to Mankind in the Sacred Scripture: for the understanding of which, he seemed to be assisted by the same Spirit with which they were written: He *that regardeth truth in the inward parts,* making him to understand *wisdom secretly.* And the good man would often say, that *God abhors confusion as contrary to his nature,* and as often say, that the Scripture was not writ to beget *Disputations,* and *Pride,* and *Opposition* to *Government*; but *Charity* and *Humility, Moderation, Obedience* to *Authority,* and peace to Mankind: of which vertues, he would as often say, no man did ever repent himself on his deathbed. And that this was really his judgment, did appear in his future writings, and in all the actions of his life. Nor was this excellent man a stranger to the more light and airy parts of Learning, as *Musick* and *Poetry*; all which he had digested, and made useful: and of all which the Reader will have a fair testimony in what will follow.

In the Year 1579. the Chancellor of the University was given to understand, that the publick *Hebrew Lecture* was not read according to the Statutes; nor could be, by reason of a distemper that had then seiz'd the brain of Mr. *Kingsmill,* who was to read it; so that it lay long unread, to the great detriment of those that were studious of that language: Therefore, the *Chancellor* writ to his *Vice-chancellor,* and the *University,* that he had heard such commendations of the excellent knowledge of Mr. *Richard Hooker* in that tongue, that he desired he might be procured to read it: And he did, and continued to do so, till he left *Oxford.*

Within three months after his undertaking this

Lecture (namely in *October* 1579.) he was with Dr. *Reynolds*, and others expell'd his *Colledge*; and this Letter transcrib'd from Dr. *Reynolds* his own hand, may give some account of it.

To Sir *Francis Knolles.*

I *Am sorry, Right Honourable, that I am enforced to make unto you such a suit, which I cannot move, but I must complain of the unrighteous dealing of one of our* Colledge; *who hath taken upon him against all Law and Reason, to expell out of our House, both me and Mr.* Hooker, *and three other of our Fellows, for doing that which by Oath we were bound to do. Our matter must be heard before the Bishop of Winchester, with whom I do not doubt, but we shall find equity. Howbeit, forasmuch as some of our adversaries have said, that the* Bishop *is already forestalled, and will not give us such audience as we look for; therefore I am humbly to beseech your Honour, that you will desire the* Bishop, *by your Letters, to let us have Justice; though it be with rigour, so it be Justice: our Cause is so good, that I am sure we shall prevail by it. Thus much I am bold to request of your Honour for* Corpus-Christi *Colledge sake, or rather for* Christs *sake; whom I beseech to bless you with daily encrease of his manifold gifts, and the blessed graces of his holy Spirit.*

London,
Octob. 9.
1579.

Your HONOURS
in Christ to command,
JOHN REYNOLDS.

This Expulsion was by Dr. *John Barfoote*, then Vice-president of the Colledge, and Chaplain to

Ambrose Earl of *Warwick*. I cannot learn the pretended cause; but, that they were restor'd the same Month is most certain.

I return to Mr. *Hooker* in his *Colledge*, where he continued his studies with all quietness, for the space of three years; about which time, he enter'd into Sacred Orders, being then made Deacon and Priest; and, not long after, was appointed to preach at St. *Pauls Cross*.

In order to which Sermon, to *London* he came, and immediately to the *Shunamites house*; (which is a House so called, for that, besides the Stipend paid the Preacher, there is provision made also for his Lodging and Diet for two days before, and one day after his Sermon;) this house was then kept by *John Churchman*, sometimes a Draper of good Note in *Watling-street*, upon whom poverty had at last come like an armed man, and brought him into a necessitous condition; which, though it be a punishment, is not always an argument of Gods disfavour, for he was a vertuous man: I shall not yet give the like testimony of his Wife, but leave the Reader to judge by what follows. But to this house Mr. *Hooker* came so wet, so weary, and weather-beaten, that he was never known to express more passion, than against a Friend that dissuaded him from footing it to *London*, and for finding him no easier an Horse; supposing the Horse trotted, when he did not: And at this time also, such a faintness and fear possest him, that he would not be perswaded two days rest and quietness, or any other means could be used to make him able to preach his Sunday Sermon; but a warm Bed, and Rest, and Drink, proper for a Cold, given him by Mrs. *Churchman*, and her diligent attendance added unto it, enabled him to perform the office of the day, which was in or about the Year 1581.

And in this first publick appearance to the World, he was not so happy as to be free from Exceptions against a point of Doctrine delivered in his Sermon; which was, *That in God there were two Wills, an Antecedent, and a Consequent Will; his first Will, that all Mankind should be saved; but his second Will was, that those only should be saved, that did live answerable to that degree of Grace which he had offered, or afforded them.* This seemed to cross a late Opinion of Mr. *Calvins*, and then taken for granted by many that had not a capacity to examine it, as it had been by him before, and hath been since by Master *Henry Mason*, Dr. *Jackson*, Dr. *Hammond*, and others of great Learning, who believ'd that a contrary Opinion intrenches upon the Honour and Justice of our merciful God. How he justified this, I will not undertake to declare, but it was not excepted against (as Mr. *Hooker* declares in his rational Answer to Mr. *Travers*) by *John Elmer*, then Bishop of *London*; at this time one of his Auditors, and at last one of his Advocates too, when Mr. *Hooker* was accused for it.

But the justifying of this Doctrine did not prove of so bad consequence, as the kindness of Mrs. *Churchmans* curing him of his late Distemper and Cold; for that was so gratefully apprehended by M. *Hooker*, that he thought himself bound in conscience to believe all that she said; so that the good man came to be perswaded by her, *that he was a man of a tender constitution*, and *that it was best for him to have a Wife, that might prove a Nurse to him*; such an one as *might both prolong his life, and make it more comfortable; and such a one she could and would provide for him, if he thought fit to marry.* And he not considering, that *the children of this world are wiser in their generation, than the children of light*; but, like a true *Nathanael,* fearing no guile, because he meant none, did give her such a power as *Eleazar* was trusted with, (you may read it in the book of *Genesis*) when he was sent to choose a Wife for *Isaac*; for even so he trusted her to choose for him, promising upon a fair summons to return to *London*, and accept of her choice; and he did so in that or about the year following. Now the Wife provided for him, was her Daughter *Joan*, who brought him neither Beauty nor Portion; and for her Conditions, they were too like that Wife's which is by *Solomon* compar'd to a *dripping house*; so that the good man had no reason to *rejoice in the Wife of his Youth*; but too just cause to say with the holy Prophet, *Wo is me that I am constrained to have my habitation in the tents of Kedar.*

This choice of Mr. *Hookers* (if it were his choice) may be wondred at; but let us consider that the Prophet *Ezekiel* says, *There is a wheel within a wheel*, a secret Sacred wheel of Providence (most visible in Marriages) guided by his hand, that *allows not the race to the swift*, nor *bread to the wise*, nor good wives to good men : and he that can bring good out of evil, (for Mortals are blind to this Reason) only knows why this blessing was denied to patient *Job*, to meek *Moses*, and to our as meek and patient Mr. *Hooker*. But so it was; and let the Reader cease to wonder, for *Affliction is a Divine diet*, which though it be not pleasing to Mankind, yet Almighty God hath often, very often imposed it as good, though bitter Physick to those children whose Souls are dearest to him.

And by this marriage the good man was drawn from the tranquillity of his Colledge, from that Garden of Piety, of Pleasure, of Peace, and a sweet Conversation, into the thorny Wilderness of a busie World; into those corroding cares that attend a married Priest,

and a Countrey Parsonage: which was *Draiton Beauchamp* in *Buckinghamshire*, not far from *Alesbury*, and
in the Diocess of *Lincoln*; to which he was presented
by *John Cheny* Esquire, then Patron of it, the 9*th*
of *December* 1584. where he behaved himself so as
to give no occasion of evil, but (as St. *Paul* adviseth
a Minister of God) *in much patience, in afflictions,
in anguishes, in necessities; in poverty, and no doubt
in long-suffering*: yet troubling no man with his discontents and wants.

And in this condition he continued about a year,
in which time his two Pupils, *Edwin Sandys* and
George Cranmer, took a journey to see their Tutor,
where they found him with a Book in his hand (it
was the *Odes* of *Horace*) he being then like humble
and innocent *Abel*, tending his small allotment of
sheep in a common field, which he told his Pupils
he was forced to do then, for that his servant was
gone home to Dine, and assist his Wife to do some
necessary houshold business. But when his servant
returned and released him, then his two Pupils attended
him unto his house, where their best entertainment
was his quiet company, which was presently denied
them: for, *Richard was call'd to rock the Cradle*; and
the rest of their welcom was so like this, that they
staid but till next morning, which was time enough
to discover and pity their Tutors condition; and they
having in that time rejoiced in the remembrance, and
then paraphrased on many of the innocent recreations
of their younger days, and other like diversions, and
thereby given him as much present comfort as they
were able, they were forced to leave him to the company of his wife *Joan*, and seek themselves a quieter
Lodging for next night: But at their parting from
him, Mr. *Cranmer* said, *Good Tutor, I am sorry your*

lot is fall'n in no better ground as to your Parsonage; and more sorry that your Wife proves not a more comfortable Companion after you have wearied your self in your restless studies. To whom the good man replied, *My dear* George, *If Saints have usually a double share in the miseries of this life, I that am none, ought not to repine at what my wise Creator hath appointed for me, but labour, (as indeed I do daily) to submit mine to his Will, and possess my soul in patience, and peace.*

At their return to *London, Edwin Sandys* acquaints his father, who was then Archbishop of *York*, with his Tutors sad condition, and sollicits for his removal to some Benefice that might give him a more quiet and a more comfortable subsistence; which his father did most willingly grant him, when it should next fall into his power. And not long after this time, which was in the year 1585. Mr. *Alvie* (Master of the Temple) died, who was *a man of a strict Life, of great Learning, and of so venerable Behaviour, as to gain so high a degree of love and reverence from all men, that he was generally known by the name of* Father Alvie. And at the Temple-Reading, next after the death of this *Father Alvie*, he the said Archbishop of *York* being then at Dinner with the *Judges*, the *Reader*, and *Benchers* of that Society, met with a general Condolement for the death of *Father Alvie*, and with a high commendation of his Saint-like life, and of his great merit both towards God and man: and as they bewail'd his death, so they wish't for a like pattern of Virtue and Learning to succeed him. And here came in a fair occasion for the Bishop to commend Mr. *Hooker* to *Father Alvies* place, which he did with so effectual an earnestness, and that seconded with so many other Testimonies of his worth, that Mr. *Hooker* was sent for from *Draiton Beauchamp* to

London, and there the Mastership of the Temple proposed unto him by the Bishop, as a greater freedom from his Country cares, the advantage of a better Society, and a more liberal Pension than his Countrey Parsonage did afford him. But these Reasons were not powerful enough to incline him to a willing acceptance of it; his wish was rather to gain a better Countrey living, where he might *see Gods blessings spring out of the Earth, and be free from Noise* (so he exprest the desire of his heart) *and eat that bread which he might more properly call his own in privacy and quietness.* But, notwithstanding this aversness, he was at last perswaded to accept of the Bishops proposal, and was by * Patent for Life, made Master of the Temple the 17*th* of *March* 1585. he being then in the 34*th* year of his age.

* *This you may find in the Temple Records.*

William Ermstead *was Master of the Temple at the Dissolution of the Priory; and died* 2 Eliz.

Richard Alvey *Bat. Divinity*, Pat. 13. Febr. 2 Eliz. *Magister sive Custos Domùs & Ecclesiæ novi Templi,* died 27 Eliz.

Richard Hooker *succeeded that year by Patent* in terminis, *as* Alvey *had it, and he left it,* 33 Eliz.

That year Dr. Balgey *succeeded* Richard Hooker.

And here I shall make a stop; and, that the Reader may the better judge of what follows, give him a character of the Times, and Temper of the people of this Nation, when Mr. *Hooker* had his admission into this place; a place which he accepted, rather than desired; and yet here he promised himself a virtuous quietness, that blessed Tranquillity which he always prayed and labour'd for, that so he might in peace bring forth the fruits of peace, and glorifie God by uninterrupted prayers and praises: for this he always thirsted and prayed: but Almighty God did not grant it, for his admission into this place, was the very beginning of those oppositions and anxieties, which till then this good man was a stranger to; and of which the Reader may guess by what follows.

In this character of the Times, I shall, by the Readers favour, and for his information, look so far back as to the beginning of the Reign of Queen *Elizabeth*; a time, in which *the many pretended Titles to the Crown, the frequent Treasons, the Doubts of her Successor, the late Civil War, and the sharp Persecution for Religion that raged to the effusion of so much blood in the Reign of Queen* Mary, were fresh in the memory of all men; and begot fears in the most pious and wisest of this Nation, lest the like days should return again to them, or their present posterity. And the apprehension of these dangers begot a hearty desire of a settlement in the Church and State; believing, there was no other probable way left to make them sit quietly under their own Vines and Fig-trees, and enjoy the desired fruit of their Labours. But *Time*, and *Peace*, and *Plenty*, begot *Self-ends*, and these begot *Animosities*, *Envy*, *Opposition*, and *Unthankfulness* for those very blessings for which they lately thirsted, being then the very utmost of their desires, and even beyond their hopes.

This was the temper of the Times in the beginning of her Reign; and thus it continued too long; for, those very people that had enjoyed the desires of their hearts in a Reformation from the Church of *Rome*, became at last so like the grave, as never to be satisfied, but were still thirsting for more and more; neglecting to pay that Obedience, and perform those Vows which they made in their days of adversities and fear: so that in short time, there appeared three several Interests, each of them fearless and restless in the prosecution of their designs; they may for distinction be called, The active *Romanists*, The restless *Nonconformists* (of which there were many sorts) and The passive *peaceable Protestant*. The Counsels of the first considered, and resolved on in *Rome*: the second both in *Scotland*, in *Geneva*, and in divers selected, secret, dangerous Conventicles, both there, and within the bosom of our own Nation: the third pleaded and defended their Cause by establisht Laws, both Ecclesiastical and Civil; and, if they were active, it was to prevent the other two from destroying what was by those known Laws happily establisht to them and their Posterity.

I shall forbear to mention the very many and dangerous Plots of the Romanists against the Church and State, because what is principally intended in this digression, is an account of the Opinions and Activity of the Non-conformists; against whose judgment and practice, Mr. *Hooker* became at last, but most unwillingly, to be ingaged in a Book-war; a War, which he maintained not as against an Enemy, but with the spirit of meekness and reason.

In which number of Non-conformists, though some might be sincere, well-meaning men, whose *indiscreet Zeal* might be so like *Charity*, as thereby to cover a multitude of their Errors; yet, of this party, there were many that were possest with a high degree of *spiritual wickedness*; I mean, with an innate restless *pride*, and *malice*. I do not mean the visible carnal sins of *Gluttony*, and *Drunkenness*, and the like (from which good Lord deliver us) but sins of a higher nature, because they are more unlike God, who is the God of *love* and *mercy*, and *order*, and *peace*; and more like the *Devil*, who is not a *Glutton*, nor can be *drunk*, and yet is a Devil; but I mean those spiritual wickednesses of *malice* and *revenge,* and an *opposition* to *Government*: Men that joyed to be the Authors of misery, which is properly his work that is *the enemy and disturber of Mankind*; and thereby, greater sinners then the *glutton* or *drunkard,* though some will not believe it. And of this party, there were also many, whom prejudice and a furious zeal had so blinded, as to make them neither to hear reason, nor adhere to the ways of peace: Men, that were the very dregs and pest of Mankind; men whom *Pride* and *Self-conceit,* had made to over-value their own pitiful, crooked wisdom so much, as not to be asham'd to hold foolish and unmannerly Disputes against those men whom they ought to reverence; and those Laws which they ought to obey: Men, that labour'd and joyed first to find out the faults, and then to speak evil of Government; and to be the Authors of Confusion: Men, whom Company, and Conversation, and Custom, had at last so blinded, and made so insensible that these were sins, that, like those that perisht in the *gainsaying of Core,* so these died without repenting of these *spiritual wickednesses*: of which the practises of *Copinger,* and *Hacket* in their lives; and the death of them and their adherents, are God knows too sad examples; and, ought to be cautions to those men that are inclin'd to the like *spiritual wickednesses.*

And in these Times which tended thus to Confusion, there were also many of these scruple-mongers that pretended a tenderness of Conscience, refusing to take an Oath before a lawful Magistrate, and yet these very men, in their secret Conventicles, did covenant and swear to each other, to be assiduous and faithful in using their best endeavours to set up the *Presbyterian Doctrine* and *Discipline*; and both in such a manner as they themselves had not yet agreed on,

but up that government must. To which end, there
were many that wandred up and down, and were
active in sowing Discontents and Sedition, by venomous
and secret murmurings, and a dispersion of scurrilous
Pamphlets and Libels against the Church and State,
but especially against the Bishops; by which means,
together with venomous and indiscreet Sermons, the
common people became so phanatick, as to believe
the Bishops to be Antichrist, and the only obstructers
of Gods Discipline; and at last some of them were
given over to so bloody a Zeal, and such other desperate
delusions, as to find out a Text in the *Revelation* of St.
John, that *Antichrist was to be overcome by the Sword.*
So that those very men, that began with *tender* and
meek Petitions, proceeded to *Admonitions,* then to
Satyrical Remonstrances, and at last, having like
Absolom numbred who was not, and who was, for
their Cause, they got a supposed certainty of so great
a Party, that they durst threaten *first the Bishops,* and
then *the Queen and Parliament*; to all which they
were secretly encouraged by the *Earl of Leicester,* then
in great favour with Her Majesty, and the reputed
Cherisher and Patron-general of these pretenders to
Tenderness of Conscience; his design being, by their
means, to bring such an *odium* upon the *Bishops,* as to
procure an Alienation of their Lands, and a large proportion of them for himself: which avaritious desire
had at last so blinded his reason, that his ambitious
and greedy hopes seem'd to put him into a present
possession of *Lambeth-house.*

And to these undertakings, the Non-conformists of
this Nation were much encouraged and heightned by
a Correspondence and Confederacy
with that Brotherhood in *Scotland*; so
that here they became so bold, that * one told the

* Mr. *Dering.*

Queen openly in a Sermon, *She was like an untamed Heyfer, that would not be ruled by Gods people, but obstructed his Discipline*. And in *Scotland* they were

* Vide Bishop *Spotswoods* History of the Church of *Scotland*.

more confident, for, there * they declared Her an *Atheist*, and grew to such an height, as not to be accountable for any thing spoken against Her, *nor for Treason against their own King, if it were but spoken in the Pulpit*; shewing at last such a disobedience to Him, that His Mother being in *England*, and then in distress, and in prison, and in danger of death, the Church denied the King their prayers for her : and, at another time, when He had appointed a day of Feasting, the Church declared for a general Fast, in opposition to His Authority.

To this height they were grown in both Nations; and by these means there was distill'd into the minds of the common people such other venomous and turbulent principles, as were inconsistent with the safety of the Church and State : and these opinions vented so daringly, that, beside the loss of life and limbs, the governors of the Church and State were forced to use such other severities as will not admit of an excuse, if it had not been to prevent the gangrene of Confusion, and the perilous consequences of it; which, without such prevention, would have been first Confusion, and then Ruine and Misery to this numerous Nation.

These Errors and Animosities were so remarkable, that they begot wonder in an ingenious *Italian*, who being about this time come newly into this Nation, and considering them, writ scoffingly to a friend in his own Country, to this purpose, *That the Common people of* England *were wiser than the wisest of his*

Nation; for here the very Women *and* Shopkeepers, *were able to judge of* Predestination, *and to determine what Laws were fit to be made concerning Church-government ; and then, what were fit to be obeyed or abolisht : That they were more able (or at least thought so) to raise and determine perplext Cases of Conscience, than the wisest of the most learned Colledges in* Italy ; *That men of the slightest Learning, and the most ignorant of the Common people, were mad for a new, or,* Super- *or* Re-reformation *of Religion; and that in this* they appeared like that man, who would never cease to whet and whet his knife, till there was no steel left to make it useful. And he concluded his Letter with this observation, *That those very men that were most busie in* Oppositions, *and* Disputations, *and* Contro-*versies, and finding out the faults of their Governors, had usually the least of* Humility *and* Mortification, *or of the* power *of* Godliness.

And to heighten all these Discontents and Dangers there was also sprung up a generation of Godless men ; men that had so long given way to their own lusts and delusions, and so highly opposed the blessed motions of his Spirit, and the inward light of their own Consciences, that they became the very slaves of vice, and had thereby sinned themselves into a belief of that which they would, but could not believe ; into a belief which is repugnant even to humane Nature (for the Heathens believe that there are many gods) but these had sin'd themselves into a belief that there was no God ; and so, finding nothing in themselves but what was worse than nothing, began to wish what they were not able to hope for ; namely, *that they might be like the beasts that perish* : And in wicked company (which is the Atheists Sanctuary) were so bold as to say so, though the worst of Mankind when he is left alone at midnight, may wish, but is not then able to think it : even into a belief that there is no God. Into this wretched, this reprobate condition, many had then sinned themselves.

And now, when the Church was pestered with them, and with all those other forenamed Irregularities; when her Lands were in danger of Alienation, her Power at least neglected, and her Peace torn to pieces by several Schisms, and such Heresies as do usually attend that sin, (for Heresies do usually out-live their first Authors) when the Common people seemed ambitious of doing those very things that were forbidden and attended with most dangers, that thereby they might be punish'd, and then applauded and pitied ; when they called the Spirit of opposition a Tender Conscience, and complained of persecution, because they wanted power to persecute others ; when the giddy multitude raged, and became restless to find out misery for themselves and others ; and the Rabble would herd themselves together, and endeavour to govern and act in spight of Authority. In this extremity of fear, and danger of the Church and State, when to suppress the growing evils of both, they needed a man of prudence and piety, and of an high and fearless fortitude, they were blest in all by *John Whitgift* his being made Archbishop of *Canterbury*; of whom Sir *Henry Wotton* that knew him well in his youth, and had studied him in his age, gives this true Character : *That he was a man of Reverend and Sacred memory : and of the primitive temper ; such a temper, as when the Church by lowliness of Spirit did flourish in highest examples of Virtue.* And indeed, this man prov'd so.

And though I dare not undertake to add to this excellent and true character of Sir *Henry Wotton* : yet

I shall neither do right to this Discourse, nor to my Reader, if I forbear to give him a further and short account of the life and manners of this excellent man ; and it shall be short, for I long to end this digression, that I may lead my Reader back to Mr. *Hooker*, where we left him at the *Temple*.

John Whitgift was born in the County of *Lincoln*, of a Family that was ancient, and noted to be both prudent, and affable, and Gentile by nature ; he was educated in *Cambridge*, much of his Learning was acquired in *Pembroke Hall*, (where Mr. *Bradford* the Martyr was his Tutor) from thence he was remov'd to *Peter-house*, from thence to be Master of *Pembroke Hall*, and from thence to the Mastership of *Trinity* Colledge : About which time, the Queen made him Her Chaplain, and not long after Prebend of *Ely*, and then Dean of *Lincoln* ; and having for many years past look't upon him with much reverence and favour, gave him a fair testimony of both, by giving him the Bishoprick of *Worcester,* and (which was not with her a usual favour) forgiving him his First-fruits ; then by constituting him Vice-president of the principality of *Wales*. And having experimented his Wisdom, his Justice, and Moderation in the menage of Her affairs, in both these places ; She, in the 26*th* of Her Reign, made him Archbishop of *Canterbury*, and not long after of Her Privy Council, and trusted him to manage all Her Ecclesiastical Affairs and Preferments. In all which Removes, he was like the Ark, which left a blessing upon the place where it rested ; and in all his Imployments was like *Jehoiada*, that did good unto *Israel*.

These were the steps of this Bishops ascension to this place of dignity and cares : in which place (to speak Mr. *Cambdens* very words in his Annals of Queen *Elizabeth*) *he devoutly consecrated both his whole life to*

God, and his painful labours to the good of his Church.
And yet in this place he met with many oppositions
in the regulation of Church-affairs, which were
much disordered at his entrance, by reason of the age
and remisness of Bishop *Grindall,* his immediate
Predecessor, the activity of the Non-conformists, and
their chief assistant the *Earl* of *Leicester;* and indeed,
by too many others of the like Sacrilegious principles.
With these he was to encounter; and though he
wanted neither courage, nor a good cause; yet he
foresaw that without a great measure of the Queens
favour, it was impossible to stand in the breach that
had been lately made into the Lands and Immunities
of the Church, or indeed to maintain the remaining
lands and rights of it. And therefore by justifiable
sacred Insinuations, such as St. *Paul* to *Agrippa,*
(*Agrippa, believest thou? I know thou believest*) he
wrought himself into so great a degree of favour with
Her, as by his pious use of it hath got both of them
a great degree of Fame in this World, and of Glory
in that into which they are now both entred.

His merits to the Queen, and Her favours to him
were such, that *She called him her little black Husband,*
and *called his Servants Her Servants:* and She saw
so visible and blessed a sincerity shine in all his cares
and endeavours for the Churches, and for Her good,
that She was supposed to trust him with the very
secrets of Her Soul, and to make him Her Confessor;
of which She gave many fair testimonies, and of which
one was, that *She would never eat Flesh in Lent without
obtaining a Licence from her little black Husband:* and
would often say, *She pitied him because She trusted him,
and had thereby eased Her self, by laying the burthen of
all Her Clergy-cares upon his shoulders; which he
managed with prudence & piety.*

I shall not keep my self within the promised Rules of brevity in this account of his Interest with Her Majesty, and his care of the Churches Rights, if in this digression I should enlarge to particulars; and therefore my desire is, that one Example may serve for a Testimony of both. And, that the Reader may the better understand it, he may take notice, that not many years before his being made Archbishop, there passed an Act or Acts of Parliament, intending the better preservation of the Church-lands, by recalling a power which was vested in others to Sell or Lease them, by lodging and trusting the future care and protection of them only in the Crown: And amongst many that made a bad use of this power or trust of the Queens, the *Earl of Leicester* was one; and the Bishop having by his Interest with Her Majesty, put a stop to the Earls sacrilegious designs, they two fell to an open opposition before Her; after which they both quitted the Room, not friends in appearance; but the Bishop made a sudden and a seasonable return to Her Majesty (for he found Her alone) and spake to Her with great humility and reverence, to this purpose.

I *Beseech Your Majesty to hear me with patience, and to believe that Yours, and the Churches safety, are dearer to me than my Life; but my Conscience dearer than both: and therefore give me leave to do my Duty, and tell You,* That Princes are deputed Nursing Fathers of the Church, and owe it a pro-tection; *and therefore God forbid that You should be so much as Passive in her Ruines, when You may prevent it; or that I should behold it without horror and detesta-tion, or should forbear to tell Your Majesty of the sin and danger of* Sacriledge: *And though You and my self were born in an Age of Frailties, when the primitive piety and care of the Churches Lands and Immunities are much decayed; yet (Madam) let me beg that you would first consider that there are such sins as* Prophaneness *and* Sacriledge; *and that if there were not, they could not have names in Holy Writ, and particularly in the New Testament. And I beseech You to consider, that though our Saviour said,* He judged no man; *and to testifie it, would not judge nor divide the inheritance betwixt the two Brethren; nor would judge the Woman taken in Adultery: yet in this point of the Churches Rights he was so zealous, that he made himself both the* Accuser, *and the* Judge, *and the* Executioner *too, to punish these sins; witnessed, in that he himself made the Whip to drive the Prophaners out of the* Temple, *overthrew the Tables of the* Money-changers, *and drove them out of it. And I beseech you to consider that it was St.* Paul *that said to those Christians of his time that were offended with Idolatry, and yet committed* Sacriledge; Thou that abhorrest Idols, dost thou commit Sacriledge? *Supposing (I think) Sacriledge the greater sin. This may occasion Your Majesty to consider that there is such a sin as Sacriledge; and to incline You to prevent the Curse that will follow it, I beseech You also to consider, that* Constantine *the first Christian Emperor, and* Helena *his Mother; that King* Edgar, *and* Edward the Confessor, *and indeed many others of Your Predecessors, and many private Christians, have also given to God, and to his Church, much Land, and many Immunities, which they might have given to those of their own Families, and did not: but gave them for ever as* an absolute Right and Sacrifice to God: *And with these Immunities and Lands they have entail'd a Curse upon the Alienators of them;* God prevent Your Majesty and Your Successors from being liable to that Curse which will cleave unto Church-lands, as the Leprosie to the Jews.

And, to make You that are trusted with their preservation, the better to understand the danger of it, I beseech You forget not, that to prevent these Curses, the Churches Land and Power have been also endeavoured to be preserved (as far as Humane Reason, and the Law of this Nation have been able to preserve them) by an immediate and most sacred Obligation on the Consciences of the Princes of this Realm : For they that consult Magna Charta, *shall find, that as all Your Predecessors were at their Coronation, so You also were sworn before all the Nobility and Bishops then present, and in the presence of God, and in his stead to him that anointed You,* To maintain the Church-lands, and the Rights belonging to it ; *and this you Your self have testified openly to God at the holy Altar, by laying Your hands on the Bible then lying upon it : And not only* Magna Charta, *but many modern Statutes, have denounced a Curse upon those that break* Magna Charta : *A Curse like the* Leprosie, *that was intail'd on the* Jews ; *for, as that, so these Curses have and will cleave to the very stones of those buildings that have been consecrated to God ; and the fathers sin of* Sacriledge, *hath and will prove to be intail'd on his Son and Family. And now Madam, what account can be given for the breach of this Oath at the last great day, either by Your Majesty, or by me, if it be wilfully, or but negligently violated, I know not ?*

And therefore, good Madam, let not the late Lords Exceptions against the failings of some few Clergymen, prevail with You to punish Posterity, for the Errors of this present Age ; let particular men suffer for their particular Errors ; but let God and his Church have their Inheritance : And though I pretend not to Prophesie ; yet I beg Posterity to take notice of what is already become visible in many Families ; That Church-land added to an ancient and just Inheritance, hath proved like a Moth fretting a Garment, and secretly consumed both: Or like the Eagle that stole a coal from the Altar, and thereby set her Nest on fire, which consumed both her young Eagles, and her self that stole it. *And though I shall forbear to speak reproachfully of Your Father, yet I beg You to take notice, that a part of the Churches Rights, added to the vast Treasure left him by his Father, hath been conceived to bring an unavoidable Consumption upon both, notwithstanding all his diligence to preserve them.*

And consider that after the violation of those Laws, to which he had sworn in Magna Charta, *God did so far deny him his restraining Grace, that as King Saul after he was forsaken of God, fell from one sin to another; so he, till at last he fell into greater sins than I am willing to mention. Madam,* Religion is the Foundation and Cement of humane Societies: *and when they that serve at Gods Altar, shall be exposed to Poverty, then Religion it self will be exposed to scorn, and become contemptible, as You may already observe it to be in too many poor Vicaridges in this Nation. And therefore, as You are by a late Act or Acts of Parliament entrusted with a great power to preserve or waste the Churches Lands, yet dispose of them* for Jesus sake, as you have promised to men, and vowed to God, that is, as the Donors intended; *let neither Falshood nor Flattery beguile You to do otherwise: but, put a stop to Gods and the* Levites *portion (I beseech You) and to the approaching Ruines of his Church, as You expect comfort at the last great day; for Kings must be judged; Pardon this affectionate plainness, my most dear Soveraign; and let me beg to be still continued in Your favour, and the Lord still continue You in his.*

The Queens patient hearing this affectionate Speech, and her future Care to preserve the Churches Rights,

which till then had been neglected, may appear a fair
Testimony, that he made hers and the Churches Good
the chiefest of his Cares, and that she also thought so.
And of this there were such daily testimonies given, as
begot betwixt them so mutual a joy and confidence,
that they seemed born to believe and do good to each
other; she not doubting his Piety to be more than all
his Opposers, which were many; nor doubting his
Prudence to be equal to the chiefest of her Council,
who were then as remarkable for active Wisdom, as
those dangerous Times did require, or this Nation did
ever enjoy. And in this condition he continued
twenty years; in which time, he saw some Flowings,
but many more Ebbings of her Favour towards all
men that had opposed him, especially the *Earl of
Leicester*: so that God seemed still to keep him in her
Favour, that he might preserve the remaining Church
Lands and Immunities from Sacrilegious Alienations.
And this Good man deserved all the Honour and Power
with which she gratified and trusted him; for he was
a pious man, and naturally of Noble and Grateful
Principles: he eased her of all her Church-cares by
his wise Menage of them; he gave her faithful and
prudent Counsels in all the Extremities and Dangers
of her Temporal Affairs, which were very many; he
lived to be the chief Comfort of her Life in her Declining age, and to be then most frequently with her, and
her Assistant at her private Devotions, he liv'd to be
the greatest Comfort of her Soul upon her Death-
bed; to be present at the Expiration of her last Breath,
and to behold the closing of those Eyes that had long
looked upon him with Reverence and Affection. And
let this also be added, that he was the Chief Mourner
at her sad Funeral; nor let this be forgotten, that
within a few hours after her death, he was the happy

Proclaimer, that King *James* (her peaceful Successor) was Heir to the Crown.

Let me beg of my Reader to allow me to say a little, and but a little, more of this good Bishop, and I shall then presently lead him back to Mr. *Hooker*; and, because I would hasten, I will mention but one part of the Bishops Charity and Humility; but this of both: He built a large Alms-house near to his own Palace at *Croydon* in *Surry*, and endowed it with Maintenance for a Master and twenty eight poor Men and Women; which he visited so often, that he knew their Names and Dispositions, and was so truly humble, that he called them *Brothers* and *Sisters*: and whensoever the Queen descended to that lowliness to dine with him at his Palace in *Lambeth* (which was very often) he would usually the next day shew the like lowliness to his poor Brothers and Sisters at *Croydon*, and dine with them at his Hospital; at which time, you may believe, there was Joy at the Table. And at this place he built also a fair Free-School, with a good Accommodation and Maintenance for the Master and Scholars; Which gave just occasion for *Boyse Sisi*, then Embassador for the French King, and Resident here, at the Bishops death to say, *The Bishop had published many learned Books, but a Free-school to train up Youth, and an Hospital to lodge and maintain aged and poor People, were the best Evidences of Christian Learning that a Bishop could leave to Posterity*. This good Bishop lived to see King *James* setled in Peace, and then fell into an extream sickness at his Palace in *Lambeth*; of which when the King had notice, he went presently to visit him, and found him in his Bed in a declining condition, and very weak; and after some short discourse betwixt them, the King, at his departure assured him, *He had a great Affection for him, and a very high value for his Prudence and Vertues, and would indeavour to beg his life of God for the good of his Church.* To which the good Bishop replied, *Pro Ecclesia Dei, Pro Ecclesia Dei:* which were the last words he ever spake; therein testifying, that as in his Life, so at his Death, his chiefest care was of Gods Church.

This *John Whitgift* was made Archbishop in the year 1583. In which busie place, he continued twenty years and some moneths; and in which time, you may believe, he had many Trials of his Courage and Patience; but his Motto was, *Vincit, qui patitur:* and he made it good.

Many of his many Trials were occasioned by the then powerful *Earl of Leicester,* who did still (but secretly) raise and cherish a Faction of *Non-conformists* to oppose him; especially one *Thomas Cartwright,* a man of noted Learning, sometime Contemporary with the Bishop in *Cambridge,* and of the same Colledge, of which the Bishop had been Master; in which place there began some Emulations (the particulars I forbear) and at last open and high Oppositions betwixt them; and in which you may believe Mr. *Cartwright* was most faulty, if his Expulsion out of the University can incline you to it.

And in this discontent after the Earls death (which was 1588.) Mr. *Cartwright* appeared a chief Cherisher of a Party that were for the *Geneva* Church-government; and to effect it, he ran himself into many dangers both of Liberty and Life; appearing at the last to justifie himself and his Party in many Remonstrances, which he caused to be printed, and to which the Bishop made a first Answer, and *Cartwright* replied upon him; and then the Bishop having rejoined to his first Reply, Mr. *Cartwright* either was, or was perswaded to be, satisfied: for he wrote no more, but left the Reader to be judge which had maintained their Cause with most Charity and Reason. After some silence, Mr. *Cartwright* received from the Bishop many personal Favours, and betook himself to a more private Living, which was at *Warwick*, where he was made Master of an Hospital, and lived quietly, and grew rich; and where the Bishop gave him a Licence to preach, upon promises not to meddle with Controversies, but incline his Hearers to Piety and Moderation; and this Promise he kept during his Life, which ended 1602. the Bishop surviving him but some few months; each ending his days in perfect Charity with the other.

And now after this long Digression made for the Information of my Reader concerning what follows, I bring him back to venerable Mr. *Hooker*, where we left him in the *Temple*; and, where we shall find him as deeply engaged in a Controversie with *Walter Trevers*, a Friend and Favorite of Mr. *Cartwrights*, as the Bishop had ever been with Mr. *Cartwright* himself; and of which I shall proceed to give this following account.

And first this; That though the Pens of Mr. *Cartwright* and the Bishop were now at rest, yet there was sprung up a new Generation of restless men, that by Company and Clamours became possest of a Faith which they ought to have kept to themselves, but could not; men that were become positive in asserting, *That a Papist cannot be saved*: insomuch that about this time, at the Execution of the Queen of Scots, the Bishop that preached her Funeral Sermon (which was Doctor *Howland*, then Bishop of *Peterborough*) was reviled for not being positive for her Damnation. And beside this boldness of their becoming Gods, so far as to set limits to his Mercies; there was not only one *Martin Mar-prelate*, but other venomous Books daily printed and dispersed; Books, that were so absurd and scurrilous, that the graver Divines disdained them an Answer. And yet these were grown into high esteem with the Common people, till *Tom Nash* appeared against them all; who was a man of a sharp wit, and the Master of a scoffing Satyrical merry Pen, which he imployed to discover the Absurdities of those blind malitious sensless Pamphlets, and Sermons as sensless as they; *Nash* his Answers being like his Books, which bore these or like Titles, *An Almond for a Parrot. A Fig for my God-son. Come crack me this Nut*, and the like: so that his merry Wit made some sport, and such a discovery of their Absurdities as (which is strange) he put a greater stop to these malicious Pamphlets, than a much wiser man had been able.

And now the Reader is to take notice, That at the Death of *Father Alvie*, who was Master of the *Temple*, this *Walter Travers* was Lecturer there for the Evening Sermons, which he preach'd with great approbation, especially of some Citizens, and the younger Gentlemen of that Society; and for the most part approved by Mr. *Hooker* himself, in the midst of their oppositions. For he continued Lecturer a part of his time, Mr. *Travers* being indeed a man of Competent Learning, of a winning Behaviour, and of a blameless Life. But he had taken Orders by the Presbytery in *Antwerp* (and with them some opinions, that could never be eradicated) and if in any thing he was transported, it was in an extream desire to set up that Government in this Nation: For the promoting of which, he had a correspondence with *Theodore Beza* at *Geneva*, and others in *Scotland*; and was one of the chiefest assistants to Mr. *Cartwright* in that Design.

Mr. *Travers* had also a particular hope to set up this Government in the *Temple,* and to that end used his most zealous endeavours to be Master of it; and his being disappointed by Mr. *Hookers* admittance, proved the occasion of a publick opposition betwixt them, in their Sermons. Many of which were concerning the Doctrine, and Ceremonies of this Church: Insomuch that, as St. *Paul* withstood St. *Peter* to his face, so did they withstand each other in their Sermons; for, as one hath pleasantly exprest it, *The Forenoon Sermon spake* Canterbury, *and the Afternoon,* Geneva.

In these Sermons there was little of bitterness, but each party brought all the Reasons he was able to prove his Adversaries Opinion erroneous. And thus it continued a long time, till the Oppositions became so visible, and the Consequences so dangerous, especially in that place, that the prudent Archbishop put a stop to Mr. *Travers* his Preaching by a positive Prohibition: Against which Mr. *Travers* Appeal'd and Petition'd Her Majesties Privy Council to have it recalled: where besides his Patron the *Earl of Leicester,* he met also with many assisting Friends; but they were not able to prevail with, or against the Arch-bishop, whom the Queen had intrusted with all Church-power: and, he had received so fair a Testimony of Mr. *Hookers* Principles, and of his Learning and Moderation, that he withstood all Sollicitations.——But the denying this Petition of Mr. *Travers* was unpleasant to divers of his Party; and the Reasonableness of it became at last to be so publickly magnified by them and many others of that party, as never to be answered; so that intending the Bishops and Mr. *Hookers* disgrace, they procured it to be privately printed, and scattered abroad: and then Mr. *Hooker* was forced to appear and make as publick an answer: which he did, and

Dedicated it to the Arch-bishop; and it proved so full an Answer, an answer that had in it so much of clear Reason, and writ with so much Meekness and Majesty of Style, that the Bishop began to have him in admiration, and to rejoice that he had appeared in his Cause, and disdained not earnestly to beg his Friendship, even a familiar Friendship, with a man of so much *quiet Learning* and *Humility*.

To enumerate the many particular points, in which Mr. *Hooker* and Mr. *Travers* dissented, (all or most of which, I have seen written) would prove at least tedious; and therefore, I shall impose upon my Reader no more then two, which shall immediately follow, and by which he may judge of the rest.

Mr. *Travers* excepted against Mr. *Hooker*, for that in one of his Sermons he declared, *That the assurance of what we believe by the Word of God, is not to us so certain as that which we perceive by sense.* And Mr. *Hooker* confesseth he said so; and endeavours to justifie it by the Reasons following.

First, I taught, That the things which God promises in his Word are surer than what we touch, handle, or see; but are we so sure and certain of them? if we be, why doth God so often prove his Promises to us, as he doth, by Arguments drawn from our sensible Experience? For we must be surer of the Proof than of the things Proved; otherwise it is no Proof. For Example: How is it that many men looking on the Moon at the same time, every one knoweth it to be the Moon, as certainly as the other doth: but many believing one and the same Promise, have not all one and the same Fulness of Perswasion? For how falleth it out, that men being assured of any thing by Sense, can be no surer of it than they are; when as the strongest in Faith that liveth upon the Earth, hath always need to labour, strive and pray, that his

Assurance concerning Heavenly and Spiritual things may grow, increase, and be augmented ?

The Sermon that gave him the cause of this his Justification makes the Case more plain, by declaring *that there is besides this Certainty of Evidence, a Certainty of Adherence* : in which having most excellently demonstrated what the *Certainty of Adherence* is, he makes this comfortable use of it, *Comfortable* (he says) *as to weak Believers, who suppose themselves to be faithless, not to believe, when notwithstanding they have their* Adherence ; *the Holy Spirit hath his private operations, and worketh secretly in them, and effectually too, though they want the inward Testimony of it.*

Tell this, saith he, to a man that hath a mind too much dejected by a sad sense of his sin ; to one that by a too severe judging of himself, concludes that he wants Faith, because he wants the comfortable Assurance of it ; and his Answer will be, *Do not perswade me against my knowledge, against what I find and feel in my self* ; I do not, I know, *I do not believe.* (Mr. *Hookers* own words follow) *Well then, to favour such men a little in their weakness, Let that be granted which they do imagine ; be it that they adhere not to Gods Promises, but are faithless and without belief; but are they not grieved for their unbelief ? they confess they are; do they not wish it might, and also strive that it may be otherways ? we know they do; whence cometh this, but from a secret Love and Liking that they have of those things believed ? For,* no man can love those things which in his own opinion are not; *and, if they think those things to be, which they shew they love when they desire to believe them ; then must it be, that by desiring to believe, they prove themselves true believers ; For,* without Faith no man thinketh that things believed are: *which argument all the Subtilties of infernal powers will never be able to dissolve.* This is an abridgment of part of the Reasons Mr. *Hooker* gives for his Justification of this his Opinion for which he was excepted against by Mr. *Travers*.

Mr. *Hooker* was also accused by Mr. *Travers*, for that he in one of his Sermons had declared, that *he doubted not but that God was merciful to many of our fore-fathers living in Popish Superstition, for as much as they Sinned ignorantly*: and Mr. *Hooker* in his answer professeth it to be his Judgment, and declares his Reasons for this Charitable opinion to be as followeth.

But first, he states the question about *Justification* and *Works*, and how the *Foundation of Faith without works is overthrown*; and then he proceeds to discover that way which *Natural men* and some others have mistaken to be the way by which they hope to attain true and everlasting happiness; and having discovered the mistaken, he proceeds to direct to that True way, by which, and no other, everlasting life and blessedness is attainable; and, these two ways he demonstrates thus: (they be his own words that follow) ' *That, the way of Nature, This, the way of* ' *Grace; the end of that way, Salvation merited, pre-* ' *supposing the righteousness of mens works; their* ' *Righteousness, a Natural ability to do them; that* ' *ability, the goodness of God which created them in* ' *such perfection.* But, *the end of this way, Salvation* ' *bestowed upon men as a gift: presupposing not their* ' *righteousness, but the forgiveness of their Vnrighteous-* ' *ness,* Justification; *their Justification, not their Natural* ' *ability to do good, but their hearty Sorrow for not doing,* ' *and unfeigned belief in him for whose sake not doers* ' *are accepted,* which is their vocation; *their Vocation,* ' *the Election of God, taking them out of the number of*

' *lost Children ; their Election a Mediator in whom to*
' *be elected ; this mediation inexplicable mercy ; this*
' *mercy, supposing their misery for whom he vouchsafed*
' *to dye, and make himself a Mediator.*'

And he also declareth, *There is no meritorious cause
for our Justification but Christ; no effectual but his
Mercy*; and says also, *We deny the Grace of our Lord
Jesus Christ, we abuse, disanul, and annihilate the
benefit of his Passion, if by a proud imagination we
believe we can merit everlasting life, or can be worthy of
it.* This belief (he declareth) is to destroy the very
essence of our Justification : and he makes all opinions
that border upon this, to be very dangerous. *Yet nevertheless* (and for this he was accused) ' *Considering how
' *many vertuous and just men, how many Saints and
' *Martyrs have had their dangerous opinions, amongst
' *which this was one, that they hoped to make God some
' *part of amends by voluntary punishments which they
' *laid upon themselves*; because by this or the like
' erroneous opinions which do by consequence over-
' throw the merits of Christ, shall man be so bold as
' to write on their Graves, *such men are damned, there
' *is for them no Salvation ?* St. Austin says, *errare
' *possum, Hæreticus esse nolo.* And except we put a
' difference betwixt them that err Ignorantly, and them
' that Obstinately persist in it, how is it possible that
' any man should hope to be saved ? give me a Pope
' or a Cardinal, whom great afflictions have made to
' know himself, whose heart God hath touched with
' true sorrow for all his sins, and filled with a Love of
' Christ and his Gospel, whose eyes are willingly open
' to see the truth, and his mouth ready to renounce all
' errour, this one opinion of merit excepted, which he
' thinketh God will require at his hands, and because
' he wanteth, trembleth, and is discouraged, and yet

'can say, *Lord cleanse me from all my secret sins*, shall
'I think because of this or a like errour such men touch
'not so much as the Hem of Christs Garment; if
'they do, wherefore should I doubt but that vertue
'may proceed from Christ to save them? no, I will
'not be afraid to say to such a one, *you err in your*
'*opinion: but be of good comfort, you have to do with a*
'*merciful God who will make the best of that little*
'*which you hold well; and not with a captious Sophister,*
'*who gathereth the worst out of every thing in which you*
'*are mistaken.*'

But it will be said (says Mr. *Hooker*) *The admittance*
of Merit in any degree, overthroweth the foundation,
excludeth from the hope of mercy, from all possibility
of Salvation. (And now Mr. *Hookers* own words
follow)

'What, though they hold the truth sincerely in all
'other parts of Christian Faith; although they have
'in some measure all the Vertues and Graces of the
'Spirit; although they have all other tokens of Gods
'Children in them; although they be far from having
'any proud opinion that they shall be saved by the
'worthiness of their deeds; although the only thing
'that troubleth and molesteth them be a little too much
'dejection, somewhat too great a fear arising from an
'erroneous conceit, that God will require a worthiness
'in them, which they are grieved to find wanting in
'themselves? although they be not obstinate in this
'opinion? although they be willing and would be
'glad to forsake it, if any one reason were brought
'sufficient to disprove it? although the only cause
'why they do not forsake it ere they dye, be their
'Ignorance of that means by which it might be dis-
'prov'd? although the cause why the Ignorance in
'this point is not removed, be the want of knowledge

' in such as should be able, and are not to remove it ;
Let me dye (says Mr. *Hooker*) *if it be ever proved, that
simply an Errour doth exclude a Pope or Cardinal in
such a case utterly from hope of life.* ' Surely I must
' confess, that if it be an Error to think that God may
' be merciful to save men even when they err ; my
' greatest comfort is my error : were it not for the love
' I bear to this error : I would never wish to speak or
' to live.'

I was willing to take notice of these two points, as
supposing them to be very material ; and that as they
are thus contracted, they may prove useful to my
Reader ; as also, for that the Answers be arguments of
Mr. *Hookers* great and clear Reason, and equal Charity.
Other exceptions were also made against him by Mr.
Travers, as, *That he prayed before and not after his
Sermons ; that in his Prayers he named Bishops ; that
he kneeled both when he prayed and when he received the
Sacrament,* and (says Mr. *Hooker* in his defence) *other
exceptions so like these, as but to name, I should have
thought a greater fault then to commit them.*

And 'tis not unworthy the noting, that in the
manage of so great a controversie, a sharper reproof
than this, and one like it, did never fall from the happy
pen of this Humble man. That like it was upon a
like occasion of exceptions, to which his answer was,
*Your next argument consists of railing and of reasons ;
to your Railing, I say nothing, to your Reasons, I say what
follows.* And I am glad of this fair occasion, to testifie
the Dove-like temper of this meek, this matchless man ;
and doubtless, if Almighty God had blest the Dissenters
from the Ceremonies and Discipline of this Church,
with a like measure of Wisdom and Humility, instead
of their pertinacious zeal : then Obedience and Truth
had kissed each other ; then Peace and Piety had

flourished in our Nation, and this Church and State had been blest like *Jerusalem that is at unity with it self*; but this can never be expected, till God shall bless the common people of this Nation with a belief *that Schism is a Sin; and they not fit to judge what is Schism*: and bless them also with a belief, *That there may be offences taken which are not given*; and *That Laws are not made for private men to dispute, but to Obey*.

And this also may be worthy of noting, That these Exceptions of Mr. *Travers* against Mr. *Hooker*, prov'd to be *Felix error*, for they were the cause of his Transcribing those few of his Sermons, which we now see printed with his Books, and of his Answer to Mr. *Travers*, his Supplication, and of his most learned and useful discourse of *Justification* of *Faith* and *Works*; and by their Transcription they fell into such hands as have preserved them from being lost, as too many of his other matchless writings were; and from these I have gathered many observations in this Discourse of his Life.

After the publication of his Answer to the Petition of Mr. *Travers*, Mr. *Hooker* grew daily into greater repute with the most learned and wise of the Nation; but it had a contrary effect in very many of the Temple that were zealous for Mr. *Travers* and for his Church Discipline: insomuch, that though Mr. *Travers* left the place, yet the seeds of Discontent could not be rooted out of that Society, by the great Reason, and as great Meekness of this humble man: for though the chief Benchers gave him much Reverence and Incouragement, yet he there met with many neglects and oppositions by those of Master *Travers* Judgment; in so much, that it turned to his extream grief: and that he might unbeguile and win them, he designed to write a deliberate sober Treatise of the Churches power to make Canons for the use of Ceremonies, and by Law to impose an obedience to them, as upon her Children; and this he proposed to do in *eight Books of the Laws of Ecclesiastical Polity*; intending therein to shew such Arguments as should force an assent from all men, if Reason, delivered in sweet Language, and void of any provocation, were able to do it; And that he might prevent all prejudice, he wrote before it a large Preface or Epistle to the *Dissenting Brethren*, wherein there were such Bowels of Love, and such a Commixture of that *Love* with *Reason*, as was never exceeded but in Holy Writ, and particularly by that of St. *Paul* to his dear Brother and fellow Labourer *Philemon*: than which, none ever was more like this Epistle of Mr. *Hookers*; so that his dear friend and Companion in his Studies Doctor *Spenser*, might after his death justly say, *What admirable height of Learning and depth of Judgment dwelt in the lowly mind of this truly humble man, great in all wise mens eyes except his own; with what gravity and Majesty of speech his Tongue and Pen uttered Heavenly Mysteries; whose eyes in the Humility of his Heart were always cast down to the ground; how all things that proceeded from him were breathed as from the Spirit of Love, as if he, like the Bird of the Holy Ghost, the Dove, had wanted Gall; let those that knew him not in his Person, judge by these living Images of his soul, his Writings.*

The foundation of these Books was laid in the Temple; but he found it no fit place to finish what he had there designed; and he therefore earnestly solicited the Archbishop for a remove from that place, to whom he spake to this purpose. *My Lord, When I lost the freedom of my Cell, which was my Colledge, yet I found some degree of it in my quiet Country*

Parsonage: but I am weary of the noise and oppositions of this place; and indeed, God and Nature did not intend me for Contentions, but for Study and quietness: My Lord, *My particular contests with Mr.* Travers *here have proved the more unpleasant to me, because I believe him to be a good man; and, that belief hath occasioned me to examine mine own Conscience concerning his Opinions: and, to satisfie that, I have consulted the Scripture, and other Laws both Humane and Divine, whether the Conscience of him and others of his judgment ought to be so far complyed with as to alter our frame of Church Government, our manner of Gods Worship, our Praising and Praying to him, and, our established Ceremonies as often as his and others tender Consciences shall require us; and, in this examination, I have not only satisfied my self, but have begun a treatise, in which I intend a Justification of the Laws of our Ecclesiastical Polity: in which design God and his holy Angels shall at the last great day bear me that witness which my Conscience now does; that my meaning is not to provoke any, but rather to satisfie all tender Consciences, and I shall never be able to do this, but where I may Study, and pray for Gods blessing upon my indeavours, and keep my self in Peace and Privacy, and behold Gods blessing spring out of my Mother Earth, and eat my own bread without oppositions; and therefore, if your Grace can Judge me worthy of such a favour, let me beg it, that I may perfect what I have begun.*

About this time the Parsonage or Rectory of *Boscum*, in the Diocess of *Sarum*, and six miles from that City, became void. The Bishop of *Sarum* is Patron of it; but in the vacancy of that See (which was three years betwixt the Translation of Bishop *Peirce* to the See of *York*, and Bishop *Caldwells* admission into it) the disposal of that and all Benefices belonging to that See, during this said vacancy, came to be disposed of by the Archbishop of *Canterbury*, and he presented *Richard Hooker* to it, in the year 1591. And *Richard Hooker* was also in the said year Instituted, *July* 17. to be a minor Prebend of *Salisbury*, the Corps to it being *Nether-Havin*, about ten miles from that City: which Prebend was of no great value, but intended chiefly to make him capable of a better preferment in that Church. In this *Boscum* he continued till he had finished four of his eight proposed Books of the Laws of Ecclesiastical Polity, and these were entered into the register Book in Stationers Hall, the 9*th* of *March* 1592. but not published till the year 1594. and then were with the before-mentioned large and affectionate Preface, which he directs *to them that seek (as they term it) the Reformation of the Laws and Orders Ecclesiastical in the Church of England*; of which Books I shall yet say nothing more, but that he continued his laborious diligence to finish the remaining four during his life (of all which more properly hereafter) but at *Boscum* he finisht and publisht but only the first four; being then in the 39*th* year of his Age.

He left *Boscum* in the year 1595. by a surrender of it into the hands of Bishop *Caldwell*, and he presented *Benjamin Russel*, who was Instituted into it the 23 of *June* in the same year.

The Parsonage of *Bishops Borne* in *Kent*, three miles from *Canterbury*, is in that Archbishops gift; but, in the latter end of the year 1594. Doctor *William Redman* the Rector of it was made *Bishop* of *Norwich*, by which means the power of presenting to it was *pro ea vice* in the Queen; and she presented *Richard Hooker*, whom she loved well, to this good living of *Borne* the 7*th* of *July* 1595. in which living he continued till his Death, without any addition of Dignity or Profit.

And now having brought our *Richard Hooker*, from his Birth-place to this where he found a Grave, I shall only give some account of his Books, and of his behaviour in this Parsonage of *Borne*, and then give a rest both to my self and my Reader.

His first four Books and large Epistle have been declared to be printed at his being at *Boscum*, *Anno* 1594. Next I am to tell that at the end of these four Books, there was when he first printed them this Advertisement to the Reader.——' I have for ' some causes thought it at this time more fit to let go ' these first four Books by themselves, than to stay ' both them and the rest, till the whole might together ' be published. Such generalities of the cause in ' question as are here handled, it will be perhaps not ' amiss to consider apart, by way of Introduction unto ' the Books that are to follow concerning particulars ; ' in the mean time the Reader is requested to mend the ' Printers errours, as noted underneath.

And I am next to declare, that his fifth Book (which is larger than his first four) was first also printed by it self *Anno* 1597. and dedicated to his Patron (for till then he chose none) the Archbishop. These Books were read with an admiration of their excellency in This, and their just fame spread it self also into foreign Nations. And I have been told more than forty years past, that either Cardinal *Allen*, or learned Doctor *Stapleton* (both English men, and in *Italy* about the time when *Hookers* four Books were first printed :) meeting with this general fame of them, were desirous to read an Author that both the Reformed and the learned of their own *Romish* Church did so much magnifie, and therefore caused them to be sent for to

Rome; and after reading them, boasted to the Pope (which then was *Clement* the eighth) *that though he had lately said he never met with an English Book whose Writer deserved the name of Author*; yet there now appear'd a wonder to them, and it would be so to his Holiness, if it were in Latin, for *a poor obscure English Priest had writ four such Books of Laws, and Church Polity, and in a Style that exprest such a Grave, and so Humble Majesty, with such clear demonstration of Reason, that in all their readings they had not met with any that exceeded him*; and this begot in the Pope an earnest desire that Doctor *Stapleton* should bring the said four Books, and looking on the English read a part of them to him in Latin; which Doctor *Stapleton* did, to the end of the first Book; at the conclusion of which, the Pope spake to this purpose; *There is no Learning that this man hath not searcht into; nothing too hard for his understanding: this man indeed deserves the name of an Author; his Books will get reverence by Age, for there is in them such seeds of Eternity, that if the rest be like this, they shall last till the last fire shall consume all Learning.*

Nor was this high, the only testimony and commendations given to his Books; for at the first coming of King *James* into this Kingdom, he inquired of the Archbishop *Whitgift* for his friend Mr. *Hooker* that writ the Books of Church Polity; to which the answer was, that he dyed a year before Queen *Elizabeth*, who received the sad news of his Death with very much Sorrow; to which the King replied, *and I receive it with no less, that I shall want the desired happiness of seeing and discoursing with that man, from whose Books I have received such satisfaction: Indeed, my Lord, I have received more satisfaction in reading a leaf, or paragraph in* Mr. *Hooker*, though it were but about the *fashion* of *Churches,* or *Church musick,* or the like, but especially *of the Sacraments, than I have had in the reading particular large Treatises written but of one of those Subjects by others, though very learned men*; and, I observe *there is in* Mr. Hooker *no affected language, but a grave, comprehensive, clear manifestation of Reason, and that back't with the Authority of the* Scripture, *the* Fathers and School-men, *and with all* Law *both* Sacred and Civil. *And, though many others write well, yet in the next Age they will be forgotten; but doubtless there is in every page of* Mr. Hookers Book *the picture of a Divine Soul, such Pictures of* Truth *and* Reason, *and drawn in so sacred Colours, that they shall never fade, but give an immortal memory to the Author.* And it is so truly true, that the King thought what he spake, that as the most learned of the Nation have and still do mention Mr. *Hooker* with reverence, so he also did never mention him but with the Epithite of *Learned,* or *Judicious,* or *Reverend,* or *Venerable* Mr. Hooker.

Nor did his Son, our late King *Charles* the First, ever mention him but with the same reverence, enjoining his Son, our now gracious King, to be studious in Mr. *Hookers* Books. And our learned Antiquary Mr. *Cambden* * mentioning the death, the modesty, and other vertues of Mr. *Hooker,* and magnifying his Books, wish't, *That for the honour of this, and benefit of other Nations, they were turn'd into the Vniversal Language.* Which work, though undertaken by many, yet they have been weary, and forsaken it; but the Reader may now expect it, having been long since begun, and lately finisht, by the happy Pen of Dr. *Earl,* now Lord Bishop of *Salisbury,* of whom I may justly say (and let it not offend him, because it is such a truth as ought

* *In his Annals* 1599.

not to be conceal'd from Posterity, or those that now live, and yet know him not) that since Mr. *Hooker* dyed, none have liv'd whom God hath blest with more innocent Wisdom, more sanctified Learning, or a more pious, peaceable, primitive temper: so that this excellent person seems to be only like himself, and our Venerable *Richard Hooker*; and only fit to make the learned of all Nations happy, in knowing what hath been too long confin'd to the language of our little Island.

There might be many more and just occasions taken to speak of his Books, which none ever did, or can commend too much, but I decline them, and hasten to an account of his Christian behaviour and death at *Borne*: in which place he continued his customary Rules of Mortification and Self-denial; was much in Fasting, frequent in Meditation and Prayers, enjoying those blessed returns, which only men of strict lives feel and know, and of which men of loose and godless lives, cannot be made sensible; for spiritual things are spiritually discerned.

At his entrance into this place, his friendship was much sought for by Dr. *Hadrian Saravia*, then or about that time made one of the Prebends of *Canterbury*; a German by Birth, and sometimes a Pastor both in *Flanders* and *Holland*, where he had studied and well considered the controverted points concerning Episcopacy and Sacriledge; and in *England* had a just occasion to declare his judgment concerning both, unto his Brethren Ministers of the Low Countreys; which was excepted against by *Theodor Beza*, and others; against whose exceptions, he rejoined, and thereby became the happy Author of many learned Tracts, writ in Latin; especially of three; one, of the *Degrees of Ministers*, and *of the Bishops superiority above the Presbytery*; a second against *Sacriledge*; and, a third of *Christian Obedience to Princes*; the last being occasioned by *Gretzerus* the Jesuite. And it is observable, that when in a time of Church-tumults, *Beza* gave his reasons to the Chancellor of *Scotland* for the abrogation of Episcopacy in that Nation, partly by Letters, and more fully in a Treatise of a threefold Episcopacy (which he calls *Divine*, *Humane*, and *Satanical*) this Dr. *Saravia* had by the help of Bishop *Whitgift* made such an early discovery of their intentions, that he had almost as soon answered that Treatise as it became publick; and he therein discovered how *Beza's* opinion did contradict that of *Calvins*, and his adherents, leaving them to interfere with themselves in point of *Episcopacy*; but of these Tracts it will not concern me to say more, than that they were most of them dedicated to his and the Church of *Englands* watchful Patron *John Whitgift* the Archbishop, and printed about the time in which Mr. *Hooker* also appeared first to the World in the publication of his first four Books of Ecclesiastical Polity.

This friendship being sought for by this learned Doctor, you may believe was not denied by Mr. *Hooker*, who was by fortune so like him, as to be engaged against Mr. *Travers*, Mr. *Cartwright*, and others of their judgment, in a Controversie too like Dr. *Saravia's*; so that in this year of 1595, and in this place of *Borne*, these two excellent persons began a holy friendship, increasing daily to so high and mutual affections, that their two wills seemed to be but one and the same: and their designs both for the glory of God, and peace of the Church, still assisting and improving each others vertues, and the desired comforts of a peaceable piety. Which I have willingly mentioned, because it gives a foundation to some things that follow.

This Parsonage of *Borne* is from *Canterbury* three miles, and near to the common Road that leads from that City to *Dover*: in which Parsonage Mr. *Hooker* had not been Twelve months, but his Books, and the innocency and sanctity of his life became so remarkable, that many turn'd out of the Road, and others (Scholars especially) went purposely to see the man, whose life and learning were so much admired; and alas, as our Saviour said of St. *John* Baptist, *What went they out to see? a man cloathed in purple and fine linnen?* no indeed, but an *obscure, harmless man, a man in poor Cloaths, his Loyns usually girt in a course Gown, or Canonical Coat; of a mean stature, and stooping, and yet more lowly in the thoughts of his Soul; his Body worn out, not with Age, but Study, and Holy Mortifications; his Face full of Heat-pimples, begot by his unactivity and sedentary life.* And to this true character of his person, let me add this of his disposition and behaviour; God and Nature blest him with so blessed a bashfulness, that as in his younger days his Pupils might easily look him out of countenance; so neither then, nor in his age, *did he ever willingly look any man in the face; and was of so mild and humble a nature, that his poor Parish Clerk and he did never talk but with both their Hats on, or both off, at the same time*: And to this may be added, that though he was not pur-blind, yet he was short or weak-sighted; and where he fixt his eyes at the beginning of his Sermon, there they continued till it was ended; and the Reader has a liberty to believe, that his modesty and dim sight, were some of the reasons why he trusted Mrs. *Churchman* to choose his Wife.

This Parish-Clerk lived till the third or fourth year

of the late Long Parliament: betwixt which time and Mr. *Hookers* death, there had come many to see the place of his Burial, and the Monument dedicated to his memory by Sir *William Cooper* (who still lives) and the poor Clerk had many rewards for shewing Mr. *Hookers* Grave-place, and his said Monument, and did always hear Mr. *Hooker* mentioned with commendations and reverence: to all which, he added his own knowledge and observations of his humility and holiness; and in all which Discourses, the poor man was still more confirm'd in his opinion of Mr. *Hookers* vertues and learning; but it so fell out, that about the said third or fourth year of the Long Parliament, the then present Parson of *Borne* was Sequestred (you may guess why) and a *Genevian* Minister put into his good Living; this, and other like Sequestrations, made the Clerk express himself in a wonder, and say, *They had Sequestred so many good men, that he doubted if his good Master Mr.* Hooker *had lived till now, they would have Sequestred him too.*

It was not long, before this intruding Minister had made a Party in and about the said Parish, that were desirous to receive the Sacrament as in *Geneva*; to which end, the day was appointed for a select Company, and Forms and Stools set about the Altar or Communion-Table, for them to sit and eat, and drink; but when they went about this work, there was a want of some Joint-stools, which the Minister sent the Clerk to fetch, and then to fetch Cushions (but not to kneel upon); when the Clerk saw them begin to sit down, he began to wonder; but the Minister bad him *cease wondring, and lock the Church-door*; to whom he replied, *Pray take you the Keys, and lock me out, I will never come more into this Church; for all men will say, my Master* Hooker *was a good Man, and a good Scholar, and I am sure it was not used to be thus in his days.* And, report says, the old man went presently home, and died; I do not say died immediately, but within a few days after.

But let us leave this grateful Clerk in his quiet Grave, and return to Mr. *Hooker* himself, continuing our observations of his Christian behaviour in this place, where he gave a holy Valediction to all the pleasures and allurements of Earth, possessing his Soul in a vertuous quietness, which he maintained by constant Study, Prayers, and Meditations; his use was to preach once every *Sunday*, and he or his Curate to Catechise after the second Lesson in the Evening Prayer; his Sermons were neither long nor earnest, but uttered with a grave zeal, and an humble voice; his eyes always fixt on one place to prevent his imagination from wandring, insomuch, that he seem'd to study as he spake; the design of his Sermons (as indeed of all his Discourses) was to shew Reasons for what he spake; and with these Reasons, such a kind of Rhetorick, as did rather convince and perswade, than frighten men into piety; studying not so much for matter (which he never wanted) as for apt illustrations to inform and teach his unlearned Hearers by familiar Examples, and then make them better by convincing Applications; never labouring by hard words, and then by needless distinctions and sub-distinctions, to *amuse* his Hearers, and get glory to himself; but glory only to God. Which intention, he would often say, was as discernable in a Preacher, *as a Natural from an Artificial beauty.*

He never failed the *Sunday* before every *Ember-week*, to give notice of it to his Parishioners, perswading them both to fast, and then to double their devotions for a learned and pious Clergy: but especially the last, saying often, *That the Life of a pious Clergy-man was visible Rhetorick, and so convincing, that the most Godless men, (though they would not deny them-selves the enjoyment of their present lusts) did yet secretly wish themselves like those of the strictest lives*: And to what he perswaded others, he added his own example of Fasting and Prayer; and did usually every *Ember-week*, take from the Parish-Clerk the Key of the Church-door; into which place he retir'd every day, and lockt himself up for many hours; and did the like most *Fridays*, and other days of Fasting.

He would by no means omit the customary time of *Procession*, perswading all both rich and poor, if they desired the preservation of Love, and their Parish Rights and Liberties, to accompany him in his Per-ambulation, and most did so; in which Perambula-tion, he would usually express more pleasant Discourse than at other times, and would then always drop some loving and facetious observations to be remem-bred against the next year, especially by the boys and young people; still inclining them and all his pres-ent Parishioners, to meekness, and mutual kindnesses, and love; because *Love thinks not evil, but covers a multitude of Infirmities.*

He was diligent to inquire who of his Parish were sick, or any ways distrest, and would often visit them, unsent for; supposing, that the fittest time to discover to them those Errors to which health and prosperity had blinded them; and having by pious reasons and prayers, moulded them into holy resolutions for the time to come, he would incline them to confession, and bewailing their sins, with purpose to forsake them, and then to receive the Communion, both as a strengthning of those holy resolutions, and as a seal betwixt God and them of his Mercies to their Souls, in case that present sickness did put a period to their lives.

And as he was thus watchful and charitable to the sick, so he was as diligent to prevent Law-suits, still urging his Parishioners and Neighbours, to bear with each others infirmities, and live in love, because (as St. *John* says) *he that lives in love, lives in God, for God is love.* And to maintain this holy fire of love constantly burning on the Altar of a pure heart, his advice was to watch and pray, and always keep themselves fit to receive the Communion; and then to receive it often, for it was both a confirming and strengthning of their graces; this was his advice: And at his entrance or departure out of any house, he would usually speak to the whole Family, and bless them by name; insomuch, that as he seem'd in his youth to be taught of God, so he seem'd in this place to teach his precepts, as *Enoch* did by walking with him, in all holiness and humility, making each day a step towards a blessed Eternity. And though in this weak and declining Age of the World, such Examples are become barren, and almost incredible, yet let his memory be blest with this true Recordation, because he that praises *Richard Hooker*, praises God, who hath given such gifts to men; and let this humble and affectionate Relation of him, become such a pattern, as may invite Posterity to imitate these his vertues.

This was his constant behaviour both at *Borne* and in all the places in which he lived: thus did he walk with God, and tread the footsteps of primitive piety; and yet, as that great example of meekness and purity, even our blessed *Jesus*, was not free from false accusations, no more was this Disciple of his, this most humble, most innocent, holy man; his was a slander parallel to that of chaste *Susannah's* by the wicked

Elders, or that against St. *Athanasius,* as it is recorded
in his life, (for that holy man had heretical enemies)
a slander which this Age calls *Trepanning*; the particulars need not a repetition; and that it was false,
needs no other Testimony than the publick punishment of his Accusers, and their open confession of his
Innocency; 'twas said that the accusation was con-
triv'd by a dissenting Brother, one that endur'd not
Church-Ceremonies, hating him for his Books sake,
which he was not able to answer; and his name hath
been told me, but I have not so much confidence in
the relation, as to make my Pen fix a scandal on him
to posterity; I shall rather leave it doubtful till the
great day of Revelation: But this is certain, that he
lay under the great charge, and the anxiety of this
accusation, and kept it secret to himself for many
months; and being a helpless man, had lain longer
under this heavy burthen, but that the protector of
the innocent gave such an accidental occasion as
forced him to make it known to his two dearest friends,
Edwin Sandys, and *George Cranmer*: who were so
sensible of their Tutors sufferings, that they gave
themselves no rest, till by their disquisitions and
diligence they had found out the fraud, and brought
him the welcom News, that his Accusers did confess
they had wrong'd him, and beg'd his pardon: To
which, the good mans reply was to this purpose, *The
Lord forgive them,* and *the Lord bless you for this comfortable News*: Now I have a just occasion to say with
Solomon, Friends are born for the days of adversity,
and such you have prov'd to me; and to my God I
say, as did the mother of St. *John Baptist, Thus hath
the Lord dealt with me, in the day wherein he looked upon
me, to take away my reproach among men. And, oh my
God! neither my life, nor my reputation are safe in mine*

own keeping, but in thine, who didst take care of me,
when I yet hanged upon my mothers breast; blessed are
they, that put their trust in Thee O Lord; for when false
witnesses were risen up against me; when shame was ready
to cover my face, when my nights were restless, when my
Soul thirsted for a deliverance, as the Hart panteth after
the rivers of waters, then thou Lord didst hear my com-
plaints, pity my condition, and art now become my
deliverer; and as long as I live I will hold up my hands in
this manner, and magnifie thy mercies, who didst not give
me over as a prey to mine enemies, the net is broken and
they are taken in it. Oh blessed are they that put their
trust in thee; and no prosperity shall make me forget
those days of sorrow; or to perform those vows that I have
made to thee in the days of my affliction; for with such
Sacrifices, thou, O God, art well pleased, and I will
pay them.

Thus did the joy and gratitude of this good mans
heart break forth. And 'tis observable, that as the
invitation to this slander was his meek behaviour and
Dove-like simplicity, for which he was remarkable;
so his Christian charity ought to be imitated: for,
though the spirit of revenge is so pleasing to Mankind,
that it is never conquered but by a supernatural grace,
revenge being indeed so deeply rooted in Humane
Nature, that to prevent the excesses of it (for men would
not know Moderation) Almighty God allows not any
degree of it to any man, but says, *Vengeance is mine*:
And, though this be said positively by God himself,
yet this revenge is so pleasing, that man is hardly perswaded to submit the menage of it to the Time, and
Justice, and Wisdom of his Creator, but would hasten
to be his own Executioner of it: And yet nevertheless,
if any man ever did wholly decline, and leave this
pleasing passion to the time and measure of God alone,

it was this *Richard Hooker* of whom I write; for when his Slanderers were to suffer, he laboured to procure their pardon; and when that was denied him, his Reply was, *That however he would fast and pray, that God would give them repentance, and patience to undergo their punishment.* And his prayers were so far returned into his own bosom, that the first was granted, if we may believe a penitent behaviour, and an open confession. And 'tis observable, that after this time he would often say to Doctor *Saravia*, *Oh with what quietness did I enjoy my Soul after I was free from the fears of my Slander! and how much more after a conflict and victory over my desires of Revenge!*

About the Year 1600, and of his Age 46, he fell into a long and sharp sickness, occasioned by a cold taken in his passage by water betwixt *London* and *Gravesend*; from the malignity of which he was never recovered; for after that time till his death he was not free from thoughtful Days, and restless Nights; but a submission to his Will that makes the sick mans Bed easie by giving rest to his Soul, made his very languishment comfortable: and yet all this time he was sollicitous in his Study, and said often to Dr. *Saravia* (who saw him daily, and was the chief comfort of his life) *That he did not beg a long life of God, for any other reason, but to live to finish his three remaining Books of POLITY; and then, Lord, let thy servant depart in peace,* which was his usual expression. And God heard his prayers, though he denied the Church the benefit of them, as compleated by himself; and 'tis thought he hastened his own death, by hastening to give life to his Books: But this is certain, that the nearer he was to his death, the more he grew in *Humility*, in *Holy Thoughts* and *Resolutions*.

About a month before his death, this good man,

that never knew, or at least never consider'd, the pleasures of the Palate, became first to lose his appetite, and then, to have an aversness to all food; insomuch, that he seem'd to live some intermitted weeks by the smell of meat only, and yet still studied and writ. And now his guardian Angel seem'd to foretell him, that the day of his dissolution drew near; for which his vigorous Soul appear'd to thirst. In this time of his sickness, and not many days before his death, his House was rob'd; of which he having notice, his Question was, *Are my Books and written Papers safe?* And being answered, *That they were*; his Reply was, *then it matters not; for no other loss can trouble me.*

About one day before his Death, Dr. *Saravia*, who knew the very secrets of his Soul, (for they were supposed to be Confessors to each other) came to him, and after a Conference of the Benefit, the Necessity, and Safety of the Churches Absolution, it was resolved the Doctor should give him both that and the Sacrament the day following. To which end, the Doctor came, and after a short retirement and privacy, they two return'd to the company, and then the Doctor gave him, and some of those friends which were with him, the blessed Sacrament of the body and blood of our Jesus. Which being performed, the Doctor thought he saw a reverend gaity and joy in his face; but it lasted not long: for his bodily Infirmities did return suddenly, and became more visible, in so much that the Doctor apprehended death ready to seize him; yet, after some amendment, left him at Night, with a promise to return early the day following, which he did, and then found him better in appearance, deep in Contemplation, and not inclinable to Discourse; which gave the Doctor occasion to require his present Thoughts? to which he replied, *That he was meditating*

*the number and nature of Angels, and their blessed
obedience and order, without which peace could not be
in Heaven ; and oh that it might be so on Earth !* After
which words he said, *I have lived to see this world is
made up of perturbations, and I have been long preparing
to leave it, and gathering comfort for the dreadful hour
of making my account with God, which I now apprehend
to be near ; and though I have by his grace lov'd him in
my youth, and fear'd him in mine age, and labour'd to
have a conscience void of offence to him, and to all men ;
yet, if thou, O Lord, be extream to mark what I have done
amiss, who can abide it ? and therefore, where I have
failed, Lord shew mercy to me for I plead not my
righteousness, but the forgiveness of my unrighteousness,
for his merits who died to purchase pardon for penitent
sinners ; and since I owe thee a death, Lord let it not be
terrible, and then take thine own time, I submit to it ;
let not mine, O Lord, but let thy Will be done* ; with
which expression he fell into a dangerous slumber ;
dangerous, as to his recovery ; yet recover he did, but
it was to speak only these few words, *Good Doctor,
God hath heard my daily petitions, for I am at peace with
all men, and he is at peace with me ; and from that
blessed assurance I feel that inward joy, which this
world can neither give nor take from me : my Conscience
beareth me this witness, and this witness makes the
thoughts of death joyful. I could wish to live to do the
Church more service, but cannot hope it, for my dayes
are past as a shadow that returnes not*: More he would
have spoken, but his spirits failed him ; and after
a short conflict betwixt Nature and Death, a quiet
Sigh put a period to his last breath, and so he fell
asleep. And now he seems to rest like *Lazarus* in
Abrahams bosom ; let me here draw his Curtain, till
with the most glorious company of the *Patriarchs* and

Apostles, the most Noble Army of *Martyrs* and *Confessors*, this most learned, most humble, holy man, shall also awake to receive an eternal Tranquillity: and with it, a greater degree of Glory than common Christians shall be made partakers of.

> *In the mean time, bless* O Lord! *Lord bless his Brethren*, the Clergy of this Nation, *with effectual endeavours to attain, if not to his great learning, yet to his* remarkable meekness, *his* godly simplicity, *and his* Christian moderation; *for these will bring peace at the last: And, Lord! let his most excellent Writings be blest with what he design'd, when he undertook them: which was,* Glory to Thee O God on High, Peace in thy Church, and Good Will to Mankind. *Amen, Amen.*

Izaak Walton.

This following Epitaph was long since presented to the World, in memory of Mr. *Hooker*, by Sir *William Cooper*, who also built him a fair Monument in *Borne Church*, and acknowledges him to have been his Spiritual Father.

Though nothing can be spoke worthy his fame,
Or the remembrance of that precious name,
Judicious Hooker ; though this cost be spent
On him, that hath a lasting Monument
In his own Books, yet ought we to express,
If not his Worth, yet our Respectfulness.
Church-Ceremonies he maintain'd, then why
Without all Ceremony should he dye ?
Was it because his Life and Death should be
Both equal patterns of Humility ?
Or that perhaps this only glorious one
Was above all to ask, why had he none ?
Yet he that lay so long obscurely low,
Doth now preferr'd to greater Honours go.
Ambitious men, learn hence to be more wise,
Humility is the true way to rise :
And God in me this Lesson did inspire,
To bid this humble man, Friend sit up higher.

AN

APPENDIX

To the LIFE of

Mr. *RICHARD HOOKER.*

AND now having by a long and laborious search satisfied my self, and I hope my Reader, by imparting to him the true Relation of Mr. *Hookers* Life : I am desirous also, to acquaint him with some Observations that relate to it, and which could not properly fall to be spoken till after his death, of which my Reader may expect a brief and true account in the following Appendix.

And first it is not to be doubted, but that he died in the Forty-seventh, if not in the Forty-sixth year of his Age; which I mention, because many have believed him to be more aged ; but I have so examined it, as to be confident I mistake not; and for the year of his death, Mr. *Cambden*, who in his Annals of Queen *Elizabeth* 1599. mentions him with a high commendation of his Life and Learning, declares him to dye in the year 1599. and yet in that Inscription of his Monument set up at the charge of Sir *William Cooper* in *Borne Church*, where Mr. *Hooker* was buried : his death is there said to be in *Anno* 1603. but doubtless both mistaken ; for I have it attested under the hand of *William Somner* the Archbishops Register for the Province of *Canterbury*, that *Richard Hookers* Will bears date *Octob.* 26. in *Anno* 1600. and that it was prov'd the third of *December* following*.

* And the Reader may take notice, that since I first writ this Appendix to the Life of Mr. *Hooker*, Mr. *Fulman* of *Corpus Christi Colledge*, hath shewed me a good Authority for the very day and hour of Mr. *Hookers* death, in one of his Books of *Polity*, which had been *Archbishop Lauds*. In which Book, beside many considerable Marginal Notes of some passages of his time, under the *Bishops* own hand, there is also written in the Title page of that Book (which now is Mr. *Fulmans*) this Attestation:

Richardus Hooker *vir summis Doctrinæ dotibus ornatus, de Ecclesia præcipuè Anglicana optimè meritus, obiit* Novemb. 2. *circiter horam secundam postmeridianam.* Anno 1600.

And that at his death he left four Daughters, *Alice, Cicily, Jane* and *Margaret*; that he gave to each of them an hundred pound; that he left *Jone* his Wife his sole Executrix, and that by his Inventory, his Estate (a great part of it being in Books) came to 1092 *l.* 9 *s.* 2. *d.* which was much more than he thought himself worth; and which was not got by his care, much less by the good huswifery of his Wife, but saved by his trusty servant *Thomas Lane*, that was wiser than his Master in getting money for him, and more frugal than his Mistress in keeping of it; of which Will of Mr. *Hookers* I shall say no more, but that his dear friend *Thomas*, the father of *George Cranmer* (of whom I have spoken, and shall have occasion to say more) was one of the witnesses to it.

One of his elder Daughters was married to one *Chalinor*, sometime a School-master in *Chichester*, and are both dead long since: *Margaret* his youngest Daughter was married unto *Ezekiel Chark*, Batchelor in Divinity, and Rector of St. *Nicholas* in *Harble-down* near *Canterbury*, who died about 16 years past, and had a son *Ezekiel*, now living, and in Sacred Orders; being at this time Rector of *Waldron* in *Sussex*; she left also a Daughter, with both whom I have spoken not many months past, and find her to be a Widow in a condition that wants not, but very far from abounding; and these two attested unto me, that *Richard Hooker* their Grandfather had a Sister, by name *Elizabeth Harvey*, that liv'd to the Age of 121 Years, and dyed in the month of *September*, 1663.

For his other two Daughters I can learn little certainty, but have heard they both died before they were marriageable; and for his Wife, she was so unlike *Jeptha*'s Daughter, that she staid not a comely time to bewail her Widow-hood; nor liv'd long enough to repent her second marriage, for which doubtless she would have found cause, if there had been but four months betwixt Mr. *Hookers* and her death: But she is dead, and let her other infirmities be buried with her.

Thus much briefly for his Age, the Year of his Death, his Estate, his Wife, and his Children. I am next to speak of his Books: concerning which, I shall have a necessity of being longer, or shall neither do right to my self, or my Reader, which is chiefly intended in this Appendix.

I have declared in his Life, that he proposed eight Books, and that his first four were printed *Anno* 1594. and his fifth Book first printed, and alone, *Anno* 1597. and that he liv'd to finish the remaining three of the proposed eight, but whether we have the last three as finish't by himself, is a just and material Question; concerning which I do declare, that I have been told almost 40 Years past, by one that very well knew Mr. *Hooker*, and the affairs of his Family, that about a month after the death of Mr. *Hooker*, Bishop *Whitgift*, then Archbishop of *Canterbury*, sent one of his Chaplains to enquire of Mrs. *Hooker*, for the three remaining Books of Polity, writ by her Husband : of which she would not, or could not give any account ; and that about three months after that time the Bishop procured her to be sent for to *London*, and then by his procurement she was to be examined, by some of her Majesties Council, concerning the disposal of those Books ; but by way of preparation for the next dayes examination, the Bishop invited her to *Lambeth*, and, after some friendly questions, she confessed to him, *That one Mr.* Charke, *and another Minister that dwelt near* Canterbury, *came to her, and desired that they might go into her Husbands Study, and look upon some of his Writings: and that there they two burnt and tore many of them, assuring her, that they were Writings not fit to be seen, & that she knew nothing more concerning them.* Her lodging was then in *King-street* in *Westminster*, where she was found next morning dead in her Bed, and her new husband suspected and questioned for it ; but he was declared innocent of her death.

And I declare also, that Dr. *John Spencer* (mentioned in the Life of Mr. *Hooker*) who was of Mr. *Hookers* Colledge, and of his time there, and betwixt whom there was so friendly a friendship, that they continually advised together in all their Studies, and particularly in what concern'd these Books of Polity : This Dr. *Spencer*, the 3 perfect Books being lost, had delivered into his hands (I think by Bishop *Whitgift*) the imperfect Books, or first rough draughts of them, to be made as perfect as they might be, by him, who both knew Mr. *Hookers* hand-writing, and was best acquainted with his intentions. And a fair Testimony of this may appear by an Epistle first and usually printed before Mr. *Hookers* five Books (but omitted, I know not why, in the last impression of the eight printed together in *Anno* 1662, in which the Publishers seem to impose the three doubtful Books to be the undoubted Books of Mr. *Hooker*) with these two Letters *J. S.* at the end of the said Epistle, which was meant for this *John Spencer*: in which Epistle, the Reader may find these words, which may give some Authority to what I have here written of his last three Books.

And though Mr. Hooker *hastened his own death by hastening to give life to his Books, yet he held out with his eyes to behold these* Benjamins, *these sons of his right hand, though to him they prov'd* Benonies, *sons of pain and sorrow. But some evil disposed minds, whether of malice, or covetousness, or wicked blind zeal, it is uncertain, as soon as they were born, and their father dead, smother'd them, and, by conveying the perfect Copies, left unto us nothing but the old imperfect mangled draughts dismembred into pieces ; no favour, no grace, not the shadow of themselves remaining in them ; had the father lived to behold them thus defaced, he might rightly have named them* Benonies, *the sons of sorrow ; but being the learned will not suffer them to dye and be buried, it is intended the world shall see them as they are ; the learned will find in them some shadows and resemblances of their fathers face. God grant, that as they were with their Brethren dedicated to the Church for messengers of peace ; so, in the strength of that little breath of life that remaineth in them, they may prosper in their work, and by satisfying the doubts of such as are willing to learn, they may help to give an end to the calamities of these our Civill Wars.*

J.S.

And next the Reader may note, that this Epistle of Dr. *Spencers*, was writ and first printed within four years after the death of Mr. *Hooker*, in which time all diligent search had been made for the perfect Copies; and then granted not recoverable, and therefore endeavored to be compleated out of M. *Hookers* rough draughts, as is exprest by the said D. *Spencer*, in the said Epistle, since whose death it is now 50 Years.

And I do profess by the faith of a Christian, that Dr. *Spencers* Wife (who was my Aunt and Sister to *George Cranmer*, of whom I have spoken) told me forty Years since, in these, or in words to this purpose, *That her Husband had made up, or finish't Mr.* Hookers *last three Books; and that upon her Husbands Deathbed, or in his last Sickness, he gave them into her hand, with a charge they should not be seen by any man, but be by her delivered into the hands of the then Archbishop of* Canterbury, *which was Dr.* Abbot, *or unto Dr.* King *then Bishop of* London, *and that she did as he injoin'd her.*

I do conceive, that from D. *Spencers*, and no other Copy, there have been divers Transcripts, and I know that these were to be found in several places, as namely, Sir *Thomas Bodlies* Library, in that of D. *Andrews*, late Bishop of *Winton*, in the late Lord *Conwayes*, in the Archbishop of *Canterburies*, and in the Bishop of *Armaghs*, and in many others: and most of these pretended to be the Authors own hand, but much disagreeing, being indeed altered and diminisht, as men have thought fittest to make Mr. *Hookers* judgment suit with their fancies, or give authority to their corrupt designs; and for proof of a part of this, take these following Testimonies.

Dr. *Barnard*, sometime Chaplain to Dr. *Vsher*, late Lord Archbishop of *Armagh*, hath declar'd in a late Book called *Clavi Trebales*, printed by *Richard*

Hodgkinson, Anno 1661. that in his search and examination of the said Bishops Manuscripts, he found the three written Books which were supposed the 6, 7, and 8, of Mr. *Hookers* Books of Ecclesiastical Polity; and that in the said three Books (now printed as Mr. *Hookers*) there are so many omissions, that they amount to many Paragraphs, and which cause many incoherencies; the omissions are by him set down at large in the said printed Book, to which I refer the Reader for the whole; but think fit in this place to insert this following short part of some of the said omissions.

First, as there could be in Natural Bodies no Motion of any thing, unless there were some first which moved all things, and continued unmoveable; even so in Politick Societies, there must be some unpunishable, or else no man shall suffer punishment; for sith punishments proceed always from Superiors, to whom the administration of justice belongeth, which administration must have necessarily a fountain that deriveth it to all others, and receiveth not from any, because otherwise the course of justice should go infinitely in a Circle, every Superior having his Superior without end, which cannot be; therefore, a Well-spring, it followeth, there is, a Supream head of Justice whereunto all are subject, but it self in subjection to none. Which kind of preheminency if some ought to have in a Kingdom, who but the King shall have it? Kings therefore, or no man an have lawful power to judge.

If private men offend? there is the Magistrate over them which judgeth; if Magistrates? they have their Prince; if Princes? there is Heaven, a Tribunal, before which they shall appear, on Earth they are not accomptable to any. Here, says the Doctor, it breaks off abruptly.

And I have these words also attested under the hand of Mr. *Fabian Philips*, a man of Note for his useful Books. *I will make Oath, if I shall be required, that Dr.* Sanderson, *the late Bishop of* Lincoln, *did a little before his death, affirm to me, he had seen a Manuscript affirmed to him to be the hand-writing of Mr.* Richard Hooker, *in which there was no mention made of the King or Supream Governours being accomptable to the People; this I will make Oath, that that good man attested to me.* Fabian Philips.

So that there appears to be both Omissions and Additions in the said last three printed Books; and this may probably be one reason why Dr. *Sanderson*, the said learned Bishop (whose Writings are so highly and justly valued) gave a strict charge near the time of his Death, or in his last Will, *That nothing of his that was not already printed, should be printed after his Death.*

It is well known how high a value our learned King *James* put upon the Books writ by Mr. *Hooker*, and known also that our late King *Charles* (the Martyr for the Church) valued them the second of all Books, testified by his commending them to the reading of his Son *Charles*, that now is our gracious King; and you may suppose that this *Charles* the First, was not a stranger to the pretended three Books, because in a Discourse with the Lord *Say*, in the time of the *Long Parliament*, when the said Lord required the King to grant the truth of his Argument, because it was the judgment of Mr. *Hooker* (quoting him in one of the three written Books) the King replied, *They were not allowed to be Mr.* Hookers *Books*; but however *he would allow them to be Mr.* Hookers, *and consent to what his Lordship proposed to prove out of those doubtful Books, if he would but consent to the Judgment of Mr. Hooker in the other five that were the undoubted Books of Mr. Hooker.*

' In this relation concerning these three doubtful
' Books of Mr. *Hookers*, my purpose was to enquire,
' then set down what I observ'd and know, which I
' have done, not as an engaged person, but indifferently ;
' and now, leave my Reader to give sentence, for their
' legitimation, as to himself ; but so, as to leave others
' the same liberty of believing, or disbelieving them to
' be Mr. *Hookers* ; and 'tis observable, that as Mr.
' *Hooker* advis'd with Dr. *Spencer*, in the design and
' manage of these Books, so also, and chiefly with his
' dear Pupil *George Cranmer* (whose *Sister* was the
' Wife of Dr. *Spencer*) of which this following Letter
' may be a Testimony, and doth also give Authority to
' some things mentioned both in this Appendix, and in
' the life of Mr. *Hooker*, and is therefore added.

J.W.

George Cranmers Letter unto Mr. *Richard Hooker.* Feb. 1598.

WHat Posterity is likely to judge of these matters concerning *Church-Discipline*, we may the better conjecture, if we call to mind what our own Age, within few years, upon better Experience, hath already judged concerning the same. It may be remembred, that at first the greatest part of the Learned in the Land, were either eagerly affected, or favourably inclined that way. The Books then written for the most part savoured of the Disciplinary stile ; it sounded every where in Pulpits, and in common phrase of mens speech: the contrary part began to fear they had taken a wrong course, many which impugned the Discipline, yet so impugned it, not as not being the better Form of Government, but as not being so convenient for our State, in regard of dangerous Innovations there-   * *John Whitgift* by like to grow; * one man alone there   the Archbishop. was, to speak of (whom let no suspition of flattery deprive of his deserved commendation) who in the defiance of the one part, and courage of the other, stood in the gap, and gave others respite to prepare themselves to the defence, which by the sudden eagerness and violence of their adversaries, had otherwise been prevented, wherein God hath made good unto him his own Impress, *Vincit qui patitur*; for what contumelious indignities he hath at their hands sustained, the World is witness; and what reward of Honour above his Adversaries God hath bestowed upon him, themselves (though nothing glad thereof) must needs confess. Now of late years the heat of men towards the Discipline is greatly decayed, their judgments begin to sway on the other side: the Learned have weighed it, and found it light; wise men conceive some fear, lest it prove not only not the best kind of Government, but the very bane and destruction of all Government. The cause of this change in mens Opinions, may be drawn from the general nature of Error, disguised and cloathed with the name of Truth; which did mightily and violently possess men at first, but afterwards, the weakness thereof being by time discovered, it lost that reputation, which before it had gained; as by the outside of an house the passers by are oftentimes deceived, till they see the conveniency of the Rooms within: so by the very name of *Discipline* and *Reformation*, men were drawn at first to cast a fancy towards it, but now they have not contented themselves only to pass by and behold afar off the Fore-front of this reformed house ; they have entered in, even at the special request of Master-workmen and chief builders thereof : they have perused the Rooms, the Lights, the Conveniencies, and they find them not answerable to that report which was made of them, nor to that opinion which upon report they had conceived : So as now, the Discipline which at first triumphed over all, being unmasked, beginneth to droop and hang down her head.

This cause of change in opinion concerning the Discipline, is proper to the Learned, or to such as by them have been instructed ; another cause there is more open, and more apparent to the view of all, namely, the course of Practice, which the Reformers have had with us from the beginning ; the first degree was onely some small difference about the *Cap* and *Surplice,* but not such as either bred division in the Church, or tended to the ruine of the Government established. This was peaceable ; the next degree more stirring. *Admonitions* were directed to the Parliament in peremptory sort against our whole Form of Regiment ; in defence of them, Volumes were published in English, and in Latin ; yet this was no more than writing. Devices were set on foot to erect the Practice of the Discipline without Authority ; yet herein some regard of Modesty, some moderation was used ; Behold, at length it brake forth into open outrage, first in writing by *Martin*, in whose kind of dealing these things may be observed ; first, that whereas *T.C.* and others his great Masters had always before set out the Discipline as a Queen, and as the Daughter of God ; He contrarywise, to make her more acceptable to the people, brought her forth as a Vice upon the Stage.

2. This conceit of his was grounded (as may be supposed) upon this rare policy, that seeing the Discipline was by writing refuted, in Parliament rejected, in secret corners hunted out and decryed, it was imagined that by open rayling (which to the Vulgar is commonly most plausible) the State Ecclesiastical might have been drawn into such contempt and hatred, as the overthrow thereof should have been most grateful to all men, and in a manner desired by all the Common people. 3. It may be noted, (and this I know my self to be true) how some of them, although they could not for shame approve so lewd an Action : yet were content to lay hold on it to the advancement of their cause, by acknowledging therein the secret Judgments of God against the Bishops : and hoping that some good might be wrought thereby for his Church ; as indeed there was, though not according to their construction. For, 4. contrary to their expectation, that railing Spirit did not only not further, but extremely disgrace and prejudice their Cause, when it was once perceived from how low degrees of contradiction, at first, to what outrage of Contumely and Slander they were at length proceeded ; and were also likely to proceed further.

A further degree of outrage was also in Fact ; Certain * Prophets did arise, who deeming it not possible that God should suffer that to be undone, which they did so *Hacket and Coppinger.* fiercely desire to have done, Namely, that his holy Saints, the favourers and Fathers of the Discipline, should be enlarged, and delivered from persecution ; and seeing no means of Deliverance Ordinary, were fain to perswade themselves that God must needs raise some extraordinary means ; and being perswaded of none so well as of themselves, they forthwith must needs be the instruments of this great work. Hereupon they framed unto themselves an assured hope that upon their Preaching out of a Pease Cart in *Cheapside*, all the multitude would have presently joyned unto them; and in amazement of mind have asked them, *Viri fratres, quid agimus?* whereunto it is likely they would have returned an answer far unlike to that of St. Peter, *Such and such are men unworthy to govern, pluck them down; Such and such are the dear Children of God, let them be advanced.*

Of two of these men it is meet to speak with all Commiseration: yet so, that others by their example may receive instruction, and withal some light may appear, what stirring affections the Discipline is like to inspire, if it light upon apt and prepared minds.

Now, if any man doubt of what Society they were? or, if the Reformers disclaim them, pretending, that by them they were condemned; let these points be considered. 1. *Whose associates were they before they entered into this frantick Passion? whose Sermons did they frequent? whom did they admire?* 2. *Even when they were entering into it, whose advice did they require?* and when they were in, *whose approbation? whom advertised they of their purpose? whose assistance by Prayer did they request?* But we deal injuriously with them to lay this to their charge; for they reproved and condemned it. How? did they disclose it to the Magistrate, that it might be suppressed? or were they not rather content to stand aloof of, and see the end of it, as being loath to quench that Spirit, No doubt these mad practitioners were of their society, with whom before, and in the practice of their madness they had most affinity. Hereof read Dr. *Bancrofts* Book.

A third inducement may be to dislike of the Discipline, if we consider not only how far the Reformers themselves have proceeded, but what others upon their Foundations have built. Here come the *Brownists* in the first rank: their lineal descendants: who have seised upon a number of strange opinions: whereof, although their Ancestors, the Reformers, were never actually possessed, yet by right and interest from them derived, the *Brownists* and *Barrowists* have taken possession of them; for if the positions of the Reformers be true, I cannot see how the main and general Conclusions of *Brownism* should be false; for, upon these two points, as I conceive, they stand.

1. That because we have no Church, they are to sever themselves from us. 2. That without Civil Authority they are to erect a Church of their own. And if the former of these be true, the latter, I suppose will follow; for if above all things, men be to regard their Salvation; and if out of the Church there be no Salvation; it followeth, that if we have no Church, we have no means of Salvation; and therefore separation from us, in that respect, is both lawful and necessary; as also that men so separated from the false and counterfeit Church, are to associate themselves unto some Church; not to ours; to the Popish much less; therefore to one of their own making: Now the ground of all these Inferences being this, (*That in our Church there is no means of Salvation*) is out of the Reformers Principles most clearly to be proved. For wheresoever any matter of Faith unto Salvation necessary is denyed, there can be no means of Salvation; But in the Church of *England*, the Discipline, by them accounted a matter of Faith, and necessary to Salvation, is not onely denyed, but impugned, and the Professors thereof oppressed. *Ergo.*

Again, (but this reason perhaps is weak) Every true

Church of Christ acknowledgeth the whole Gospel of Christ : The Discipline, in their opinion, is a part of the Gospel, and yet by our Church resisted. *Ergo.*

Again, the Discipline is essentially united to the Church : by which term *Essentially*, they must mean either an essential part, or an essential property. Both which ways it must needs be, that where that essential Discipline is not, neither is there any Church. If therefore between them and the *Brownists*, there should be appointed a Solemn disputation, whereof with us they have been oftentimes so earnest Challengers : it doth not yet appear what other answer they could possibly frame to these and the like arguments, wherewith they may be pressed, but fairly to deny the Conclusion (for all the Premisses are their own) or rather ingeniously to reverse their own Principles, before laid, whereon so foul absurdities have been so firmly built. What further proofs you can bring out of their high words, magnifying the Discipline, I leave to your better remembrance : but above all points, I am desirous this one should be strongly inforced against them, because it wringeth them most of all, and is of all others (for ought I see) the most unanswerable ; you may notwithstanding say, that you would be heartily glad these their positions might be salved as the Brownists might not appear to have issued out of their Loyns : but until that be done, they must give us leave to think that *they have cast the Seed whereout these tares are grown.*

Another sort of men there are, which have been content to run on with the Reformers for a time, and to make them poor instruments of their own designs : These are a sort of *Godless Politicks*, who perceiving the Plot of *Discipline* to consist of these two parts, the overthrow of Episcopal, and erections of Presbyterial Authority, and that this latter can take no place till the former be removed, are content to joyn with them in the Destructive part of Discipline, bearing them in hand, that in the other also they shall find them as ready. But when time shall come, it may be they would be as loath to be yoaked with that kind of Regiment, as now they are willing to be released from this; These mens ends in all their actions, is Distraction, their pretence and colour, Reformation. Those things which under this colour they have effected to their own good, are, 1. By maintaining a contrary faction, they have kept the Clergy alwayes in Awe, and thereby made them more pliable and willing to buy their peace. 2. By maintaining an Opinion of Equality among Ministers, they have made way to their own purposes for devouring Cathedral Churches, and Bishops livings. 3. By exclaiming against abuses in the Church, they have carried their own corrupt dealings in the Civil State more covertly; for such is the Nature of the multitude, that they are not able to apprehend many things at once; so as being possessed with a dislike or liking of any one thing, many other in the mean time may escape them without being perceived. 4. They have sought to disgrace the Clergy, in entertaining a conceit in mens minds, and confirming it by continual practice, *That men of Learning, and specially of the Clergy, which are imployed in the chiefest kind of Learning, are not to be admitted, or sparingly admitted to matter of State*; contrary to the practice of all well-governed Commonwealths, and of our own till these late years.

A third sort of men there are, though not descended from the Reformers, yet in part raised and greatly strengthened by them; namely, the *cursed crew of Atheists*. This also is one of those points, which I am desirous you should handle most effectually, and strain your self therein to all points of motion and affection ; as, in that of the *Brownists*, to all strength and sinews of Reason. This is a sort most damnable, and yet by the general suspition of the world at this day most common. The causes of it, which are in the parties themselves (although you handle in the beginning of the fifth Book,) yet here again they may be touched ; but the occasions of help and furtherance, which by the Reformers have been yielded unto them, are, as I conceive, two ; namely, *Senseless Preaching*, and *disgracing of the Ministry* ; for how should not men dare to impugn that, which neither by force of Reason, nor by Authority of Persons is maintained ; But in the parties themselves these two causes I conceive of Atheism, 1. more abundance of Wit then Judgment, and of Witty than Judicious Learning, whereby they are more inclined to contradict any thing, than willing to be informed of the Truth. They are not therefore men of sound Learning for the most part, but Smatterers ; neither is their kind of Dispute so much by force of Argument, as by Scoffing ; which humour of scoffing, and turning matters most serious into merriment, is now become so common, as we are not to marvel what the Prophet means by the *Seat of Scorners*, nor what the Apostles by foretelling of *Scorners to come* ; for our own age hath verified their speech unto us ; which also may be an Argument against these Scoffers and Atheists themselves, seeing it hath been so many ages ago foretold, that such men the later dayes of the world should afford : which could not be done by any other Spirit, save that whereunto *things future and present are alike*. And even for the main question of the Resurrection, whereat they stick so mightily ! was it not plainly foretold, that men should in the latter

times say, *Where is the Promise of his Coming?*
Against the Creation, the Ark, and divers other points,
exceptions are said to be taken, the ground whereof
is superfluity of Wit, without ground of Learning and
Judgment. A second cause of Atheism is *Sensuality*,
which maketh men desirous to remove all stops and
impediments of their wicked life; among which,
because Religion is the chiefest, so as neither in this
life without shame they can persist therein, nor (if
that be true) without Torment in the life to come:
they therefore whet their wits to annihilate the joys
of Heaven, wherein they see (if any such be) they can
have no part, and likewise the pains of Hell, wherein
their portion must needs be very great. They labour
therefore, not that they may not deserve those pains,
but that deserving them, there may be no such pains
to seize upon them; But what conceit can be
imagined more base, than that man should strive to
perswade himself even against the secret Instinct (no
doubt) of his own Mind, that his Soul is as the Soul
of a Beast, mortal and corruptible with the Body?
Against which barbarous Opinion, their own Atheism
is a very strong Argument. For were not the Soul a
Nature separable from the Body, how could it enter
into discourse of things meerly Spiritual, and nothing
at all pertaining to the Body? Surely the Soul were
not able to conceive any thing of Heaven, no not so
much as to dispute against Heaven and against God,
if there were not in it somewhat Heavenly and derived
from God.

The last which have received strength and encouragement from the Reformers are *Papists*; against whom
although they are most bitter Enemies, yet unwittingly
they have given them great advantage. For what
can any Enemy rather desire than the Breach and

Dissention of those which are Confederates against him ? Wherein they are to remember, that if our Communion with Papists in some few Ceremonies do so much strengthen them as is pretended, how much more doth this Division and Rent among our selves, especially seeing it is maintained to be, not in light matters only, but even in matter of Faith and Salvation ? Which over-reaching Speech of theirs, because it is so open an advantage for the *Barrowist* and the *Papist*, we are to wish and hope for, that they will acknowledge it to have been spoken rather in heat of Affection, than with soundness of Judgment ; and that through their exceeding love to that Creature of *Discipline* which themselves have bred, nourished, and maintained, their mouth in commendation of her did so often overflow.

From hence you may proceed (but the means of connexion I leave to your self) to another discourse, which I think very meet to be handled either here or elsewhere at large ; the parts whereof may be these. 1. That in this cause between them and us, men are to sever the proper and essential points and controversie, from those which are accidental. The most essential and proper are these two : overthrow of Episcopal, and erection of Presbyterial Authority. But in these two points whosoever joineth with them is accounted of their number ; whosoever in all other points agreeth with them, yet thinketh the Authority of Bishops not unlawful, and of Elders not necessary, may justly be severed from their retinue. Those things therefore, which either in the Persons, or in the Laws and Orders themselves are faulty, may be complained on, acknowledged and amended ; yet they no whit the nearer their main purpose ; for what if all errors by them supposed in our Liturgy were amended, even according to their own hearts desire ? if *Non-residence*, *Pluralities*, and the like, were utterly taken away ? are their *Lay-Elders* therefore presently Authorized ? or their Soveraign Ecclesiastical Jurisdiction established ?

But even in their complaining against the outward and accidental matters in Church-government, they are many ways faulty : 1. In their end, which they propose to themselves. For in Declaming against Abuses, their meaning is not to have them redressed, but by disgracing the present State, to make way for their own Discipline. As therefore in *Venice*, if any Senatour should discourse against the Power of their Senate, as being either *too Soveraign*, or *too weak* in Government, with purpose to draw their Authority to a Moderation, it might well be suffered ; but not so, if it should appear he spake with purpose to induce another State by depraving the present : So, in all Causes belonging either to Church or Commonwealth, we are to have regard what mind the Complaining part doth bear, whether of Amendment or Innovation ; and accordingly either to suffer or suppress it. Their Objection therefore is frivolous, *Why may not men speak against Abuses ?* Yes ; but with desire to *cure the part affected, not to destroy the whole.* 2. A second fault is in their Manner of Complaining, not only because it is for the most part in bitter and reproachful Terms, but also it is to the Common people, who are Judges incompetent and insufficient, both to determine any thing amiss, and for want of Skill and Authority to amend it. Which also discovereth their Intent and Purpose to be rather Destructive than Corrective. 3. Thirdly, those very exceptions which they take are frivolous and impertinent : Some things indeed they accuse as impious, which if they may appear to be such, God forbid they should be maintained.

Against the rest it is only alledged, that they are Idle Ceremonies without use, and that better and more profitable might be devised. Wherein they are doubly deceived ; for neither is it a sufficient Plea to say, This must give place, because a Better may be devised ; because in our Judgments of Better and Worse, we oftentimes conceive amiss, when we compare those things which are in Devise, with those which are in Practice ; *for the Imperfections of the one are hid, till by Time and Trial they be discovered* : The others are already manifest and open to all. But last of all (which is a Point in my Opinion of great regard, and which I am desirous to have enlarg'd) they do not see that for the most part when they strike at the State Ecclesiastical, they secretly wound the Civil State : for Personal faults, *What can be said against the Church, which may not also agree to the Commonwealth ?* In both States Men have always been, and will be always, Men ; sometimes blinded with Error, most commonly perverted by passions : many Unworthy have been and are advanced in both, many Worthy not regarded. And as for Abuses which they pretend to be in the Laws themselves, when they inveigh against *Non-residence*, do they take it a matter lawful or expedient in the Civil State for a man to have a great and gainful Office in the North, himself continually remaining in the South ? *He that hath an Office, let him attend his Office.* When they condemn *Plurality* of Livings Spiritual to the pit of Hell, what think they of the Infinite of Temporal Promotions ? By the great Philosopher, *Pol.lib.2.c.9.* it is forbidden as a thing most dangerous to Commonwealths, that by the same man many great Offices should be exercised : When they deride our Ceremonies as vain and frivolous, were it hard to apply their Exceptions even to those

Civil Ceremonies, which at the Coronation, in Parliament, and all Courts of Justice, are used ; Were it hard to argue even against Circumcision, the Ordinance of God, as being a cruel Ceremony ? against the Passeover, as being ridiculous, should be girt, a Staff in their hand, to eat a Lamb.

To conclude ; you may exhort the Clergy (or what if you direct your Conclusion not to the Clergy in general, but only to the Learned in or of both Universities ?) you may exhort them to a due Consideration of all things, and to a right Esteem and Valuing of each thing in that degree wherein it ought to stand. For it oftentimes falleth out, that what Men have either devised themselves, or greatly delighted in, the Price and the Excellency thereof they do admire above desert. The chiefest Labour of a Christian should be to know ; of a Minister, to preach Christ crucified : in regard whereof, not only Worldly things, but things otherwise precious, even the Discipline it self is vile and base : Whereas now by the heat of Contention, and violence of Affection, the Zeal of men towards the one hath greatly decayed their Love to the other. Hereunto therefore they are to be exhorted, to *Preach Christ crucified*, the *Mortification* of the *Flesh*, the Renewing of the *Spirit* ; not those things which in time of Strife seem precious, but (Passions being allayed) are vain and childish.

G. C.

FINIS

THE

LIFE

OF

Mr. *GEORGE HERBERT.*

Wisdom of Salom. 4. 10.

He pleased God, and was beloved of him: so that whereas
he lived among sinners, he translated him.

LONDON,
Printed in the Year 1675.

*To his very Worthy and much Hon-
oured Friend Mr.* Izaak Walton,
upon his Excellent Life of Mr.
GEORGE HERBERT.

I.

Heav'ns youngest Son, its *Benjamin*,
　　Divinity's next Brother, *Sacred Poesie*,
　　No longer shall a Virgin reckoned be,
　(What ere with others 'tis) by me,
　A Female Muse, as were the Nine :
　　But (full of Vigor Masculine)
An Essence Male, with Angels his Companions shine.
With Angels first the heavenly youth was bred ;
And, when a Child, instructed them to sing,
　　The praises of th'Immortal King,
　　Who *Lucifer* in Triumph led :
For, as in Chains the Monster sank to Hell,
And tumbling headlong down the precipice fell,
By him first taught, *How art thou fallen thou morning*
　　　　　　　　　　　　　　[*star ?* they said
Too fondly then, we have fancy'd him a Maid :
We, the vain Brethren of the rhyming trade ;
A femal Angel less would * *Urbins* skill upbraid.

　　* *Raphael Urbin* the famous painter.

II.

Thus 'twas in Heaven: This, *Poesy*'s Sex and Age;
And, when he thence t'our lower World came down.
    He chose a Form more like his own,
And *Jesse*'s youngest Son inspir'd with holy rage,
The sprightly Shepherd felt unusual Fire,
    And up he took his tuneful Lyre;
He took it up, and struck't, and his own soft touches
                            [did admire.
    Thou, Poesie, on him didst bestow
Thy choicest gift, a honor shew'd before to none;
And, to prepare his way to th'Hebrew Throne,
Gav'st him thy Empire, and Dominion;
    The happy Land of Verse, where flow
Rivers of Milk, and Woods of Laurel grow;
    Wherewith thou didst adorn his brow,
And mad'st his first, more flourishing, and triumphant
                            [Crown.
Assist me thy great Prophets praise to sing,
David, the Poets, and bless'd *Israels* King;
And, with the dancing Echo, let the mountains ring!
Then, on the wings of some auspicious wind,
Let his great name from earth be rais'd on high,
And in the starry volume of the Sky,
    A lasting Record find:
    Be with his mighty *Psaltery* join'd;
Which, taken long since up into the Air,
And call'd the *Harp*, makes a bright Constellation
                            [there.

III.

Worthy it was to be translated hence,
And, there, in view of all, exalted hang:

To which so oft the Princely Prophet sang,
  And mystick Oracles did dispence.
    Though, had it still remain'd below,
    More wonders of it we had seen,
How great the mighty *Herberts* skill had been;
Herbert, who could so much without it do;
Herbert, who did its Chords distinctly know,
More perfectly, than any Child of Verse below.
  O! Had we known him half so well!
But then, my friend, there had been left for you
Nothing so fair, and worthy praise to do;
Who so exactly all his Story tell,
    That, though he did not want his Bays,
    Nor all the Monuments vertue can raise,
Your hand, he did, to Eternize his Praise.
  Herbert, and *Donne*, again are join'd,
    Now here below, as they're above;
These friends are in their old embraces twin'd;
And, since by you the Enterview's design'd,
    Too weak, to part them, death does prove;
For in this book they meet again; as in one **Heav'n**
              [they love.

Bensted,
Apr. 3.
1670.

Sam. Woodforde D.D.

In Vitam *Georgii Herberti* ab *Isaaco Waltono* Scriptam.

O Quàm erubesco cum tuam vitam lego,
    Herberte *Sancte*, quamq̇; me pudet meæ!
    Ego talpa cæcus hic humi fodiens miser,
Aquila volatu tu petens nubes tuo,
Ego Choicum vas terreas fæces olens,
Tu (sola namq̇, Vrania tibi ex musis placet)
Nil tale spiras; sed sapis cœlum & Deum,
Omniq̇; vitæ, libri & omni, lineâ;
Templûmq̇; tecum ubiq̇; circumfers tuum:
Domi-porta cœli, cui domus propria, optima:
Vbi Rex, ibi Roma, Imperii sedes; ubi
Tu sancte vates, templum ibi, & cœlum, & Deus.
Tu quale nobis intuendum clericis
Speculum Sacerdotale, tu qualem piis
Pastoris ideam & libro & vitâ tuâ
Tu quale Sanctitatis elementis bonæ,
Morumq̇; nobis tradis exemplum ac typum!
Typum,* Magistro nempe proximum Tuo,
Exemplar illud grande qui solus fuit.
Canonizet ergò quos velit Dominus Papa;
Sibiq̇; sanctos, quos facit, servet suos
Colátque; sancte Herberte, tu Sanctus meus;
Oraq̇; pro me, dicerem, si fas, tibi.
Sed hos honores par nec est sanctis dari;
Velis nec ipse; recolo te, sed non colo.
Talis legenda est vita Sancti, concio
Ad promovendum quàm potens & efficax!

* Sic Christum solens vocavit quoties ejus mentionem fecit.

256

Per talia exempla est breve ad cœlos iter.
Waltone, macte, perge vitas scribere,
Et penicillo, quo Vales, insigni adhuc
Sanctorum imagines coloribus suis
Plures repræsentare; quod tu dum facis
Vitamq; & illis & tibi das Posthumam,
Lectoris æternæq; vitæ consulis.
Vrge ergò pensum; at interim scias velim,
Plutarchus alter sis licèt Biogræphus,
Herberto, Amice, vix Parallelum dabis.
Liceat Libro addere hanc coronidem tuo;
Vir, an Poeta, Orator an melior fuit,
Meliornè amicus, sponsus, an Pastor Gregis,
Herbertus, incertum; & quis hoc facilè sciat,
Melior ubi ille, qui fuit ubiq; optimus.

Jacob. Duport. *S.T.P.*
Decanus Petr.

THE
LIFE
OF
Mr. *GEORGE HERBERT.*

The Introduction.

IN *a late retreat from the business of this World, and those many little cares with which I have too often cumbred my self, I fell into a Contemplation of some of those Historical passages that are recorded in* Sacred Story ; *and, more particularly, of what had past betwixt our* Blessed Saviour, *and that wonder of Women, and Sinners, and Mourners,* Saint Mary Magdalen. *I call her* Saint, *because I did not then, nor do now consider her, as when she was possest with seven Devils; not as when her wanton Eyes, and dissheveld Hair, were designed and manag'd, to charm and insnare amorous Beholders: But I did then, and do now consider her, as after she had exprest a visible and sacred sorrow for her sensualities; as after those Eyes had wept such a flood of penitential tears as did wash, and that hair had wip't, and she most passionately kist the feet of hers, and our blessed* Jesus. *And I do now consider, that because she lov'd much, not only much was forgiven her : but that,*

258

*beside that blessed blessing of having her sins pardoned,
and the joy of knowing her happy Condition, she also had
from him a testimony, that her* Alablaster *box of precious
oyntment poured on his head and feet, and that* Spike-
nard, *and those* Spices *that were by her dedicated to
embalm and preserve his sacred body from putrefaction,
should so far preserve her own memory, that these demonstrations of her sanctified love, and of her officious, and
generous gratitude, should be recorded and mentioned
wheresoever his Gospel should be read: intending thereby,
that as his, so her name should also live to succeeding
generations, even till time it self shall be no more.*

*Upon occasion of which fair example, I did lately
look back, and not without some content* (at least
to my self) *that I have endeavour'd to deserve the love,
and preserve the memory of my two deceased friends,*
Dr. Donne, *and* Sir Henry Wotton, *by declaring the
several employments and various accidents of their Lives :
And though Mr.* George Herbert (whose Life I now
intend to write) *were to me a stranger as to his person,
for I have only seen him: yet since he was, and was
worthy to be their friend, and very many of his have
been mine; I judge it may not be unacceptable to those
that knew any of them in their lives, or do now know
them by mine, or their own Writings, to see this Conjunction
of them after their deaths ; without which, many things
that concern'd them, and some things that concern'd the
Age in which they liv'd, would be less perfect, and lost
to posterity.*

For these Reasons I have undertaken it, and if I
have prevented any abler person, I beg pardon of him,
and my Reader.

The *LIFE*.

George Herbert was born the third day of *April,* in the Year of our Redemption 1593. The place of his Birth was near to the Town of *Montgomery,* and in that *Castle* that did then bear the name of that Town and County; that *Castle* was then a place of state and strength, and had been successively happy in the Family of the *Herberts,* who had long possest it: and, with it, a plentiful Estate, and hearts as liberal to their poor Neighbours. A Family, that hath been blest with men of remarkable wisdom, and a willingness to serve their Country, and indeed, to do good to all Mankind; for which they are eminent: But alas! this Family did in the late Rebellion suffer extreamly in their Estates; and the Heirs of that *Castle* saw it laid level with that earth that was too good to bury those Wretches that were the cause of it.

The Father of our *George,* was *Richard Herbert* the Son of *Edward Herbert* Knight, the Son of *Richard Herbert* Knight, the Son of the famous Sir *Richard Herbert* of *Colebrook* in the County of *Monmouth* Banneret, who was the youngest Brother of that memorable *William Herbert* Earl of *Pembroke,* that liv'd in the Reign of our King *Edward* the fourth.

His Mother was *Magdalen Newport,* the youngest Daughter of Sir *Richard,* and Sister to Sir *Francis Newport* of *High Arkall* in the County of *Salop* Kt. and Grand-father of *Francis* Lord *Newport,* now Comptroller of His Majesties Houshold. A Family, that for their Loyalty, have suffered much in their

Estates, and seen the ruine of that excellent Structure, where their Ancestors have long liv'd, and been memorable for their Hospitality.

This Mother of *George Herbert* (of whose person and wisdom, and vertue, I intend to give a true account in a seasonable place) was the happy Mother of seven Sons, and three Daughters, which she would often say, was *Job's number*, and *Job's distribution* ; and as often bless God, that they were neither defective in their shapes, or in their reason ; and very often reprove them that did not praise God for so great a blessing. I shall give the Reader a short accompt of their names, and not say much of their Fortunes.

Edward the eldest was first made Kt. of the *Bath*, at that glorious time of our late Prince *Henries* being install'd Knight of the Garter ; and after many years useful travel, and the attainment of many Languages, he was by King *James* sent Ambassador Resident to the then *French* King, *Lewis* the Thirteenth. There he continued about two Years ; but he could not subject himself to a compliance with the humors of the Duke *de Luines*, who was then the great and powerful Favourite at Court : so that upon a complaint to our King, he was call'd back into *England* in some displeasure ; but at his return he gave such an honourable account of his employment, and so justified his Comportment to the Duke, and all the Court, that he was suddenly sent back upon the same Embassie, from which he return'd in the beginning of the Reign of our good King *Charles* the first, who made him first Baron of *Castle-Island* ; and not long after of *Cherbery* in the County of *Salop* : *He was a man of great learning and reason, as appears by his printed Book* de veritate ; *and by his History of the Reign of K. Hen. the Eight, &* *by several other Tracts.*

The second and third Brothers were *Richard* and *William*, who ventur'd their lives to purchase Honour in the Wars of the *Low Countries*, and died Officers in that employment. *Charles* was the fourth, and died Fellow of *New-Colledge* in *Oxford*. *Henry* was the sixth, who became a menial servant to the Crown in the daies of King *James*, and hath continued to be so for fifty years : during all which time he hath been Master of the Revels ; a place that requires a diligent wisdom, with which God hath blest him. The seventh Son was *Thomas*, who being made Captain of a Ship in that Fleet with which Sir *Robert Mansel* was sent against *Algiers*, did there shew a fortunate and true English valor. Of the three Sisters, I need not say more, then that they were all married to persons of worth, and plentiful fortunes ; and liv'd to be examples of *vertue*, and to do good in their generations.

I now come to give my intended account of *George*, who was the fifth of those seven Brothers.

George Herbert spent much of his Childhood in a sweet content under the eye and care of his prudent mother, and the tuition of a Chaplain or Tutor to him, and two of his Brothers, in her own Family (for she was then a Widow) where he continued, till about the age of twelve years ; and being at that time well instructed in the Rules of Grammar, he was not long after commended to the care of Dr. *Neale*, who was then Dean of *Westminster* ; and by him to the care of Mr. *Ireland*, who was then chief Master of that School ; where the beauties of his pretty behaviour and wit, shin'd and became so eminent and lovely in this his innocent age, that he seem'd to be marked out for piety, and to become the care of Heaven, and of a particular good Angel to guard and guide him. And thus, he continued in that School, till he came to be perfect in the learned Languages, and especially in the Greek Tongue, in which he after prov'd an excellent Critick.

About the age of Fifteen, he, being then a Kings Scholar, was elected out of that School for *Trinity Colledge* in *Cambridge*, to which place he was transplanted about the year 1608. and his prudent mother well knowing, that he might easily lose, or lessen that virtue and innocence which her advice and example had planted in his mind; did therefore procure the generous and liberal Dr. *Nevil*, who was then Dean of *Canterbury*, and Master of that Colledge, to take him into his particular care, and provide him a Tutor; which he did most gladly undertake, for he knew the excellencies of his Mother, and how to value such a friendship.

This was the method of his Education, till he was setled in *Cambridge*, where we will leave him in his Study, till I have paid my promis'd account of his excellent Mother, and I will endeavour to make it short.

I have told her birth, her Marriage, and the Number of her Children, and have given some short account of them: I shall next tell the Reader, that her husband dyed when our *George* was about the Age of four years: I am next to tell that she continued twelve years a Widow: that she then married happily to a Noble Gentleman, the Brother and Heir of the Lord *Danvers* Earl of *Danby*, who did highly value both her person and the most excellent endowments of her mind.

In this time of her Widowhood, she being desirous to give *Edward* her eldest son, such advantages of Learning, and other education as might suit his birth and fortune: and thereby make him the more fit for the service of his Country: did at his being of a fit age, remove from *Montgomery Castle* with him, and some of her younger sons to *Oxford*; and having entred *Edward* into *Queens Colledge*, and provided him a fit *Tutor*, she commended him to his Care; yet she continued there with him, and still kept him in a moderate awe of her self: and so much under her own eye, as to see and converse with him daily; but she managed this power over him without any such rigid sourness, as might make her company a torment to her Child; but with such a sweetness and complyance with the recreations and pleasures of youth, as did incline him willingly to spend much of his time in the company of his dear and careful Mother: which was to her great content: for, she would often say, "That as our bodies take a nourishment sutable to "the meat on which we feed: so, our souls do as "insensibly take in vice by the example or Conversation "with wicked Company: and would therefore as "often say, "That ignorance of Vice was the best "preservation of Vertue: and, that the very knowledge "of wickedness was as tinder to inflame and kindle "sin, and to keep it burning. For these reasons she indeared him to her own Company: and continued with him in *Oxford* four years: in which time, her *great* and *harmless wit*, her *chearful gravity*, and her *obliging behaviour*, gain'd her an acquaintance and friendship with most of any eminent worth or learning, that were at that time in or near that University; and particularly, with Mr. *John Donne*, who then came accidentally to that place, in this time of her being there: it was that *John Donne* who was after *Doctor Donne*, and Dean of *Saint Pauls London*: and he at his leaving *Oxford*, writ and left there in verse a Character of the Beauties of her body, and mind; of the first, he saies,

No Spring nor Summer-Beauty, *has such grace*
As I have seen in an Autumnal *face.*

Of the latter he sayes,

In all her words to every hearer fit
You may at Revels, *or at* Council *sit.*

The rest of her Character may be read in his printed
Poems, in that Elegy which bears the name of the
Autumnal Beauty. For both he and she were then past
the meridian of mans life.

This Amity, begun at this time, and place, was not
an *Amity* that polluted their Souls; but an *Amity*
made up of a chain of sutable inclinations and vertues;
an *Amity*, like that of St. *Chrysostoms* to his dear and
vertuous *Olimpias*; whom, in his Letters, he calls his
Saint: Or, an *Amity* indeed more like that of St.
Hierom to his *Paula*; whose affection to her was such,
that he turn'd Poet in his old Age, and then made
her *Epitaph*; *wishing all his Body were turn'd into*
Tongues, that he might declare her just praises to posterity.
——And this *Amity* betwixt her and Mr. *Donne*, was
begun in a happy time for him, he being then near to
the Fortieth year of his Age (which was some years
before he entred into Sacred Orders :) A time, when
his necessities needed a daily supply for the support of
his Wife, seven Children, and a Family : And in this
time she prov'd one of his most bountiful Benefactors;
and he, as grateful an acknowledger of it. You may
take one testimony for what I have said of these two
worthy persons, from this following *Letter*, and *Sonnet.*

MADAM,

'YOur Favours to me are every where; I use
     'them, and have them. I enjoy them at
     'London, and leave them there; and yet
'find them at *Micham*: such Riddles as these become

'things unexpressible ; and such is your goodness. I
'was almost sorry to find your Servant here this day,
'because I was loth to have any witness of my not
'coming home last Night, and indeed of my coming
'this Morning : But my not coming was excusable,
'because earnest business detein'd me ; and my
'coming this day, is by the example of your St. *Mary*
'*Magdalen*, who rose early upon *Sunday*, to seek that
'which she lov'd most ; and so did I. And from
'her and my self, I return such thanks as are due to
'one to whom we owe all the good opinion, that
'they whom we need most, have of us——by this
'Messenger, and on this good day, I commit the
'inclosed *Holy Hymns* and *Sonnets* (which for the
'matter, not the workmanship, have yet escap'd the
'fire) to your judgment, and to your protection too,
'if you think them worthy of it ; and I have appointed
'this inclosed *Sonnet* to usher them to your happy
'hand.

Your unworthiest Servant,

Micham,
July 11.
1607.

*unless your accepting him to be so,
have mended him.*

JO. DONNE.

To the Lady *Magdalen Herbert* ; of St. *Mary
Magdalen.*

H*ER of your name, whose fair inheritance*
    Bethina was, and jointure Magdalo :
        An active faith so highly did advance,
    That she once knew, more than the Church did know,
The Resurrection ; *so much good there is*
    Deliver'd of her, that some Fathers be

Loth to believe one Woman *could do this ;*
  But think these Magdalens *were two or three.*
Increase their number, Lady, *and their fame:*
  To their Devotion, *add your* Innocence :
Take so much of th' example, as of the name ;
  The latter half; and in some recompence
That they did harbour Christ *himself, a* Guest,
  Harbour these Hymns, *to his dear name addrest.*

J. D.

These *Hymns* are now lost to us; but doubtless they were such, as they two now sing in *Heaven.*

There might be more demonstrations of the Friendship, and the many sacred Indearments betwixt these two excellent persons (for I have many of their Letters in my hand) and much more might be said of her great prudence and piety : but my design was not to write hers, but the Life of her Son ; and therefore I shall only tell my Reader, that about that very day twenty years that this Letter was dated, and sent her, I saw and heard this Mr. *John Donne* (who was then Dean of *St. Pauls*) weep, and preach her Funeral Sermon, in the Parish-Church of *Chelsey* near *London,* where she now rests in her quiet Grave : and where we must now leave her, and return to her Son *George,* whom we left in his Study in *Cambridge.*

And in *Cambridge* we may find our *George Herberts* behaviour to be such, that we may conclude, he consecrated the first-fruits of his early age to vertue, and a serious study of learning. And that he did so, this following Letter and Sonnet which were in the first year of his going to *Cambridge* sent his dear Mother for a New-years gift, may appear to be some testimony.

———' But I fear the heat of my late *Ague* hath
' dried up those springs, by which Scholars say, the
' *Muses* use to take up their habitations. However,
' I need not their help, to reprove the vanity of those
' many Love-poems, that are daily writ and consecrated
' to *Venus*; nor to bewail that so few are writ, that look
' towards *God* and *Heaven*. For my own part, my
' meaning (*dear Mother*) is in these Sonnets, to declare
' my resolution to be, that my poor Abilities in *Poetry*
' shall be all, and ever consecrated to Gods glory; and
I beg you to receive this as one testimony.

M Y *God, where is that ancient heat towards thee,*
  Wherewith whole showls of Martyrs *once did*
  burn,
Besides their other flames? Doth Poetry
Wear Venus Livery? *only serve her turn?*
Why are not Sonnets *made of thee? and layes*
  Vpon thine Altar burnt? Cannot thy love
  Heighten a spirit to sound out thy praise
As well as any she? Cannot thy Dove
Out-strip their Cupid *easily in flight?*
  Or, since thy ways are deep, and still the same,
  Will not a verse run smooth that bears thy name!
Why doth that fire, which by thy power and might
  Each breast does feel, no braver fuel choose
  Than that, which one day, Worms *may chance refuse.*
Sure Lord, there is enough in thee to dry
  Oceans of Ink; *for, as the Deluge did*
  Cover the Earth, so doth thy Majesty:
Each cloud distils thy praise, and doth forbid
Poets *to turn it to another use.*
  Roses and Lillies *speak thee; and to make*
  A pair of Cheeks *of them, is thy abuse.*
Why should I Womens *eyes for* Chrystal *take?*

Such poor invention burns in their low mind
Whose fire is wild, and doth not upward go
To praise, and, on thee Lord, some Ink *bestow.*
Open the bones, and you shall nothing find
In the best face *but* filth ; *when Lord, in thee*
The beauty *lies, in the* discovery.

G. H.

This was his resolution at the sending this Letter to his dear Mother ; about which time, he was in the Seventeenth year of his Age ; and, as he grew older, so he grew in learning, and more and more in favour both with God and man : insomuch, that in this morning of that short day of his life, he seem'd to be mark'd out for vertue, and to become the care of Heaven ; for God still kept his soul in so holy a frame, that he may, and ought to be a pattern of vertue to all posterity ; and especially, to his Brethren of the Clergy, of which the Reader may expect a more exact account in what will follow.

I need not declare that he was a strict Student, because, that he was so, there will be many testimonies in the future part of his life. I shall therefore only tell, that he was made *Batchelor of Art* in the year 1611. *Major Fellow* of the *Colledge, March* 15. 1615. And that in that year, he was also made *Master of Arts,* he being then in the 22*d* year of his Age ; during all which time, all, or the greatest diversion from his Study, was the practice of Musick, in which he became a great Master ; and of which, he would say, ' That ' it did relieve his drooping spirits, compose his dis- ' tracted thoughts, and raised his weary soul so far ' above Earth, that it gave him an earnest of the joys ' of Heaven, before he possest them. And it may be noted, that from his first entrance into the Colledge, the generous Dr. *Nevil* was a cherisher of his Studies, and such a lover of his person, his behaviour, and the excellent endowments of his mind, that he took him often into his own company; by which he confirm'd his native gentileness; and, if during this time he exprest any Error, it was, that he kept himself too much retir'd, and at too great a distance with all his inferiours: and his cloaths seem'd to prove, that he put too great a value on his parts and Parentage.

This may be some account of his disposition, and of the employment of his time, till he was Master of Arts, which was *Anno* 1615. and in the year 1619. he was chosen Orator for the University. His two precedent Orators, were Sir *Robert Nanton*, and Sir *Francis Nethersoll*: The first was not long after made Secretary of State; and Sir *Francis*, not very long after his being Orator, was made Secretary to the Lady *Elizabeth* Queen of *Bohemia*. In this place of Orator, our *George Herbert* continued eight years; and manag'd it with as becoming, and grave a gaiety, as any had ever before, or since his time. For *He had acquir'd great Learning, and was blest with a high fancy, a civil and sharp wit, and with a natural elegance, both in his behaviour, his tongue, and his pen.* Of all which, there might be very many particular evidences, but I will limit my self to the mention of but three.

And the first notable occasion of shewing his fitness for this employment of *Orator*, was manifested in a Letter to King *James*, upon the occasion of his sending that University his Book, called *Basilicon Doron*; and their Orator was to acknowledge this great honour, and return their gratitude to His Majesty for such a condescension; at the close of which Letter, he writ,

Quid Vaticanam Bodleianamque objicis hospes!
Vnicus est nobis Bibliotheca Liber.

This Letter was writ in such excellent Latin, was so
full of Conceits, and all the expressions so suted to the
genius of the King, that he inquired the Orators
name, and then ask'd *William* Earl of *Pembroke*, if he
knew him ? whose answer was, ' That he knew him
' very well; and that he was his Kinsman, but he
' lov'd him more for his learning and vertue, than for
' that he was of his name and family.' At which
answer, the King smil'd, and asked the Earl leave,
' that he might love him too; for he took him to be
' the Jewel of that University.

The next occasion he had and took to shew his
great Abilities, was, with them, to shew also his great
affection to that Church in which he received his
Baptism, and of which he profest himself a member;
and the occasion was this : There was one *Andrew
Melvin*, a Minister of the Scotch Church, and Rector
of St. *Andrews* ; who, by a long and constant Converse,
with a discontented part of that Clergy which oppos'd
Episcopacy, became at last to be a chief leader of that
Faction : and, had proudly appear'd to be so, to
King *James*, when he was but King of tha Nation,
who the second year after his Coronation in *England*,
conven'd a part of the *Bishops* and otherLearned Divines
of his Church, to attend him at *Hampton-Court*, in
order to a friendly Conference with some Dissenting
Brethren, both of this, and the Church of *Scotland:* of
which Scotch party, *Andrew Melvin* was one ; and,
he being a man of learning, and inclin'd to *Satyrical
Poetry*, had scatter'd many malicious bitter Verses
against our *Liturgy*, our *Ceremonies*, and our *Church-
government:* which were by some of that party, so
magnified for the wit, that they were therefore brought
into *Westminster-School*, where Mr. *George Herbert*
then, and often after, made such answers to them,

and such reflexion on him and his *Kirk*, as might unbeguile any man that was not too deeply pre-ingaged in such a quarrel.——But to return to Mr. *Melvin* at *Hampton-Court-Conference*, he there appear'd to be a man of an unruly wit, of a strange confidence, of so furious a Zeal, and of so ungovern'd passions, that his insolence to the King, and others at this conference, lost him both his Rectorship of St. *Andrews*, and his liberty too: for, his former Verses, and his present reproaches there used against the Church and State, caus'd him to be committed prisoner to the Tower of *London*: where he remained very angry for three years. At which time of his commitment, he found the Lady *Arabella* an innocent prisoner there; and he pleas'd himself much in sending the next day after his Commitment, these two Verses to the good Lady, which I will under-write, because they may give the Reader a taste of his others, which were like these.

Causa tibi mecum est communis, Carceris, Ara-
Bella; tibi causa est, Araque sacra mihi.

I shall not trouble my Reader with an account of his enlargement from that Prison, or his Death; but tell him, Mr. *Herberts* Verses were thought so worthy to be preserv'd, that Dr. *Duport* the learned Dean of *Peterborough*, hath lately collected, and caus'd many of them to be printed, as an honourable memorial of his friend Mr. *George Herbert*, and the Cause he undertook.

And, in order to my third and last observation of his great Abilities, it will be needful to declare, that about this time King *James* came very often to hunt at *New-Market* and *Royston*; and was almost as often invited to *Cambridge*, where his entertainment was Comedies suted to his pleasant humor; and where Mr.

George Herbert was to welcome him with *Gratulations*, and the *Applauses* of an *Orator*; which he alwaies perform'd so well, that he still grew more into the Kings favour, insomuch, that he had a particular appointment to attend His Majesty at *Royston*, where after a Discourse with him, His Majesty declar'd to his Kinsman, the Earl of *Pembroke*, ' That he found ' the Orators learning and wisdom, much above his ' age or wit. The year following, the King appointed to end His progress at *Cambridge*, and to stay there certain days; at which time, he was attended by the great Secretary of Nature, and all Learning, Sir *Francis Bacon* (Lord *Verulam*) and by the ever memorable and learned Dr. *Andrews* Bishop of *Winchester*, both which did at that time begin a desir'd friendship with our *Orator*. Upon whom, the first put such a value on his judgment, that he usually desir'd his approbation, before he would expose any of his Books to be printed, and thought him so worthy of his friendship, that having translated many of the Prophet *Davids* Psalms into English Verse, he made *George Herbert* his Patron, by a publick dedication of them to him, as the best Judge of *Divine Poetry*. And for the learned Bishop, it is observable, that at that time, there fell to be a modest debate betwixt them two about *Predestination*, and *Sanctity of life*; of both which, the *Orator* did not long after send the Bishop some safe and useful *Aphorisms*, in a long Letter written in Greek; which Letter was so remarkable for the language, and reason of it, that after the reading it, the Bishop put it into his bosom, and did often shew it to many Scholars, both of this, and forreign Nations; but did alwaies return it back to the place where he first lodg'd it, and continu'd it so near his heart, till the last day of his life.

To these, I might add the long and intire friendship betwixt him and Sir *Henry Wotton*, and Doctor *Donne*, But I have promis'd to contract my self, and shall therefore only add one testimony to what is also mentioned in the Life of Doctor *Donne*; namely, that a little before his death, he caused many Seals to be made, and in them to be ingraven the figure of *Christ crucified* on an *Anchor* (the emblem of hope) and of which Doctor *Donne* would often say, *Crux mihi Anchora.*——These Seals, he gave or sent to most of those friends on which he put a value; and, at Mr. *Herberts* death, these Verses were found wrapt up with that Seal which was by the Doctor given to him.

When my dear Friend could write no more,
He gave this Seal, and so gave ore.

When winds and waves rise highest, I am sure,
This Anchor keeps my faith, that me secure.

At this time of being *Orator*, he had learnt to understand the *Italian*, *Spanish*, and *French* Tongues very perfectly; hoping, that as his Predecessors, so he might in time attain the place of a *Secretary of State*, he being at that time very high in the Kings favour; and not meanly valued and lov'd by the most eminent and most powerful of the Court-Nobility: This, and the love of a Court-conversation mixt with a laudible ambition to be something more than he then was, drew him often from *Cambridge* to attend the *King* wheresoever the Court was, who then gave him a *Sine Cure*, which fell into his Majesties disposal, I think, by the death of the Bishop of St. *Asaph*. It was the same, that Queen *Elizabeth* had formerly given to her Favourite Sir *Philip Sidney*; and valued to be worth an hundred and twenty pound *per Annum*. With this, and his

Annuity, and the advantage of his Colledge, and of his
Oratorship, he enjoyed his gentile humor for cloaths,
and Court-like company, and seldom look'd towards
Cambridge, unless the King were there, but then he
never fail'd; and, at other times, left the manage of
his Orators place, to his learned friend Mr. *Herbert
Thorndike*, who is now Prebend of *Westminster*.

I may not omit to tell, that he had often design'd
to leave the University, and decline all Study, which he
thought did impair his health; for he had a body
apt to a *Consumption*, and to *Fevers*, and other infirmities
which he judg'd were increas'd by his Studies; for
he would often say, ' He had too thoughtful a Wit:
' a Wit, like a Pen-knife in too narrow a sheath, too
' sharp for his Body: But his Mother would by no
means allow him to leave the University, or to travel;
and, though he inclin'd very much to both, yet he
would by no means satisfie his own desires at so dear
a rate, as to prove an undutiful Son to so affectionate a
Mother; but did always submit to her wisdom.
And what I have now said, may partly appear in a
Copy of Verses in his printed Poems; 'tis one of those
that bears the title of *Affliction*: And it appears to
be a pious reflection on Gods providence, and some
passages of his life, in which he saies,

> Whereas my birth and spirit rather took
> 　　The way that takes the Town:
> 　Thou didst betray me to a lingring Book,
> 　　And wrap me in a Gown:
> I was intangled in a World of strife,
> Before I had the power to change my life.
>
> Yet, for I threatned oft the Siege to raise,
> 　　Not simpring all mine age:
> Thou often didst with Academick praise,

Melt, and dissolve my rage:
I took the sweetned Pill, till I came where
I could not go away, nor persevere.

Yet, least perchance, I should too happy be
In my unhappiness;
Turning my purge to food, thou throwest me
Into more sicknesses.
Thus doth thy power Cross-byass me, not making
Thine own gifts good; yet me from my ways taking.

Now I am here, what thou wilt do with me
None of my Books will shew:
I read, and sigh, and wish I were a Tree,
For then sure I should grow
To fruit or shade, at least, some Bird would trust
Her Houshold with me, and I would be just.

Yet, though thou troublest me, I must be meek;
In weakness must be stout:
Well, I will change my service, and go seek
Some other Master out:
Ah my dear God! though I am clean forgot,
Let me not love thee, if I love thee not.

G. H.

In this time of Mr. *Herberts* attendance and expectation of some good occasion to remove from *Cambridge,*
to Court; God, in whom there is an unseen Chain of
Causes, did in a short time put an end to the lives of
two of his most obliging and most powerful friends,
Lodowick Duke of *Richmond,* and *James* Marquess of
Hamilton; and not long after him, King *James* died
also, and with them, all Mr. *Herbert's* Court-hopes:
So that he presently betook himself to a Retreat from

London, to a Friend in *Kent*, where he liv'd very privately, and was such a lover of solitariness, as was judg'd to impair his health, more then his Study had done. In this time of Retirement, he had many Conflicts with himself, Whether he should return to the painted pleasures of a Court-life, or betake himself to a study of Divinity, and enter into Sacred Orders ? (to which his dear Mother had often persuaded him.) These were such Conflicts, as they only can know, that have endur'd them ; for ambitious Desires, and the outward Glory of this World, are not easily laid aside ; but, at last, God inclin'd him to put on a resolution to serve at his Altar.

He did at his return to *London*, acquaint a Court-friend with his resolution to enter into *Sacred Orders*, who persuaded him to alter it, as too mean an employment, and too much below his birth, and the excellent abilities and endowments of his mind. To whom he replied, ' It hath been formerly judged that the ' Domestick Servants of the King of Heaven, should ' be of the noblest Families on Earth : and, though ' the Iniquity of the late Times have made Clergy-men ' meanly valued, and the sacred name of *Priest* con- ' temptible ; yet I will labour to make it honourable, ' by consecrating all my learning, and all my poor ' abilities, to advance the glory of that God that gave ' them ; knowing, that I can never do too much for ' him, that hath done so much for me, as to make me ' a Christian. And I will labour to be like my Saviour, ' by making Humility lovely in the eyes of all men, ' and by following the merciful and meek example of ' my *dear Jesus*.

This was then his resolution, and the God of Constancy, who intended him for a great example of virtue, continued him in it ; for within that year he was made Deacon, but the day when, or by whom, I cannot learn ; but that he was about that time made Deacon, is most certain ; for I find by the Records of *Lincoln*, that he was made Prebend of *Layton Ecclesia*, in the Diocess of *Lincoln*, *July* 15. 1626. and that this Prebend was given him, by *John*, then *Lord Bishop of that See*. And now, he had a fit occasion to shew that Piety and Bounty that was deriv'd from his generous Mother, and his other memorable Ancestors, and the occasion was this.

This *Layton Ecclesia*, is a Village near to *Spalden* in the County of *Huntington*, and the greatest part of the Parish Church was fallen down, and that of it which stood, was so decayed, so little, and so useless, that the Parishioners could not meet to perform their Duty to God in publick prayer and praises ; and thus it had been for almost 20 years, in which time there had been some faint endeavours for a publick Collection, to enable the Parishioners to rebuild it, but with no success, till Mr. *Herbert* undertook it ; and he, by his own, and the contribution of many of his Kindred, and other noble Friends, undertook the Re-edification of it ; and made it so much his whole business, that he became restless, till he saw it finisht as it now stands ; being, for the workmanship, a costly *Mosaick:* for the form, an *exact Cross* ; and for the decency and beauty, I am assur'd it is the most remarkable Parish-Church, that this Nation affords. He lived to see it so wainscoated, as to be exceeded by none ; and, by his order, the Reading Pew, and Pulpit, were a little distant from each other, and both of an equal height ; for he would often say, ' They should neither have a pre-
' cedency or priority of the other : but that *Prayer* and
' *Preaching* being equally useful, might agree like
' Brethren, and have an equal honour and estimation.

Before I proceed farther, I must look back to the time of Mr. *Herberts* being made Prebend, and tell the Reader, that not long after, his Mother being inform'd of his intentions to Re-build that Church: and apprehending the great trouble and charge that he was like to draw upon himself, his Relations, and Friends, before it could be finisht; sent for him from *London* to *Chelsey* (where she then dwelt) and at his coming, said——' *George*, I sent for you, to perswade ' you to commit Simony, by giving your Patron as good ' a gift as he has given to you; namely, that you give ' him back his Prebend; for, *George*, it is not for your ' weak body, and empty purse, to undertake to build ' *Churches*. Of which, he desir'd he might have a Days time to consider, and then make her an Answer: And at his return to her the next Day, when he had first desired her blessing, and she given it him, his next request was, ' That she would at the Age of Thirty ' three Years, allow him to become an *undutiful* ' *Son*; for he had made a Vow to God, that if he were ' able, he would Re-build that Church': And then, shew'd her such reasons for his resolution, that she presently subscribed to be one of his Benefactors: and undertook to sollicit *William* Earl of *Pembroke* to become another, who subscribed for fifty pounds; and not long after, by a witty, and persuasive Letter from Mr. *Herbert*, made it fifty pounds more. And in this nomination of some of his Benefactors, *James* Duke of *Lenox*, and his brother Sir *Henry Herbert*, ought to be remembred; as also, the bounty of Mr. *Nicholas Farrer*, and Mr. *Arthur Woodnot*; the one, a Gentleman in the Neighbourhood of *Layton*, and the other, a Goldsmith in *Foster-lane*, *London*, ought not to be forgotten: for the memory of such men ought to out-live their lives. Of Master *Farrer*, I shall hereafter give an account in a more seasonable place; but before I proceed farther, I will give this short account of Master *Arthur Woodnot*.

He was a man, that had consider'd, overgrown Estates do often require more care and watchfulness to preserve, than get them, and consider'd that there be many Discontents, that Riches cure not; and did therefore set limits to himself as to desire of wealth: And having attain'd so much as to be able to shew some mercy to the Poor, and preserve a competence for himself, he dedicated the remaining part of his life to the service of God; and to be useful for his Friends: and he prov'd to be so to Mr. *Herbert*; for, beside his own bounty, he collected and return'd most of the money that was paid for the Re-building of that Church; he kept all the account of the charges, and would often go down to state them, and see all the Workmen paid. When I have said, that this good man was a useful Friend to Mr. *Herberts* Father, and to his Mother, and continued to be so to him, till he clos'd his eyes on his Death-bed; I will forbear to say more, till I have the next fair occasion to mention the holy friendship that was betwixt him and Mr. *Herbert*.——From whom Mr. *Woodnot* carryed to his Mother this following Letter, and delivered it to her in a sickness which was not long before that which prov'd to be her last.

A Letter of Mr. George Herbert to his Mother, in her Sickness.

MADAM,

AT my last parting from you, I was the better content because I was in hope I should my self carry all sickness out of your family: but, since I know I did not, and that your share continues, or rather increaseth, I wish earnestly that I were again with you: and would quickly make good my wish, but that my employment does fix me here, it being now but a month to our Commencement: wherein, my absence by how much it naturally augmenteth suspicion, by so much shall it make my prayers the more constant and the more earnest for you to the God of all Consolation.——In the mean time, I beseech you to be chearful, and comfort your self in the God of all Comfort, who is not willing to behold any sorrow but for sin.——What hath Affliction grievous in it more then for a moment? or why should our afflictions here, have so much power or boldness as to oppose the hope of our Joys hereafter?——Madam! As the Earth is but a point in respect of the heavens, so are earthly Troubles compar'd to heavenly Joys; therefore, if either Age or Sickness lead you to those Joys, consider what advantage you have over Youth and Health, who are now so near those true Comforts.——Your last Letter gave me Earthly preferment, and I hope kept Heavenly for your self: but, wou'd you divide and choose too? our Colledge Customs allow not that, and I shou'd account *my self most happy if I might change with you ; for, I have always observ'd the thred of Life to be like other threds or skenes of silk, full of snarles and incumbrances: Happy is he, whose bottom is wound up and laid ready for work in the New Jerusalem.——For my self,* dear Mother, *I alwaies fear'd sickness more then death, because sickness hath made me unable to perform those Offices for which I came into the world, and must yet be kept in it ; but you are freed from that fear, who have already abundantly discharg'd that part, having both ordered your Family, and so brought up your Children that they have attain'd to the years of Discretion, and competent Maintenance.——So that now if they do not well the fault cannot be charg'd on you, whose Example and Care of them, will justifie you both to the world and your own Conscience: insomuch, that whether you turn your thoughts on the life past, or on the Joys that are to come, you have strong preservatives against all disquiet.——And for temporal Afflictions : I beseech you consider all that can happen to you, are either afflictions of* Estate, *or* Body, *or* Mind.——*For those of* Estate, *of what poor regard ought they to be, since if we had Riches we are commanded to give them away : so that the best use of them is, having, not to have them.——But perhaps being above the Common people, our Credit and estimation calls on us to live in a more splendid fashion ?——but, O God! how easily is that answered, when we consider that the Blessings in the holy Scripture, are never given to the rich, but to the poor. I never find Blessed be the Rich ; or, Blessed be the Noble ; but,* Blessed be the Meek, *and,* Blessed be the poor, *and,* Blessed be the Mourners, *for they shall be comforted——And yet, Oh God! most carry themselves so, as if they not only not desir'd, but even fear'd to be blessed.——And for Afflictions of the Body,* dear Madam, *remember the holy Martyrs of God, how they have been burnt by thousands, and have endur'd such other Tortures, as the very mention of them might beget amazement; but their Fiery-trials have had an end: and yours (which praised be God are less) are not like to continue long.——I beseech you let such thoughts as these, moderate your present fear and sorrow ; and know, that if any of yours shou'd prove a Goliah-like trouble, yet you may say with* David,——That God who hath delivered me out of the paws of the Lion and Bear, will also deliver me out of the hands of this uncircumcised *Philistin.*——*Lastly, for those Afflictions of the Soul: consider, that God intends that to be as a* sacred Temple *for himself to dwell in, and will not allow any room there for such an in-mate as* Grief; *or allow that any sadness shall be his Competitor.*——*And above all, If any care of future things molest you, remember those admirable words of the Psalmist:* Cast thy Care on the Lord and he shall nourish thee. *To which join that of* St. Peter, Casting all your Care on the Lord, for he careth for you.——*What an admirable thing is this, that God puts his shoulder to our burthen ! and, entertains our Care for us that we may the more quietly intend his service.*——*To Conclude, Let me commend only one place more to you* (Philip. 4. 4.) St. Paul *saith there:* Rejoice in the Lord alwaies, and again I say rejoice. *He doubles it to take away the scruple of those that might say,* What shall we rejoice in afflictions ? *yes, I say again rejoice; so that it is not left to us to rejoice or not rejoice : but whatsoever befalls us we must always, at all times rejoice in the Lord, who taketh care for us : and it follows in the next verse :* Let your moderation appear to all men, the Lord is at hand : be careful for nothing. *What can be said more comfortably ? trouble not your selves, God is at hand to*

Psal. 55.
1 Pet. 5. 7.

deliver us from all, or in all.——Dear Madam, *pardon my boldness, and accept the good meaning of,*

Trin. Col.　　　　Your most obedient Son,
May 25.
1622.　　　　　　*George Herbert.*

About the year 1629. and the 34*th* of his Age, Mr. *Herbert* was seiz'd with a sharp *Quotidian Ague*, and thought to remove it by the change of Air; to which end, he went to *Woodford* in Essex, but thither more chiefly, to enjoy the company of his beloved Brother Sir *Henry Herbert,* and other Friends then of that Family. In his House he remain'd about Twelve Months, and there became his own Physitian, and cur'd himself of his Ague, by forbearing Drink, and not eating any Meat, no not Mutton, nor a Hen, or Pidgeon, unless they were salted; and by such a constant Dyet, he remov'd his Ague, but with inconveniencies that were worse; for he brought upon himself a disposition to Rheums, and other weaknesses, and a supposed Consumption. And it is to be Noted, that in the sharpest of his extream Fits, he would often say, *Lord abate my great affliction, or increase my patience; but, Lord, I repine not, I am dumb, Lord, before thee, because thou doest it.* By which, and a sanctified submission to the Will of God, he shewed he was inclinable to bear the sweet yoke of *Christian Discipline*, both then, and in the latter part of his life, of which there will be many true Testimonies.

And now his care was to recover from his Consumption by a change, from *Woodford* into such an air as was most proper to that end. And his remove was to *Dantsey* in *Wiltshire*, a noble House which stands in a choice Air; the owner of it then was the Lord *Danvers* Earl of *Danby*, who lov'd Mr. *Herbert* so

very much, that he allow'd him such an apartment
in it, as might best sute with his accommodation and
liking. And, in this place, by a *spare Dyet*, declining all
perplexing Studies, moderate exercise, and a *chearful
conversation*, his health was apparently improv'd to a
good degree of strength and chearfulness : And then,
he declar'd his resolution both to marry, and to enter
into the Sacred Orders of Priesthood. These had
long been the desires of his Mother, and his other
Relations ; but she liv'd not to see either, for she
died in the year 1627. And, though he was dis-
obedient to her about *Layton* Church, yet, in conformity
to her will, he kept his Orators place, till after her
death ; and then presently declin'd it : And, the more
willingly, that he might be succeeded by his friend
Robert Creighton, who now is Dr. *Creighton*, and the
worthy Bishop of *Wells*.

I shall now proceed to his Marriage ; in order to
which, it will be convenient, that I first give the
Reader a short view of his person, and then an
account of his Wife, and of some circumstances concerning both.—*He was for his person of a stature inclining towards Tallness; his Body was very strait, and so
far from being cumbred with too much flesh, that he was
lean to an extremity. His aspect was chearful, and his
speech and motion did both declare him a Gentleman ;
for they were all so meek and obliging, that they purchased
love and respect from all that knew him.*

These, and his other visible vertues, begot him
much love from a Gentleman, of a Noble fortune, and
a near kinsman to his friend the Earl of *Danby ;*
namely, from Mr. *Charles Danvers* of *Bainton*, in the
County of *Wilts* Esq ; this Mr. *Danvers* having known
him long, and familiarly, did so much affect him,
that he often and publickly declar'd a desire that

Mr. *Herbert* would marry any of his Nine Daughters (for he had so many) but rather his Daughter *Jane*, than any other, because *Jane was his beloved Daughter*: And he had often said the same to Mr. *Herbert* himself; and that if he could like her for a Wife, and she him for a Husband, *Jane* should have a *double blessing*: and Mr. *Danvers* had so often said the like to *Jane*, and so much commended Mr. *Herbert* to her, that *Jane* became so much a Platonick, as to fall in love with Mr. *Herbert* unseen.

This was a fair preparation for a Marriage; but alas, her father died before Mr. *Herberts* retirement to *Dantsey*; yet some friends to both parties, procur'd their meeting; at which time a mutual affection entred into both their hearts, as a Conqueror enters into a surprized City, and Love having got such possession govern'd, and made there such Laws and Resolutions, as neither party was able to resist; insomuch, that she chang'd her name into *Herbert*, the third day after this first interview.

This haste might in others be thought a *Lovephrensie*, or worse: but it was not; for they had wooed so like Princes, as to have select Proxies: such, as were true friends to both parties; such as well understood Mr. *Herberts*, and her temper of mind; and also their Estates so well, before this Interview, that the suddenness was justifiable, by the strictest Rules of prudence: And the more, because it prov'd so happy to both parties; for the eternal lover of Mankind, made them happy in each others mutual and equal affections, and compliance; indeed, so happy, that there never was any opposition betwixt them, unless it were a Contest which should most incline to a compliance with the others desires. And though this begot, and continued in them, such a mutual *love* and *joy*, and *content*, as was no way defective: yet this mutual *content* and *love*, and *joy*, did receive a daily augmentation, by such daily obligingness to each other, as still added such new affluences to the former fulness of these divine Souls, as was only improvable in Heaven, where they now enjoy it.

About three months after his Marriage, Dr. *Curle*, who was then Rector of *Bemerton* in *Wiltshire*, was made Bishop of *Bath* and *Wells* (and not long after translated to *Winchester*, and by that means the presentation of a Clerk to *Bemerton*, did not fall to the Earl of *Pembroke* (who was the undoubted Patron of it) but to the King, by reason of Dr. *Curles* advancement: but *Philip*, then Earl of *Pembroke* (for *William* was lately dead) requested the King to bestow it upon his kinsman *George Herbert*; and the King said, *Most willingly to Mr. Herbert, if it be worth his acceptance*: and the Earl as willingly and suddenly sent it him, without seeking; but though Mr. *Herbert* had formerly put on a resolution for the Clergy: yet, at receiving this presentation, the apprehension of the last great Account that he was to make for the Cure of so many Souls, made him fast and pray often, and consider, for not less than a month: in which time he had some resolutions to decline both the Priesthood, and that Living. And in this time of considering, *He endur'd* (as he would often say) *such spiritual Conflicts, as none can think, but only those that have endur'd them*.

In the midst of these Conflicts, his old and dear friend Mr. *Arthur Woodnot*, took a journey to salute him at *Bainton* (where he then was with his Wives Friends and Relations) and was joyful to be an Eyewitness of his Health, and happy Marriage. And after they had rejoyc'd together some few days, they

took a Journey to *Wilton*, the famous Seat of the
Earls of *Pembroke*; at which time, the King, the
Earl, and the whole Court were there, or at *Salisbury*,
which is near to it. And at this time Mr. *Herbert*
presented his Thanks to the Earl, for his presentation
to *Bemerton*, but had not yet resolv'd to accept it, and
told him the reason why; but that Night, the Earl
acquainted Dr. *Laud*, then Bishop of *London*, and
after Archbishop of *Canterbury*, with his Kinsmans
irresolution. And the Bishop did the next day so
convince Mr. *Herbert*, *That the refusal of it was a sin*;
that a Taylor was sent for to come speedily from
Salisbury to *Wilton*, to take measure, and make him
Canonical Cloaths, against next day: which the
Taylor did; and Mr. *Herbert* being so habited, went
with his presentation to the learned Dr. *Davenant*,
who was then Bishop of *Salisbury*, and he gave him
Institution immediately (for Mr. *Herbert* had been
made Deacon some years before) and he was also the
same day (which was *April 26.* 1630) inducted into
the good, and more pleasant, than healthful Parsonage
of *Bemerton*: which is a Mile from *Salisbury*.

I have now Brought him to the Parsonage of Bemerton,
*and to the thirty sixth Year of his Age, and must stop
here, and bespeak the Reader to prepare for an almost
incredible story, of the great sanctity of the short remainder
of his holy life; a life so full of* Charity, Humility,
*and all Christian vertues, that it deserves the eloquence
of St.* Chrysostom *to commend and declare it! A life,
that if it were related by a Pen like his, there would
then be no need for this Age to look back into times past
for the examples of primitive piety: for they might be
all found in the life of* George Herbert. *But now, alas!
who is fit to undertake it! I confess I am not: and am
not pleas'd with my self that I must; and profess my*

self amaz'd, when I consider how few of the Clergy liv'd like him then, and how many live so unlike him now: But, it becomes not me to censure: my design is rather to assure the Reader, that I have used very great diligence to inform my self, that I might inform him of the truth of what follows; and though I cannot adorn it with eloquence, yet I will do it with sincerity.

When at his Induction he was shut into *Bemerton* Church, being left there alone to Toll the Bell, (as the Law requires him :) he staid so much longer than an ordinary time, before he return'd to those Friends that staid expecting him at the Church-door, that his Friend, Mr. *Woodnot*, look'd in at the Church-window, and saw him lie prostrate on the ground before the Altar: at which time and place (as he after told Mr. *Woodnot*) he set some Rules to himself, for the future manage of his life; and then and there made a vow, to labour to keep them.

And the same night that he had his Induction, he said to Mr. *Woodnot, I now look back upon my aspiring thoughts, and think my self more happy than if I had attain'd what then I so ambitiously thirsted for: And, I can now behold the Court with an impartial Eye, and see plainly, that it is made up of* Fraud, *and* Titles, *and* Flattery, *and many other such empty, imaginary painted Pleasures: Pleasures, that are so empty, as not to satisfy when they are enjoy'd; but in God and his service, is a fulness of all* joy *and* pleasure, *and no satiety: And I will now use all my endeavours to bring my Relations and Dependants to a love and relyance on him, who never fails those that trust him. But above all, I will be sure to live well, because the vertuous life of a Clergyman, is the most powerful eloquence to perswade all that see it, to reverence and love, and at least, to desire to live like him. And this I will do, because I know* we live in an Age that hath more need of good examples, than precepts. *And I beseech that God, who hath honour'd me so much as to call me to serve him at his Altar : that as by his special grace he hath put into my heart these good desires, and resolutions : so, he will by his assisting grace give me ghostly strength to bring the same to good effect: and I beseech him that my humble and charitable life may so win upon others, as to bring glory to my* JESUS, whom I have this day taken to be my Master and Governour ; *and I am so proud of his service, that I will alwaies observe, and obey, and do his Will; and alwaies call him* Jesus my Master, *and I will always contemn my birth, or any title or dignity that can be conferr'd upon me, when I shall compare them with my title of being a* Priest, *and serving at the* Altar *of* Jesus my Master.

And that he did so, may appear in many parts of his Book of *Sacred Poems*; especially, in that which he calls *the Odour.* In which he seems to rejoyce in the thoughts of that word *Jesus,* and say that the adding these words *my Master* to it, and the often repetition of them, seem'd to perfume his mind, and leave an oriental fragrancy in his very breath. And for his unforc'd choice to serve at Gods Altar, he seems in another place of his Poems (*the Pearl,* Matth. 13.) to rejoyce and say——*He knew the waies of Learning: knew, what nature does willingly; and what, when 'tis forc'd by fire : knew the waies of honour, and when glory inclines the Soul to noble expressions: knew the Court: knew the waies of pleasure, of love, of wit, of musick, and upon what terms he declined all these for the service of his* Master JESUS, and then concludes, saying,

That, through these Labyrinths, not my groveling Wit,
But thy Silk-twist, let down from Heaven to me ;
Did both conduct, and teach me, how by it,
                              To climb to thee.

The third day after he was made Rector of *Bemerton*,
and had chang'd his sword and silk Cloaths into a
Canonical Coat; he return'd so habited with his
friend Mr. *Woodnot* to *Bainton* : And, immediately
after he had seen and saluted his Wife, he said to her
——*You are now a Ministers Wife, and must now so far
forget your fathers house, as not to claim a precedence of
any of your Parishioners; for you are to know, that a
Priests Wife can challenge no precedence or place, but
that which she purchases by her obliging humility ; and,
I am sure, places so purchased, do best become them.*
And let me tell you, *That I am so good a Herald, as to
assure you that this is truth.* And she was so meek a
Wife, *as to assure him it was no vexing News to her, and
that he should see her observe it with a chearful willingness.*
And indeed her unforc'd humility, that humility that was
in her so original, as to be born with her, made her so
happy as to do so; and her doing so, begot her an unfeigned love, and a serviceable respect from all that con-
verst with her ; and this love followed her in all places,
as inseparably, as shadows follow substances in Sunshine.

It was not many days before he return'd back to
Bemerton, to view the Church, and repair the Chancel ;
and indeed, to rebuild almost three parts of his house
which was fall'n down, or decayed by reason of his Predecessors living at a better Parsonage-house ; namely,
at *Minal*, 16 or 20 miles from this place. At which
time of Mr. *Herberts* coming alone to *Bemerton*, there
came to him a poor old Woman, with an intent to
acquaint him with her necessitous condition, as also, with

some troubles of her mind; but after she had spoke some few words to him, she was surpriz'd with a fear, and that begot a shortness of breath, so that her spirits and speech fail'd her; which he perceiving, did so compassionate her, and was so humble, that he took her by the hand, and said, *Speak good Mother, be not afraid to speak to me; for I am a man that will hear you with patience; and will relieve your necessities too, if I be able: and this I will do willingly, and therefore, Mother, be not afraid to acquaint me with what you desire.* After which comfortable speech, he again took her by the hand, made her sit down by him, & understanding she was of his Parish, he told her, *He would be acquainted with her, and take her into his care:* And having with patience heard and understood her wants (and it is some relief for a poor body to be but hear'd with patience) he like a Christian Clergyman comforted her by his meek behaviour and counsel; but because that cost him nothing, he reliev'd her with money too, and so sent her home with a chearful heart, praising God, and praying for him. *Thus worthy, and* (like *Davids* blessed man) *thus lowly, was Mr.* George Herbert *in his own eyes*: and thus lovely in the eyes of others.

At his return that Night to his Wife at *Bainton*, he gave her an account of the passages 'twixt him and the poor Woman: with which she was so affected, that she went next day to *Salisbury*, and there bought a pair of Blankets and sent them as a Token of her love to the poor Woman: and with them a Message, *That she would see and be acquainted with her, when her house was built at* Bemerton.

There be many such passages both of him and his Wife, of which some few will be related; but I shall first tell, that he hasted to get the Parish-Church repair'd; then, to beautifie the Chappel (which stands near his House) and that at his own great charge. He then proceeded to re-build the greatest part of the Parsonage-house, which he did also very compleatly, and at his own charge; and having done this good work, he caus'd these Verses to be writ upon, or ingraven in the Mantle of the Chimney in his Hall.

To my Successor.
If thou chance for to find
A new House to thy mind,
And built without thy Cost:
Be good to the Poor,
As God gives thee store,
And then my Labour's not lost.

We will now by the Readers favour suppose him fixt at *Bemerton*, and grant him to have seen the Church repair'd, and the Chappel belonging to it very decently adorn'd, at his own great charge (which is a real Truth) and having now fixt him there, I shall proceed to give an account of the rest of his behaviour both to his Parishioners, and those many others that knew and convers'd with him.

Doubtless Mr. *Herbert* had consider'd and given Rules to himself for his Christian carriage both to God and man before he enter'd into *Holy Orders*. And 'tis not unlike, but that he renewed those resolutions at his prostration before the *Holy Altar*, at his Induction into the Church of *Bemerton*; but as yet he was but a *Deacon*, and therefore long'd for the next *Ember-week*, that he might be ordain'd *Priest*, and made capable of Administring both the Sacraments. At which time, the Reverend Dr. *Humphrey Hinchman*, now Lord Bishop of *London* (who does not mention him, but with some veneration for his life and excellent learning) tells me, *He laid his hand on Mr.* Herberts

*Head, and (alas!) within less then three Years, lent his
Shoulder to carry his dear Friend to his Grave.*

And that Mr. *Herbert* might the better preserve
those holy Rules which such a *Priest* as he intended
to be, ought to observe; and that time might not
insensibly blot them out of his memory, but that the
next year might shew him his variations from this
years resolutions; he therefore did set down his
Rules, then resolv'd upon, in that order, as the World
now sees them printed in a little Book, call'd, *The
Country Parson*, in which some of his Rules are:

The Parsons Knowledge.	*The Parson Condescending.*
The Parson on Sundays.	
The Parson Praying.	*The Parson in his Journey.*
The Parson Preaching.	*The Parson in his Mirth.*
The Parsons Charity.	*The Parson with his Church-wardens.*
The Parson comforting the Sick.	
The Parson Arguing.	*The Parson Blessing the People.*

And his behaviour toward God and man, may be said
to be a practical Comment on these, and the other
holy Rules set down in that useful Book. A Book,
so full of plain, prudent and useful Rules, that that
Country Parson, that can spare 12 *d.* and yet wants
it, is scarce excusable; because it will both direct him
what he ought to do, and convince him for not having
done it.

At the Death of Mr. *Herbert*, this Book fell into
the hands of his friend Mr. *Woodnot*; and he commended it into the trusty hands of Mr. *Barnabas Oly*,
who publisht it with a most conscientious, and
excellent Preface; from which I have had some of
those Truths, that are related in this life of Mr.

Herbert. The Text for his first Sermon was taken out of *Solomons Proverbs,* and the words were, *Keep thy heart with all diligence.* In which first Sermon, he gave his Parishioners many necessary, holy, safe Rules for the discharge of a good Conscience, both to God and man. And deliver'd his Sermon after a most florid manner; both with great learning and eloquence. But at the close of this Sermon, told them, *That should not be his constant way of Preaching, for, since Almighty God does not intend to lead men to heaven by hard Questions, he would not therefore fill their heads with unnecessary Notions; but that for their sakes, his language and his expressions should be more plain and practical in his future Sermons.* And he then made it his humble request, *That they would be constant to the Afternoons Service, and Catechising.* And shewed them convincing reasons why he desir'd it; and his obliging example and perswasions brought them to a willing conformity to his desires.

The Texts for all his future Sermons (which God knows were not many) were constantly taken out of the Gospel for the day; and, he did as constantly declare why the Church did appoint that portion of Scripture to be that day read: And in what manner the *Collect* for every Sunday does refer to the *Gospel,* or to the *Epistle* then read to them; and that they might pray with understanding, he did usually take occasion to explain, not only the *Collect* for every particular Sunday, but the reasons of all the other *Collects* and *Responses* in our Church-Service; and, made it appear to them, that *the whole Service of the Church,* was a reasonable, and therefore an acceptable Sacrifice to God; as namely, that we begin with *Confession of our selves to be vile, miserable sinners:* and that we begin so, because till we have confess'd our selves to be such, we are not capable of that mercy which we acknowledge we need, and pray for; but having in the prayer of our Lord, begg'd pardon for those sins which we have confest: And hoping, that as the *Priest* hath declar'd our Absolution, so by our publick Confession, and real Repentance, we have obtain'd that pardon: Then we dare and do proceed to beg of the Lord, *to open our lips, that our mouths may shew forth his praise,* for, till then, we are neither able, nor worthy to praise him. But this being suppos'd, we are then fit to say, *Glory be to the Father, and to the Son, and to the Holy Ghost;* and fit to proceed to a further service of our God, in the *Collects,* and *Psalms,* and *Lauds* that follow in the Service.

And as to these *Psalms* and *Lauds,* he proceeded to inform them, why they were so often, and some of them daily repeated in our *Church-service:* namely, the *Psalms* every Month, because they be an *Historical* and thankful repetition of mercies past; and such a composition of prayers and praises, as ought to be repeated often, and publickly; for *with such Sacrifices, God is honour'd, and well-pleased.* This, for the *Psalms.*

And for the *Hymns* and *Lauds,* appointed to be daily repeated or sung after the first and second Lessons are read to the Congregation: he proceeded to inform them, that it was most reasonable, after they have heard the will and goodness of God declar'd or preach't by the *Priest* in his reading the two Chapters, that it was then a seasonable duty to rise up and express their gratitude to Almighty God for those his mercies to them, and to all Mankind; and then to say with the *blessed Virgin, That* their *Souls do magnifie the Lord, and that* their *spirits do also rejoyce in God their Saviour;* And that it was their Duty also to rejoice with *Simeon*

in his Song, and say with him, *That their eyes have* also
seen their salvation ; for they have seen that salvation
which was but prophesied till his time : and he then
broke out into those expressions of joy that he did
see it : but they live to see it daily, in the History of
it, and therefore ought daily to rejoice, and daily to
offer up their Sacrifices of praise to their God, for that
particular mercy. A service, which is now the constant employment of that *blessed Virgin*, and *Simeon*,
and all those blessed Saints that are possest of Heaven :
and where they are at this time interchangeably and
constantly singing, *Holy, Holy, Holy Lord God, Glory
be to God on High, and on Earth peace.*——And he
taught them, that to do this, was an acceptable service
to God, because the Prophet *David* says in his Psalms,
He that praiseth the Lord, honoureth him.

He made them to understand, how happy they be
that are freed from the incumbrances of that Law
which our Fore-fathers groan'd under : namely, from
the *Legal Sacrifices* : and from the many *Ceremonies
of the Levitical Law* : freed from *Circumcision*, and
from the strict observation of the *Jewish Sabbath*,
and the like : And he made them know that having
receiv'd so many, and so great blessings, by being born
since the days of our Saviour, it must be an acceptable
Sacrifice to Almighty God, for them to acknowledge
those blessings daily, and stand up and worship, and
say as *Zacharias* did, *Blessed be the Lord God of* Israel,
for he hath (in our days) *visited and redeemed his people*;
and (he hath in our days) *remembred, and shewed that
mercy which by the mouth of the Prophets, he promised
to our Fore-fathers* : and this he hath done, *according to
his holy Covenant made with them* : And he made them
to understand that we live to see and enjoy the benefit
of it, in his *Birth*, in his *Life*, his *Passion*, his *Resurrec-*

tion and *Ascension* into Heaven, where he now sits sensible of all our temptations and infirmities: and, where he is at this present time making intercession for us, to his and our Father: and therefore they ought daily to express their publick gratulations, and say daily with *Zacharias, Blessed be that Lord God of* Israel, *that hath thus visited, and thus redeemed his people.*——— These were some of the reasons by which Mr. *Herbert* instructed his Congregation for the use of the *Psalms,* and the *Hymns* appointed to be daily sung or said in the Church-service.

He inform'd them also, when the *Priest* did pray only for the Congregation, and not for himself; and when they did only pray for him, as namely, after the repetition of the *Creed,* before he proceeds to pray the Lords prayer, or any of the appointed Collects, the Priest is directed to kneel down, and pray for them, saying———*The Lord be with you*———And when they pray for him, saying———*And with thy spirit*; and then they join together in the following Collects, and he assur'd them, that when there is such mutual love, and such joint prayers offer'd for each other, then the holy Angels look down from Heaven, and are ready to carry such charitable desires to God Almighty; and he as ready to receive them; and that a Christian Congregation calling thus upon God, with one heart, and one voice, and in one reverend and humble posture, look as beautifully as *Jerusalem,* that is at peace with it self.

He instructed them also, why the prayer of our Lord was pray'd often in every full service of the Church: namely, at the conclusion of the several parts of that Service; and pray'd then, not only because it was compos'd and commanded by our *Jesus* that made it, but as a perfect pattern for our less perfect Forms of prayer, and therefore fittest to sum up and conclude all our imperfect Petitions.

He instructed them also, that as by the second Commandment we are requir'd not to bow down, or worship an *Idol*, or *false God*; so, by the contrary Rule, we are to bow down and kneel, or stand up and *worship* the true God. And he instructed them, why the Church requir'd the Congregation to stand up, at the repetition of the Creeds; namely, because they did thereby declare both their obedience to the Church, and an assent to that faith into which they had been baptiz'd. And he taught them, that in that shorter Creed, or Doxology so often repeated daily; they also stood up to testify their belief to be, that, *the God that they trusted in was one God, and three persons; the Father, the Son, and the Holy Ghost, to whom they & the Priest gave glory*: And because there had been Hereticks that had deny'd some of these three persons to be God; therefore the Congregation stood up and honour'd him, by confessing and saying, *It was so in the beginning, is now so, and shall ever be so World without end*. And all gave their assent to this belief, by standing up and saying, *Amen*.

He instructed them also, what benefit they had, by the Churches appointing the Celebration of Holy-dayes, and the excellent use of them; namely, that they were set apart for particular Commemorations of particular mercies received from Almighty God; and (as Reverend Mr. *Hooker* saies) to be the *Landmarks* to distinguish times; for by them we are taught to take notice how time passes by us; and that we ought not to let the Years pass without a Celebration of praise for those mercies which those days give us occasion to remember; & therefore they were to note that the Year is appointed to begin the 25*th* day of *March*; **a** day in which we commemorate the *Angels* appearing to the *B. Virgin*, with the joyful tidings that *she should conceive and bear a Son, that should be the redeemer of Mankind*; and she did so Forty weeks after this joyful salutation; namely, at our *Christmas*: a day in which we commemorate his Birth, with joy and praise; and that eight days after this happy Birth, we celebrate his *Circumcision*; namely, in that which we call *New-years day*. And that upon that day which we call *Twelfth-day*, we commemorate the manifestation of the unsearchable riches of Jesus to the Gentiles: And that that day we also celebrate the memory of his goodness in sending a *Star* to guide the *three wise men* from the *East* to *Bethlem*, that they might there *worship*, and present him with their oblations of *Gold, Frankincense*, and *Myrrhe*. And he (Mr. *Herbert*) instructed them, that *Jesus* was Forty days after his Birth, presented by his blessed mother in the *Temple*; namely, on that day which we call, *the Purification of the blessed Virgin, Saint* Mary. And he instructed them, that by the *Lent-fast*, we imitate and commemorate our Saviours humiliation in fasting Forty days; and, that we ought to endeavour to be like him in purity. And, that on *Good-friday* we commemorate and condole his *Crucifixion*. And at *Easter*, commemorate his *glorious Resurrection*. And he taught them, that after Jesus had manifested himself to his Disciples, to be *that Christ that was crucified, dead and buried*; and by his appearing and conversing with his Disciples for the space of Forty days after his *Resurrection*, he then, and not till then, *ascended into Heaven*, in the sight of those Disciples; namely, on that day which we call the *Ascension*, or *Holy Thursday*. And that we then celebrate the performance of the promise which he made to his Disciples, at or before his

Ascension : namely, *that though he left them, yet he would send them the Holy Ghost to be their Comforter*; and that he did so on that day which the Church calls *Whitsunday*.——Thus the Church keeps an Historical and circular Commemoration of times, as they pass by us ; of such times, as ought to incline us to occasional praises, for the particular blessings which we do, or might receive by those holy Commemorations.

He made them know also, why the Church hath appointed *Ember-weeks*; and to know the reason why the *Commandments*, and the *Epistles* and *Gospels* were to be read at the *Altar*, or *Communion Table* : why the Priest was to pray the *Litany* kneeling ; and, why to pray some *Collects* standing ; and he gave them many other observations, fit for his plain Congregation, but not fit for me now to mention ; for I must set limits to my Pen, and not make that a Treatise, which I intended to be a much shorter account than I have made it ;—but I have done, when I have told the Reader, that he was constant in *Catechising* every *Sunday* in the After-noon, and that his Catechising was after his second lesson, and in the Pulpit, and that he never exceeded his half hour, and was always so happy as to have an obedient, and a full Congregation.

And to this I must add, That if he were at any time too zealous in his Sermons, it was in reproving the indecencies of the peoples behaviour, in the time of Divine Service ; and of those Ministers that hudled up the Church-prayers, without a visible reverence and affection ; namely, *such as seem'd to say the Lords prayer, or a Collect in a breath* ; but for himself, his custom was, to stop betwixt every Collect, and give the people time to consider what they had pray'd, and to force their desires affectionately to God, before he engag'd them into new Petitions.

And by this account of his diligence, to make his Parishioners understand what they pray'd, and why they prais'd, and ador'd their Creator: I hope I shall the more easily obtain the Readers belief to the following account of Mr. *Herberts* own practice; which was, to appear constantly with his Wife, and three Neeces (the daughters of a deceased Sister) and his whole Family, twice every day at the Church-prayers, in the Chappel which does almost joyn to his Parsonage-house. And for the time of his appearing, it was strictly at the Canonical hours of 10 and 4; and then and there, he lifted up pure and charitable hands to God in the midst of the Congregation. And he would joy to have spent that time in that place, where the honour of his *Master Jesus* dwelleth; and there, by that inward devotion which he testified constantly by an humble behaviour, and visible adoration, he, like *Josua* brought not only *his own Houshold thus to serve the Lord*; but brought most of his Parishioners, and many Gentlemen in the Neighbourhood, constantly to make a part of his Congregation twice a day; and some of the meaner sort of his Parish, did so love and reverence Mr. *Herbert*, that they would let their Plow rest when Mr. *Herberts Saints-Bell* rung to Prayers, that they might also offer their devotions to God with him: and would then return back to their Plow. And his most holy life was such, that it begot such reverence to God, and to him, that they thought themselves the happier, when they carried Mr. *Herberts* blessing back with them to their labour.——Thus powerful was his reason, and example, to perswade others to a practical piety, and devotion.

And his constant publick prayers did never make him to neglect his own private devotions, nor those prayers that he thought himself bound to perform with his Family, which alwaies were a Set-form, and not long; and he did alwaies conclude them with that Collect which the Church hath appointed for the day or week.——*Thus he made every days sanctity a step towards that Kingdom where Impurity cannot enter.*

His chiefest recreation was Musick, in which heavenly Art he was a most excellent Master, and did himself compose many *divine Hymns* and *Anthems*, which he set and sung to his *Lute* or *Viol*; and, though he was a lover of retiredness, yet his love to *Musick* was such, that he went usually twice every week on certain appointed days, to the *Cathedral Church* in *Salisbury*; and at his return would say, *That his time spent in Prayer, and Cathedral Musick, elevated his Soul, and was his Heaven upon Earth:* But before his return thence to *Bemerton*, he would usually sing and play his part, at an appointed private Musick-meeting; and, to justifie this practice, he would often say, *Religion does not banish mirth, but only moderates, and sets rules to it.*

And as his desire to enjoy *his Heaven upon Earth*, drew him twice every week to *Salisbury*, so his walks thither, were the occasion of many happy accidents to others: of which, I will mention some few.

In one of his walks to *Salisbury*, he overtook a Gentleman that is still living in that City, and in their walk together, Mr. *Herbert* took a fair occasion to talk with him, and humbly begg'd to be excus'd, if he ask'd him some account of his faith, and said, *I do this the rather, because though you are not of my Parish, yet I receive Tythe from you by the hand of your Tenant; and, Sir, I am the bolder to do it, because I know there be some Sermon-hearers, that be like those Fishes, that always live in salt water, and yet are always fresh.*

After which expression, Mr. *Herbert* asked him

some needful Questions, and having received his answer, gave him such Rules for the trial of his sincerity, and for a practical piety, and in so loving and meek a manner, that the Gentleman did so fall in love with him, and his discourse, that he would often contrive to meet him in his walk to *Salisbury*, or to attend him back to *Bemerton*; and still mentions the name of Mr. *George Herbert* with veneration, and still praiseth God for the occasion of knowing him.

In another of his *Salisbury* walks, he met with a Neighbour Minister, and after some friendly Discourse betwixt them, and some Condolement for the decay of Piety, and too general Contempt of the Clergy, Mr. *Herbert* took occasion to say,

One Cure for these Distempers would be for the Clergy themselves to keep the Ember-Weeks *strictly, and beg of their Parishioners to joyn with* them *in* Fasting *and* Prayers, *for a more Religious Clergy.*

And another Cure would be, *for themselves to restore the great and neglected duty of* Catechising, *on which the salvation of so many of the poor and ignorant Lay-people does depend; but principally, that the Clergy themselves would be sure to live unblameably; and that the dignif'd Clergy especially, which preach Temperance, would avoid Surfeiting, and take all occasions to express a visible humility and charity in their lives; for this would force a love & an imitation, and an unfeigned reverence from all that knew them to be such.* (And for proof of this, we need no other Testimony, than the life and death of Dr. *Lake*, late Lord Bishop of *Bath* and *Wells*) *This* (said Mr. *Herbert*) *would be a cure for the wickedness and growing Atheism of our Age. And,* my dear Brother, *till this be done by us, and done in earnest, let no man expect a reformation of the manners of the* Laity: *for 'tis not learning, but this,*

this only, that must do it; and till then, the fault must lye at our doors.

In another walk to *Salisbury*, he saw a poor man, with a poorer horse, that was fall'n under his Load; they were both in distress, and needed present help; which Mr. *Herbert* perceiving, put off his Canonical Coat, and help'd the poor man to unload, and after, to load his horse: The poor man blest him for it: and he blest the poor man; and was so like the *good Samaritan*, that he gave him money to refresh both himself and his horse; and told him, *That if he lov'd himself, he should be merciful to his Beast.*——Thus he left the poor man, and at his coming to his musical friends at *Salisbury*, they began to wonder that Mr. *George Herbert* which us'd to be so trim and clean, came into that company so soyl'd and discompos'd; but he told them the occasion: And when one of the company told him, *He had disparag'd himself by so dirty an employment*; his answer was, *That the thought of what he had done, would prove Musick to him at Midnight; and that the omission of it, would have upbraided and made discord in his Conscience, whensoever he should pass by that place; for, if I be bound to pray for all that be in distress, I am sure that I am bound so far as it is in my power to practise what I pray for. And though I do not wish for the like occasion every day, yet let me tell you, I would not willingly pass one day of my life without comforting a sad soul, or shewing mercy; and I praise God for this occasion*: And now let's tune our Instruments.

Thus, as our blessed Saviour after his Resurrection did take occasion to interpret the Scripture to *Cleopas*, and that other Disciple which he met with and accompanied in their journey to *Emmaus*; so Mr. *Herbert*, in his path toward Heaven, did daily take any fair occasion to instruct the ignorant, or comfort any that were in affliction; and did alwaies confirm his precepts, by shewing humility and mercy, and ministring grace to the hearers.

And he was most happy in his Wifes unforc'd compliance with his acts of Charity, whom he made his *Almoner*, and paid constantly into her hand, *a tenth penny* of what money he receiv'd for Tythe, and gave her power to dispose that to the poor of his Parish, and with it a power to dispose a tenth part of the Corn that came yearly into his Barn; which trust she did most faithfully perform, and would often offer to him *an account of her stewardship*, and as often beg an inlargement of his bounty, for she rejoyc'd in the employment; and this was usually laid out by her in *Blankets* and *Shooes*, for some such poor people, as she knew to stand in most need of them. This, as to her Charity.——And for his own, he set no limits to it; nor did ever turn his face from any that he saw in want, but would relieve them; especially his poor Neighbours; to the meanest of whose Houses, he would go and inform himself of their wants, and relieve them chearfully if they were in distress; and would alwaies praise God, as much for being willing, as for being able to do it.——And when he was advis'd by a friend to be more frugal, because he might have Children, his answer was, *He would not see the danger of want so far off; but, being the Scripture does so commend Charity, as to tell us, that Charity is the top of Christian vertues, the covering of sins, the fulfilling of the Law, the life of Faith: And that Charity hath a promise of the blessings of this life, and of a reward in that life which is to come, being these, and more excellent things are in Scripture spoken of thee O Charity, and that, being all my Tythes, and Church-dues, are a*

Deodate from thee O my God! make me, O my God, so far to trust thy promise, as to return them back to thee; and, by thy grace, I will do so, in distributing them to any of thy poor members that are in distress, or do but bear the image of Jesus my Master. *Sir* (said he to his friend) *my Wife hath a competent maintenance secur'd her after my death, and therefore as this is my prayer, so this my resolution shall by Gods grace be unalterable.*

This may be some account of the excellencies of the active part of his life; and thus he continued, till a Consumption so weakned him, as to confine him to his House, or to the Chappel, which does almost joyn to it; in which he continued to read Prayers constantly twice every day, though he were very weak; in one of which times of his reading, his Wife observ'd him to read in pain, and told him so, and that it wasted his spirits, and weakned him: and he confess'd it did, but said, *His life could not be better spent, than in the service of his Master Jesus, who had done and suffered so much for him:* But, said he, *I will not be wilful: for though my spirit be willing, yet I find my flesh is weak; and therefore Mr.* Bostock *shall be appointed to read Prayers for me to morrow, and I will now be only a hearer of them, till this mortal shall put on immortality.* And Mr. *Bostock* did the next day undertake and continue this happy employment, till Mr. *Herberts* death.——This Mr. *Bostock* was a learned and vertuous man, an old friend of Mr. *Herberts*, and then his Curate to the Church of *Fulston*, which is a mile from *Bemerton*, to which Church, *Bemerton* is but a *Chappel of ease.*—— And, this Mr. *Bostock* did also constantly supply the *Church-service* for Mr. *Herbert* in that Chappel, when the Musick-meeting at *Salisbury* caus'd his absence from it.

About one month before his death, his friend Mr. *Farrer* (for an account of whom I am by promise indebted to the Reader, and intend to make him sudden payment) hearing of Mr. *Herberts* sickness, sent Mr. *Edmund Duncon* (who is now Rector of *Fryer Barnet* in the County of *Middlesex*) from his House of *Gidden Hall*, which is near to *Huntington*, to see Mr. *Herbert*, and to assure him, he wanted not his daily prayers for his recovery; and Mr. *Duncon* was to return back to *Gidden*, with an account of Mr. *Herberts* condition. Mr. *Duncon* found him weak, and at that time lying on his Bed, or on a Pallat; but at his seeing Mr. *Duncon*, he rais'd himself vigorously, saluted him, and with some earnestness *inquir'd the health of his brother* Farrer? of which Mr. *Duncon* satisfied him; and after some discourse of Mr. *Farrers* holy life, and the manner of his constant serving God, he said to Mr. *Duncon——Sir, I see by your habit that you are a Priest, and I desire you to pray with me;* which being granted, Mr. *Duncon* ask'd him, *what Prayers?* to which, Mr. *Herberts* answer was, *O Sir, the Prayers of my Mother, the Church of* England, *no other Prayers are equal to them! but, at this time, I beg of you to pray only the* Litany, *for I am weak and faint;* and Mr. *Duncon* did so. After which, and some other discourse of Mr. *Farrer,* Mrs. *Herbert* provided Mr. *Duncon* a plain Supper, and a clean Lodging, and he betook himself to rest.——*This Mr.* Duncon *tells me;* and tells me, that at his first view of Mr. *Herbert,* he saw *majesty* and *humility* so reconcil'd in his looks and behaviour, as begot in him an awful reverence for his person: and saies, *his discourse was so pious, and his motion so gentile and meek, that after almost forty years, yet they remain still fresh in his memory.*

The next morning Mr. *Duncon* left him, and betook himself to a Journey to *Bath,* but with a promise to return back to him within five days, and he did so;

but before I shall say any thing of what discourse then fell betwixt them two, I will pay my promis'd account of Mr. *Farrer*.

Mr. *Nicholas Farrer* (who got the reputation of being call'd Saint *Nicholas*, at the age of six years) was born in *London*: and doubtless had good education in his youth; but certainly was at an early age made Fellow of *Clare-Hall* in *Cambridge*, where he continued to be eminent for his *piety*, *temperance*, and *learning*.——About the 26*th* year of his Age, he betook himself to Travel: in which he added to his *Latin* and *Greek*, a perfect knowledge of all the Languages spoken in the Western parts of our Christian world; and understood well the principles of their Religion, and of their manner, and the reasons of their worship.——In this his Travel he m̄et with many perswasions to come into a communion with that Church which calls it self *Catholick*: but he return'd from his Travels as he went, eminent for his obedience to his Mother, *the Church of England*. In his absence from *England*, Mr. *Farrers* father (who was a Merchant) allow'd him a liberal maintenance; and, not long after his return into *England*, Mr. *Farrer* had by the death of his father, or an elder brother, or both, an Estate left him, that enabled him to purchase Land to the value of 4 or 500 *l.* a year; the greatest part of which Land was at *Little Gidden*, 4 or 6 miles from *Huntington*, and about 18 from *Cambridge*: which place, he chose for the privacy of it, and for the Hall, which had the Parish-Church, or Chappel belonging, and adjoining near to it; for Mr. *Farrer* having seen the manners and vanities of the World, and found them to be, as Mr. *Herbert* says, *A nothing between two Dishes*; did so contemn it, that he resolv'd to spend the remainder of his life in mortifications, and in devotion, and

charity, and to be alwaies prepar'd for Death :——
And his life was spent thus.

He, and his Family, which were like a little
Colledge, and about Thirty in number, did most of
them keep *Lent*, and all *Ember-weeks* strictly, both in
fasting, and using all those mortifications and prayers
that the Church hath appointed to be then used : and,
he and they, did the like constantly on *Fridays*, and
on the *Vigils*, or Eves appointed to be fasted before
the Saints-days ; and this frugality and abstinence,
turn'd to the relief of the Poor : but this was but a
part of his charity, none but God and he knew the
rest.

This Family, which I have said to be in number
about Thirty, were a part of them his Kindred, and
the rest chosen to be of a temper fit to be moulded into
a devout life ; and all of them were for their dispositions *serviceable* and *quiet*, and *humble*, and *free from
scandal*. Having thus fitted himself for his Family,
he did about the year 1630. betake himself to a constant and methodical service of God, and it was in
this manner.——He being accompanied with most of
his Family, did himself use to read the Common
prayers (for he was a Deacon) every day, at the
appointed hours of Ten and Four, in the Parish Church
which was very near his House, and which he had both
repair'd and adorn'd ; for it was fallen into a great
ruine, by reason of a depopulation of the Village before
Mr. *Farrer* bought the Mannor : And he did also
constantly read the *Mattins* every Morning at the
hour of six, either in the Church, or in an Oratory,
which was within his own House : And many of the
Family did there continue with him after the Prayers
were ended, and there they spent some hours in
singing *Hymns*, or *Anthems*, sometimes in the Church,

and often to an Organ in the Oratory. And there they sometimes betook themselves to meditate, or to pray privately, or to read a part of the New Testament to themselves, or to continue their praying or reading the Psalms : and, in case the Psalms were not all alwaies read in the day, then Mr. *Farrer*, and others of the Congregation, did at Night, at the ring of a Watch-bell, repair to the Church or Oratory, and there betake themselves to prayers, and lauding God, and reading the Psalms that had not been read in the day ; and, when these, or any part of the Congregation grew weary, or faint, the Watch-bell was Rung, sometimes before, and sometimes after Midnight : and then another part of the Family rose, and maintain'd the Watch, sometimes by praying, or singing Lauds to God, or reading the Psalms : and when after some hours they also grew weary or faint, then they rung the Watch-bell, and were also reliev'd by some of the former, or by a new part of the Society, which continued their devotions (as hath been mentioned) until morning.——And it is to be noted, that in this continued serving of God, the Psalter, or whole Book of Psalms, was in every four and twenty hours, sung or read over, from the first to the last verse : and this was done as constantly, as the Sun runs his Circle every day about the World, and then begins again the same instant that it ended.

Thus did Mr. *Farrer*, and his happy Family, serve God day and night : Thus did they alwaies behave themselves, as in his presence. And they did alwaies eat and drink by the strictest rules of Temperance ; eat and drink so, as to be ready to rise at Midnight, or at the call of a Watch-bell, and perform their devotions to God.——And 'tis fit to tell the Reader, that many of the Clergy that were more inclin'd to *practical piety*, and *devotion*, then to doubtful and needless Disputations, did often come to *Gidden Hall*, and make themselves a part of that happy Society, and stay a week or more, and then join with Mr. *Farrer* and the Family in these Devotions, and assist and ease him or them in their Watch by Night; and these various Devotions, had never less than two of the Domestick Family in the Night; and the Watch was alwaies kept in the Church or Oratory, unless in extream cold Winter nights, and then it was maintain'd in a Parlour which had a fire in it: and the Parlour was fitted for that purpose; and this course of Piety, and great liberality to his poor Neighbours, Mr. *Farrer* maintain'd till his death, which was in the year 1639.

Mr. *Farrers*, and Mr. *Herberts* devout lives, were both so noted, that the general report of their sanctity gave them occasion to renew that slight acquaintance which was begun at their being Contemporaries in *Cambridge*; and this new holy friendship was long maintain'd without any interview, but only by loving and endearing Letters. And one testimony of their friendship, and pious designs, may appear by Mr. *Farrers* commending the considerations of *John Valdesso* (a Book which he had met with in his Travels, and Translated out of *Spanish* into *English*) to be examin'd and censur'd by Mr. *Herbert* before it was made publick; which excellent Book, Mr. *Herbert* did read, and return back with many marginal Notes, as they be now printed with it: And with them, Mr. *Herberts* affectionate Letter to Mr. *Farrer*.

This *John Valdesso* was a *Spaniard*, and was for his Learning and Vertue, much valued and lov'd by the great Emperour *Charles the fifth*, whom *Valdesso* had followed as a *Cavalier* all the time of his long and dangerous Wars; and when *Valdesso* grew old, and grew weary both of War and the World, he took his fair opportunity to declare to the Emperour, that his resolution was to decline His Majesties Service, and betake himself to a quiet and contemplative life, *because there ought to be a vacancy of time, betwixt fighting and dying.*——The Emperour had himself, for the same, or other like reasons, put on the same resolution: but, God and himself did till then, only know them; and he did therefore desire *Valdesso* to consider well of what he had said, and to keep his purpose within his own breast, till they two might have a second opportunity of a friendly Discourse: which *Valdesso* promis'd to do.

In the mean time, the Emperour appoints privately a day for him and *Valdesso* to meet again, and, after a pious and free discourse they both agreed on a certain day to receive the blessed Sacrament publickly: and, appointed an eloquent and devout Fryer, to preach a Sermon of *contempt of the World*, and of the happiness and benefit of a quiet and contemplative life; which the Fryer did most affectionately.——After which Sermon, the Emperour took occasion to declare openly, *That the Preacher had begot in him a resolution to lay down his Dignities, and to forsake the World, and betake himself to a Monastical life.* And he pretended, he had perswaded *John Valdesso* to do the like; but this is most certain, that after the Emperour had called his son *Philip* out of *England*, and resign'd to him all his Kingdoms, that then the Emperour, and *John Valdesso*, did perform their resolutions.

This account of *John Valdesso*, I receiv'd from a Friend, that had it from the mouth of Mr. *Farrer*: And the Reader may note, that in this retirement, *John Valdesso* writ his 110 considerations, and many

other Treatises of worth, which want a second Mr.
Farrer to procure, and translate them.

After this account of Mr. *Farrer*, and *John Valdesso*,
I proceed to my account of Mr. *Herbert*, and Mr.
Duncon, who, according to his promise, return'd from
the Bath the fifth day, and then found Mr. *Herbert*
much weaker than he left him : and therefore their
Discourse could not be long ; but at Mr. *Duncons* parting with him, Mr. *Herbert* spoke to this purpose——
Sir, I pray give my brother Farrer *an account of the
decaying condition of my body, and tell him, I beg him
to continue his daily prayers for me : and let him know,
that I have consider'd,* That God only is what he would
bee ; *and that I am by his grace become now so like him,
as to be pleas'd with what pleaseth him ; and tell him,
that I do not repine but am pleas'd with my want of health;
and tell him, my heart is fixed on that place where true
joy is only to be found; and that I long to be there, and
do wait for my appointed change with* hope *and* patience.
Having said this, he did with so sweet a humility as
seem'd to exalt him, bow down to Mr. *Duncon,*——
with a thoughtful and contented look, say to him,——
Sir, I pray deliver this little Book to my dear brother
Farrer, *and tell him, he shall find in it a picture of the
many spiritual Conflicts that have past betwixt* God *and
my Soul, before I could subject mine to the will of* Jesus
my Master : *in whose service I have now found perfect
freedom ; desire him to read it : and then, if he can
think it may turn to the advantage of any dejected poor
Soul, let it be made publick: if not, let him burn it :
for* I *and it, are less than the least of* God's *mercies.*
——Thus meanly did this humble man think of this
excellent Book, which now bears the name of *The
TEMPLE :* Or, *Sacred Poems,* and *Private Ejaculations*; of which, Mr. *Farrer* would say, *There was in*

it the picture of a divine Soul in every page; and that the whole Book was such a harmony of holy passions, as would enrich the World with pleasure and piety. And it appears to have done so : for there have been more then Twenty thousand of them sold since the first Impression.

And this ought to be noted, that when Mr. *Farrer* sent this Book to *Cambridge* to be Licensed for the Press, the *Vice-Chancellor* would by no means allow the two so much noted Verses,

> *Religion stands a Tip-toe in our Land,*
> *Ready to pass to the* American *Strand.*

to be printed ; and Mr. *Farrer* would by no means allow the Book to be printed, and want them : But after some time, and some arguments, for and against their being made publick, the *Vice-Chancellor* said, *I knew Mr.* Herbert *well, and know that he had many heavenly Speculations, and was a Divine Poet; but I hope the World will not take him to be an inspired Prophet, and therefore I License the whole Book* : So that it came to be printed, without the diminution or addition of a syllable, since it was deliver'd into the hands of Mr. *Duncon*, save only, that Mr. *Farrer* hath added that excellent Preface that is printed before it.

At the time of Mr. *Duncons* leaving Mr. *Herbert*, (which was about three weeks before his death) his old and dear friend Mr. *Woodnot*, came from *London* to *Bemerton*, and never left him, till he had seen him draw his last breath, and clos'd his Eyes on his Death-bed. In this time of his decay, he was often visited and pray'd for by all the Clergy that liv'd near to him, especially by his friends the Bishop and Prebends of the Cathedral Church in *Salisbury*; but by none more devoutly, than his Wife, his three Neeces (then a part of his Family) and Mr. *Woodnot*, who were the sad Witnesses of his daily decay; to whom he would often speak to this purpose.——*I now look back upon the pleasures of my life past, and see the content I have taken in* beauty, *in* wit, *in* musick, *and* pleasant Conversation, *are now all past by me, like a dream, or as a shadow that returns not, and are now all become dead to me, or I to them; and I see that as my father and generation hath done before me, so I also shall now suddenly (with* Job*) make my Bed also in the dark; and I praise God I am prepared for it; and I praise him, that I am not to learn patience, now I stand in such need of it; and that I have practised Mortification, and endeavour'd to dye daily, that I might not dye eternally; and my hope is, that I shall shortly leave this valley of tears, and be free from all fevers and pain: and which will be a more happy condition, I shall be free from sin, and all the temptations and anxieties that attend it; and this being past, I shall dwell in the new* Jerusalem, *dwell there with men made perfect; dwell, where these eyes shall see my Master and Saviour* Jesus; *and with him see my dear Mother, and all my Relations and Friends:*——*But I must dye, or not come to that happy place: And this is my content, that I am going daily towards it; and that every day which I have liv'd, hath taken a part of my appointed time from me; and that I shall live the less time, for having liv'd this, and the day past.*——These, and the like expressions, which he utter'd often, may be said to *be his* enjoyment of Heaven, before he enjoy'd it.——The *Sunday* before his death, he rose suddenly from his Bed or Couch, call'd for one of his Instruments, took it into hand, and said——

> *My God, My God,*
> *My Musick shall find thee,*
>   *And every string*
> *shall have his attribute to sing.*

And having tun'd it, he play'd and sung :
> *The Sundays of Mans life,*
> *Thredded together on times string,*
> *Make Bracelets, to adorn the Wife*
> *Of the eternal glorious King :*
> *On Sundays, Heavens dore stands ope ;*
> *Blessings are plentiful and rife,*
>   *More plentiful than hope.*

Thus he sung on Earth such Hymns and Anthems, as the Angels and he, and Mr. *Farrer*, now sing in Heaven.

Thus he continued meditating and praying, and rejoicing, till the day of his death ; and on that day, said to Mr. *Woodnot*, *My dear Friend, I am sorry I have nothing to present to my merciful God but sin and misery; but the first is pardoned: and a few hours will now put a period to the latter*; for I shall suddenly go hence and be no more seen. Upon which expression, Mr. *Woodnot* took occasion to remember him of the Re-edifying *Layton* Church, and his many Acts of mercy ; to which he made answer, saying, *They be good works, if they be sprinkled with the blood of Christ, and not otherwise.* After this Discourse he became more restless, and his Soul seem'd to be weary of her earthly Tabernacle ; and this uneasiness became so visible, that his Wife, his three Neeces, and Mr. *Woodnot*, stood constantly about his bed, beholding him with sorrow, and an unwillingness to lose the sight of him whom they could not hope to see much longer.——As they stood thus beholding him, his Wife observ'd him to breath faintly, and with much trouble: and observ'd him to fall into a sudden Agony; which so surpriz'd her, that she fell into a sudden passion, and requir'd of him to know, *how he did?* to which his answer was, *That he had past a Conflict with his last Enemy, and had overcome him, by the merits of his Master Jesus.* After which answer, he look'd up, and saw his Wife and Neeces weeping to an extremity, and charg'd them, *If they lov'd him, to withdraw into the next Room, and there pray every one alone for him, for nothing but their lamentations could make his death uncomfortable.* To which request, their sighs and tears would not suffer them to make any reply: but they yielded him a sad obedience, leaving only with him Mr. *Woodnot,* and Mr. *Bostock.* Immediately after they had left him, he said to Mr. *Bostock, Pray Sir open that door, then look into that Cabinet, in which you may easily find my last Will, and give it into my hand;* which being done Mr. *Herbert* deliver'd it into the hand of Mr. *Woodnot,* and said, *My old Friend, I here deliver you my last Will, in which you will find that I have made you my sole Executor for the good of my Wife and Neeces; and I desire you to shew kindness to them, as they shall need it; I do not desire you to be just: for I know you will be so for your own sake; but I charge you, by the Religion of our friendship, to be careful of them.* And having obtain'd Mr. *Woodnots* promise to be so; he said, *I am now ready to dye:* after which words he said, *Lord, forsake me not now my strength faileth me: but grant me mercy for the merits of my Jesus; and now Lord, Lord now receive my Soul.* And, with those words he breath'd forth his Divine Soul, without any apparent disturbance: Mr. *Woodnot,* and Mr. *Bostock*, attending his last breath, and closing his eyes.

Thus he liv'd, and thus he dy'd like a Saint, unspotted of the World, full of Alms-deeds, full of Humility, and all the examples of a vertuous life; which I cannot conclude better, than with this borrowed observation :

> —— *All must to their cold Graves;*
> *But the religious actions of the just,*
> *Smell sweet in death, and blossom in the dust.*

Mr. *George Herberts* have done so to this, and will doubtless do so to succeeding Generations.——I have but this to say more of him : That if *Andrew Melvin* dyed before him, then *George Herbert* dyed without an enemy.——I wish (if God shall be so pleased) that I may be so happy as to dye like him.

Iz. Wa.

THere is a debt justly due to the memory of Mr. Herberts *vertuous Wife; a part of which I will endeavour to pay, by a very short account of the remainder of her life, which shall follow.*

She continu'd his disconsolate Widow, about six years, bemoaning her self, and complaining, *That she had lost the delight of her eyes;* but more, *that she had lost the spiritual guide for her poor soul; and would often say,* O that I had like holy *Mary,* the Mother of Jesus, treasur'd up all his sayings in my heart; but since I have not been able to do that, I will labour to live like him, that where he now is, I may be also. *And she would often say (as the Prophet* David *for his son* Absolon) O that I had dyed for him ! *Thus she continued mourning, till time and conversation had so moderated her sorrows, that she became the happy Wife of Sir* Robert Cook *of Highnam in the County of* Gloucester *Knight: And though he put a high value on the excellent accomplishments of her mind and body; and was so like Mr.* Herbert, *as not to govern like a Master, but as an affectionate Husband; yet she would even to him often take occasion to mention the name of Mr.*George Herbert, *and say,* That name must live in her memory, till she put off mortality.——*By Sir* Robert, *she had only one Child, a Daughter, whose parts and plentiful estate make her happy in this world, and her well using of them, gives a fair testimony, that she will be so in that which is to come.*

Mrs. Herbert *was the Wife of Sir* Robert *eight years, and liv'd his Widow about fifteen ; all which time, she took a pleasure in mentioning, and commending the ex-cellencies of* Mr. George Herbert. *She dyed in the year* 1663. *and lies buried at* Highnam; *Mr.* Herbert *in his own Church, under the Altar, and cover'd with a Grave-stone without any inscription.*

This Lady Cook, *had preserv'd many of Mr.* Herberts *private Writings, which she intended to make publick; but they, and* Highnam *house, were burnt together, by the late Rebels, and so lost to posterity.*

J. W.

LETTERS

Written by

Mr. *GEORGE HERBERT*,

At his being in

CAMBRIDGE:

With others to his Mother, the Lady

MAGDALEN HERBERT;

Written by

JOHN DONNE,

Afterwards

DEAN of St. *PAVLS*.

LONDON,

Printed in the Year 1675.

Mr. *GEORGE HERBERT* to *N. F.* the Translatour of *Valdesso*.

MY dear and deserving Brother, your *Valdesso* I now return with many thanks, and some notes, in which perhaps you will discover some care, which I forbear not in the midst of my griefs; First for your sake; because, I would do nothing negligently that you commit unto me; Secondly for the Authors sake, whom I conceive to have been a true servant of God; and to such, and all that is theirs, I owe diligence; Thirdly for the Churches sake, to whom by Printing it, I would have you consecrate it. You owe the Church a debt, and God hath put this into your hands (as he sent the Fish with money to St. *Peter*) to discharge it: happily also with this (as his thoughts are fruitful) intending the honour of his servant the Author, who being obscured in his own Countrey, he would have to flourish in this land of light, and region of the Gospel, among his chosen. It is true, there are some things which I like not in him, as my fragments will express, when you read them; nevertheless, I wish you by all means to publish it, for these three eminent things observable therein: First, that God in the midst of Popery should open the eyes of one to understand and express so clearly, and excellently the intent of the Gospel in the acceptation of Christs righteousness: (as he sheweth through all his Considerations,) a thing strangely buried, and darkned by the Adversaries, and their great stumbling block. Secondly, the great honour and reverence which he every where bears towards our dear Master and Lord; concluding every Consideration almost with his holy Name, and setting his merit forth so piously; for which I do so love him, that were there nothing else, I would Print it, that with it the honour of my Lord might be published. Thirdly, the many pious rules of ordering our life, about Mortification, and observation of Gods Kingdom within us, and the working thereof; of which he was a very diligent observer. These three things are very eminent in the Author, and overweigh the Defects (as I conceive) towards the publishing thereof.

From his Parsonage
  of *Bemerton*, near
   Salisbury, Sept.
    29. 1632.

To Sir *J. D.*

SIR,

THough I had the best wit in the World, yet it would easily tire me, to find out variety of thanks for the diversity of your favours, if I sought to do so; but I profess it not: And therefore let it be sufficient for me, that the same heart, which you have won long since, is still true to you, and hath nothing else to answer your infinite kindnesses, but a constancy of obedience, only hereafter I will take heed how I propose my desires unto you, since I find you so willing to yield to my requests; for, since your favours come a Horse-back, there is reason, that my desires should go a-foot: neither do I make any question, but that you have performed your kindness to the full, and that the Horse is every way fit for me, and I will strive to imitate the compleatness of your love, with being in some proportion, and after my manner,

Your most obedient Servant,

George Herbert.

For my dear sick Sister.

Most dear Sister,

THink not my silence forgetfulness; or that my love is as dumb as my papers, though businesses may stop my hand, yet my heart, a much better member, is always with you: and which is more, with our good and gracious God, incessantly begging some ease of your pains, with that earnestness, that becomes your griefs, and my love. God who knows and sees this Writing, knows also that my solliciting him has been much, and my tears many for you; judge me then by those waters, and not by my ink, and then you shall justly value

Your most truly,

Decem. 6. 1620.
    Trin. Coll.   *most heartily,*

affectionate Brother,

and Servant,

George Herbert.

SIR,

I Dare no longer be silent, least while I think I am modest, I wrong both my self, and also the confidence my Friends have in me; wherefore I will open my case unto you, which I think deserves the reading at the least; and it is this, I want Books extreamly; You know Sir, how I am now setting foot into Divinity, to lay the platform of my future life, and shall I then be fain always to borrow Books, and build on anothers foundation? What Tradesman is there who will set up without his Tools? Pardon my boldness Sir, it is a most serious Case, nor can I write coldly in that, wherein consisteth the making good of my former education, of obeying that Spirit which hath guided me hitherto, and of atchieving my (I dare say) holy ends. This also is aggravated, in that I apprehend what my Friends would have been forward to say, if I had taken ill courses, *Follow your Book, and you shall want nothing*: You know Sir, it is their ordinary speech, and now let them make it good; for, since, I hope, I have not deceived their expectation, let not them deceive mine: But perhaps they will say, you are sickly, you must not study too hard; it is true (God knows) I am weak, yet not so, but that every day, I may step one step towards my journies end; and I love my friends so well, as that if all things proved not well, I had rather the fault should lie on me, than on them; but they will object again, What becomes of your Annuity? Sir, if there be any truth in me, I find it little enough to keep me in health. You know I was sick last Vacation, neither am I yet recovered, so that I am fain ever and anon, to buy somewhat tending towards my health, for infirmities are both painful and costly. Now this *Lent* I am forbid utterly to eat any Fish, so that I am fain to dyet in my Chamber at mine own cost; for in our publick Halls, you know, is nothing but Fish and Whit-meats: Out of *Lent* also, twice a Week, on *Fridays* and *Saturdays*, I must do so, which yet sometimes I fast. Sometimes also I ride to *New-Market*, and there lie a day or two for fresh Air; all which tend to avoiding of costlier matters, if I should fall absolutely sick: I protest and vow, I even study Thrift, and yet I am scarce able with much ado to make one half years allowance, shake hands with the other: And yet if a Book of four or five Shillings, come in my way, I buy it, though I fast for it; yea, sometimes of Ten Shillings: But, alas Sir, what is that to those infinite Volumes of Divinity, which yet every day swell, and grow bigger. Noble Sir, pardon my boldness, and consider but these three things. First, the Bulk of Divinity. Secondly, the time when I desire this (which is now, when I must lay the foundation of my whole life). Thirdly, what I desire, and to what end, not vain pleasures, nor to a vain end. If then, Sir, there be any course, either by engaging my future Annuity, or any other way, I desire you, Sir, to be my Mediator to them in my behalf.

Now I write to you, Sir, because to you I have ever opened my heart; and have reason, by the Patents of your perpetual favour to do so still, for I am sure you love

March 18. 1617.   *Your faithfullest Servant,*
  Trin. Coll.   George Herbert.

SIR,

THis Week hath loaded me with your Favours; I wish I could have come in person to thank you, but it is not possible; presently after *Michaelmas,* I am to make an Oration to the whole University of an hour long in *Latin,* and my *Lincoln* journey hath set me much behind hand: neither can I so much as go to *Bugden,* and deliver your Letter, yet have I sent it thither by a faithful Messenger this day: I beseech you all, you and my dear Mother and Sister to pardon me, for my *Cambridge* necessities are stronger to tye me here, than yours to *London:* If I could possibly have come, none should have done my message to Sir *Fr. Nethersole* for me; he and I are ancient acquaintance, and I have a strong opinion of him, that if he can do me a courtesie, he will of himself; yet your appearing in it, affects me strangely. I have sent you here inclosed a Letter from our Master in my behalf, which if you can send to Sir *Francis* before his departure, it will do well, for it expresseth the Universities inclination to me; yet if you cannot send it with much convenience, it is no matter, for the Gentleman needs no incitation to love me.

The Orators place (that you may understand what it is) is the finest place in the University, though not the gainfullest; yet that will be about 30 l. *per an.* but the commodiousness is beyond the Revenue; for the Orator writes all the University Letters, makes all the Orations, be it to King, Prince, or whatever comes to the University; to requite these pains, he takes place next the Doctors, is at all their Assemblies and Meetings, and sits above the Proctors, is Regent or Non-regent at his pleasure, and such like Gaynesses, which will please a young man well.

I long to hear from Sir *Francis*, I pray Sir send the Letter you receive from him to me as soon as you can, that I may work the heads to my purpose. I hope I shall get this place without all your *London* helps, of which I am very proud, not but that I joy in your favours, but that you may see, that if all fail, yet I am able to stand on mine own legs. Noble Sir, I thank you for your infinite favours, I fear only that I have omitted some fitting circumstance, yet you will pardon my haste, which is very great, though never so, but that I have both time and work to be

Your extream Servant,

George Herbert.

SIR,

I Have received the things you sent me, safe; and now the only thing I long for, is to hear of my dear sick Sister; first, how her health fares, next, whether my peace be yet made with her concerning my unkind departure. Can I be so happy, as to hear of both these that they succeed well? Is it not too much for me? Good Sir, make it plain to her, that I loved her even in my departure, in looking to her Son, and my charge. I suppose she is not disposed to spend her eye-sight on a piece of Paper, or else I had wrote to her; when I shall understand that a Letter will be seasonable, my Pen is ready. Concerning the Orators place all goes well yet, the next *Friday* it is tried, and accordingly you shall hear. I have forty businesses in my hands, your Courtesie will pardon the haste of

Your humblest Servant,

Jan. 19. 1619.
  Trin. Coll.

George Herbert.

SIR,

I Understand by Sir *Francis Nethersols* Letter, that he fears I have not fully resolved of the matter, since this place being civil may divert me too much from Divinity, at which, not without cause, he thinks, I aim ; but I have wrote him back, that this dignity, hath no such earthiness in it, but it may very well be joined with Heaven ; or if it had to others, yet to me it should not, for ought I yet knew ; and therefore I desire him to send me a direct answer in his next Letter. I pray Sir therefore, cause this inclosed to be carried to his brothers house of his own name (as I think) at the sign of the *Pedler* and the *Pack* on *London-bridge*, for there he assigns me. I cannot yet find leisure to write to my Lord, or Sir *Benjamin Ruddyard* ; but I hope I shall shortly, though for the reckoning of your favors, I shall never find time and paper enough, yet I am

Your readiest Servant,

Octob. 6. 1619.
  Trin. Coll.

George Herbert.

I remember my most humble duty to my Mother, who cannot think me lazy, since I rode 200 mile to see a Sister, in a way I knew not, in the midst of much business, and all in a Fortnight, not long since.

To the truly Noble Sir *J. D.*

SIR,

I Understand by a Letter from my Brother *Henry*, that he hath bought a parcel of Books for me, and that they are coming over. Now though they have hitherto travelled upon your charge, yet if my Sister were acquainted that they are ready, I dare say she would make good her promise of taking five or six pound upon her, which she hath hitherto deferred to do, not of her self, but upon the want of those Books which were not to be got in *England*; for that which surmounts, though your noble disposition is infinitely free, yet I had rather flie to my old ward, that if any course could be taken of doubling my Annuity now, upon condition that I should surcease from all title to it, after I enter'd into a Benefice, I should be most glad to entertain it, and both pay for the surplusage of these Books, and for ever after cease my clamorous and greedy bookish requests. It is high time now that I should be no more a burden to you, since I can never answer what I have already received; for your favours are so ancient, that they prevent my memory, and yet still grow upon

Your Humblest Servant,

George Herbert.

I remember my most humble duty to my Mother, I have wrote to my dear sick Sister this week already, and therefore now I hope may be excused.

I pray Sir, pardon my boldness of inclosing my Brothers
Letter in yours, for it was because I know your
Lodging, but not his.

To the worthiest Lady, Mrs.
Magdalen Herbert.

MADAM,

EVery excuse hath in it somewhat of accusation;
and since I am innocent, and yet must excuse,
how shall I do for that part of accusing. By my
troth, as desperate and perplexed men, grow from
thence bold; so must I take the boldness of accusing
you, who would draw so dark a Curtain betwixt me and
your purposes, as that I had no glimmering, neither of
your goings, nor the way which my Letters might
haunt. Yet I have given this Licence to Travel, but
I know not whether, nor it. It is therefore rather a
Pinnace to discover; and the intire Colony of Letters,
of Hundreds and Fifties, must follow; whose employment is more honourable, than that which our State
meditates to *Virginia*, because you are worthier than
all that Countrey, of which that is a wretched inch;
for you have better treasure, and a harmlessness. If
this sound like a flattery, tear it out. I am to my
Letters as rigid a Puritane, as *Cæsar* was to his Wife.
I can as ill endure a suspitious and misinterpretable
word as a fault; but remember, that nothing is
flattery which the Speaker believes; and of the
grossest flatteries there is this good use, that they tell
us what we should be. But, *Madam*, you are beyond
instruction, and therefore there can belong to you only
praise; of which, though you be no good hearer, yet

allow all my Letters leave to have in them one part of it, which is thankfulness towards you.

Your unworthiest Servant,

Michin,
July 11.   *Except your accepting*
1607.
                                        have mended him,

John Donne

To *the worthiest Lady,* Mrs. Magdalen Herbert.

MADAM,

THis is my second Letter, in which though I cannot tell you what is good, yet this is the worst, that I must be a great part of it; yet to me, that is recompensed, because you must be mingled. After I knew you were gone (for I must, little less than accusingly tell you, I knew not you would go) I sent my first Letter, like a *Bevis* of *Hampton*, to seek Adventures. This day I came to Town, and to the best part of it, your House; for your memory is a State-cloth and Presence; which I reverence, though you be away; though I need not seek that there, which I have about and within me. There, though I found my accusation, yet any thing to which your hand is, is a pardon; yet I would not burn my first Letter, because as in great destiny no small passage can be omitted or frustrated, so in my resolution of writing almost daily to you, I would have no link of the Chain broke by me, both because my Letters interpret one another, and because only their number can give them weight: If I had your Commission and Instructions to do you the service of a Legier Ambassador here, I could say something of the Countess of *Devon*: of the States, and such things.   But since to you, who are not only a World alone, but the Monarchy of the World your self, nothing can be added, especially by me; I will sustain my self with the honour of being

London,   *Your Servant Extraordinary,*
July 23.
1607.

                                    And without Place,

                                         John Donne.

To the worthiest Lady, Mrs. Magdalen Herbert.

MADAM,

AS we must dye before we can have full glory and happiness, so before I can have this degree of it, as to see you by a Letter, I must almost dye, that is, come to *London*, to plaguy *London*; a place full of danger, and vanity, and vice, though the Court be gone.   And such it will be, till your return redeem it: Not that the greatest vertue in the World, which is you, can be such a Marshal, as to defeat, or disperse all the vice of this place; but as higher bodies remove, or contract themselves when better come, so at your return we shall have one door open to innocence.   Yet

Madam, you are not such an *Ireland,* as produceth neither ill, nor good; no Spiders, nor Nightingales, which is a rare degree of perfection: But you have found and practised that experiment, That even nature, out of her detesting of emptiness, if we will make that our work, to remove bad, will fill us with good things. To abstain from it, was therefore but the Childhood, and Minority of your Soul, which had been long exercised since, in your manlier active part, of doing good. Of which since I have been a witness and subject, not to tell you sometimes, that by your influence and example I have attained to such a step of goodness, as to be thankful, were both to accuse your power and judgment of impotency and infirmity.

your Ladyships in all Services,

August 2.
1607.

John Donne.

On Mr. *George Herbert's* Book, In-tituled, *The Temple of Sacred Poems,* sent to a Gentlewoman.

> K*Now you Fair, on what you look?*
>   *Divinest Love lies in this Book:*
>   *Expecting Fire from your Eyes,*
> *To kindle this his Sacrifice.*
> *When your hands untye these strings,*
> *Think you've an Angel by the wings.*
> *One that gladly will be nigh,*
> *To wait upon each morning sigh.*

To flutter in the balmy Air,
Of your well perfumed Prayer.
These white Plumes of his Hee'll lend you,
Which every day to Heaven will send you,
To take acquaintance of the Sphere,
And all the smooth-fac'd Kindred there.
    And though Herberts Name do owe
    These Devotions, Fairest; know
    That while I lay them on the shrine
    Of your white Hand, they are mine.

               [Richard Crashaw.]

To the Right Honourable the Lady *Anne*, Countess of *Pembr.* and *Montg.* at Court.

MADAM,

WHat a trouble hath your *Goodness brought on you, by admitting our poor services? now they creep in a Vessel of* Metheglin, *and still they will be presenting or wishing to see, if at length they may find out some thing not unworthy of those hands at which they aim. In the mean time a Priests blessing, though it be none of the Court-stile, yet doubtless Madam, can do you no hurt: Wherefore the Lord make good the blessing of your Mother upon you, and cause all her wishes, diligence, prayers and tears, to bud, blow and bear fruit in your Soul, to his glory, your own good, and the great joy of*

Madam,

Dec. 10. 1631.
   Bemerton.   Your most faithful Servant

                              in Christ Jesu,

Madam, Your poor
   Colony of Servants
   present their humble
   duties.

George Herbert.

FINIS.

THE

LIFE

OF

Dr. *SANDERSON,*

LATE
Biſhop of *Lincoln.*

Written by *IZAAK WALTON.*

To which is added,
Some short Tracts or Cases of
Conscience, written by the
ſaid Bishop.

ECCLES. 3.
Mysteries are revealed to the meek.

LONDON,
Printed for *Richard Marriott.* 1678.

TO THE

RIGHT REVEREND,

AND HONOURABLE,

GEORGE

Lord Bishop of *Winchester*,
PRELATE of the *GARTER*,
and one of *his*
Majesties Privy Council.

My Lord,

IF I should undertake to enumerate the many favours
and advantages I have had by my very long acquaintance with your Lordship, I should enter upon an
Imployment, that might prove as tedious, as the Collecting of the Materials for this poor Monument, which I
have erected, and do dedicate to the Memory of your
beloved Friend Dr. Sanderson: But though I will not
venture to do that; yet I do remember with pleasure, and
remonstrate with gratitude, that your Lordship made me
known to him, Mr. Chillingworth, and Dr. Hammond;
men, whose Merits ought never to be forgotten.

My Friendship with the first was begun almost Forty
years past, when I was as far from a thought, as a desire
to out-live him; and farther from an intention to write
his life: But the wise Disposer of all mens lives and
actions hath prolong'd the first, and now permitted the

last; which is here dedicated to your Lordship (and as it ought to be) with all humility, and a desire that it may remain as a publick Testimony of my Gratitude,

> My Lord,
>> Your most affectionate
>>> Old Friend, and most
>>>> humble Servant,
>>>>> *Izaak Walton.*

THE
PREFACE.

I Dare neither think, nor assure the Reader, that I have committed no Mistakes in this Relation of the Life of Dr. *Sanderson*; but am sure, there is none that are either wilful, or very material. I confess, it was worthy the imployment of some person of more Learning and greater Abilities than I can pretend to; and I have not a little wondred that none have yet been so grateful to him and Posterity, as to undertake it. For it may be noted, That our Saviour hath had such care, that for *Mary Magdalens* kindness to him, her Name should never be forgotten: And doubtless, Dr. *Sanderson*'s meek and innocent Life, his great and useful Learning, might therefore challenge the like indeavours to preserve his Memory: And 'tis to me a wonder, that it has been already fifteen years neglected. But, in saying this, my meaning is not to upbraid others (I am far from that) but excuse my self, or beg pardon for daring to attempt it. This being premis'd, I desire to tell the Reader, that in this Relation I have been so bold, as to paraphrase and say what I think he (whom I had the happiness to know well) would have said upon the same occasions; and, if I have err'd in this kind, and cannot now beg pardon of him that lov'd me; yet I do of my Reader, from whom I desire the same favour.

And, though my Age might have procur'd me a Writ of Ease, and that secur'd me from all further trouble in this kind; yet I met with such perswasions to begin, and so many willing Informers since, and from them and others, such helps and incouragements to proceed, that when I found my self faint, and weary of the burthen with which I had loaden my self, and ready to lay it down; yet time and new strength hath at last brought it to be what it now is, and presented to the Reader, and with it this desire; That he will take notice, that Dr. *Sanderson* did in his Will or last Sickness advertise, that after his death nothing of his might be printed; because *that might be said to be his, which indeed was not*; and also for that *he might have chang'd his opinion since he first writ it.* And though these Reasons ought to be regarded, yet regarded so, as he resolves in that Case of Conscience concerning *rash Vows*, that there may appear very good second Reasons, why we may forbear to perform them. However, for his said Reasons, they ought to be read as we do *Apocriphal Scripture*; to explain, but not oblige us to so firm a belief of what is here presented as his.

And I have this to say more, That as in my Queries for writing Dr. *Sanderson*'s Life, I met with these little Tracts annex'd; so in my former Queries for my Information to write the Life of *venerable* Mr. *Hooker*, I met with a Sermon, which I also believe was really his, and here presented as his to the Reader. It is affirm'd (and I have met with reason to believe it) that there be some Artists, that do certainly know an *Original* Picture from a *Copy*; and in what Age of the World, and by whom drawn: And if so, then I hope it may be as safely affirmed, that what is here presented for theirs, is so like their temper of mind, their other writings, the times when, and the occasions upon which they were writ, that all Readers may safely conclude, they could be writ by none but *venerable* Mr. *Hooker*, and the *humble* and *learned* Dr. *Sanderson*.

And lastly, I am now glad that I have collected these Memoirs, which lay scatter'd, and contracted them into a narrower compass; and, if I have by the pleasant toyl of doing so, either pleas'd or profited any man, I have attain'd what I design'd when I first undertook it: But I seriously wish, both for the Readers, and Dr. *Sanderson*'s sake, that Posterity had known his great Learning and Vertue by a better Pen; by such a Pen, as could have made his Life as immortal as his Learning and Merits ought to be.

I. W.

May the 7th. 1678.

L ET the Life of Dr. *Sanderson*, late Bishop of *Lincoln*, with the Letters and Tracts at the end thereof, and Mr. *Hooker*'s Sermon, be printed.

> *WILL. JANE*, Chaplain to the Right Reverend Father in God, *Henry* Lord Bishop of *London*.

THE

LIFE

OF

Dr. *Robert Sanderson*,

Late

Lord Bishop of *Lincoln*.

Doctor *Robert Sanderson*, the late learned Bishop of *Lincoln*, whose Life I intend to write with all truth and equal plainness, was born the nineteenth day of *September*, in the year of our Redemption 1587. The place of his birth was *Rotheram* in the County of *York*; a Town of good note, and the more for that *Thomas Rotheram*, sometime *Archbishop* of that See was born in it; a man, whose great wisdom, and bounty, and sanctity of life, have made it the more memorable; as indeed it ought also to be, for being the birth place of our *Robert Sanderson*. And the Reader will be of my belief, if this humble Relation of his Life can hold any proportion with his great Piety, his useful Learning, and his many other extraordinary endowments.

He was the second and youngest Son of *Robert Sanderson* of *Gilthwait-hall*, in the said Parish and County, Esq; by *Elizabeth* one of the Daughters of *Richard Carr* of *Buterthwate-hall*, in the Parish of *Ecclesfield* in the said County of *York*, Gentleman.

This *Robert Sanderson* the Father, was descended from a numerous, ancient, and honourable Family of his own Name : for the search of which truth, I refer my Reader, that inclines to it, to Dr. *Thoriton's History of the Antiquities of Nottinghamshire,* and other Records ; not thinking it necessary here to ingage him into a search for bare Titles, which are noted to have in them nothing of reality : For Titles not acquir'd, but deriv'd only, do but shew us who of our Ancestors have, and how they have atchiev'd that honour which their Descendants claim, and may not be worthy to enjoy. For if those Titles descend to persons that degenerate into Vice, and break off the continued line of Learning, or Valour, or that Vertue that acquir'd them, they destroy the very foundation upon which that Honour was built ; and all the Rubbish of their Vices ought to fall heavy on such dishonourable Heads ; ought to fall so heavy, as to degrade them of their Titles, and blast their Memories with reproach and shame.

But our *Robert Sanderson* lived worthy of his Name and Family : Of which one testimony may be, That *Gilbert,* call'd the Great Earl of *Shrewsbury,* thought him not unworthy to be joyn'd with him as a God-father to *Gilbert Sheldon,* the late Lord Archbishop of *Canterbury* ; to whose Merits and Memory Posterity (the Clergy especially) ought to pay a Reverence.

But I return to my intended Relation of *Robert* the Son, who began in his Youth to make the Laws of God, and Obedience to his Parents, the rules of his life ; seeming even then to dedicate himself, and all his Studies, to Piety and Vertue.

And, as he was inclin'd to this by that native goodness, with which the wise Disposer of all hearts had endow'd his : So this calm, this quiet and happy

temper of mind (his being mild, and averse to oppositions) made the whole course of his life easie and
grateful both to himself and others : And this blessed
temper, was maintain'd and improv'd by his prudent
Fathers good Example, and by frequent conversing
with him ; and scattering short Apothegms and little
pleasant Stories, and making useful applications of
them, his Son was in his Infancy taught to abhor
Vanity and Vice as Monsters, and to discern the
loveliness of Wisdom and Vertue ; and by these means,
and God's concurring Grace, his knowledge was so
augmented, and his native goodness so confirm'd, that
all became so habitual, as 'twas not easie to determine
whether Nature or Education were his Teachers.

And here let me tell the Reader, That these early
beginnings of Vertue were by God's *assisting grace*
blest with what St. P*aul* seem'd to beg for his
Philippians [Phil. 1. 6], namely, *That he that had begun
a good work in them, would finish it.* And Almighty
God did : For his whole life was so regular and
innocent, that he might have said at his death (and
with truth and comfort) what the same St. *Paul*
said after to the same *Philippians*, when he advis'd
them to *walk as they had him for an Example* [Chap.
3. 17].

And this goodness, of which I have spoken, seem'd
to increase as his years did ; and with his goodness his
learning, the foundation of which was laid in the
Grammer School of *Rotheram* (that being one of those
three that were founded and liberally endow'd by
the said great and good Bishop of that Name.) And in
this time of his being a Scholar there, he was observ'd to
use an unwearied diligence to attain learning, and to
have a seriousness beyond his age, and with it a more
than common modesty ; and to be of so calm and

obliging a behaviour, that the Master and whole number of Scholars lov'd him, as one man.

And in this love and amity he continued at that School till about the thirteenth year of his age; at which time his Father design'd to improve his Grammer learning, by removing him from *Rotheram* to one of the more noted Schools of *Eaton* or *Westminster*: and after a years stay there, then to remove him thence to *Oxford*. But, as he went with him, he call'd on an old Friend, a Minister of noted learning, and told him his intentions; and he, after many questions with his Son, receiv'd such Answers from him, that he assur'd his Father, his Son was so perfect a Grammarian, that he had laid a good foundation to build any, or all the Arts upon; and therefore advis'd him to shorten his journey, and leave him at *Oxford*. And his Father did so.

His father left him there to the sole care and manage of Dr. *Kilbie*, who was then Rector of *Lincoln Colledge*: And he, after some time and trial of his manners and learning, thought fit to enter him of that Colledge, and after to matriculate him in the University, which he did the first of *July* 1603. but he was not chosen Fellow till the third of *May* 1606. at which time he had taken his Degree of Batchelor of Arts; at the taking of which Degree, his Tutor told the *Rector, That his Pupil* Sanderson *had a metaphysical brain, and a matchless memory: and that he thought he had improv'd, or made the last so by an Art of his own invention.* And all the future imployments of his life prov'd that his Tutor was not mistaken. I must here stop my Reader, and tell him, that this Dr. *Kilbie* was a man of so great learning and wisdom, and so excellent a Critick in the *Hebrew Tongue*, that he was made Professor of it in this University; and was also so perfect a Grecian, that

he was by King *James* appointed to be one of the
Translators of the Bible : And that this Doctor and
Mr. *Sanderson* had frequent Discourses, and lov'd as
Father and Son. The Doctor was to ride a Journey
into *Darbyshire*, and took Mr. *Sanderson* to bear him
company : and they going together on a *Sunday* with
the Doctor's Friend to that Parish Church where they
then were, found the young Preacher to have no more
discretion, than to waste a great part of the hour allotted
for his Sermon in exceptions against the late Translation of several words (not expecting such a hearer as
Dr. *Kilbie*) and shew'd three Reasons why a particular
word should have been otherwise translated. When
Evening Prayer was ended, the Preacher was invited
to the Doctor's Friends house ; where, after some other
Conference, the Doctor told him, *He might have
preach'd more useful Doctrine, and not fill'd his Auditors
ears with needless Exceptions against the late Translation ; and for that word, for which he offered to that poor
Congregation three Reasons, why it ought to have been
translated, as he said* ; *he and others had considered all
them, and found thirteen more considerable Reasons, why
it was translated as now printed:* and told him, *If his
Friend,* then attending him, *should prove guilty of such
indiscretion, he should forfeit his favour.* To which
Mr. *Sanderson* said, *He hop'd he should not.* And the
Preacher was so ingenious as to say, *He would not justifie
himself.* And so I return to *Oxford.* In the year
1608. (*July the* 11*th.*) Mr. *Sanderson* was compleated
Master of Arts. I am not ignorant, that for the
attaining these Dignities, the time was shorter than was
then, or is now required ; but either his birth, or the
well performance of some extraordinary exercise, or
some other merit, made him so : and the Reader is
requested to believe that 'twas the last ; and requested

to believe also, that, if I be mistaken in the time, the Colledge Records have mis-informed me: But I hope they have not.

In that year of 1608. he was (*November* the 7*th*.) by his Colledge chosen Reader of Logick in the House, which he performed so well, that he was chosen again the sixth of *November*, 1609. In the year 1613. he was chosen Sub-rector of the Colledge, and the like for the year 1614. and chosen again to the same Dignity and Trust for the year 1616.

In all which time and imployments, his abilities and behaviour were such, as procur'd him both love and reverence from the whole Society; there being no exception against him for any faults, but a sorrow for the infirmities of his being too timorous and bashful; both which were, God knows, so connatural, as they never left him. And I know not whether his lovers ought to wish they had; for they prov'd so like the *Radical moisture* in man's body, that they preserv'd the life of Vertue in his Soul, which by God's assisting grace never left him, till this life put on immortality. Of which happy infirmities (if they may be so call'd) more hereafter.

In the year 1614. he stood to be elected one of the Proctors for the University. And 'twas not to satisfie any ambition of his own, but to comply with the desire of the Rector and whole Society, of which he was a Member; who had not had a Proctor chosen out of their Colledge for the space of sixty years (namely, not from the year 1554. unto his standing;) and they per-swaded him, that if he would but stand for *Proctor*, his merits were so generally known, and he so well beloved, that 'twas but appearing, and he would infallibly carry it against any Opposers; and told him, *That he would by that means recover a right or reputation that was seemingly dead to his Colledge.* By these and other like perswasions he yielded up his own reason to theirs, and appear'd to stand for *Proctor.* But that Election was carried on by so sudden and secret, and by so powerful a Faction, that he mist it. Which when he understood, he profest seriously to his Friends, *That if he were troubled at the disappointment, 'twas for theirs, and not for his own sake: For he was far from any desire of such an Imployment, as must be managed with charge and trouble, and was too usually rewarded with hard censures, or hatred, or both.*

In the year following he was earnestly perswaded by Dr. *Kilbie* and others, to review the Logick Lectures which he had read some years past in his Colledge: and that done, to methodize and print them, for the ease and publick good of Posterity. But though he had an aversness to appear publickly in print; yet after many serious solicitations, and some second thoughts of his own, he laid aside his modesty, and promised he would; and he did so in that year of 1615. And the Book prov'd, as his Friends seem'd to prophecy, that is, of great and general use, whether we respect the Art or the Author. For Logick may be said to be an *Art of right reasoning:* an Art that undeceives men who take falshood for truth; enables men to pass a true Judgment, and detect those fallacies, which in some mens Understandings usurp the place of right reason. And how great a Master our Author was in this Art, will quickly appear from that clearness of method, argument, and demonstration, which is so conspicuous in all his other Writings. He who had attained to so great a dexterity in the use of reason himself, was best qualified to prescribe rules and directions for the instruction of others. And I am the more satisfied of the excellency and usefulness of this his first publick Undertaking, by hearing that most Tutors in both Universities teach Dr. *Sanderson's* Logick to their Pupils, as a Foundation upon which they are to build their future Studies in Philosophy. And for a further confirmation of my belief, the Reader may note, That since his Book of Logick was first printed, there has not been less than ten thousand sold: And that 'tis like to continue both to discover truth, and to clear and confirm the reason of the unborn world.

It will easily be believed that his former standing for a Proctors place, and being disappointed, must prove much displeasing to a man of his great wisdom and modesty, and create in him an aversness to run a second hazard of his credit and content; and yet he was assured by Dr. *Kilbie*, and the Fellows of his own Colledge, and most of those that had oppos'd him in the former Election, that his Book of Logick had purchas'd for him such a belief of his Learning and Prudence, and his behaviour at the former Election had got for him so great and so general a love, that all his former Opposers repented what they had done; and therefore perswaded him to venture to stand a second time. And upon these and other like incouragements, he did again, but not without an inward unwilling-ness, yield up his own reason to theirs, and promis'd to stand. And he did so; and was the tenth of *April*, 1616. chosen Senior Proctor for the year following, Mr. *Charles Crooke* of *Christ-Church* being then chosen the Junior.

In this year of his being Proctor there happened many memorable accidents; namely, Dr. *Robert Abbot*, Master of *Balial Colledge*, and *Regius* Professor of Divinity (who being elected or consecrated Bishop of *Sarum* some months before) was solemnly con-

ducted out of *Oxford* towards his Diocese, by the Heads
of all Houses, and the chief of all the University.   And
Dr. *Pridiaux* succeeded him in the Professorship, in
which he continued till the year 1642. (being then
elected Bishop of *Worcester*) and then our now Proctor Mr. *Sanderson* succeeded him in the *Regius*
Professorship.

And in this year Dr. *Arthur Lake* (then Warden of
New Colledge) was advanced to the Bishoprick of
Bath and *Wells* : A man of whom I take my self bound
in Justice to say, That he made the great trust
committed to him, the chief care and whole business
of his life.   And one testimony of this truth may be,
That he sate usually with his Chancellor in his
Consistory, and at least advis'd, if not assisted in most
sentences for the punishing of such Offenders as
deserved Church Censures.   And it may be noted,
That after a Sentence for Penance was pronounced, he
did very rarely or never allow of any *Commutation* for
the Offence, but did usually see the Sentence for
Penance executed ; and then as usually preach'd a
Sermon of Mortification and Repentance, and so
apply them to the Offenders, that then stood before
him, as begot in them then a devout contrition, and at
least resolutions to amend their lives ; and having done
that, he would take them (though never so poor) to
dinner with him, and use them friendly, and dismiss
them with his blessing, and perswasions to a vertuous
life, and beg them to believe him : And his Humility,
and Charity, and other Christian Excellencies were all
like this.   Of all which the Reader may inform himself in his Life, truly writ and printed before his
Sermons.

And in this year also, the very prudent and very
wise Lord *Elsmere*, who was so very long Lord

Chancellor of *England*, and then of *Oxford*, resigning up the last, the right Honourable, and as magnificent, *William Herbert* Earl of *Pembroke*, was chose to succeed him.

And in this year our late King *Charles* the First (then Prince of *Wales*) came honourably attended to *Oxford*; and having deliberately visited the University, the Schools, Colledges, and Libraries, He and his Attendants were entertained with Ceremonies and Feasting sutable to their Dignity and Merits.

And this year King *James* sent Letters to the University for the regulating their Studies; especially of the young Divines: Advising they should not rely on modern Sums and Systemes, but study the Fathers and Councils, and the more Primitive Learning. And this advice was occasioned by the indiscreet inferences made by very many Preachers out of Mr. *Calvin*'s Doctrine concerning *Predestination, Universal Redemption, the Irresistibility of God's Grace,* and of some other knotty Points depending upon these; Points which many think were not, but by Interpreters forc'd to be Mr. *Calvin*'s meaning; of the truth or falshood of which, I pretend not to have an ability to judge; my meaning in this Relation being only to acquaint the Reader with the occasion of the King's Letter.

It may be observed, that the various accidents of this year did afford our Proctor large and laudable matter to dilate and discourse upon: And, that though his Office seem'd, according to Statute and Custome, to require him to do so at his leaving it; yet he chose rather to pass them over with some very short Observations, and present the Governours, and his other Hearers, with rules to keep up Discipline and Order in the University; which at that time was either by defective Statutes, or want of the due

execution of those that were good, grown to be extreamly irregular. And in this year also, the Magis-
terial part of the Proctor requir'd more diligence, and
was more difficult to be managed than formerly, by
reason of a multiplicity of new Statutes, which begot
much confusion; some of which Statutes were then,
and others suddenly after, put into a useful execution.
And though these Statutes were not then made so
perfectly useful, as they were design'd, till Archbishop
Laud's time (who assisted in the forming and promoting
them;) yet our present Proctor made them as effectual
as discretion and diligence could do: Of which one
Example may seem worthy the noting; namely, That if
in his Night-walk he met with irregular Scholars absent
from their Colledges at University hours, or disordered
by drink, or in scandalous company, he did not use
his power of punishing to an extremity; but did
usually take their names, and a promise to appear
before him unsent for next morning: And when they
did, convinced them with such obligingness, and
reason added to it, that they parted from him with
such resolutions as the man after God's own heart was
possess'd with, when he said, *There is mercy with thee,
and therefore thou shalt be feared. Psal.* 34. 1. And
by this, and a like behaviour to all men, he was so
happy as to lay down this dangerous imployment,
as but very few, if any have done, even *without an
Enemy.*

After his Speech was ended, and he retir'd with a
Friend into a convenient privacy; he looked upon
his Friend with a more than common chearfulness, and
spake to him to this purpose. *I look back upon my late
imployment with some content to my self, and a great
thankfulness to Almighty God, that he hath made me of
a temper not apt to provoke the meanest of mankind, but*

rather to pass by infirmities, if noted; and in this Imployment I have had (God knows) many occasions to do both. And when I consider how many of a contrary temper, are by sudden and small occasions transported and hurried by Anger to commit such Errors, as they in that passion could not foresee, and will in their more calm and deliberate thoughts upbraid, and require repentance: And consider, that though Repentance secures us from the punishment of any sin, yet how much more comfortable it is to be innocent, than need pardon: And consider, that Errors against men, though pardon'd both by God and them, do yet leave such anxious and upbraiding impressions in the memory, as abates of the Offender's content: When I consider all this, and that God hath of his goodness given me a temper that hath prevented me from running into such enormities, I remember my temper with joy and thankfulness. And though I cannot say with David *(I wish I could) that therefore his praise shall always be in my mouth;* Psal. 1 3 0. *yet I hope, that by his grace, and that grace seconded by my endeavours, it shall never be blotted out of my memory; and I now beseech Almighty God that it never may.*

And here I must look back, and mention one passage more in his Proctorship, which is; That *Gilbert Sheldon*, the late Lord Archbishop of *Canterbury*, was this year sent to *Trinity Colledge* in that University; and not long after his entrance there, a Letter was sent after him from his God-father (the Father of our Proctor) to let his Son know it, and commend his God-son to his acquaintance, and to more than a common care of his behaviour; which prov'd a pleasing injunction to our Proctor, who was so gladly obedient to his Fathers desire, that he some few days after sent his Servitor to intreat Mr. *Sheldon* to his Chamber next morning. But it seems Mr. *Sheldon* having (like a young man as he was) run into some such irregularity as made him conscious he had transgress'd his Statutes, did therefore apprehend the Proctor's invitation as an introduction to punishment; the fear of which made his Bed restless that night; but at their meeting the next morning, that fear vanished immediately by the Proctor's chearful countenance, and the freedom of their discourse of Friends. And let me tell my Reader, that this first meeting prov'd the beginning of as spiritual a friendship as human nature is capable of; of a friendship free from all self ends: and it continued to be so, till death forc'd a separation of it on earth; but 'tis now reunited in heaven.

And now, having given this account of his behaviour, and the considerable accidents in his Proctorship, I proceed to tell my Reader, that this busie imployment being ended, he preach'd his Sermon for his degree of Batchelor in Divinity, in as eligant Latin, and as remarkable for the matter, as hath been preach'd in that University since that day. And having well perform'd his other Exercises for that degree, he took it the nine and twentieth of *May* following, having been ordain'd Deacon and Priest in the year 1611. by *John King*, then Bishop of *London*, who had not long before been Dean of *Christ-Church*, and then knew him so well, that he became his most affectionate Friend. And in this year, being then about the 29*th*. of his Age, he *took* from the University a Licence to preach.

In the year 1618. he was by Sir *Nicholas Sanderson*, Lord Viscount *Castleton*, presented to the Rectory of *Wibberton*, not far from *Boston*, in the County of *Lincoln*, a Living of very good value; but it lay in so low and wet a part of that Countrey, as was inconsistent with his health. And health being (next to a good

Conscience) the greatest of God's blessings in this life, and requiring therefore of every man a care and diligence to preserve it, he, apprehending a danger of losing it if he continued at *Wibberton* a second Winter, did therefore resign it back into the hands of his worthy Kinsman and Patron, about one year after his donation of it to him.

And about this time of his resignation he was presented to the Rectory of *Boothby Pannel* in the same County of *Lincoln*; a Town which has been made famous, and must continue to be famous, because *Dr. Sanderson*, the humble and learned *Dr. Sanderson*, was more than 40 years Parson of *Boothby Pannel*, and from thence dated all, or most of his matchless Writings.

To this Living (which was of less value, but a purer Air than *Wibberton*) he was presented by *Thomas Harrington* of the same County and Parish, Esq.; who was a Gentleman of a very ancient Family, and of great use and esteem in his Countrey during his whole life. And in this *Boothby Pannel* the meek and charitable *Dr. Sanderson* and his Patron liv'd with an endearing, mutual, and comfortable friendship, till the death of the last put a period to it.

About the time that he was made Parson of *Boothby Pannel*, he resign'd his Fellowship of *Lincoln Colledge* unto the then Rector and Fellows : And his resignation is recorded in these words :

Ego Robertus Sanderson *per, &c.*

I Robert Sanderson, *Fellow of the Colledge of* St. Maries *and* All-Saints, *commonly call'd* Lincoln Colledge, *in the University of* Oxford, *do freely and willingly resign into the hands of the Rector and fellows, all the Right and Title that I have in the said Colledge, wishing to them and their Successors, all peace, and piety, and happiness, in the Name of the Father, and of the Son, and of the Holy Ghost.   Amen.*

May 6. 1619.

Robert Sanderson.

And not long after this resignation, he was by the then Bishop of *York*, or the King, *Sede vacante*, made Prebend of the Collegiate Church of *Southwell* in that Diocese; and shortly after of *Lincoln* by the Bishop of that See.

And being now resolv'd to set down his rest in a quiet privacy at *Boothby Pannel*, and looking back with some sadness upon his removal from his general Acquaintance left in *Oxford*, and the peculiar pleasures of a University life; he could not but think the want of Society would render this of a Countrey Parson the more uncomfortable, by reason of that want of conversation; and therefore he did put on some faint purposes to marry. For he had considered, that though marriage be cumbred with more worldly care than a single life; yet a complying and a prudent Wife changes those very cares into so mutual a content, as makes them become like the Sufferings of St. *Paul*, *Colos.* i. 24, which he would not have wanted, because *they occasioned his rejoycing in them.* And he having well considered this, and observ'd the secret unutterable joys that Children beget in Parents, and the mutual pleasures and contented trouble of their daily care and constant endeavours to bring up those little Images of themselves so, as to make them as happy as all those cares and endeavours can make them: He having considered all this, the hopes of such happiness turn'd his faint purpose into a positive resolution to marry. And he was so happy as to obtain *Anne*, the daughter of *Henry Nelson* Batchelor in Divinity, then Rector of *Haugham* in the County of *Lincoln* (a man of noted worth and learning.) And the Giver of all good things was so good to him, as to give him such a Wife as was sutable to his own desires; a Wife, that made his life happy by being always content when he was chearful; that divided her joys with him, and abated of his sorrow, by bearing a part of that burthen; a Wife, that demonstrated her affection by a chearful obedience to all his desires, during the whole course of his life; and at his death too, for she outliv'd him.

And in this *Boothby Pannel* he either found or made his Parishioners peaceable, and complying with him in the decent and regular service of God. And thus his Parish, his Patron, and he liv'd together in a religious love, and a contented quietness. He not troubling their thoughts by preaching high and useless notions, but such plain truths as were necessary to be known, believed, and practised, in order to their salvation. And their assent to what he taught was testified by such a conformity to his Doctrine, as declared they believ'd and lov'd him. For he would often say, *That without the last, the most evident truths (heard as from an enemy, or an evil liver) either are not, or are at least the less effectual; and do usually rather harden, than convince the hearer.*

And this excellent man did not think his duty discharged by only reading the Church Prayers, Catechizing, Preaching, and administring the Sacraments seasonably; but thought (if the Law or the Canons may seem to injoyn no more, yet) that God would require more than the defective Laws of man's making,

can or does injoyn ; the performance of that inward
Law, which Almighty God hath imprinted in the
Conscience of all good Christians, and inclines those
whom he loves to perform. He considering this, did
therefore become a law to himself, practising what his
Conscience told him was his duty, in reconciling
differences, and preventing Law-suits, both in his
Parish and in the Neighbourhood. To which may be
added his often visiting sick and disconsolate Families,
perswading them to patience, and raising them from
dejection by his advice and chearful discourse, and by
adding his own Alms, if there were any so poor as to
need it ; considering how acceptable it is to Almighty
God, when we do as we are advis'd by St. *Paul,
Gal* 6. 2, *help to bear one anothers burthen,* either of
sorrow or *want :* and what a comfort it will be, when
the Searcher of all hearts shall call us to a strict account
for that evil we have done, and the good we have
omitted, to remember we have comforted and been
helpful to a dejected or distressed Family.

And that his practice was to do good, one Example
may be, That he met with a poor dejected Neighbour
that complain'd he had taken a Meadow, the Rent of
which was 9 *l.* a year ; and when the Hay was made
ready to be carried into his Barn, several days constant
rain had so raised the water, that a sudden Flood carried
all away, and his rich Landlord would bate him no
rent ; and that unless he had half abated, he and seven
children were utterly undone. It may be noted,
That in this Age there are a sort of people so unlike
the God of mercy, so void of the bowels of pity, that
they love only themselves and children ; love them so,
as not to be concern'd, whether the rest of mankind
waste their days in sorrow or shame ; People that are
curst with riches, and a mistake that nothing but riches

can make them and theirs happy. But 'twas not so with Dr. *Sanderson*; for he was concern'd, and spoke comfortably to the poor dejected man; bade him go home and pray, and not load himself with sorrow, for he would go to his Landlord next morning, and if his Landlord would not abate what he desired, he and a Friend would pay it for him.

To the Landlord he went the next day; and in a conference, the Doctor presented to him the sad condition of his poor dejected Tenant; telling him how much God is pleas'd when men compassionate the poor: and told him, That though God loves Sacrifice, yet he loves Mercy so much better, that he is pleas'd when call'd *the God of mercy*. And told him, the riches he was possest of were given him by that *God of mercy*, who would not be pleas'd, if he that had so much given, yea, and forgiven him too, should prove like the rich Steward in the Gospel, *that took his fellow servant by the throat to make him pay the utmost farthing*. This he told him. And told him, That the Law of this Nation (by which Law he claims his Rent) does not undertake to make men *honest* or *merciful*; but does what it can to restrain men from being *dishonest* or *unmerciful*, and yet was defective in both: and that taking any Rent from his poor Tenant, for what God suffered him not to enjoy, though the Law allowed him to do so, yet if he did so, he was too like that rich Steward which he had mentioned to him; and told him that riches so gotten, and added to his great Estate, would, as *Job* says, *prove like gravel in his teeth*, would in time so corrode his Conscience, or become so nauseous when he lay upon his Death-bed, that he would then labour to vomit it up, and not be able: and therefore advis'd him, being very rich, **to make Friends of his *unrighteous Mammon*,** before that evil day come upon him : But however, neither for his own sake, nor for God's sake, to take any Rent of his poor dejected sad Tenant, for that were to gain a temporal, and lose his eternal happiness. These and other such reasons, were urg'd with so grave and so compassionate an earnestness, that the Landlord forgave his Tenant the whole Rent.

The Reader will easily believe that Dr. *Sanderson*, who was himself so meek & merciful, did suddenly and gladly carry this comfortable news to the dejected Tenant ; and will believe, that at the telling of it there was a mutual rejoycing. 'Twas one of *Job*'s boasts, *That he had seen none perish for want of clothing : and that he had often made the heart of the widow to rejoyce. Job* 31. And doubtless Dr. *Sanderson* might have made the same religious boast of this, and very many like occasions. But since he did not, I rejoyce that I have this just occasion to do it for him ; and that I can tell the Reader, I might tire my self and him in telling how like the whole course of Dr. *Sanderson*'s life was to this which I have now related.

Thus he went on in an obscure and quiet privacy, doing good daily both by word and by deed, as often as any occasion offer'd it self ; yet not so obscurely, but that his very great learning, prudence, and piety were much noted and valued by the Bishop of his Diocese, and by most of the Nobility and Gentrey of that County. By the first of which he was often summon'd to preach many Visitation Sermons, and by the latter at many Assizes. Which Sermons, though they were much esteemed by them that procur'd and were fit to judge them ; yet they were the less valued, because he read them, which he was forc'd to do ; for though he had an extraordinary memory (even the Art of it) yet he had such an innate, invincible **fear** and bashfulness, that his memory was wholly useless, as to the repetition of his Sermons as he had writ them, which gave occasion to say, when they were first printed and expos'd to censure (which was in the year 1632.) That *the best Sermons that were ever read, were never preach'd.*

In this contented obscurity he continued, till the learned and good Archbishop *Laud*, who knew him well in *Oxford* (for he was his contemporary there) told the King ('twas the knowing and conscientious King *Charles* the I.) that there was one Mr. *Sanderson*, an obscure Countrey Minister, that was of such sincerity, and so excellent in all Casuistical learning, that he desir'd his Majesty would make him his Chaplain. The King granted it most willingly, & gave the Bishop charge to hasten it, for he long'd, to discourse with a man that had dedicated his Studies to that useful part of learning. The Bishop forgot not the King's desire, and Mr. *Sanderson* was made his Chaplain in Ordinary in *November* following, 1631. And when they became known to each other, the King did put many Cases of Conscience to him, and receiv'd from him such deliberate, safe, and clear solutions, as gave him great content in conversing with him : so that at the end of his months attendance, the King told him, *He should long for the next* November ; *for he resolv'd to have a more inward acquaintance with him, when that month and he return'd.* And when the month and he did return, the good King was never absent from his Sermons, and would usually say, *I carry my ears to hear other Preachers, but I carry my conscience to hear Mr.* Sanderson, and to act accordingly. And this ought not to be conceal'd from Posterity, That the King thought what he spake : For he took him to be his Adviser in that quiet part of his life, and he prov'd to be his

Comforter in those days of his affliction, when he apprehended himself to be in danger of Death or Deposing. Of which more hereafter.

In the first Parliament of this good King (which was 1625.) he was chosen to be a Clerk of the Convocation for the Diocese of *Lincoln*, which I here mention, because about that time did arise many disputes about Predestination, and the many Critical Points that depend upon, or are interwoven in it; occasioned, as was said, by a disquisition of new Principles of Mr. *Calvin's* (though others say they were before his time.) But of these Dr. *Sanderson* then drew up for his own satisfaction such a Scheme (he call'd it *Pax Ecclesiæ*) as then gave himself, and hath since given others such satisfaction, that it still remains to be of great estimation among the most learned. He was also chosen Clerk of all the Convocations during that good Kings reign. Which I here tell my Reader, because I shall hereafter have occasion to mention that Convocation in 1640. the unhappy long Parliament, and some debates of the Predestinarian Points, as they have been since charitably handled betwixt him, the learned Dr. *Hammond*, and Dr. *Peirce*, the now reverend Dean of *Salisbury*.

In the year 1636. his Majesty then in his Progress took a fair occasion to visit *Oxford*, and to take an entertainment for two days for himself and honourable Attendants, which the Reader ought to believe was sutable to their dignities: But this is mentioned, because at the King's coming thither Dr. Sanderson did attend him, and was then (the 31 of *August*) created Doctor of Divinity; which honour had an addition to it, by having many of the Nobility of this Nation then made *Doctors* and *Masters of Art with him:* Some of whose names shall be recorded and live with his (and none shall out-live it.)   First Dr. *Curle* and Dr. *Wren*, who were then Bishops of *Winton* and of *Norwich* (and had formerly taken their degrees in *Cambridge*) were with him created Doctors of Divinity in his University. So was *Merick* the Son of the learned *Izaak Casaubon*; and Prince *Rupert* (who still lives) the then *Duke* of *Lenox*, Earl of *Hereford*, Earl of *Essex*, of *Barkshire*, and very many others of noble birth (too many to be named) were then created Masters of Arts.

Some years before the unhappy long Parliament, this Nation being then happy and in peace (though inwardly sick of being well) namely in the year 1639. a discontented party of the *Scots* Church were zealously restless for another Reformation of their Kirk Government; and to that end created a new Covenant, for the general taking of which they pretended to petition the King for his assent, and that he would injoyn the taking of it by all of that Nation : but this Petition was not to be presented to him by a Committee of eight or ten men of their Fraternity, but by so many thousands, and they so arm'd, as seem'd to force an assent to what they seem'd to request ; so that though forbidden by the King, yet they entred *England*, and in their heat of Zeal took and plunder'd *New-Castle*, where the King was forc'd to meet them with an Army ; but upon a Treaty and some concessions, he sent them back (though not so rich as they intended, yet) for that time without blood-shed : But oh, this Peace and this Covenant were but the forerunners of War and the many miseries that followed : For in the year following there were so many chosen into the long Parliament, that were of a conjunct Council with these very zealous, and as factious Reformers, as begot such a confusion by the several desires and designs in many of the Members of that Parliament, and at last in the very common people of this Nation, that they were so lost by contrary designs, fears and confusions, as to believe the *Scots* and their Covenant would restore them to their former tranquillity. And to that end the Presbyterian party of this Nation did again, in the year 1643. invite the Scotch Covenanters back into *England*: and hither they came marching with it gloriously upon their Pikes, and in their Hats, with this motto, *For the Crown and Covenant of both Kingdoms.* This I saw, and suffer'd by it. But when I look back upon the ruine of Families, the bloodshed, the decay of common honesty, and how the former piety and plain dealing of this now sinful Nation is turned into cruelty and cunning, I praise God that he prevented me from being of that party which help'd to bring in this Covenant, and those sad Confusions that have follow'd it. And I have been the bolder to say this of my self, because in a sad discourse with Dr. *Sanderson* I heard him make the like grateful acknowledgment.

This digression is intended for the better information of the Reader in what will follow concerning Dr. *Sanderson.* And first, That the Covenanters of this Nation, and their party in Parliament, made many Exceptions against the Common Prayer and Ceremonies of the Church, and seem'd restless for a Reformation : And though their desires seem'd not reasonable to the King and the learned Dr. *Laud,* then Archbishop of *Canterbury* ; yet to quiet their Consciences, and prevent future confusion, they did in the year 1641. desire Dr. *Sanderson* to call two more of the Convocation to advise with him, and that he would then draw up some such safe alterations as he thought fit in the Service Book, and abate some of the Ceremonies that were least material, for satisfying their consciences ; and to this end they did meet together privately twice a week at the *Dean* of *Westminster*'s House (for the space of 3 months or more.) But not long after that time, when Dr. *Sanderson* had made the Reformation ready for a view, the Church and State were both fall'n into such a confusion, that Dr. *Sanderson*'s Model for Reformation became then useless. Nevertheless, his Reputation was such, that he was in the year 1642. propos'd by both Houses of Parliament to the King then in *Oxford*, to be one of their Trustees for the settling of Church affairs, and was allowed of by the King to be so; but that Treaty came to nothing.

In the year 1643. the 2 Houses of Parliament took upon them to make an Ordinance, and call an Assembly of Divines, to debate and settle some Church controversies (of which many were very unfit to judge :) in which Dr. *Sanderson* was also named; but did not appear, I suppose for the same reason that many other worthy and learned men did forbear, the Summons wanting the King's Authority. And here I must look back and tell the Reader, that in the year 1642. he was (*July* 21.) named by a more undoubted Authority to a more noble imployment, which was to be *Professor Regius of Divinity in Oxford*; but though *knowledge be said to puff up*, yet his modesty and too mean an opinion of his great Abilities, and some other real or pretended reasons (exprest in his Speech, when he first appeared in the Chair, and since printed) kept him from entring into it till *October* 1646.

He did for about a years time continue to read his matchless Lectures, which were first *de Juramento*, a Point very difficult, and at that time very dangerous to be handled as it ought to be. But this learned man, as he was eminently furnished with Abilities to satisfie the consciences of men upon that important Subject; so he wanted not courage to assert the true obligation of Oaths in a degenerate Age, when men had made perjury a main part of their Religion. How much the learned world stands obliged to him for these and his following Lectures *de Conscientia*, I shall not attempt to declare, as being very sensible, that the best Pens must needs fall short in the commendation of them: So that I shall only add, That they continue to this day, and will do for ever, as a compleat standard for the resolution of the most material doubts in Casuistical Divinity. And therefore I proceed to tell the Reader, That about the time of his reading those Lectures (the King being then Prisoner in the *Isle of Wight*) the Parliament had sent the *Covenant*, the *Negative Oath*, and I know not what more, to be taken by the *Doctor* of the *Chair*, and all Heads of Houses: and all other inferiour Scholars of what degree soever, were *all to take these Oaths* by a fixed day, and those that did not, to abandon their Colledge and the University too, within 24 hours after the beating of a Drum; for if they remain'd longer, they were to be proceeded against as Spies.

Dr. *Laud* then Archbishop of *Canterbury*, the Earl of *Strafford*, and many others, had been formerly murthered by this wicked Parliament, but the King yet was not; and the University had yet some faint hopes that in a Treaty then in being, or pretended to be suddenly, there might be such an Agreement made between King and Parliament, that the dissenters in the University might both preserve their Consciences and Subsistance which they then enjoyed by their Colledges.

And being possess'd of this mistaken hope, That the Parliament were not yet grown so merciless as not to allow manifest reason for their not submitting to the enjoyn'd Oaths, the University appointed twenty

Delegates to meet, consider, and draw up a *Manifesto*
to the Parliament, why they could not take those
Oaths but by violation of their Consciences : And of
these Delegates Dr. *Sheldon* (late Archbishop of
Canterbury), Dr. *Hammond*, Dr. *Sanderson*, Dr. *Morley*
(now Bishop of *Winchester*) and that most honest, and
as judicious Civil Lawyer, Dr. *Zouch*, were a part, the
rest I cannot now name ; but the whole number of the
Delegates requested Dr. *Zouch* to draw up the Law
part, and give it to Dr. *Sanderson*, and he was requested
to methodize and add what referr'd to reason and
conscience, and put it into form.   He yielded to their
desires, and did so.   And then after they had been
read in a full Convocation, and allow'd of, they were
printed in *Latin*, that the Parliaments proceedings and
the Universities sufferings might be manifested to
all Nations ; and the Imposers of these Oaths might
repent, or answer them : But they were past the first ;
and for the latter, I might swear they neither can, nor
ever will.   And these reasons were also suddenly
turn'd into English by *Dr. Sanderson*, that those of these
three Kingdoms might the better judge of the Loyal
Parties sufferings.

About this time the Independents (who were then
grown to be the most powerful part of the Army) had
taken the King from a close to a more large imprisonment, and by their own pretences to *liberty of Conscience*,
were obliged to allow somewhat of that to the King,
who had in the year 1646. sent for *Dr. Sanderson, Dr.
Hammond, Dr. Sheldon* (the late Archbishop of *Canterbury*) and *Dr. Morley* (the now Bishop of *Winchester*)
to attend him, in order to advise with them, how far he
might with a good Conscience comply with the Proposals of the Parliament for a Peace in Church and
State ; but these having been then denied him by the

Presbyterian Parliament, were now allow'd him by those in present power. And as those other Divines, so *Dr. Sanderson* gave his attendance on his Majesty also in the *Isle of Wight*, preach'd there before him, and had in that attendance many, both publick and private Conferences with him, to his Majesties great satisfaction. At which time he desir'd *Dr. Sanderson*, that being the Parliament had propos'd to him the abolishing of Episcopal Government in the Church, as inconsistent with Monarchy, that he would consider of it, and declare his judgment: He undertook to do so, and did it; but it might not be printed till our King's happy Restoration, and then it was. And at *Dr. Sanderson's* taking his leave of his Majesty in his last attendance on him, the King requested him *to betake himself to the writing Cases of Conscience for the good of Posterity.* To which his answer was, *That he was now grown old, and unfit to write Cases of Conscience.* But the King was so bold with him, as to say, *It was the simplest answer he ever heard from Dr.* Sanderson; *for no young man was fit to be a Judge, or write Cases of Conscience.* And let me here take occasion to tell the Reader this truth, not commonly known, that in one of these Conferences this conscientious King told Dr. *Sanderson,* or one of them that then waited with him, *That the remembrance of two Errors did much afflict him,* which were, *his assent to the Earl of* Strafford's *death, and the abolishing Episcopacy in* Scotland; *and that if God ever restored him to be in a peaceable possession of his Crown, he would demonstrate his Repentance by a publick Confession and a voluntary penance* (I think barefoot) *from the* Tower *of* London, *or* Whitehall, *to St.* Paul's *Church, and desire the people to intercede with God for his pardon.* I am sure one of them told it me, lives still, and will witness it. And it ought to be observ'd, that Dr. *Sanderson*'s Lectures *de Juramento* were so approv'd and valu'd by the King, that in this time of his imprisonment and solitude, he translated them into exact English, desiring Dr. *Juxson* (then Bishop of *London*) *Dr. Hammond*, and Sir *Thomas Herbert* (who then attended him) to compare them with the Original. The last still lives, and has declared it, with some other of that King's excellencies, in a Letter under his own hand, which was lately shew'd me by Sir *William Dugdale*, King at Arms. The Book was design'd to be put into the King's Library at St. *James*'s, but I doubt not now to be found there. I thought the honour of the Author and the Translator to be both so much concern'd in this Relation, that it ought not to be conceal'd from the Reader, and 'tis therefore here inserted.

I now return to Dr. *Sanderson* in the Chair in *Oxford*, where they that comply'd not in taking the *Covenant*, *Negative Oath*, and *Parliament Ordinance* for Church Discipline and Worship, were under a sad and daily apprehension of Expulsion; for the Visiters were daily expected, and both City and University full of Souldiers, and a party of Presbyterian Divines, that were as greedy and ready to possess, as the ignorant and ill-natur'd Visiters were to eject the dissenters out of their Colledges and Livelyhoods: But notwithstanding Dr. *Sanderson* did still continue to read his Lecture, and did to the very faces of those Presbyterian Divines and Souldiers, read with so much reason, and with a calm fortitude make such applications, as if they were not, they ought to have been asham'd, and beg'd pardon of God and him, and forborn to do what follow'd. But these thriving sinners were hardned; and as the Visiters expel'd the Orthodox, they, without scruple or shame, possest themselves of their Colledges;

so that with the rest, *Dr. Sanderson* was (in *June* 1648.) forc'd to pack up and be gone, and thank God he was not imprison'd, as *Dr. Sheldon*, *Dr. Hammond*, and others then were.

I must now again look back to *Oxford*, and tell my Reader, that the year before this expulsion, when the University had deny'd this Subscription, & apprehended the danger of that Visitation which followed, they sent *Dr. Morley*, then Canon of *Christ-Church* (now Lord Bishop of *Winchester*) and others, to petition the Parliament for recalling the Injunction, or a mitigation of it, or accept of their Reasons why they could not take the Oaths injoyn'd them ; and the Petition was by Parliament referr'd to a Committee to hear and report the Reasons to the House, and a day set for hearing them. This done, *Dr. Morley* and the rest went to inform and fee Counsel, to plead their Cause on the day appointed : but there had been so many committed for pleading, that none durst undertake it ; for at this time the Priviledges of that Parliament were become a *Noli me tangere*, as sacred and useful to them, as Traditions ever were, or are now to the Church of *Rome*, their number must never be known, and therefore not without danger to be meddled with. For which Reason *Dr. Morley* was forc'd, for want of Counsel, to plead the Universities Reasons for not complyance with the Parliaments injunctions ; and though this was done with great reason, and a boldness equal to the Justice of his Cause ; yet the effect of it was, but that he and the rest appearing with him were so fortunate, as to return to *Oxford* without commitment. This was some few days before the Visiters and more Soldiers were sent down to drive the Dissenters out of the University. And one that was at this time of *Dr. Morley*'s pleading a powerful man in the Parliament, and of that Committee, observing *Dr. Morley's* behaviour and reason, and inquiring of him, and hearing a good report of his Morals, was therefore willing to afford him a peculiar favour ; and that he might express it, sent for me that relate this Story, and knew *Dr. Morley* well, and told me, *He had such a love for Dr. Morley, that knowing he would not take the Oaths, and must therefore be ejected his Colledge, and leave Oxford, he desired I would therefore write to him to ride out of* Oxford *when the Visiters came into it, and not return till they left it, and he should be sure then to return in safety ; and that he should without taking any Oath or other molestation, enjoy his Canons place in his Colledge.* I did receive this intended kindness with a sudden gladness, because I was sure the party had a power, and as sure he meant to perform it, and did therefore write the Doctor word ; and his Answer was, *That I must not fail to return my Friend* (who still lives) *his humble and undissembled thanks, though he could not accept of his intended kindness ; for when the Dean, Dr.* Gardner, *Dr.* Paine, *Dr.* Hammond, *Dr.* Sanderson, *and all the rest of the Colledge were turn'd out, except Dr.* Wall, *he should take it to be, if not a sin, yet a shame, to be left behind with him only.* Dr. *Wall* I knew, and will speak nothing of him, for he is *dead*.

It may be easily imagined, with what a joyful willingness these self-loving Reformers took possession of all vacant preferments, and with what reluctance others parted with their beloved Colledges and Subsistance ; but their Consciences were dearer than their Subsistance, and out they went ; the Reformers possessing them without shame or scruple, where I will leave these Scruple-mongers, and make an account of the then present affairs of *London*, to be the next imployment of my Readers patience.

And in *London* all the Bishops Houses were turn'd to be Prisons, and they fill'd with Divines, that would not take the Covenant, or forbear reading Common Prayer, or that were accus'd for some faults like these. For it may be noted, That about this time the Parliament set out a Proclamation to incourage all Lay-men that had occasion to complain of their Ministers for being troublesome or scandalous, or that conformed not to Orders of Parliament, to make their complaint to a Committee for that purpose ; and the Minister, though 100 miles from *London*, should appear there and give satisfaction, or be sequestred ; (and you may be sure no Parish could want a covetous, or malicious, or cross-grain'd complainant :) by which means all Prisons in *London*, and in some other places, became the sad habitations of Conforming Divines.

And about this time the Bishop of *Canterbury* having been by an unknown Law condemned to die, and the execution suspended for some days, many of the malicious Citizens fearing his pardon, shut up their Shops, professing not to open them till Justice was executed. This malice and madness is scarce credible, but I saw it.

The Bishops had been voted out of the House of Parliament, & some upon that occasion sent to the *Tower*, which made many Covenanters rejoyce, and believe Mr. *Brightman* (who probably was a good and well meaning man) to be inspir'd in this Comment on the *Apocalyps*, an Abridgment of which was now printed, and cal'd Mr. Brightman's *Revelation of the Revelation*. And though he was grosly mistaken in other things, yet ; because he had made the Churches of *Geneva* and *Scotland*, which had no Bishops, to be *Philadelphia* in the *Apocalyps*, *the Angel that God loved* ; and the power of Prelacy to be Antichrist, the evil Angel, which the House of Commons had now so spued up, as never to recover their dignity : Therefore did those Covenanters approve and applaud Mr. *Brightman* for discovering and foretelling the Bishops downfall; so that they both rail'd at them, and rejoyc'd to buy good pennyworths of their Land, which their Friends of the House of Commons, did afford them as a reward of their diligent assistance to pull them down.

And the Bishops power being now vacated, the common people were made so happy, as every Parish might choose their own Minister, and tell him when he did, and when he did not preach true Doctrine : and by this and like means several Churches had several Teachers, that pray'd and preach'd for and against one another ; and ingag'd their hearers to contend furiously for truths which they understood not ; some of which I shall mention in the discourse that follows.

I have heard of two men that in their discourse undertook to give a character of a third person ; and one concluded he was a very honest man, *for he was beholding to him* ; and the other that he was not, *for he was not beholden to him.* And something like this was in the designs both of the Covenanters and Independants (the last of which were now grown both as numerous and as powerful as the former :) for though they differed much in many Principles, and preach'd against each other, one making it a sign of being in the state of grace, if we were but zealous for the Covenant : and the other, that we ought to buy and sell by a Measure, and to allow the same liberty of Conscience to others, which we by Scripture claim to our selves ; and therefore not to force any to swear the Covenant contrary to their consciences, and loose both their Livings and Liberties too. Though these differed thus in their conclusions, yet they both agreed in their practice to preach down *Common Prayer*, and get into the best sequestred Livings; and whatever became of the true Owners, their Wives and Children, yet to continue in them without the least scruple of Conscience.

They also made other strange Observations of *Election*, *Reprobation*, and *Free-will*, and the other Points dependent upon these; such as the wisest of the common people were not fit to judge of: I am sure I am not; though I must mention some of them historically in a more proper place, when I have brought my Reader with me to Dr. *Sanderson* at *Boothby Pannel*.

And in the way thither I must tell him, That a very Covenanter and a Scot too, that came into *England* with this unhappy Covenant, was got into a good sequestred Living by the help of a Presbyterian Parish, which had got the true Owner out. And this Scotch Presbyterian being well settled in this good Living, began to reform the Church-yard, by cutting down a large Ewe Tree, and some other Trees that were an ornament to the place, and very often a shelter to the Parishioners; who excepting against him for so doing, were answered, *That the Trees were his, and 'twas lawful for every man to use his own as he, and not as they thought fit.* I have hear'd (but do not affirm it) That no Action lies against him that is so wicked as to steal the winding sheet of a dead body after 'tis buried; and have heard the reason to be, because none were supposed to be so void of humanity, and that such a Law would vilifie that Nation that would but suppose so vile a man to be born in it: nor would one suppose any man to do what this Covenanter did. And whether there were any Law against him, I know not; but pity the Parish the less for turning out their legal Minister.

We have now overtaken Dr. *Sanderson* at *Boothby* Parish, where he hop'd to have enjoy'd himself, though in a poor, yet in a quiet and desir'd privacy; but it prov'd otherwise: For all corners of the Nation were fill'd with Covenanters, Confusion, Committee-men and Soldiers, serving each other to their several ends, of revenge, or power, or profit; and these Committee-men and Soldiers were most of them so possest with this Covenant, that they became like those that were infected with that dreadful Plague of *Athens*; the Plague of which Plague was, that they by it became maliciously restless to get into company, and to joy (so the Historian * saith) when they had infected others, even those of their

   * *Theucidides.*

most beloved or nearest Friends or Relations; and though there might be some of these Covenanters that were beguil'd, and meant well; yet such were the generality of them, and temper of the times, that you may be sure Dr. *Sanderson,* who though quiet and harmless, yet an eminent dissenter from them, could not live peaceably; nor did he: For the Soldiers would appear, and visibly disturb him in the Church when he read Prayers, pretending to advise him how God was to be serv'd most acceptably: which he not approving, but continuing to observe order and decent behaviour in reading the Church Service, they forc'd his Book from him, and tore it, expecting extemporary Prayers.

At this time he was advis'd by a Parliament man of power and note, that lov'd and valued him much, not to be strict in reading all the *Common Prayer*, but make some little variation, especially if the Soldiers came to watch him; for then it might not be in the power of him and his other Friends to secure him from taking the Covenant, or Sequestration: for which Reasons he did vary somewhat from the strict Rules of the Rubrick. I will set down the very words of Confession which he us'd, as I have it under his own hand; and tell the Reader that all his other variations were as little, & much like to this.

His Confession.

O Almighty God and merciful Father, we thy unworthy Servants do with shame and sorrow confess, that we have all our life long gone astray out of thy ways like lost sheep; and that by following too much the vain devices and desires of our own hearts, we have grievously offended against thy holy Laws both in thought, word and deed; we have many times left undone those good duties, which we might and ought to have done; and we have many times done those evils, when we might have avoided them, which we ought not to have done. We confess, O Lord, that there is no health at all, nor help in any Creature to relieve us; but all our hope is in thy mercy, whose justice we have by our sins so far provoked: Have mercy therefore upon us, O Lord, have mercy upon us miserable offenders: spare us good God, who confess our faults, that we perish not; but according to thy gracious promises declared unto mankind in Christ Jesus our Lord, restore us upon our true Repentance into thy grace and favour. And grant, O most merciful Father, for his sake, that we henceforth study to serve and please thee by leading a godly, righteous, and a sober life, to the glory of thy holy Name, and the eternal comfort of our own souls, through Jesus Christ our Lord. Amen.

In these disturbances of tearing his Service Book, a Neighbour came on a Sunday, after the Evening Service was ended, to visit and condole with him for the affront offered by the Soldiers. To whom he spake with a composed patience, and said; *God hath restored me to my desir'd privacy, with my wife and children, where I hop'd to have met with quietness, and it proves not so; but I will labour to be pleas'd, because God, on whom I depend, sees 'tis not fit for me to be quiet. I praise him, that he hath by his grace prevented me from making shipwrack of a good Conscience to maintain me in a place of great reputation and profit : and though my condition be such, that I need the last; yet I submit, for God did not send me into this world to do my own, but suffer his will, and I will obey it.* Thus by a sublime depending on his wise, and powerful, and pitiful Creator, he did chearfully submit to what God had appointed, justifying the truth of that Doctrine which he had preach'd.

About this time that excellent Book of the *King's Meditations in his Solitude* was printed, and made publick : and Dr. *Sanderson* was such a lover of the Author, and so desirous that the whole world should see the character of him in that Book, and something of the cause for which they suffer'd, that he design'd to turn it into Latin : but when he had done half of it most excellently, his friend Dr. *Earle* prevented him, by appearing to have done the whole very well before him.

About this time his dear and most intimate Friend, the learned Dr. *Hammond*, came to enjoy a conversation and rest with him for some days, and did so. And having formerly perswaded him to trust his excellent memory, and not read, but try to speak a Sermon as he had writ it, Dr. *Sanderson* became so complyant as to promise he would. And to that end they two went early the Sunday following to a Neighbour Minister, and requested to exchange a Sermon; and they did so. And at Dr. *Sanderson*'s going into the Pulpit, he gave his Sermon (which was a very short one) into the hand of Dr. *Hammond*, intending to preach it as 'twas writ; but before he had preach'd a third part, Dr. *Hammond* (looking on his Sermon as written) observed him to be out, and so lost as to the matter, that he also became afraid for him; for 'twas discernable to many of the plain Auditory: But when he had ended this short Sermon, as they two walk'd homeward, Dr. *Sanderson* said with much earnestness, *Good Doctor give me my Sermon, and know, that neither you, nor any man living, shall ever perswade me to preach again without my Books.* To which the reply was, *Good Doctor be not angry; for if I ever perswade you to preach again without Book, I will give you leave to burn all those that I am Master of.*

Part of the occasion of Dr. *Hammond*'s visit was at this time, to discourse Dr. *Sanderson* about some Opinions, in which, if they did not then, they had doubtless differed formerly; 'twas about those knotty Points, which are by the Learned call'd the *Quinquarticular Controversie*; of which I shall proceed, not to give any Judgment (I pretend not to that) but some short Historical account which shall follow.

There had been, since the unhappy Covenant was brought, and so generally taken in *England*, a liberty given or taken by many Preachers (those of *London* especially) to preach and be too positive in the Points of *Universal Redemption*, *Predestination*, and those other depending upon these. Some of which preach'd, *That all men were, before they came into this world, so predestinated to salvation or damnation, that 'twas not in their power to sin so, as to lose the first, nor by their most diligent endeavour to avoid the latter.* Others, *That 'twas not so; because then God could not be said to grieve for the death of a sinner, when he himself had made him so by an inevitable decree, before he had so much as a being in this world*; affirming therefore, *that man had some power left him to do the will of God, because he was advised to work out his salvation with fear and trembling*; maintaining, *that 'tis most certain, every man can do what he can to be saved*; and that *he that does what he can to be saved, shall never be damned*: And yet many that affirmed this, would confess, *That that grace, which is but a perswasive offer, and left to us to receive or refuse, is not that grace which shall bring men to heaven.* Which truths, or untruths, or both, be they which they will, did upon these or the like occasions come to be searched into, and charitably debated betwixt Dr. *Sanderson*, Dr. *Hammond*, and Dr. *Pierce* (the now Reverend Dean of *Salisbury*) of which I shall proceed to give some account, but briefly.

In the year 1648. the 52 *London* Ministers (then a Fraternity of *Sion Colledge* in that City) had in a printed Declaration aspers'd Dr. *Hammond* most heinously, for that he had in his *Practical Catechism* affirm'd, *That our Saviour died for the sins of all mankind.* To justifie which truth, he presently makes a charitable Reply (as 'tis now printed in his Works.) After which there were many Letters past betwixt the said Dr. *Hammond*, Dr. *Sanderson*, and Dr. *Pierce*, concerning God's grace and decrees. Dr. *Sanderson* was with much unwillingness drawn into this Debate; for he declared it would prove uneasie to him, who in his judgment of God's decrees differ'd with Dr. *Hammond* (whom he reverenced and loved dearly) and would not therefore ingage him into a Controversie, of which he could never hope to see an end: but they did all enter into a charitable disquisition of these said Points in several Letters, to the full satisfaction of the Learned; those betwixt Dr.

Sanderson and *Dr. Hammond* being printed in his Works; and for what past betwixt him and the Learned *Dr. Pierce*, I refer my Reader to a Letter annext to the end of this Relation.

I think the Judgment of *Dr. Sanderson* was by these Debates altered from what it was at his entrance into them; for in the year 1632. when his excellent Sermons were first printed in 4°. the Reader may on the Margent find some accusation of *Arminius* for false Doctrine; and find, that upon a review and reprinting those Sermons in folio in the year 1657. that accusation of *Arminius* is omitted. And the change of his judgment seems more fully to appear in his said Letter to *Dr. Pierce*. And let me now tell the Reader, which may seem to be perplex'd with these several affirmations of God's decrees before mentioned, that *Dr. Hammond*, in a Postscript to the last Letter of *Dr. Sanderson's*, says, *God can reconcile his own contradictions, and therefore advises all men, as the Apostle does, to study mortification, and be wise to sobriety.* And let me add further, that if these 52 Ministers of *Sion Colledge* were the occasion of the Debates in these Letters; they have, I think, been the occasion of giving an end to the *Quinquarticular Controversie*, for none have since undertaken to say more; but seem to be so wise, as to be content to be ignorant of the rest, till they come to that place, where the secrets of all hearts shall be laid open. And let me here tell the Reader also, that if the rest of mankind would, as *Dr. Sanderson*, not conceal their alteration of Judgment, but confess it to the honour of God and themselves, then our Nation would become freer from pertinacious Disputes, and fuller of Recantations.

I cannot lead my Reader to *Dr. Hammond* and *Dr. Sanderson* where we left them at *Boothby Pannel*, till

I have look'd back to the long Parliament, the Society of Covenanters in *Sion Colledge*, and those others scattered up and down in *London*, and given some account of their proceedings and usage of the late learned *Dr. Laud*, then Archbishop of *Canterbury*. And though I will forbear to mention the injustice of his death, and the barbarous usage of him, both then and before it; yet my desire is, that what follows may be noted, because it does now, or may hereafter concern us, namely, That in his last sad Sermon on the Scaffold at his death, he having freely pardoned all his Enemies, and humbly begg'd of God to pardon them, and besought those present to pardon and pray for him; yet he seem'd to accuse the Magistrates of the City, for suffering a sort of wretched people, that could not know why he was condemned, to go visibly up and down to gather hands to a Petition, *That the Parliament would hasten his Execution.* And having declar'd how unjustly he thought himself to be condemned, and accus'd for endeavouring to bring in *Popery* (for that was one of the Accusations for which he died) he declar'd with sadness, *That the several Sects and Divisions then in* England (which he had laboured to prevent) *were like to bring the Pope a far greater harvest, than he could ever have expected without them.* And said, *these Sects and Divisions introduce prophaneness under the cloak of an imaginary Religion;* and *that we have lost the substance of Religion by changing it into Opinion;* and *that by these means this Church, which all the Jesuits machinations could not ruine, was fall'n into apparent danger by those which were his Accusers.* To this purpose he spoke at his death: for this, & more of which, the Reader may view his last sad Sermon on the Scaffold. And 'tis here mentioned, because his dear Friend Dr. *Sanderson* seems to demonstrate the same in his two large and remarkable Prefaces before his two Volumes of Sermons; and seems also with much sorrow to say the same again in his last Will, made when he apprehended himself to be very near his death. And these Covenanters ought to take notice of it, and to remember, that by the late wicked War began by them, *Dr. Sanderson* was ejected out of the Professors Chair in *Oxford*; and that if he had continued in it (for he lived 14 years after) both the Learned of this and other Nations, had been made happy by many remarkable *Cases of Conscience*, so rationally stated, and so briefly, so clearly, and so convincingly determin'd, that Posterity might have joyed and boasted, that *Dr. Sanderson* was born in this Nation, for the ease and benefit of all the Learned that shall be born after him: But this benefit is so like *time past*, that they are both irrecoverably lost.

I should now return to *Boothby Pannel*, where we left Dr. *Hammond* and Dr. *Sanderson* together, but neither can be found there. For the first was in his Journey to *London*, and the second seiz'd upon the day after his Friends departure, and carried Prisoner to *Lincoln*, then a Garison of the Parliaments. For the pretended reason of which Commitment, I shall give this following account.

There was one Mr. *Clarke*, the Minister of *Alington*, a Town not many miles from *Boothby Pannel*, who was an active man for the Parliament and Covenant; one that, when *Belvoire Castle* (then a Garison for the Parliament) was taken by a party of the King's Soldiers, was taken in it, & made a Prisoner of War in *Newark*, then a Garison of the Kings; a man so active and useful for his party, that they became so much concern'd for his inlargement, that the

Committee of *Lincoln* sent a Troop of Horse to seize and bring *Dr. Sanderson* a Prisoner to that Garison; and they did so. And there he had the happiness to meet with many, that knew him so well as to treat him kindly; but told him, *He must continue their Prisoner, till he should purchase his own inlargement by procuring an Exchange for Mr.* Clarke *then Prisoner in the King's Garison of* Newark. There were many Reasons given by the Doctor of the Injustice of his Imprisonment, and the Inequality of the Exchange, but all were uneffectual: For done it must be, or he continue a Prisoner. And in time done it was upon the following Conditions.

First, that Dr. *Sanderson* and Mr. *Clarke* being Exchanged, should live undisturb'd at their own Parishes; and if either were injur'd by the Soldiers of the contrary party, the other having notice of it, should procure him a Redress, by having satisfaction made for his loss, or for any other injury; or if not, he to be us'd in the same kind by the other party. Nevertheless, *Dr. Sanderson* could neither live safe, nor quietly, being several times plundered, and once wounded in three places; but he, apprehending the remedy might turn to a more intolerable burthen by impatience or complying, forbore both; and possess'd his Soul in a contented quietness, without the least repining. But though he could not enjoy the safety he expected by this Exchange, yet by his Providence that can bring good out of evil, it turn'd so much to his advantage, that whereas his Living had been sequestred from the year 1644. and continued to be so till this time of his Imprisonment, he, by the *Articles* of *War* in this Exchange for Mr. *Clarke*, procur'd his Sequestration to be recall'd, and by that means injoy'd a poor but contented subsistence for himself, wife, and children, till the happy Restoration of our King and Church.

In this time of his poor, but contented privacy of life, his Casuistical Learning, peaceful moderation and sincerity, became so remarkable, that there were many that apply'd themselves to him for Resolution in Cases of Conscience; some known to him, many not; some requiring satisfaction by Conference, others by Letters; so many, that his life became almost as restless as their minds; yet he denied no man: And if it be a truth which *holy* Mr. *Herbert* says, *That all worldly joys seem less, when compared with shewing mercy or doing kindnesses*; then doubtless *Dr. Sanderson* might have boasted for relieving so many restless and wounded Consciences; which, as *Solomon* says, *are a burthen that none can bear*, though their fortitude may sustain their other Infirmities: and if words cannot express the joy of a Conscience relieved from such restless Agonies; then *Dr. Sanderson* might rejoyce, that so many were by him so clearly and conscientiously satisfied; for he denied none, and would often praise God for that ability, and as often for the occasion, and that God had inclin'd his heart to do it, to the meanest of any of those poor, but precious Souls, for which his Saviour vouchsafed to be crucified.

Some of those very many Cases that were resolved by Letters, have been preserv'd and printed for the benefit of Posterity; as namely,

1. *Of the Sabbath.*
2. *Marrying with a Recusant.*
3. *Of unlawful Love.*
4. *Of a Military life.*
5. *Of Scandal.*
6. *Of a Bond taken in the King's Name.*
7. *Of the Ingagement.*
8. *Of a rash Vow.*

But many more remain in private hands, of which one is of *Symony* ; and I wish the World might see it, that it might undeceive some Patrons, who think they have discharg'd that great and dangerous trust, both to God and man, if they take no money for a Living, though it may be parted with for other ends less justifiable.

And in this time of his retirement, when the common people were amaz'd & grown giddy by the many falshoods and misapplications of Truths frequently vented in Sermons ; when they wrested the Scripture by challenging God to be of their party, and call'd upon him in their prayers to patronize their Sacriledge & zealous Frenzies, in this time he did so compassionate the generality of this misled Nation, that though the times threatned danger, yet he then hazarded his safety by writing the large and bold Preface now extant before his last 20 Sermons (first printed in the year 1655.) In which there was such strength of reason, with so powerful and clear convincing applications made to the Non-conformists, as being read by one of those dissenting Brethren, who was possess'd with such a spirit of contradiction, as being neither able to defend his error, nor yield to truth manifest (his Conscience having slept long and quietly in a good sequestred Living) was yet at the reading of it so awakened, that after a conflict with the reason he had met, and the dammage he was to sustain if he consented to it (and being still unwilling to be so convinced, as to lose by being over-reason'd) he went in haste to the Bookseller of whom 'twas bought, threatned him, and told him in anger, *he had sold a Book in which there was false Divinity* ; *and that the Preface had upbraided the Parliament, and many godly Ministers of that party for unjust dealing.* To which his Reply was ('twas *Tim. Garthwaite*) *That 'twas not his*

Trade to judge of true or false Divinity, but to print and sell Books; and yet if he, or any friend of his would write an Answer to it, and own it by setting his Name to it, he would print the Answer, and promote the selling of it.

About the time of his printing this excellent Preface, I met him accidentally in *London* in sad-coloured clothes, and God knows, far from being costly : the place of our meeting was near to *little Britain*, where he had been to buy a Book, which he then had in his hand : we had no inclination to part presently ; and therefore turn'd to stand in a corner under a Penthouse (for it began to rain) and immediately the wind rose, and the rain increased so much, that both became so inconvenient, as to force us into a cleanly house, where we had *Bread*, *Cheese*, *Ale*, & a *Fire* for our money. This rain and wind were so obliging to me, as to force our stay there for at least an hour, to my great content and advantage ; for in that time he made to me many useful observations with much clearness and conscientious freedom. I shall relate a part of them, in hope they may also turn to the advantage of my Reader. He seem'd to lament, that the Parliament had taken upon them to abolish our Liturgy, to the scandal of so many devout and learned men, and the disgrace of those many Martyrs, who had seal'd the truth and use of it with their blood : and that no Minister was now thought godly that did not decry it ; and, at least, pretend to make better Prayers *ex tempore :* and that they, and only they that could do so, prayed by the Spirit, and were godly ; though in their Sermons they disputed, and evidently contradicted each other in their Prayers. And as he did dislike this, so he did most highly commend the *Common Prayer* of the Church, saying, *The Collects were the most passionate, proper, and most elegant expressions that any language ever afforded; and that there was in them such piety, and that so interwoven with* instructions, *that they taught us to know the power, the wisdom, the majesty, and mercy of God, and much of our duty both to him and our Neighbour; and that a Congregation behaving themselves reverently, & putting up to God these joynt and known desires for pardon of sins, and praises for mercies receiv'd, could not but be more pleasing to God, than those raw, unpremeditated expressions, to which many of the hearers could not say* Amen.

And he then commended to me the frequent use of the *Psalter* or *Psalms of David;* speaking to this purpose, *That they were the Treasury of Christian Comfort, fitted for all persons and all necessities; able to raise the soul from dejection by the frequent mention of God's mercies to repentant sinners; to stir up holy desires; to increase joy; to moderate sorrow; to nourish hope, and teach us patience, by waiting God's leasure; to beget a trust in the mercy, power, & providence of our Creator; & to cause a resignation of our selves to his will; & then (and not till then) to believe our selves happy.* This he said the *Liturgy* and *Psalms* taught us; and that by the frequent use of the last they would not only prove to be our souls comfort, but would become so habitual, as to transform them into the image of his soul that composed them. After this manner he express'd himself concerning the Liturgy & Psalms; & seem'd to lament that this, which was the Devotion of the more Primitive times, should in common Pulpits be turn'd into needless debates about *Free-will, Election,* and *Reprobation,* of which, and many like Questions, we may be safely ignorant, because Almighty God intends not to lead us to Heaven by hard Questions, but by meekness and charity, and a frequent practice of Devotion.

And he seem'd to lament very much, that by the means of irregular and indiscreet preaching, the generality of the Nation were possess'd with such dangerous mistakes, as to think, *They might be religious first, and then just and merciful; that they might sell their Consciences, and yet have something left that was worth keeping; that they might be sure they were elected, though their lives were visibly scandalous; that to be cunning was to be wise; that to be rich was to be happy, though their wealth was got without justice or mercy; that to be busie in things they understood not, was no sin.* These, and the like mistakes he lamented much, and besought God to remove them, and restore us to that humility, sincerity, and singleheartedness, with which this Nation was blest, before the unhappy Covenant was brought into the Nation, and every man preach'd and pray'd what seem'd best in his own eyes. And he then said to me, *That the way to restore this Nation to a more meek and Christian temper, was to have the Body of Divinity (or so much of it as was needful to be known) to be put into* 52 *Homilies or Sermons, of such a length as not to exceed a third or fourth part of an hours reading; and these needful Points to be made so clear and plain, that those of a mean capacity might know what was necessary to be believed, and what God requires to be done; and then some applications of trial and conviction: and these to be read every Sunday of the year, as infallibly as the blood circulates the body; and then as certainly begun again, and continued the year following: and that this being done, it might probably abate the inordinate desire of knowing what we need not, and practising what we know, and ought to do.* This was the earnest desire of this prudent man. And, O that Dr. *Sanderson* had undertaken it! for then in all probability it would have prov'd effectual.

At this happy time of injoying his company and this discourse, he express'd a sorrow by saying to me, *O that I had gone Chaplain to that excellently accomplish'd Gentleman, your Friend, Sir* Henry Wootton*! which was once intended, when he first went Ambassador to the State of* Venice : *for by that imployment I had been forc'd into a necessity of conversing, not with him only, but with several men of several Nations ; and might thereby have kept my self from my unmanly bashfulness, which has prov'd very troublesome, and not less inconvenient to me ; and which I now fear is become so habitual as never to leave me : and by that means I might also have known, or at least have had the satisfaction of seeing one of the late miracles of general learning, prudence, and modesty,* Sir Henry Wottons *dear Friend,* Padria Paulo, *who, the Author of his life says, was born with a bashfulness as invincible, as I have found my own to be :* A man whose fame must never die, till vertue and learning shall become so useless as not to be regarded.

This was a part of the benefit I then had by that hours conversation : and I gladly remember and mention it, as an Argument of my happiness, and his great humility and condescention. I had also a like advantage by another happy conference with him, which I am desirous to impart in this place to the Reader. He lamented much, that in many Parishes, where the maintenance was not great, there was no Minister to officiate ; and that many of the best sequestred Livings were possess'd with such rigid Covenanters as denied the Sacrament to their Parishioners, unless upon such conditions, and in such a manner as they could not take it. This he mentioned with much sorrow, saying, *The blessed Sacrament did, by way of preparation for it, give occasion to all conscientious Receivers to examine the performance of their*

Vows, since they received their last seal for the pardon of their sins past; and to examine and research their hearts, and make penitent reflexions on their failings; and that done, to bewail them, and then make new vows or resolutions to obey all God's Commands, and beg his grace to perform them. And this done, the Sacrament *repairs the decays of grace, helps us to conquer infirmities, gives us grace to beg God's grace, and then gives us what we beg; makes us still hunger and thirst after his righteousness, which we then receive, and being assisted with our endeavours, will still so dwell in us, as to become our satisfaction in this life, and our comfort on our last Sick-beds.* The want of this blessed benefit he lamented much, and pitied their condition that desired, but could not obtain it.

I hope I shall not disoblige my Reader, if I here inlarge into a further Character of his person and temper. As first, That he was moderately tall; his behaviour had in it much of a plain comliness, and very little (yet enough) of ceremony or courtship; his looks and motion manifested affability and mildness, and yet he had with these a calm, but so matchless a fortitude, as secur'd him from complying with any of those many Parliament injunctions, that interfer'd with a doubtful conscience. His Learning was methodical and exact; his wisdom useful; his integrity visible; and his whole life so unspotted, that all ought to be preserved as Copies for Posterity to write after; the Clergy especially, who with impure hands ought not to offer Sacrifice to that God, whose pure eyes abhorr iniquity.

There was in his Sermons no improper Rhetorick, nor such perplex'd divisions, as may be said to be like too much light, that so dazles the eyes that the sight becomes less perfect: But there was therein no want of useful matter, nor waste of words; and yet such clear distinctions as dispel'd all confus'd Notions, and made his hearers depart both wiser, and more confirm'd in vertuous resolutions.

His memory was so matchless and firm, as 'twas only overcome by his bashfulness; for he alone, or to a friend, could repeat all the *Odes of Horace*, all *Tully's Offices*, and much of *Juvenal* and *Persius* without Book; and would say, *The repetition of one of the* Odes *of* Horace *to himself was to him such musick, as a Lesson on the* Viol *was to others, when they play'd it to themselves or friends*. And though he was blest with a clearer Judgment than other men, yet he was so distrustful of it, that he did over-consider of consequences, and would so delay and reconsider what to determine, that though none ever determin'd better, yet, when the Bell toll'd for him to appear and read his Divinity Lectures in *Oxford*, and all the Scholars attended to hear him, he had not then, or not till then, resolv'd and writ what he meant to determine; so that that appear'd to be a truth, which his old dear Friend Dr. *Sheldon* would often say, namely, *That his judgment was so much superiour to his phancy, that whatsoever this suggested, that dislik'd and controul'd; still considering and reconsidering, till his time was so wasted, that he was forc'd to write, not (probably) what was best, but what he thought last*. And yet what he did then read, appear'd to all hearers to be so useful, clear, and satisfactory, as none ever determin'd with greater applause. These tiring and perplexing thoughts begot in him an aversness to enter into the toyl of considering and determining all Casuistical Points; because during that time, they neither gave rest to his body or mind. But though he would not be always loden with these knotty Points and Distinctions; yet the study of old

Records, Genealogies, and *Heraldry,* were a recreation, and so pleasing, that he would say they gave rest to his mind. Of the last of which I have seen two remarkable Volumes; and the Reader needs neither to doubt their truth or exactness.

And this humble man had so conquer'd all repining and ambitious thoughts, and with them all other unruly passions, that, if the accidents of the day prov'd to his danger or dammage, yet he both began and ended it with an even and undisturbed quietness; always praising God that he had not withdrawn food and raiment from him and his poor Family; nor suffered him to violate his Conscience for his safety, or to support himself or them in a more splendid or plentiful condition; and that he therefore resolv'd with *David, That his praise should be always in his mouth.*

I have taken a content in giving my Reader this Character of his person, his temper, and some of the accidents of his life past; and more might be added of all: But I will with sorrow look forward to the sad days, in which so many good men suffered, about the year 1658. at which time Dr. *Sanderson* was in a very low condition as to his Estate: and in that time Mr. *Robert Boyle* (a Gentleman of a very Noble Birth, and more eminent for his Liberality, Learning, and Vertue, and of whom I would say much more, but that he still lives) having casually met with, and read his Lectures *de Juramento,* to his great satisfaction, and being informed of Dr. *Sanderson's* great innocence and sincerity, and that he and his Family were brought into a low condition by his not complying with the Parliaments injunctions, sent him by his dear Friend Dr. *Barlow* (the now learned Bishop of *Lincoln*) 50*l.* and with it a request and promise: The request was, That he would review the Lectures *de Conscientia*, which he had read when he was Doctor of the Chair in *Oxford*, and print them for the good of Posterity; (and this Dr. *Sanderson* did in the year 1659.) And the Promise was, That he would pay him that, or a greater sum if desir'd, during his Life, to inable him to pay an *Amanuensis*, to ease him from the trouble of writing what he should conceive or dictate. For the more particular account of which, I refer my Reader to a Letter writ by the said Dr. *Barlow*, which I have annexed to the end of this Relation.

Towards the end of this year 1659. when the many mixt Sects, and their Creators and merciless Protectors, had led or driven each other into a Whirl-pool of Confusion: when amazement and fear had seiz'd them, and their accusing Consciences gave them an inward and fearful intelligence, that the God which they had long serv'd, was now ready to pay them such wages as he does always reward *Witches* with for their obeying him: When these wretches were come to foresee an end of their cruel reign, by our King's return; and such Sufferers as Dr. *Sanderson* (and with him many of the oppressed Clergy and others) could foresee the cloud of their afflictions would be dispers'd by it: Then, in the beginning of the year following, the King was by God restored to us, and we to our known Laws and Liberties; and a general joy and peace seem'd to breath through the 3 Nations. Then were the suffering Clergy freed from their Sequestration, restor'd to their Revenues, and to a liberty to adore, praise, and pray to God in such order as their Consciences and Oaths had formerly obliged them. And the Reader will easily believe that *Dr. Sanderson* and his dejected Family rejoyc'd to see this day, and be of this number.

It ought to be considered (which I have often heard or read) that in the Primitive times men of learning and vertue were usually sought for, and sollicited to accept of *Episcopal Government*, and often refus'd it. For they conscientiously considered, that the Office of a Bishop was made up of labour and care : that they were trusted to be God's Almoners of the Churches Revenue, and double their care for the poor : to live strictly themselves, and use all diligence to see that their Familie, Officers, and Clergy did so ; and that the account of that Stewardship must at the last dreadful day be made to the Searcher of all hearts : and that in the primitive times they were therefore timorous to undertake it. It may not be said that *Dr. Sanderson* was accomplish'd with these, and all the other requisites requir'd in a Bishop, so as to be able to answer them exactly; but it may be affirm'd, as a good preparation, that he had at the Age of 73 years (for he was so old at the King's return) fewer faults to be pardon'd by God or man, than are apparent in others in these days, in which (God knows) we fall so short of that visible sanctity and zeal to God's glory, which was apparent in the days of primitive Christianity. This is mentioned by way of preparation to what I shall say more of *Dr. Sanderson* ; and namely, That at the King's return *Dr. Sheldon*, the late prudent Bishop of *Canterbury* (than whom none knew, valued, or lov'd *Dr. Sanderson* more or better) was by his Majesty made a chief Trustee to commend to him fit men to supply the then vacant Bishopricks. And *Dr. Sheldon* knew none fitter than *Dr. Sanderson*, and therefore humbly desired the King that he would nominate him : and that done, he did as humbly desire *Dr. Sanderson* that he would for Gods and the Churches sake, take that charge and care upon him. *Dr. Sanderson* had, if not an unwillingness, certainly no forwardness to undertake it; and would often say, *He had not led himself, but his Friend would now lead him into a temptation, which he had daily pray'd against; and besought God, if he did undertake it, so to assist him with his grace, that the example of his life, his cares and endeavours, might promote his glory, and help forward the salvation of others.*

This I have mentioned as a happy preparation to his Bishoprick; and am next to tell that he was consecrated Bishop of *Lincoln* at *Westminster* the 28*th* of *October*, 1660.

There was about this time a Christian care taken, that those whose Consciences were (as they said) tender, and could not comply with the Service and Ceremonies of the Church, might have satisfaction given by a friendly debate betwixt a select number of them, and some like number of those that had been Sufferers for the *Church Service* and *Ceremonies*, and now restor'd to liberty; of which last some were then preferr'd to power and dignity in the Church. And of these Bishop *Sanderson* was one, and then chose to be a Moderator in that debate: and he perform'd his trust with much mildness, patience, and reason; but all prov'd uneffectual: For there be some propositions like jealousies, which (though causeless, yet) cannot be remov'd by reasons as apparent as demonstration can make any truth. The place appointed for this debate was the *Savoy* in the *Strand*: and the Points debated were, I think, many; some affirmed to be truth and reason, some denied to be either; and these debates being then in words, proved to be so loose and perplex'd, as satisfied neither party. For sometime that which had been affirmed was immediately forgot or deny'd, and so no satisfaction given to either party.

But that the debate might become more useful, it was therefore resolv'd that the day following the desires and reasons of the *Non-conformists* should be given in writing, and they in writing receive Answers from the conforming party. And though I neither now can, nor need to mention all the Points debated, nor the names of the dissenting Brethren : yet I am sure Mr. *Baxter* was one, and am sure what shall now follow, was one of the Points debated.

Concerning a Command of lawful Superiors, what was sufficient to its being a lawful Command ; this Proposition was brought by the conforming Party.

That Command which commands an act in it self lawful, and no other act or circumstance unlawful, is not sinful.

Mr. *Baxter* denied it for two Reasons, which he gave in with his own hand in writing thus :

One was, *Because that may be a sin* per accidens, *which is not so in it self, and may be unlawfully commanded, though that accident be not in the command.* Another was, *That it may be commanded under an unjust penalty.*

Again, this Proposition being brought by the Conformists, *That Command which commandeth an act in it self lawful, and no other act whereby any unjust penalty is injoyned, nor any circumstance whence* per accidens *any sin is consequent which the Commander ought to provide against, is not sinful.*

Mr. *Baxter* denied it for this reason then given in with his own hand in writing, thus : *Because the first act commanded may be* per accidens *unlawful, and be commanded by an unjust penalty, though no other act or circumstance commanded be such.*

Again, this Proposition being brought by the Conformists, *That Command which commandeth an act in it self lawful, and no other Act whereby any unjust penalty is injoyned, nor any circumstance whence directly or per accidens any sin is consequent, which the Commander ought to provide against, hath in it all things requisite to the lawfulness of a Command, and particularly cannot be guilty of commanding an act per accidens unlawful, nor of commanding an act under an unjust penalty.*

Mr. *Baxter* denied it upon the same Reasons.

Peter Gunning.
John Pearson.

These were then two of the Disputants, still alive, and will attest this; one being now Lord Bishop of *Ely,* and the other of *Chester.* And the last of them told me very lately, that one of the Dissenters (which I could, but forbear to name) appear'd to *Dr. Sanderson* to be so bold, so troublesome, and so illogical in the dispute, as forc'd *patient Dr. Sanderson* (who was then Bishop of *Lincoln,* and a Moderator with other Bishops) to say with an unusual earnestness, *That he had never met with a man of more pertinacious confidence, and less abilities in all his conversation.*

But though this debate at the *Savoy* was ended without any great satisfaction to either party, yet both parties knew the desires, and understood the abilities of the other much better than before it: and the late distressed Clergy, that were now restor'd to their former rights and power, did at their next meeting in Convocation contrive to give the dissenting party satisfaction by alteration, explanation, and addition to some part both of the *Rubrick* and *Common Prayer,* as also by adding some new necessary Collects, and a particular Collect of Thanksgiving. How many of those new Collects were worded by *Dr. Sanderson*, I cannot say ; but am sure the whole Convocation valued him so much, that he never undertook to speak to any Point in question, but he was heard with great willingness and attention ; and when any Point in question was determin'd, the Convocation did usually desire him to word their intentions, and as usually approve & thank him.

At this Convocation the *Common Prayer* was made more compleat, by adding 3 new necessary Offices ; which were, *A form of Humiliation for the murther of King* Charles *the Martyr*; *a Thanksgiving for the Restoration of his Son our King*; *and for the baptizing of persons of riper age.* I cannot say *Dr. Sanderson* did form or word them all, but doubtless more than any single man of the Convocation ; and he did also, by desire of the Convocation, alter & add to the forms of Prayers to be used at Sea (now taken into the *Service Book.*) And it may be noted, That *William,* the now right Reverend Bishop of *Canterbury,* was in these imployments diligently useful, especially in helping to rectifie the *Kalendar* and *Rubrick.* And lastly it may be noted, That for the satisfying all the dissenting Brethren and others, the Convocations Reasons for the alterations and additions to the Liturgy, were by them desir'd to be drawn up by *Dr. Sanderson*; which being done by him, and approv'd by them, was appointed to be printed before the Liturgy, and may be known by this Title,—*The Preface:* and begins thus—*It hath been the Wisdom of the Church—.*

I shall now follow him to his Bishoprick, and declare a part of his behaviour in that busie and weighty imployment. And first, That it was with such condescention and obligingness to the meanest of his Clergy, as to know and be known to them. And indeed he practis'd the like to all men of what degree soever, especially to his old Neighbours or Parishioners of *Boothby Pannel*; for there was all joy at his Table when they came to visit him : then they pray'd for him, and he for them with an unfeigned affection.

I think it will not be deny'd, but that the care and toyl required of a Bishop, may justly challenge the riches & revenue with which their Predecessors had lawfully endow'd them; and yet he sought not that so much, as doing good both to the present Age and Posterity; and he made this appear by what follows.

The Bishops chief House at *Buckden*, in the County of *Huntington*, the usual Residence of his Predecessors (for it stands about the midst of his Diocese) having been at his Consecration a great part of it demolish'd, and what was left standing under a visible decay, was by him undertaken to be erected and repair'd; and it was perform'd with great speed, care, and charge. And to this may be added, That the King having by an *Injunction* commended to the care of the Bishops, Deans, and Prebends of all Cathedral Churches, *the repair of them, their Houses, and augmentation of small Vicarages*; He, when he was repairing *Bugden*, did also augment the last, as fast as Fines were paid for renewing Leases : so fast, that a Friend taking notice of his bounty, was so bold as to advise him to remember; *he was under his first fruits, and that he was old, and had a wife and children yet but meanly provided for, especially if his dignity were considered.* To whom he made a mild and thankful answer, saying, *It would not become a Christian Bishop to suffer those houses built by his Predecessors, to be ruin'd for want of repair; and less justifiable to suffer any of those that were call'd to so high a calling as* to sacrifice at God's altar, *to eat the bread of sorrow constantly, when he had a power by a small augmentation to turn it into the bread of cheerfulness: and wish'd, that as this was, so it were also in his power to make all mankind happy, for he desired nothing more. And for his wife and children, he hop'd to leave them a competence; and in the hands of a God, that would provide for all that kept innocence, and trusted his providence and protection, which he had always found enough to make and keep him happy.*

There was in his Diocese a Minister of almost his Age, that had been of *Lincoln Colledge* when he left it, who visited him often, and always welcome, because he was a man of innocence and open-heartedness: This Minister asked the Bishop what Books he studied most, when he laid the foundation of his great and clear Learning? To which his Answer was, That he declin'd reading many; but what he did read, were well chosen, and read so often, that he became very familiar with them; and said they were chiefly three, *Aristotle's Rhetorick, Aquinas's Secunda Secundæ,* and *Tully,* but chiefly his *Offices,* which he had not read over less than 20 times; and could at this Age say without Book. And told him also, the learned Civilian Doctor *Zouch* (who died lately) had writ *Elementa jurisprudentiæ,* which was a Book that he could also say without Book; and that no wise man could read it too often, or love, or commend too much; and told him these had been his toyl: But for himself, he always had a natural love to *Genealogies* and *Heraldry;* and that when his thoughts were harassed with any perplext Studies, he left off, and turned to them as a recreation; and that his very recreation had made him so perfect in them, that he could in a very short time give an account of the Descent, Arms, & Antiquity of any Family of the Nobility or Gentry of this Nation.

Before I give an account of Dr. *Sanderson*'s last sickness, I desire to tell the Reader that he was of a healthful constitution, chearful and mild, of an even temper, very moderate in his diet, and had had little sickness, till some few years before his death ; but was then every Winter punish'd with a *Diarrhea*, which left him not till warm weather return'd and remov'd it : And this distemper did, as he grew elder, seize him oftner, and continue longer with him. But though it weakned him, yet it made him rather indispos'd than sick; and did no way disable him from studying (indeed too much.) In this decay of his strength, but not of his memory or reason (for this distemper works not upon the understanding), he made his last Will, of which I shall give some account for confirmation of what hath been said, and what I think convenient to be known, before I declare his death and burial.

He did in his last Will give an account of his Faith and Perswasion in point of Religion and Church Government, in these very words :

I, Robert Sanderson *Dr. of Divinity, an unworthy Minister of Jesus Christ, and by the providence of God Bishop of* Lincoln, *being by the long continuance of an habitual distemper brought to a great bodily weakness and faintness of spirits, but (by the great mercy of God) without any bodily pain otherwise, or decay of understanding, do make this my Will and Testament (written all with my own hand) revoking all former Wills by me heretofore made, if any such shall be found. First, I commend my Soul into the hands of Almighty God, as of a faithful Creator, which I humbly beseech him mercifully to accept, looking upon it, not as it is in it self (infinitely polluted with sin) but as it is redeemed and purged with the precious blood of his only beloved Son, and my most sweet Saviour Jesus Christ, in confidence of whose merits and mediation alone it is, that I cast my self upon the mercy of God for the pardon of my sins, and the hopes of eternal life. And here I do profess, that as I have lived, so I desire, and (by the grace of God) resolve to dye in the Communion of the Catholick Church of Christ, and a true son of the Church of England; which, as it stands by Law established, to be both in Doctrine and Worship agreeable to the Word of God, and in the most, and most material Points of both, conformable to the faith and practice of the godly Churches of Christ in the primitive and purer times, I do firmly believe: led so to do, not so much from the force of custom and education (to which the greatest part of mankind owe their particular different perswasions in point of Religion) as upon the clear evidence of truth and reason, after a serious and unpartial examination of the grounds, as well of Popery as Puritanism, according to that measure of understanding, and those opportunities which God hath afforded me: and herein I am abundantly satisfied, that the Schism which the Papists on the one hand, and the Superstition which the Puritan on the other hand, lay to our charge, are very justly chargeable upon themselves respectively. Wherefore I humbly beseech Almighty God, the Father of Mercies, to preserve the Church by his power and providence, in peace, truth, and godliness, evermore to the worlds end: which doubtless he will do, if the wickedness and security of a sinful people (and particularly those sins that are so rife, and seem daily to increase among us, of Unthankfulness, Riot, and Sacriledge) do not tempt his patience to the contrary. And I also farther humbly beseech him, that it would please him to give unto our gracious Sovereign, the Reverend Bishops, and the Parliament, timely to consider the great danger that visibly threatens this Church in*

*point of Religion by the late great increase of Popery, and
in point of Revenue by sacrilegious Inclosures ; and to
provide such wholesome and effectual remedies as may
prevent the same before it be too late.*

And for a further manifestation of his humble
thoughts and desires, they may appear to the Reader,
by another part of his Will which follows.

*As for my corruptible Body, I bequeath it to the Earth
whence it was taken, to be decently buried in the Parish
Church of Bugden, towards the upper end of the Chancel,
upon the second, or (at the farthest) the third day after my
decease ; and that with as little noise, pomp, and charge
as may be, without the invitation of any person how near
soever related unto me, other than the Inhabitants of
Bugden ; without the unnecessary expence of Escocheons,
Gloves, Ribons, &c. and without any Blacks to be hung
any where in or about the House or Church, other than a
Pulpit Cloth, a Hearse Cloth, and a Mourning Gown for
the Preacher ; whereof the former (after my Body shall
be interred) to be given to the Preacher of the Funeral
Sermon, and the latter to the Curat of the Parish for the
time being. And my will further is, That the Funeral
Sermon be preached by my own Houshold Chaplain,
containing some wholesome discourse concerning Mortality,
the Resurrection of the Dead, and the last Judgment ;
and that he shall have for his pains 5l. upon condition,
that he speak nothing at all concerning my person, either
good or ill, other than I my self shall direct ; only signfy-
ing to the Auditory that it was my express will to have it so.
And it is my will, that no costly Monument be erected for
my memory, but only a fair flat Marble stone to be laid
over me, with this Inscription in legible Roman characters,*
Depositum Roberti Sanderson nuper Lincolniensis
Episcopi, qui obiit Anno Domini MDCLXII. &
ætatis suæ septuagesimo sexto, Hic requiescit in spe

beatæ resurrectionis. *This manner of burial, although
I cannot but foresee it will prove unsatisfactory to sundry
my nearest Friends and Relations, and be apt to be
censured by others, as an evidence of my too much parsi-
mony and narrowness of mind, as being altogether unusual,
and not according to the mode of these times; yet it is
agreeable to the sense of my heart, and I do very
much desire my Will may be carefully observed herein,
hoping it may become exemplary to some or other: at
least howsoever testifying at my death (what I have so
often and earnestly professed in my life time) my utter
dislike of the flatteries commonly used in Funeral Sermons,
and of the vast Expences otherwise laid out in Funeral
Solemnities and Entertainments, with very little benefit
to any, which (if bestowed in pious and charitable works)
might redound to the publick or private benefit of many
persons.*

I am next to tell, that he died the 29*th* of *January*,
1662. and that his Body was buried in *Bugden* the
third day after his death; and for the manner, that
'twas as far from ostentation as he desir'd it; and all
the rest of his Will was as punctually performed. And
when I have (to his just praise) told this truth, *That he
died far from being rich*, I shall return back to visit, and
give a further account of him on his last Sick-bed.

His last Will (of which I have mentioned a part)
was made about three weeks before his death, about
which time finding his strength to decay by reason of
his constant infirmity, and a consumptive cough added
to it, he retir'd to his Chamber, expressing a desire to
enjoy his last thoughts to himself in private, without
disturbance or care, especially of what might concern
this world. And that none of his Clergy (which are
more numerous than any other Bishops) might suffer
by his retirement, he did by Commission impower his

Chaplain, Mr. *Pullin*, with Episcopal Power to give Institutions to all Livings or Church Preferments, during this his disability to do it himself. In this time of his retirement he long'd for his Dissolution; and when some that lov'd him pray'd for his recovery, if he at any time found any amendment, he seem'd to be displeas'd, by saying, *His Friends said their Prayers backward for him*: *and that 'twas not his desire to live a useless life, and by filling up a place keep another out of it, that might do God and his Church service.* He would often with much joy and thankfulness mention, *That during his being a House-keeper (which was more than 40 years) there had not been one buried out of his Family, and that he was now like to be the first.* He would also often mention with thankfulness, *That till he was three-score years of Age, he had never spent 5s. in Law, nor (upon himself) so much in Wine*: *and rejoyc'd much that he had so liv'd, as never to cause an hours sorrow to his good Father; and hop'd he should die without an Enemy.*

He in this retirement had the Church Prayers read in his Chamber twice every day; and at nine at night some Prayers read to him and a part of his Family out of the *Whole Duty of Man*. As he was remarkably punctual and regular in all his studies and actions; so he used himself to be for his Meals. And his dinner being appointed to be constantly ready at the ending of Prayers, and he expecting and calling for it, was answered, *It would be ready in a quarter of an hour.* To which his reply was, *A quarter of an hour? Is a quarter of an hour nothing to a man that probably has not many hours to live.* And though he did live many hours after this, yet he liv'd not many days; for the day after (which was three days before his death) he was become so weak and weary of either motion or sitting, that he was content, or forc'd to keep his bed.

In which I desire he may rest, till I have given some account of his behaviour there, and immediately before it.

The day before he took his bed (which was three days before his death) he, that he might receive a new assurance for the pardon of his sins past, and be strengthned in his way to the *new Jerusalem*, took the blessed Sacrament of the Body and Blood of his, and our blessed *Jesus*, from the hands of his Chaplain Mr. *Pullin*, accompanied with his Wife, Children, and a Friend, in as awful, humble, and ardent a manner, as outward reverence could express.   After the praise and thanksgiving for it was ended, he spake to this purpose ; *Thou, O God, took'st me out of my mothers womb, and hast been the powerful Protector of me to this present moment of my life ; thou hast neither forsaken me now I am become grey-headed, nor suffered me to forsake thee in the late days of temptation, and sacrifice my Conscience for the preservation of my liberty or estate. 'Twas by grace that I have stood, when others have fallen under my trials : and these mercies I now remember with joy and thankfulness ; and my hope and desire is, that I may die praising thee.*

The frequent repetition of the *Psalms of David* hath been noted to be a great part of the Devotion of the Primitive Christians : The Psalms having in them not only Prayers and holy Instructions, but such Commemorations of God's Mercies, as may preserve comfort, and confirm our dependence on the power, and providence, and mercy of our Creator.   And this is mention'd in order to telling, that as the holy Psalmist said, that *his eyes should prevent both the dawning of the day and the night watches*, by meditating on *God's word* : so 'twas Dr.   Psal. 119. 147.

Sanderson's constant practice every morning to entertain his first waking thoughts with a repetition of those very Psalms, that the Church hath appointed to be constantly read in the daily Morning Service; and having at night laid him in his bed, he as constantly clos'd his eyes with a repetition of those appointed for the Service of the Evening, remembring & repeating the very Psalms appointed for every day; and as the month had formerly ended and began again, so did this Exercise of his Devotion. And if his first waking thoughts were of the World, or what concern'd it, he would arraign and condemn himself for it. Thus he began that work on earth, which is now his imployment in heaven.

After his taking his Bed, and about a day before his death, he desir'd his Chaplain, Mr. *Pullin*, to give him Absolution: And at his performing that Office, he pull'd off his Cap, that Mr. *Pullin* might lay his hand upon his bare head. After this desire of his was satisfied, his Body seem'd to be at more ease, and his mind more chearful; and he said, *Lord, forsake me not now my strength faileth me, but continue thy mercy, and let my mouth be filled with thy praise.* He continued the remaining night and day very patient, and thankful for any of the little Offices that were perform'd for his ease and refreshment: and during that time, did often say the 103 *Psalm* to himself, and very often these words, *My heart is fixed, O God, my heart is fixed where true joy is to be found.* His thoughts seem'd now to be wholly of death, for which he was so prepar'd, that that *King of Terrors* could not surprise him *as a thief in the night*; for he had often said, *he was prepar'd, and long'd for it.* And as this desire seem'd to come from Heaven; so it left him not, till his Soul ascended to that Region of blessed Spirits, whose Imployments are to joyn in consort with him, and sing *praise* and *glory* to that God, who hath brought them to that place, *into which sin and sorrow cannot enter.*

Thus this pattern of *meekness* and primitive *innocence* chang'd this for a better life. 'Tis now too late to wish that my life may be like his; for I am in the eighty fifth year of my Age; but I humbly beseech Almighty God, that my death may; and do as earnestly beg of every Reader to say Amen.

Blessed is the man in whose Spirit there is no guile.   Psal. 32. 2.

Postscript

IF I had had time to have review'd this Relation, as I intended, before it went to the Press, I could have contracted some, and altered other parts of it; but 'twas hastned from me, and now too late for this impression. If there be a second (which the Printer hopes for) I shall both do that, and, upon information, mend any mistake, or supply what may seem wanting.

I. W.

Dr. *PIERCE*'s
LETTER.

Good Mr. Walton,

AT my return to this place, I made a yet stricter search after the Letters long ago sent me from our most excellent Dr. *Sanderson* before the happy Restoration of the King and Church of *England* to their several Rights ; in one of which Letters more especially, he was pleas'd to give me a Narrative both of the rise, and the progress, and reasons also, as well of his younger, as of his last and riper Judgment, touching the famous Points controverted between the *Calvinians* and the *Arminians,* as they are commonly (though unjustly & unskilfully) miscalled on either side.

The whole Letter I allude to does consist of several sheets, whereof a good part has been made publick long ago by the most learned, most judicious, most pious Dr. *Hammond* (to whom I sent it both for his private, and for the publick satisfaction, if he thought fit) in his excellent Book, entituled [*A Pacifick Discourse of God's Grace and Decrees, in full accordance with Dr.* Sanderson :] To which Discourse I referr you for an account of Dr. *Sanderson,* and the History of his Thoughts in his *own hand-writing,* wherein I sent it to *Westwood,* as I receiv'd it from *Boothby Pannel.* And although the whole Book (printed in the year 1660.

and reprinted since with his other Tracts in Folio) is very worthy of your perusal; yet for the Work you are about, you shall not have need to read more at present, than from the *8th* to the *23th* page, and as far as the end of §. 33. There you will find in what year the excellent man, whose life you write, became a Master of Arts. How his first reading of *learned Hooker* had been occasioned by certain *Puritanical Pamphlets*; and how good a *preparative* he found it for his reading of *Calvin's Institutions*, the *honour of whose name* (at that time especially) *gave such credit to his Errors.* How he erred with Mr. *Calvin* (whilst he *took things upon trust*) in the *sublapsarian way*. How being chosen to be *a Clerk of the Convocation for the Diocese of* Lincoln, 1625. He reduced the *Quinquartic-ular Controversie* into *five Schemes or Tables*; and thereupon *discerned a necessity of quitting the Sublap-sarian way* (*of which he had before a better liking*) *as well as the Supralapsarian, which he could never phancy. There* you will meet with *his two weighty Reasons against them both*; and find his happy *change of Judg-ment* to have been ever since the year 1625, even 34 years before the World either *knew*, or (at least) *took notice of it.* And more particularly his reasons for *rejecting Dr. Twiss* (or the way *He* walks in) although his acute, and very learned and ancient Friend.

* I now proceed to let you know from Dr. *Sanderson's* own hand, which was never printed (and which you can hardly know from any, unless from his Son, or from my self) That, when that Parliament was broken up, and the Convocation therewith dissolved, a Gentle-

Sir, I pray note, That all that follows in the Italian Character are Dr. *Sanderson's* own words, excellently worthy, but no where else extant; and commend him as much, as any thing you can say of him. *T. P.*

man of his Acquaintance, by occasion of some discourse about these Points, told him of a Book not long before published at *Paris* (*A.D.* 1623.) by a
* Arriba. *Spanish Bishop, who had undertaken to clear the Differences in the great Controversie *De Concordiâ Gratiæ & Liberi Arbitrij.* And because his Friend perceived he was greedily desirous to see the Book; he sent him one of them, containing the four first Books of twelve which he intended then to publish. *When I had read* (says Dr. *Sanderson* in the following words of the same Letter) *his Epistle Dedicatory to the Pope* (Greg. 15.) *he spake so highly of his own Invention, that I then began rather to suspect him for a Mountebank, than to hope I should find satisfaction from his perform-ances. I found much confidence, and great pomp of words, but little matter as to the main Knot of the Business, other than had been said an hundred times before, to wit, of the coexistence of all things past, present, and future,* in mente divinâ realiter ab æterno, *which is the subject of his whole third Book; only he interpreteth the word* realiter *so, as to import not only* præsentialitatem objectivam (*as others held before him*) *but* propriam & actualem existentiam. *Yet confesseth 'tis hard to make this intelligible. In his fourth Book he endeavours to declare a twofold manner of God's working* ad extra; *the one* sub ordine Prædestinationis, *of which Eternity is the proper measure; the other* sub ordine Gratiæ, *whereof Time is the measure. And that God worketh* fortiter *in the one* (*though not* irresistibiliter) *as well as* suaviter *in the other, wherein the Freewill hath his proper working also. From the Result of his whole per-formance I was confirmed in this Opinion, That we must acknowledge the work of both* (Grace and Freewill) *in the conversion of a sinner. And so likewise in all other events, the Consistency of the Infallibility of God's fore-*

knowledge at least (though not with any absolute, but conditional Predestination) with the liberty of man's will, and the contingency of inferiour causes and effects. These, I say, we must acknowledge for the ὅτι: But for the τὸ πῶς, I thought it bootless for me to think of comprehending it. And so came the two Acta Synodalia Dordrectana *to stand in my Study, only to fill up a room to this day.*

And yet see the restless curiosity of man. Not many years after, to wit, A.D. 1632. *out cometh Dr.* Twiss *his* Vindiciæ Gratiæ; *a large Volume purposely writ against* Arminius. *And then notwithstanding my former resolution, I must needs be medling again. The respect I bore to his person and great learning, and the long acquaintance I had had with him in* Oxford, *drew me to the reading of that whole Book. But from the reading of it (for I read it through to a syllable) I went away with many and great dissatisfactions. Sundry things in that Book I took notice of, which brought me into a greater dislike of his Opinion than I had before: But especially these three: First, that he bottometh very much of his Discourse upon a very erroneous Principle, which yet he seemeth to be so deeply in love with, that he hath repeated it (I verily believe) some hundreds of times in that work: to wit this, [That whatsoever is first in the intention is last in execution, and* è converso.] *Which is an Error of that magnitude, that I cannot but wonder, how a person of such acuteness and subtilty of wit could possibly be deceived with it. All Logicians know, there is no such universal Maxim as he buildeth upon. The true Maxim is but this,* Finis qui primus est in Intentione, est ultimus in Executione. *In the order of final Causes, and the Means used for that end, the Rule holdeth perpetually: But in other things it holdeth not at all, or but by chance; or not as a Rule, and necessarily.*

Secondly, that, foreseeing such Consequences would naturally and necessarily follow from his Opinion, as would offend the ear of a sober Christian at the very first sound, he would yet rather choose not only to admit the said harsh Consequences, but professedly indeavour also to maintain them, and plead hard for them in large Digressions, than to recede in the least from that opinion which he had undertaken to defend. Thirdly, that seeing (out of the sharpness of his wit) a necessity of forsaking the ordinary Sublapsarian way, and the Supralapsarian too, as it had diversly been declared by all that had gone before him (for the shunning of those Rocks, which either of those ways must unavoidably cast him upon) he was forced to seek out an untroden Path, and to frame out of his own brain a new way (like a Spider's web wrought out of her own bowels) hoping by that device to salve all Absurdities could be objected; to wit, by making the glory of God (as it is indeed the chiefest, so) the only end of all other his Decrees, and then making all those other Decrees to be but one entire coordinate Medium conducing to that one end, and so the whole subordinate to it, but not any one part thereof subordinate to any other of the same. Dr. Twiss should have done well to have been more sparing in imputing the studium Partium *to others, wherewith his own eyes (though of eminent perspicacity) were so strangely blindfolded, that he could not discern, how this his new Device, and his old dearly beloved Principle (like the* Cadmean Sparti) *do mutually destroy the one the other.*

This Relation of my pass'd thoughts having spun out to a far greater length than I intended, I shall give a shorter accompt of what they now are concerning these points.

For which account I referr you to the following parts of Dr. *Hammonds* Book aforesaid, where you may

find them already printed.   And for another account
at large of Bishop *Sanderson*'s last Judgment concerning *God's Concurrence* or *Non-concurrence* with the
Actions of men, and the *positive entity of sins of commission*, I referr you to his Letters already printed by
his consent, in my large *Appendix* to my *Impartial
inquiry into the Nature of Sin.* § 68. p. 193. as far as
p. 200.

Sir, I have rather made it my choice to transcribe all
above out of the Letters of Dr. *Sanderson* which lie
before me, than venture the loss of my Originals by
Post or Carrier, which (though not often, yet) sometimes fail.   Make use of as much, or as little as you
please, of what I send you from himself (because from
his own Letters to me) in the penning of his life, as your
own Prudence shall direct you; using my name for your
warranty in the account given of him, as much or as
little as you please too.   You have a performance of
my promise, and an obedience to your desires from

Your affectionate

North-Tidworth,
    March 5. 167⅞.

humble Servant,

Tho. Pierce.

THE
BISHOP
OF
LINCOLN'S
LETTER

My worthy Friend Mr. Walton,

I AM heartily glad, that you have undertaken to write the Life of that excellent person, and (both for learning and piety) eminent Prelate, Dr. *Sanderson*, late Bishop of *Lincoln*; because I know your ability to know, and integrity to write truth: and sure I am, that the life and actions of that pious and learned Prelate will afford you matter enough for his commendation, and the imitation of Posterity. In order to the carrying on your intended good work, you desire my assistance, that I would communicate to you such particular passages of his life, as were certainly known to me. I confess I had the happiness to be particularly known to him for about the space of 20 years, and (in *Oxon*) to enjoy his conversation, and his learned and pious Instructions while he was *Regius Professor* of Divinity there. Afterwards, when (in the time of our late unhappy confusions) he left *Oxon*, and was retir'd into the Countrey, I had the benefit of his Letters; wherein (with great candor and kindness) he

422

answered those doubts I propos'd, and gave me that satisfaction, which I neither had, nor expected from some others of greater confidence, but less judgment and humility.   Having (in a Letter) named two or three Books writ (*ex professo*) against the being of any original sin ; and that *Adam* (by his fall) transmitted some calamity only, but no Crime to his Posterity ; The good old man was exceedingly troubled, and bewailed the misery of those licentious times, and seem'd to wonder (save that the times were such) that any should write, or be permitted to publish any Error so contradictory to truth, and the Doctrine of the Church of *England*, established (as he truly said) by clear evidence of Scripture, and the just and supreme power of this Nation, both Sacred and Civil.   I name not the Books, nor their Authors, which are not unknown to learned men (and I wish they had never been known) because both *the Doctrine, and the unadvis'd Abettors of it are (and shall be)* to me *Apocryphal*.

Another little story I must not pass in silence, being an Argument of Dr. *Sanderson*'s Piety, great Ability and Judgment as a Casuist.   Discoursing with an † honourable person (whose †*Rob. Boyle*, Esq; Piety I value more than his Nobility and Learning, though both be great) about a Case of Conscience concerning Oaths and Vows, their Nature and Obligation ; in which (for some particular Reasons) he then desired more fully to be inform'd ; I commended to him Dr. *Sanderson*'s Book *De Juramento* : which having read (with great satisfaction) he ask'd me, if I thought the Doctor could be induced to write Cases of Conscience, if he might have an honorary Pension allow'd him, to furnish him with Books for that purpose ? I told him I believ'd he would : and (in a Letter to the Doctor) told him what great satisfaction that Honourable Person (and many more) had reaped by reading his Book *De Juramento*; and ask'd him, whether he would be pleased (for the benefit of the Church) to write some Tract of Cases of Conscience? He reply'd, That he was glad that any had received any benefit by his Books: and added further, That if any future Tract of his could bring such benefit to any, as we seem'd to say his former had done, he would willingly (though without any Pension) set about that work. Having receiv'd this Answer, that honourable Person (before mention'd) did (by my hands) return 50*l*. to the good Doctor (whose condition then (as most good mens at that time were) was but low) and he presently revised, finished, and published that excellent book *De Conscientiâ*. A Book little in bulk; but not so if we consider the benefit an intelligent Reader may receive by it. For there are so many general Propositions concerning Conscience, the Nature and Obligation of it, explained and proved with such firm consequence and evidence of Reason, that he who reads, remembers and can (with prudence) pertinently apply them *Hic & nunc* to particular Cases, may (by their light and help) rationally resolve a thousand particular doubts and scruples of Conscience. Here you may see the charity of that Honourable Person in promoting, and the Piety and Industry of the good Doctor in performing that excellent work.

And here I shall add the Judgment of that learned and pious Prelate concerning a passage very pertinent to our present purpose. When he was in *Oxon,* and read his publick Lectures in the Schools as *Regius Professor* of Divinity, and by the truth of his Positions, and evidences of his Proofs, gave great content and satisfaction to all his hearers; especially in his clear Resolutions of all difficult Cases which occurr'd in the Explication of the subject matter of his Lectures; a Person of Quality (yet alive) privately asked him, What course a young Divine should take in his Studies to inable him to be a good Casuist? His answer was, That a convenient understanding of the Learned Languages (at least of Hebrew, Greek and Latin) and a sufficient knowledge of Arts and Sciences presuppos'd; There were two things in humane Literature, a comprehension of which would be of very great use, to inable a man to be a rational and able Casuist, which otherwise was very difficult, if not impossible. 1. A convenient knowledge of Moral Philosophy; especially that part of it which treats of the Nature of Humane Actions: To know, *quid sit actus humanus (spontaneus, invitus, mixtus) unde habent bonitatem & malitiam moralem? an ex genere & objècto, vel ex circumstantiis?* How the variety of Circumstances varies the goodness or evil of humane Actions? How far knowledge and ignorance may aggravate or excuse, increase or diminish the goodness or evil of our Actions? For every Case of Conscience being only this—*Is this action good or bad? May I do it, or may I not?* He who (in these) knows not how and whence human Actions become morally good and evil, never can (*in Hypothesi*) rationally and certainly determine, whether this or that particular Action be so. 2. The second thing, which (he said) would be a great help and advantage to a Casuist, was a convenient knowledge of the Nature and Obligation of Laws in general: To know what a Law is; what a Natural and a Positive Law; what's required to the *Latio, dispensatio, derogatio, vel abrogatio legis*; what promulgation is antecedently required to the Obligation of any Positive Law; what ignorance takes off the Obligation of a Law, or does excuse, diminish or aggravate the transgression: For every Case of Conscience being only this—*Is this lawful for me, or is it not?* and the Law the only Rule and Measure, by which I must judge of the lawfulness or unlawfulness of any Action: It evidently follows, that he, who (in these) knows not the Nature and Obligation of Laws, never can be a good Casuist, or rationally assure himself (or others) of the lawfulness or unlawfulness of Actions in particular. This was the Judgment and good counsel of that learned and pious Prelate; and having (by long experience) found the truth and benefit of it, I conceive, I could not without ingratitude to him, and want of charity to others, conceal it.—Pray pardon this rude, and (I fear) impertinent Scrible, which (if nothing else) may signifie thus much, that I am willing to obey your Desires, and am indeed

Your affectionate

London, May 10.
    1678.

Friend,

Thomas Lincoln.

3¼.56

PRINTED IN
GREAT BRITAIN
BY
PILLANS AND WILSON LIMITED
EDINBURGH